I0100339

FROM A B to Z

A GENEALOGY

COMPILED BY

MARGARET ZELLER GARRETT

Privately printed for the compiler

by

The Daily Republican

Burlington, Kansas

From A B to Z: A Genealogy

Compiled by:
Margaret Zeller Garrett

Privately printed for the compiler by
The Daily Republican
Burlington, Kansas
ca. 1975

Reprinted by:

Janaway Publishing, Inc.
732 Kelsey Ct.
Santa Maria, California 93454
(805) 925-1038
www.JanawayGenealogy.com

2016

ISBN: 978-1-59641-367-2

Made in the United States of America

Dedicated to the memory of our mother. When Alice Bryant married Julius Zeller some of her friends laughingly said she had gone from A B to Z - thus the title of this genealogy.

Alice Bryant was born in Atlanta, Georgia during the reconstruction period. She was first taught at home by her mother, then attended the public schools in Georgia. Later she attended U. S. Grant University in Athens, Tennessee, where she graduated at the age of nineteen. After graduation she joined her parents in Mt. Vernon, N. Y. where she was a society reporter on the Newspaper.

During the early years of her marriage, she lived in various church parishes. At one time when her husband was taking special courses at the University of Chicago, she held down the pulpet with a child on either side.

When her husband was professor at Illinois Weslyan University, Bloomington, Illinois and President of the University of Puget Sound, Tacoma, Washington, she was prominent in University and Woman's Club activities and was a member of the President's Club in Tacoma. She was listed in Who's Who on the Pacific Coast.

The family also lived in Chicago, Illinois; on a plantation near Yazoo City, Mississippi; Oxford, Mississippi where our father was Vice Chancelor of the State University; and Kansas City, Missouri, where our father died. Our mother then went to East Orange, New Jersey where she lived with her daughter, Mrs. Russell Charles Gross, until her death. Her life and that of her ancestors encompasses the entire history of American life.

About 1908 our mother was very ill with Typhoid fever and Phlebitis. Later she said had she died her children would never have known about her family. She paid a genealogist twenty-five dollars to get her started and spent many years researching her various lines. Meantime she was a busy wife and mother of seven children and active in several organizations. She was Worthy Matron of the Eastern Star Chapter in Yazoo City, Mississippi, and was Regeant of her D.A.R. Chapter in East Orange, New Jersey.

As the wife of a Minister; University Professor; University President; Plantation owner and State Senator, she did a great deal of entertaining in the home and led a very active social life. She died April 26, 1946 and is buried beside her husband at Spring Bay, Illinois, the town where our father was born.

Several years after our Mother's death, I continued her research.

Margaret Zeller Garrett
Route 3, Box 66
Burlington, Kansas 66839

CHART I

Ancestors of

Alice Bryant Geller
B Nov. 16, 1871 - Atlanta, Ga.
R Atlanta + Savannah, Ga. N.Y. Ill., Wash., Miss., Mo., N.J.
M. Jan. 1, 1895 - Julius Christian Geller at Mt. Vernon, N.Y.
D. Apr. 26, 1946 - East Orange, N.J.

Paternal

Col. John Emory Bryant
B Oct. 13, 1835 - Wayne, Maine
M June 26, 1864 - Buckfield, Maine
D Feb. 27, 1900 - New York City
R Atlanta + Savannah, Ga. + Mt. Vernon, N.Y.

Benjamin Bryant, M.D.
B Apr. 25, 1803 - New Vineyard, Me.
M July 23, 1829 - Chesterville, Me.
D Feb. 5, 1870 - Wakeman, Ohio
R New Vineyard, Me., Townsend + Wakeman Ohio

Elias Bryant (Rev.)
B Sept. 8, 1772 - Middleboro, Mass.
M May 7, 1798 - Taunton, Mass.
D abt. 1830, aged 60
R Middleboro, Mass. New Vineyard, Me. + New Portland, Me.

Micah Bryant (Cont. II)
B Apr. 2, 1747 - Middleboro Mass.
D 1790
M Nov. 22, 1770 - Taunton Mass.
R Middleboro, Mass.

Margaret Paddock (Cont. III)
B Dec. 18, 1741 Yarmouth, Mass.
D Dec. 15, 1814 New Vineyard, Me.

(2) Bathsheba Hackett
B 1776
D Oct. 19, 1816 - New Vineyard, Me. Ae. 40

Ephriam Hackett R.S. (Cont. IV)
B 1746
D 1820
M May 14, 1764 - Taunton, Mass.
R Middleboro Mass. + New Vineyard, Me.

Elizabeth Paddock (Cont. III)
B
D

Lucy Ford French
B July 26, 1805 - Chesterville, Maine
D Sept. 18, 1886 - Murray, Ind. Bur. Wakeman, Ohio

Joseph French
B Oct. 4, 1770 - So. Hampton, N.H.
M before 1795
D Nov. 6, 1841 - Chesterville, Me.
R Hampton, N.H. + Chesterville, Me.

Moses French (Cont. V)
B Dec. 20, 1736
D Feb. 10, 1819
M Dec. 6, 1759 - Hampton, N.H.
R

Mary Dearborn (Cont. VI)
B June 16, 1739
D

Elizabeth Ford
B Jan. 30, 1771 - Marshfield, Mass.
D Nov. 17, 1855 - Chesterville, Maine

Isaac Ford R.S. (Cont. VII)
B June 19, 1738 Marshfield, Mass.
D Apt. Apr. 26, 1806
M Oct. 1, 1761 - Pembroke Mass.
R Marshfield, Mass. Fayette, Maine

Lucy Josselyn (Cont. VIII)
B Oct. 5, 1741
D Apt. Apr 26, 1806

Maternal

Emma Frances Spaulding
B Feb. 16, 1844 - Buckfield, Me.
D May 2, 1901 - Martins, Ill.
R Buckfield, Me. Atlanta + Savannah Ga. Mt. Vernon, N.Y. + Ill. + Athens, Tenn.

Capt. James Spaulding
B June 10, 1802 - Buckfield, Me.
M June 5, 1825 - (June 3 - Bible Rec.)
D Oct 31, 1886 - Carlinville, Ill.
R Buckfield, Me. + Carlinville, Ill.

Capt. Leonard Spaulding
B Feb. 13, 1770 - Bapt. Aug. 2, 1772, Chelmsford, Mass.
M
D Aug. 27, 1854 - Buckfield, Maine
R Chelmsford, Mass. + Buckfield, Me.

Benjamin Spaulding R.S. (Cont. IX)
B Feb. 5, 1739 - Chelmsford Mass.
D Oct. 19, 1811 - Buckfield Me.
M Nov. 29, 1764 Chelmsford Mass.
R Chelmsford + Oxley Mass. Buckfield, Maine

Patty Barrett (Cont. X)
B Jan. 20, 1740-1 Chelmsford, Mass.
D Oct. 4, 1818 Buckfield, Mass.

Margaretta Warren
B Jan. 11, 1774
D July 13, 1856. Buckfield, Me.

Capt John Warren R.S. (Cont. XI)
B March 5, 1731
D Jan. 30, 1807 Stroudwater, Me.
M Dec. 25, 1755
R Stroudwater + Westbrook, Me.

Jane Johnson (Cont. XII)
B June 15, 1740 Westbrook, Me.
D Nov. 13, 1819

Cynthia Bray
B March 25, 1802 - Minot, Maine
D Dec. 11, 1864 - Buckfield, Maine
R. Turner + Buckfield, Maine

Thomas Bray
B Sept. 20, 1769 - Minot, Me.
M Bans. Publ. Dec 30, 1797 - Hebron, Me.
D March 27, 1842
R Turner, Maine

Ebenezer Bray R.S. (Cont. XIII)
B April 19, 1732 Gloucester, Mass.
D Feb. 24, 1817 - Minot, Me.
M Jan. 19, 1762 - Gloucester Mass
R Gloucester, Mass. + Minot + Bakerstown, Me.

Judith Bennett (Cont. XIV)
B Sept. 2, 1739 Gloucester, Mass.
D June 30, 1799 Minot, Me

Cynthia Record
B Aug. 20, 1779 - Buckfield, Maine
D Sept. 20, 1819 - Minot, Maine

Simon Record R.S. (Cont. XV)
B 1753
D Oct. 5, 1843 - Buckfield Me.
M abt. 1777
R Pembroke, Mass. Buckfield, Maine

Bethiah Record (Cont. XVI)
B 1758 (?) Bridgewater, Mass.
D June 3, 1829 Buckfield, Maine

B=Born
M=Married
D=Died
R=Resided

Somerset Genealogical Form—New England Historic Genealogical Society, 101 Newbury Street, Boston, Mass.

CHART II

ANCESTORS OF I

PATERNAL

- Micah Bryant — B April 2, 1710 - Plympton, Mass. M Int. Apr. 19, 1740 Kingston, Mass. D Jan. 28, 1796 - Middleboro, Mass. R Plympton + Middleboro, Mass.
  - Benjamin Bryant — B Dec. 16, 1688 - Plympton, Mass. M July 31, 1712 - Plympton, Mass. D May 4, 1724 "Drowned on Plymouth Shore" R Plympton, Mass.
    - Lieut. John Bryant — B Aug. 17, 1644 - Situate, Mass. M Nov. 23, 1665 - Plympton, Mass. D May 12, 1715 - Situate, Mass. R Situate + Plympton, Mass.
      - John Bryant — B; M Nov. 14, 1643 Sc[...]; D Nov. 20, 1684 (Situate Rec. 1684); R Situate, Mass[...]
      - Mary Lewis — B Oct. 1623, Kent, Eng. D July 2, 1655 - Sc[...] (Co[...])
      - 110 [crossed out]; "no" written across
    - Abigail Bryant — B; D May 12, 1715 - Plympton, Mass.
      - Stephen Bryant — B; M; D; R Plympton, Mass[...]
      - Abigail Shaw — B; D Oct. 24, 1694 ? (Cont.)
  - Hannah Eaton — B Feb. 10, 1692 D March 4, 1723 or 4
    - Benjamin Eaton — B 1664 M Dec. 18, 1689 D 1745 R Plymouth, Mass.
      - Benjamin Eaton — B 1627-8; M Dec. 4, 1660; D Jan. 16, 1711-12 Plymouth, Mass.; R (Francis Eaton / Christian Penn)
      - Sarah Hoskins — B; D (Cont.)
    - Mary Combs — B Nov. 28, 1665 - Boston, Mass. D July 2, 1728 age 63, Plympton, Mass.
      - John Combs — B; M; D; R (Mr. John Combs / Sarah Priest)
      - Elizabeth (Royal ?) Barlow wid. Th[...] — B; D; M. (2) John Warren

MATERNAL

- Micah Bryant — B April 2, 1741 R Middleboro, Mass. + New Vineyard, Maine
- Elizabeth Norcutt — B Feb. 19, 1715 D June 28, 1796 - Age 80 Middleboro Mass.
  - Ephriam Norcutt — B Nov. 4, 1683 - Marshfield, Mass. M Jan. 30, 1712-13 - Marshfield, Mass. D Apr. 1757 R Marshfield, Duxbury, Middleboro, Mass.
    - William Norcutt — B; M; D Sept. 18, 1693 - Will Prob. Oct. 8, 1693; R Duxbury + Marshfield, Mass.
      - B; M; D; R
      - B; D
    - Sarah Chapman — B May 15, 1645 D Af. 1693
      - *Ralph Chapman — B Oct. 1616; M Nov. 23, 164[...]; D will prob. June 4, 1672 + dated Nov. 28, 1671; R Marshfield, [...] Duxbury, M[...]
      - Lydia Wills — B; D
  - Elizabeth Bonney — B; D
    - Thomas Bonney — B; M; D Will Prob. 8-6-1735; R Marshfield + Duxbury, Mass.
      - Thomas Bonney — B; M 1640s; D May 1, 1693; R Charlestown + [...]
      - (2) Mary Hunt — B; D (Edmund Hunt)
    - Dorcas Samson — B; D
      - Henry Sampson M.P. — B; M Feb. 6, 1635-[...]; D will prob. 5 Mar. 1684; R Plymouth + [...]
      - Ann Plummer — B; D Bu. 10 Oct. 1[...]

B=Born
M=Married
D=Died
R=Resided

MP. Mayflower Passenger
* From St. Savior's Southwark, Eng. Came in Elizabeth in Apr. 1635, Age 20.

CHART III

Capt. John Paddock
B May 5, 1669 - Yarmouth, Mass.
M 1694
D Feb. 18, 1717-18 - Yarmouth, Mass.
R Yarmouth, Mass.

Zachariah Paddock
B March 20, 1636 Plymouth, Mass.
M 1659
D May 1, 1727 - Yarmouth, Mass.
R

Robert Paddock
B Abt. 1605
M
D July 25, 1650
R Duxbury & Plymouth

Mary
B
D

Deborah Sears
B Sept. 1639 Yarmouth, Mass.
D Aug. 10, 1732 " "

Richard Sears
B 1590
M
D 1676
R

Dorothy Thacher
B
D

Joseph Paddock
B March 8, 1700 - Yarmouth, Mass.
M Nov. 29, 1739 (2nd wife) Eastham, Mass.
D April 10, 1768 - Lakeville, Mass.
R Yarmouth & Lakeville, Mass.

Priscilla Hall
B Feb. 1671 - Yarmouth, Mass.
D Jan. 2, 1724-5 " "

John Hall
B 1637 - bapt. 13 May 1638 Charlestown, Mass.
M 1666
D Oct. 24, 1718 age 73 - Yarmouth, Mass.
R Charlestown & Yarmouth, Mass.

John Hall
B 1609
M by 1637
D 23 July 1696 ae 85, will prob. Aug. 28, 1696
R Yarmouth, Mass.

Bethiah Farmer - dau. of John?
B
D
2nd wife Elizabeth Learned.

Priscilla Bearce
B 10 March 1643 - Barnstable, Mass.
D March 30, 1712 ae. 68 - Yarmouth, Mass.

Austin (Augustine) Bearse
B 1618 (Deposed 1658 age 50?)
M by 1640
D Aft. 1697
R Barnstable, Mass.

Mary Hyane
B
D

PATERNAL

ANCESTORS OF Ant. from I

Margaret Paddock
B Sep. 19, 1741
R Middleboro, Mass. & New Vineyard, Maine
M. 1814 - Micah Bryant

Elizabeth Paddock
B. Sept. 19, 1740
R. Middleboro, Mass. New Vineyard, Me.
d. abt. 1812

MATERNAL

? Thomas Mayo ?
B Jan. 3, 1678 - Eastham, Mass.
M Apr. 3, 1701 - " "
D Abt. June 1769
R Eastham, Mass.

Thomas Mayo
B Dec. 7, 1650
M June 13, 1677 - Eastham, Mass.
D Apr. 23, 1729 - Eastham, Mass.
R Eastham, Mass.

Nathaniel Mayo [Rev. John Mayo]
B abt. 1627 in Eng.
M Feb. 13, 1650
D by June 15, 1696
R Eastham, Mass.

Hannah Prence [Gov. Thomas Prence; Patience Brewster, dau. of Elder Wm. B.]
B
D

Barbara Knowles
B Sept. 29, 1653 - Eastham, Mass.
D Feb. 23, 1714-15 " "

Richard Knowles
B
M Aug. 15, 1639
D
R Plymouth & Eastham, Mass.

Ruth Bower
B
D
R Plymouth, Mass.

Elizabeth Mayo
B abt. 1700 (? May 2, 1702)
D Dec 19, 1761 - 62nd yr.

Elizabeth Higgins
B Feb. 11, 1678
D Nov. 4, 1721 - Eastham, Mass.

Jonathan Higgins
B
M 2) Jan. 1680
D
R

Richard Higgins
B
M by 1637
D
R Plymouth & Eastham, Me., New Piscataway, N.J.

1) Lydia Chandler
B
D by 1652

2) Hannah Rogers
B
D

Joseph Rogers M.P. [Thomas Rogers M.P.]
B Eng.
M by 1633
D Nov. 9, 1678 - Eastham
R Plymouth & Eastham, Mass.

Hannah
B
D

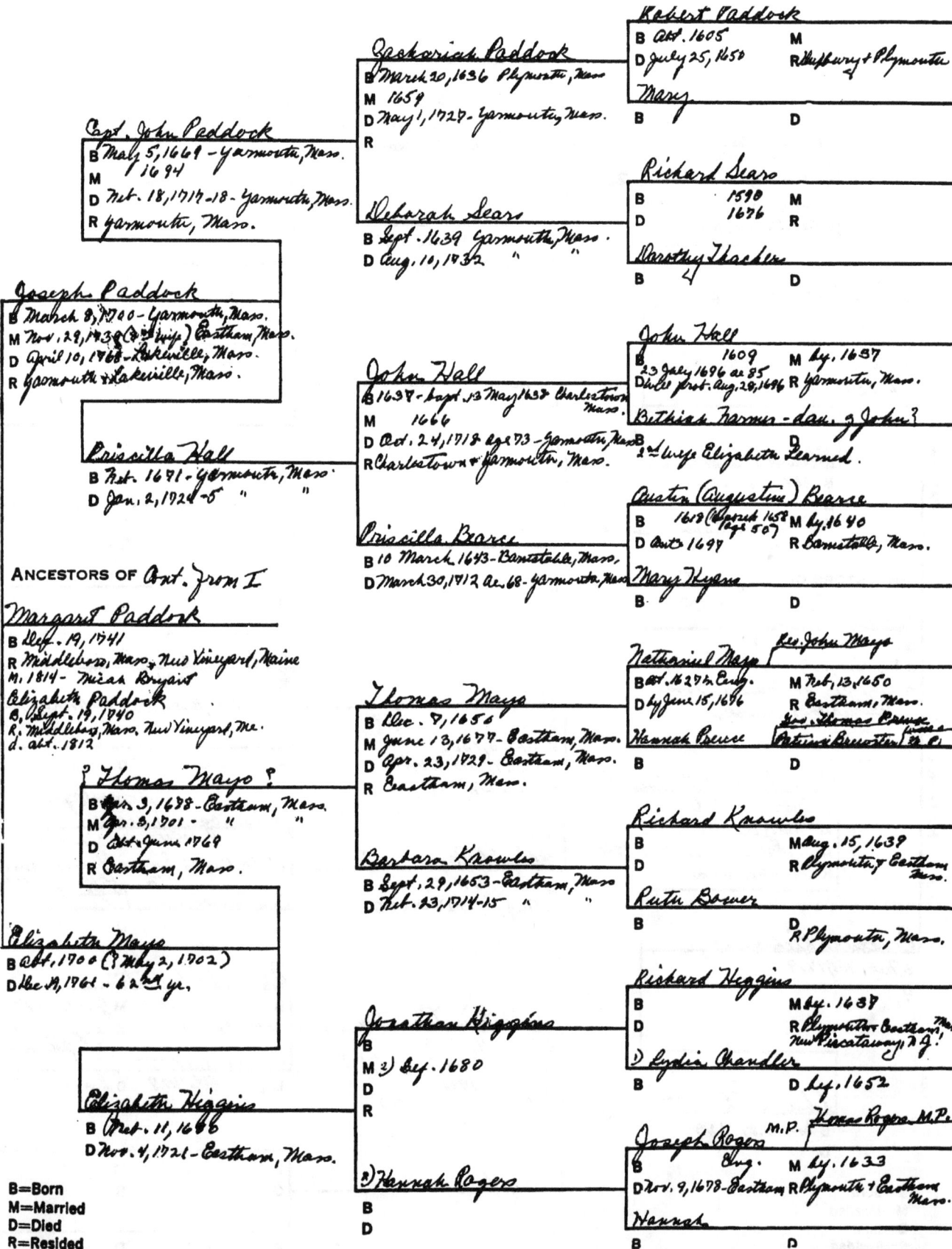

B=Born
M=Married
D=Died
R=Resided

CHART IV

Jabez Hackett
B 1624
M bef. 1654
D Nov. 4, 1686 - Taunton, Mass.
R Lynn & Taunton, Mass.

Frances Wilbor (?)
B abt. 1632
D aft. March 1695-96

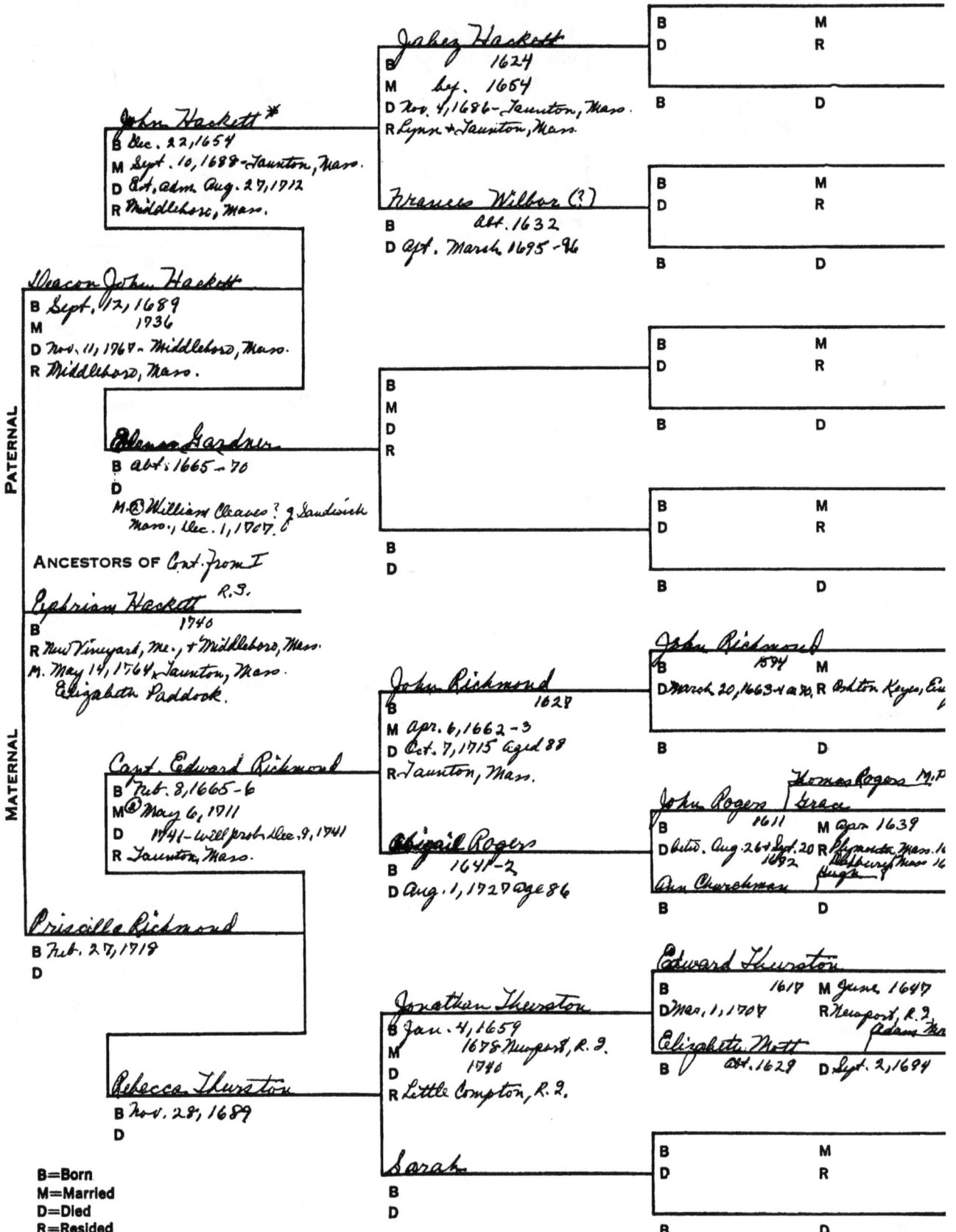

John Hackett *
B Dec. 22, 1654
M Sept. 10, 1688 - Taunton, Mass.
D Est. adm. Aug. 27, 1712
R Middleboro, Mass.

Deacon John Hackett
B Sept. 12, 1689
M 1736
D Nov. 11, 1767 - Middleboro, Mass.
R Middleboro, Mass.

Eleanor Gardner
B abt. 1665 - 70
D
M. ② William Cleaves ? of Sandwich Mass., Dec. 1, 1707.

PATERNAL

ANCESTORS OF Cont. from I

Ephriam Hackett R.S.
B 1740
R New Vineyard, Me., & Middleboro, Mass.
M. May 14, 1764 - Taunton, Mass.
Elizabeth Paddock.

MATERNAL

John Richmond
B 1594
D March 20, 1663-4 aged 70
R Ashton Keyes, En[g]

John Richmond
B 1628
M Apr. 6, 1662-3
D Oct. 7, 1715 aged 88
R Taunton, Mass.

John Rogers | Thomas Rogers M.P. | Grace
B 1611
M Apr 1639
D betw. Aug. 26 & Sept. 20 1692
R Plymouth, Mass. 16.. Duxbury, Mass. 16..
Ann Churchman | Hugh

Abigail Rogers
B 1641-2
D Aug. 1, 1727 age 86

Capt. Edward Richmond
B Feb. 8, 1665-6
M ② May 6, 1711
D 1741 - will prob. Dec. 9, 1741
R Taunton, Mass.

Priscilla Richmond
B Feb. 27, 1718
D

Edward Thurston
B 1617
M June 1647
D Mar. 1, 1707
R Newport, R.I.
Adams Mo[tt]

Elizabeth Mott
B abt. 1629
D Sept. 2, 1694

Jonathan Thurston
B Jan. 4, 1659
M 1678 Newport, R.I.
D 1740
R Little Compton, R.I.

Sarah
B
D

Rebecca Thurston
B Nov. 28, 1689
D

B=Born
M=Married
D=Died
R=Resided

* An inquest was held in the death of a John Hackett of Middleboro, Mass. Oct. 25, 1703. Suffolk Co. Court Recs. # 5919.

CHART V

Paternal

Samuel French
B Dec. 11, 1699 - Salisbury, Mass.
M Nov. 23, 1721 " & "
D will dated March 13, 1767 agreement of Heirs
R Salisbury, Mass. So. Hampton, N.H.

- Deacon Joseph French
  B Abt. 1676
  M
  D Aug. 20, 1749 - Salisbury, Mass.
  R Salisbury, Mass.
  - Samuel French
    B
    M June 1, 1664 - Salisbury, Mass.
    D July 26, 1692 " & "
    R Salisbury, Mass.
    - Edward French
      B 1590 M Aug. 1635
      D Dec. 28, 1674 R Salisbury, Mass.
    - Ann Goodale
      B D March 9, 1682-3
  - Abigail Browne
    B Oct. 23, 1643-4, Salisbury, Mass.
    D Jan. 11, 1679-80, Salisbury, Mass.
    - Deacon Henry Browne (*George Browne, Christian)
      B 1615 M
      D Aug. 6, 1701 Salisbury, Mass. R Salisbury, Mass.
    - Abigail
      B D Aug. 23, 1702
- Hannah
  B
  D
  - B M D R
    - B D M R
    - B D
  - B D
    - B D M R
    - B D

ANCESTORS OF Cont from I

Moses French
B Dec. 20, 1736
R South Hampton, N.H.
M. Mary Dearborn

Maternal

Mary Collins
B 1690-1700 Salisbury, Mass.
D

- Samuel Collins
  B Jan. 18, 1676 - Salisbury, Mass.
  M March 16, 1698-9
  D
  R Salisbury, Mass.
  - Benjamin Collins
    B
    M Nov. 5, 1668 - Salisbury, Mass.
    D Dec. 10, 1683 " & "
    R
    - B D M R
    - B D
  - Martha Eaton
    B
    D
    M. (2) Nov. 4, 1686 Philip Flanders
    - John Eaton (John Eaton, D. Oct. 29, 1668 Salisbury, Mass.)
      B Abt. 1619 M
      D Nov. 1, 1682 R
    - Martha Rowlandson (Thomas)
      B D July 1712
- Sarah White
  B
  D
  - John White Jr.?
    B Sept. 6 (?) 1652 at Roxbury, Mass.
    M
    D Mar. 28, 1695 ae 53y. at Roxbury, Mass.
    R
    - John White
      B M
      D Apr. 15, 1691 R Watertown, Boston, Roxbury, Mass.
    - Frances
      B D
  - B D
    - B D M R
    - B D

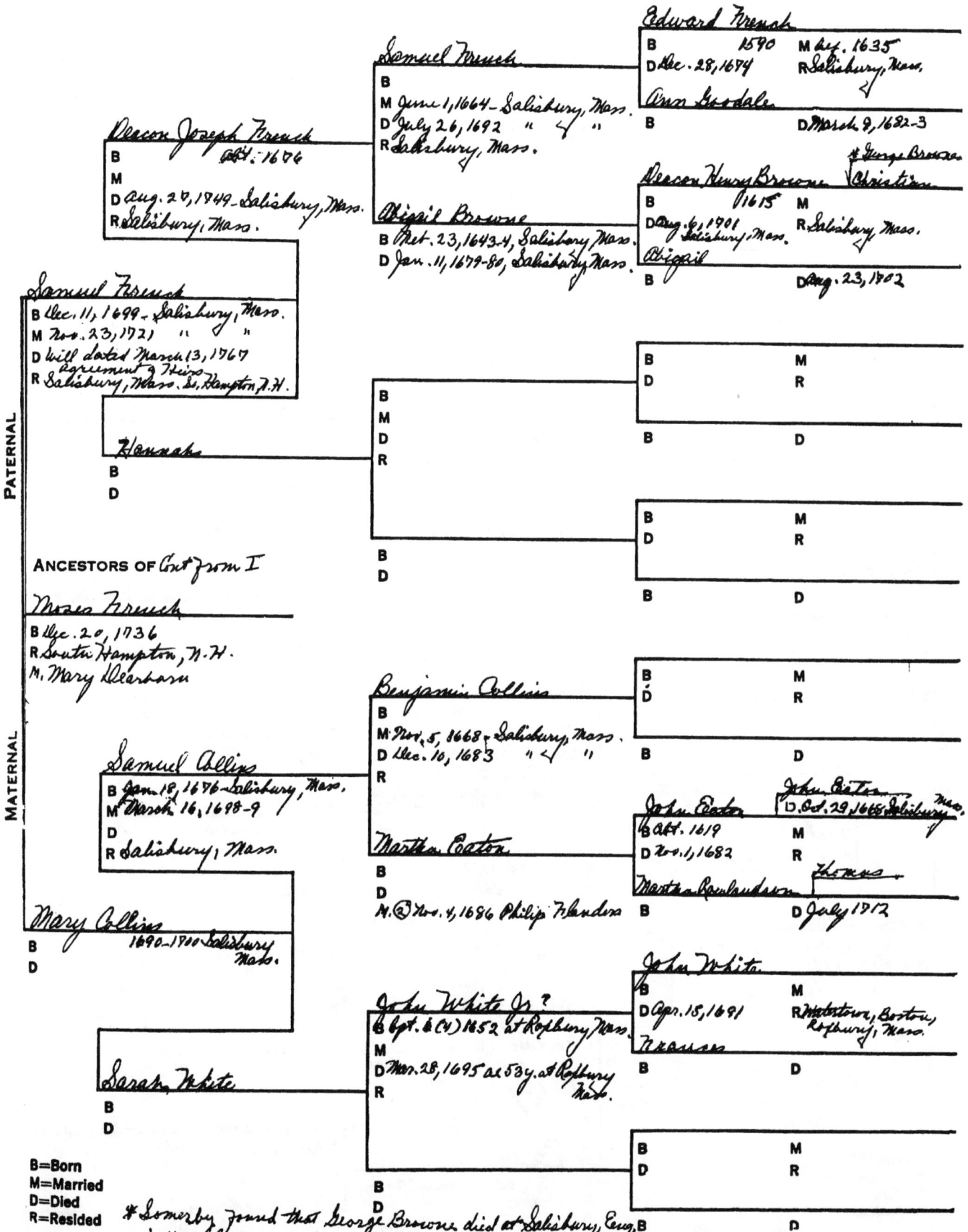

B=Born
M=Married
D=Died
R=Resided

* Somerby found that George Browne died at Salisbury, Eng. in 1633, leaving widow Christian and sons Henry, William, George + Abraham.

CHART VI

PATERNAL

Nathaniel Dearborn
B Jan. 21, 1710, No. Hampton, N. H.
M Dec. 2, 1731
D Nov. 11, 1754
R No. Hampton & Kingston, N. H.

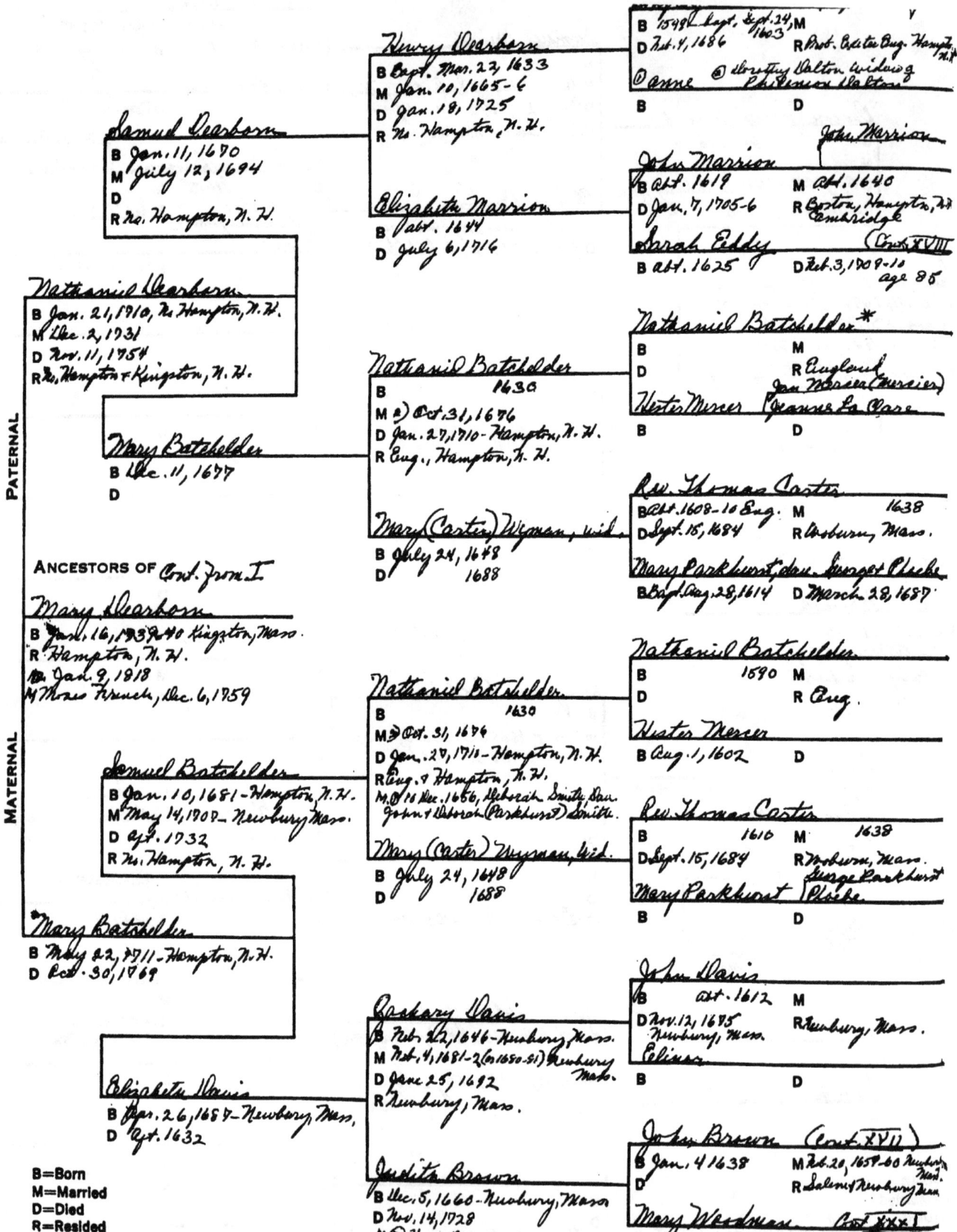

Samuel Dearborn
B Jan. 11, 1670
M July 12, 1694
D
R No. Hampton, N. H.

Henry Dearborn
B Bapt. Mar. 22, 1633
M Jan. 10, 1665-6
D Jan. 18, 1725
R No. Hampton, N. H.

B 1598 Sept. Bapt. Sept. 24, 1603 M
D Feb. 4, 1686 R Prob. Exeter Eng. Hampton, N. H.
1. Anne 2. Dorothy Dalton widow of Philemon Dalton
B D

Elizabeth Marrion
B abt. 1644
D July 6, 1716

John Marrion
John Marrion
B abt. 1619 M abt. 1640
D Jan. 7, 1705-6 R Boston, Hampton, N.H. Cambridge
Sarah Eddy (Cont. XVIII)
B abt. 1625 D Feb. 3, 1709-10 age 85

Mary Batchelder
B Dec. 11, 1677
D

Nathaniel Batchelder
B 1630
M 2) Oct. 31, 1676
D Jan. 27, 1710 - Hampton, N. H.
R Eng., Hampton, N. H.

Nathaniel Batchelder*
B M
D R England
Hester Mercer Jean Mercer (Mercier) Jeanne La Clare
B D

Mary (Carter) Wyman, wid.
B July 24, 1648
D 1688

Rev. Thomas Carter
B abt. 1608-10 Eng. M 1638
D Sept. 5, 1684 R Woburn, Mass.
Mary Parkhurst, dau. George Placke
B Bapt. Aug. 28, 1614 D March 28, 1687

ANCESTORS OF Cont. from I.

Mary Dearborn
B Jan. 16, 1739/40 Kingston, Mass.
R Hampton, N. H.
D Jan. 9, 1818
M Moses French, Dec. 6, 1759

MATERNAL

Samuel Batchelder
B Jan. 10, 1681 - Hampton, N. H.
M May 14, 1709 - Newbury, Mass.
D aft. 1732
R No. Hampton, N. H.

Nathaniel Batchelder
B 1630
M 2) Oct. 31, 1676
D Jan. 27, 1710 - Hampton, N. H.
R Eng. & Hampton, N. H.
M. 1) 10 Dec. 1656, Deborah Smith dau. John & Deborah (Parkhurst) Smith.

Nathaniel Batchelder
B 1590 M
D R Eng.
Hester Mercer
B Aug. 1, 1602 D

Mary (Carter) Wyman, wid.
B July 24, 1648
D 1688

Rev. Thomas Carter
B 1610 M 1638
D Sept. 15, 1684 R Woburn, Mass.
Mary Parkhurst George Parkhurst Placke
B D

*Mary Batchelder
B May 22, 1711 - Hampton, N. H.
D Oct. 30, 1769

Elizabeth Davis
B Apr. 26, 1687 - Newbury, Mass.
D aft. 1632

Zachary Davis
B Feb. 22, 1646 - Newbury, Mass.
M Feb. 4, 1681-2 (or 1680-81) Newbury, Mass.
D June 25, 1692
R Newbury, Mass.

John Davis
B abt. 1612 M
D Nov. 12, 1685 Newbury, Mass. R Newbury, Mass.
Elinor
B D

Judith Brown
B Dec. 5, 1660 - Newbury, Mass.
D Nov. 14, 1728
M. 2) Henry Bradley, Jan. 7, 1695-6

John Brown (Cont. XVII)
B Jan. 4 1638 M Feb. 20, 1659-60 Newbury, Mass.
D R Salem & Newbury, Mass.
Mary Woodman Cont. XXXI
B D

B=Born
M=Married
D=Died
R=Resided

The father of Nathaniel Batchelder was Rev. Stephen Batchelder, b. in Eng. d. 1660 Hackney, Co. Middlesex, Eng.
Rev. Stephen Batchelder m. 1588-9, Anne Batts, mother of all his children; m. 2) Christian Weare, 1624.
m. 3) Helena Mason, 1627, she came to America with him; m. 4) Mary Beadle, wid., of Kittery, Maine.

SOMERSET GENEALOGICAL FORM—NEW ENGLAND HISTORIC GENEALOGICAL SOCIETY. 101 NEWBURY STREET. BOSTON. MASS.

CHART VII

William Ford
B
M
D Prob. 1621 on the ship Fortune coming over.
R

Martha ( ) Ford
B
D
M.② Peter Brown of the Mayflower

William Ford *
B 1594 (Duxbury, Mass. V.R.)
M Bef. 1640
D Sept. 23, 1676 - Bur. Duxbury
R Plymouth, Duxbury, Marshfield, Mass.

Michael Ford
B 1643
M② March 29, 1683 - Duxbury, Mass.
D 1721
R Duxbury + Scituate, Mass.

B
M
D
R

Anna Winslow?
B
D Bur. Sept. 1, 1684, Marshfield, Mass.

B
D

Elisha Ford
B Jan. 19, 1696 - Marshfield, Mass.
M Jan. 13, 1719-20 - Duxbury, Mass.
D Nov. 4, 1758
R Marshfield, Mass.

Elder William Hatch (Cont. XXXVI)
B abt. 1598
M License July 9, 1624
D Nov. 6, 1651 - Scituate, Mass.
R

Walter Hatch
B abt. 1624
M May 6, 1650 - Scituate, Mass.
D May 24, 1699
R Scituate, Mass.

Jane Young
B abt. 1598
D Oct. 8, 1653
M.② Thomas King, 31 March 1653

PATERNAL

Bethiah Hatch 2nd wife
B March 31, 1661. Bapt. May 12, 1661 Scituate, Mass.
D Nov. 22, 1728

Thomas Holbrook
B 1589
M abt. 1616
D Apr. 4, 1697 - will prov.
R Weymouth, Dorchester, Sherborne, Mass.

Elizabeth Holbrook
B prob. 1630
D 1674

Jan Powyes or Page
B
D

ANCESTORS OF Cont. from I

Isaac Ford
B June 19, 1738
R Marshfield, Mass., Fayette + Wayne, Me.
M. Lucy Josselyn, Oct. 1, 1767

B
M
D
R

Samuel Oakman
B
M bef. 1664
D bef. June 28, 1676 (est. adm.)
R Spurwink (Now Cape Elizabeth) Me.

B
D

MATERNAL

Tobias Oakman
B 1664
M bef. 1696
D June 16, 1750
R Spurwink, Me. + Marshfield, Mass.

B
M
D
R

Sarah
B
D

B
D

Elizabeth Oakman
B May 10, 1701
D Nov. 15, 1768 - aged 68

Edward Doty M.D. **
B abt. 1599
M
D Aug. 23, 1655
R

Edward Doty, Jr.
B 1637
M Feb. 26, 1662-3 - Plymouth, Mass.
D Feb. 8, 1689-90 - drowned between Plymouth + Boston
R Yarmouth, Mass.

Faith Clark Cont. XXX
B 1619
D Dec. 21, 1675 Marshfield, Mass.

Elizabeth Doty
B Dec. 22, 1673
D Dec. 17, 1745 - Ae. 72 yrs.

John Faunce
B abt. 1602
M 1633-4.
D Jan. 18, 1687
R Plymouth, Mass.

Sarah
B 1645
D June 27, 1695

Patience Morton
B abt. 1615
D Aug. 16, 1691 Ae. 77
M.② — Whitney.

B=Born
M=Married
D=Died
R=Resided

* Widow Ford and son William came to Plymouth in Ship Fortune, 1621.
** 40th signer of the Mayflower Compact. In the first encounter 1620.

CHART VIII

Henry Josselyn
B March 24, 1696-7 Scituate, Mass.
M Sept. 28, 1718
D Apts Nov. 10, 1784, Pembroke
R Scarborough, Me.; Lancaster & Pembroke, Mass.

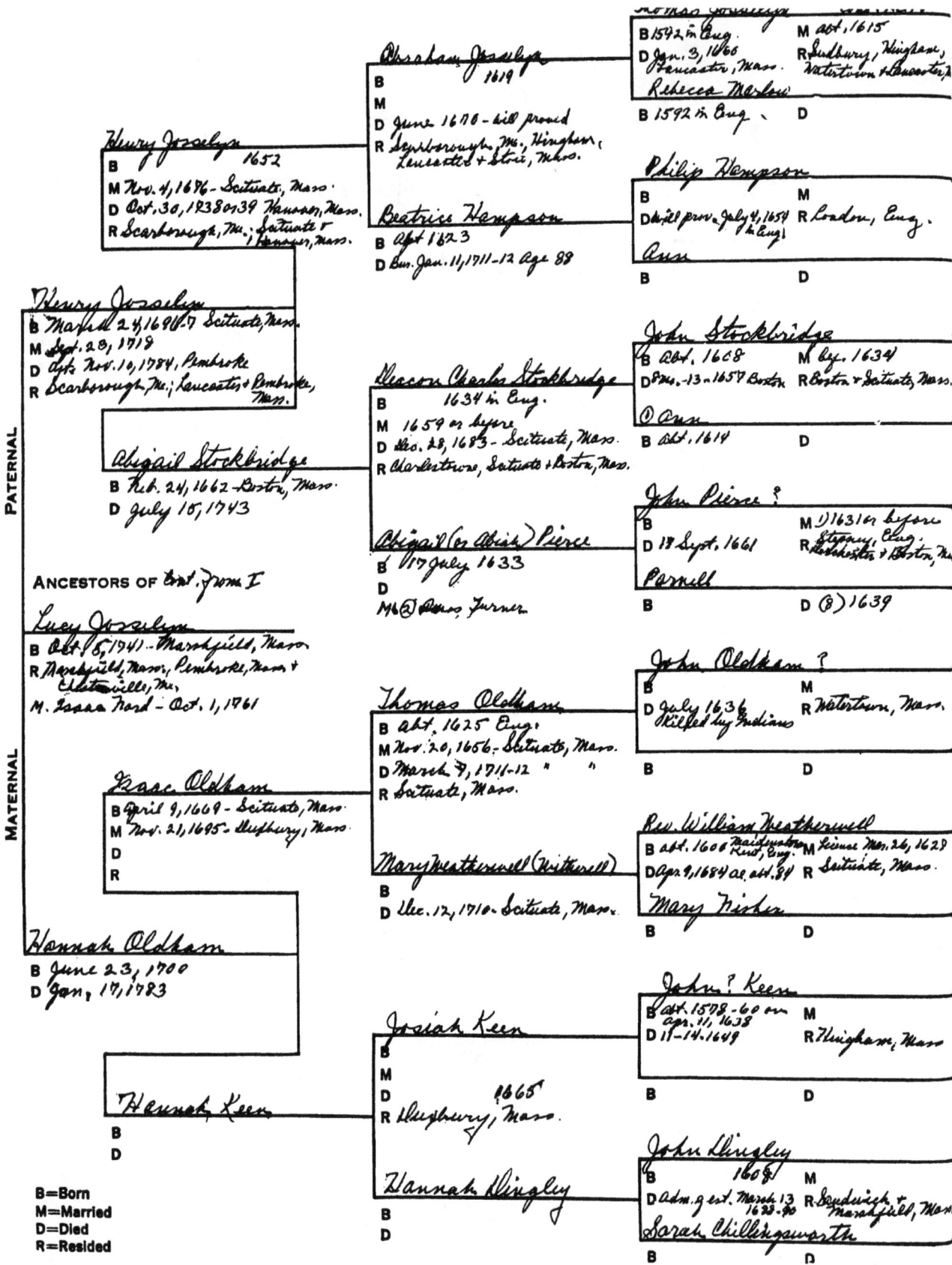

Henry Josselyn
B 1652
M Nov. 4, 1676 - Scituate, Mass.
D Oct. 30, 1738 or 39 Hanover, Mass.
R Scarborough, Me.; Scituate & Hanover, Mass.

Abraham Josselyn
B 1619
M
D June 1670 - will proved
R Scarborough, Me., Hingham, Lancaster & Stow, Mass.

Thomas Josselyn
B 1592 in Eng.
M abt. 1615
D Jan. 3, 1660 Lancaster, Mass.
R Sudbury, Hingham, Watertown & Lancaster, Mass.

Rebecca Marlow
B 1592 in Eng.
D

Beatrice Hampson
B Abt 1623
D Bur. Jan. 11, 1711-12 Age 88

Philip Hampson
B
M
D will prov. July 4, 1654 in Eng.
R London, Eng.

Ann
B
D

Abigail Stockbridge
B Feb. 24, 1662 - Boston, Mass.
D July 10, 1743

Deacon Charles Stockbridge
B 1634 in Eng.
M 1659 or before
D Dec. 28, 1683 - Scituate, Mass.
R Charlestown, Scituate & Boston, Mass.

John Stockbridge
B abt. 1608
M by. 1634
D Mo.-13-1657 Boston
R Boston & Scituate, Mass.

(1) Ann
B abt. 1614
D

Abigail (or Abiah) Pierce
B 17 July 1633
D
M (2) Amos Turner

John Pierce?
B
M (1) 1631 or before
D 18 Sept. 1661
R Stepney, Eng.; Dorchester & Boston, Mass.

Parnell
B
D (?) 1639

PATERNAL

ANCESTORS OF Cont. from I

MATERNAL

Lucy Josselyn
B Oct. 15, 1741 - Marshfield, Mass.
R Marshfield, Mass., Pembroke, Mass. & Chestersville, Me.
M. Isaac Ford - Oct. 1, 1761

Hannah Oldham
B June 23, 1700
D Jan. 17, 1783

Isaac Oldham
B April 9, 1669 - Scituate, Mass.
M Nov. 21, 1695 - Duxbury, Mass.
D
R

Thomas Oldham
B abt. 1625 Eng.
M Nov. 20, 1656 - Scituate, Mass.
D March 7, 1711-12 " "
R Scituate, Mass.

John Oldham?
B
M
D July 1636 Killed by Indians
R Watertown, Mass.

B
D

Mary Weatherwell (Witherell)
B
D Dec. 12, 1710 - Scituate, Mass.

Rev. William Weatherwell
B abt. 1600 Maidstone, Kent, Eng.
M License Mar. 26, 1623
D Apr. 9, 1684 ae. abt. 84
R Scituate, Mass.

Mary Fisher
B
D

Hannah Keen
B
D

Josiah Keen
B
M
D 1665
R Duxbury, Mass.

John? Keen
B abt. 1578-60 or Apr. 11, 1638
M
D 11-14-1649
R Hingham, Mass.

B
D

Hannah Dingley
B
D

John Dingley
B 1608
M
D Adm. g est. March 13 1689-90
R Sandwich & Marshfield, Mass.

Sarah Chillingsworth
B
D

B=Born
M=Married
D=Died
R=Resided

CHART IX

Andrew Spaulding
B Nov. 19, 1652 - Chelmsford, Mass.
M April 30, 1674 - Chelmsford, Mass.
D May 5, 1713
R Chelmsford, Mass.

B
D Feb. 26, 1670 Will Prov. Apr. 5, 1670
M ⓪ 1640
R Chelmsford, Mass. Wendham & Braintree, Mass. James City, Va.

Rachel
B
D
1st wife Margaret

Henry Spaulding
B Nov. 2, 1680
M 1703
D Apr. 5, 1718 - age 38 y. 5 m. 3 d.
R Chelmsford, Mass.

Hannah Jeffs
B Feb. 14, 1655 - Billerica, Mass.
D Jan. 21, 1730

Henry Jeffs (or Jefts)
B Abt. 1606
D May 24, 1700 ae 94 Will Prov. June 17, 1700
M May 21, 1647 - Woburn
R Billerica, Mass. Woburn, Mass.

Hannah Births
B
D Sept. 15, 1652 Billerica Mass.

Leonard Spaulding
B Dec. 1, 1713
M Int. Dec. 18, 1737
D Feb. 1758 - Concord, Mass.
R Chelmsford & Concord, Mass.

Thomas Lund
B
D bef. Feb. 5, 1687 - Est. adm.
M
R Boston, Mass.

B
D

Thomas Lund
B abt. 1660
M
D after 1721
R Dunstable, Mass.

Elizabeth Lund
B Sept. 29 - Dunstable, Mass.
D Apr. 18, 1781 - ae. 98 y. 3 m. 26 d. in Chelmsford
M ⓪ Samuel Scripture of Groton, Mass. int. Feb. 6, 1723 & Chelmsford, Mass.

Eleanor
B
D

B
D
M
R

B
D

ANCESTORS OF Cont. from I

Benjamin Spaulding R.S.
B Feb. 6, 1739 Chelmsford, Mass.
R Chelmsford, Ashby, & Townsend, Mass. Buckfield, Me.
M. Patty Barritt - Nov. 29, 1764
D. Oct. 14, 1811

John Durant
B
M Nov. 16, 1670 - Billerica, Mass.
D Oct. 27, 1692 in Prison at Cambridge during witchcraft delusion.
R Billerica, Mass.

B
D
M
R

B
D

Thomas Durant
B Jan. 7, 1674 - Billerica, Mass.
M June 12, 1702 - " "
D
R

John Button
D - 1687
R - Boston

Thomas Button
B abt. 1621 - Eng.
D Jan. 22, 1687
M
R Woburn, Reading & Billerica, Mass.

Susanna Dutton
B Feb. 27, 1653 - Reading, Mass.
D
M ⓪ Justinian Holden, bef. 1694

Susannah
B
D

Elizabeth Durant
B 1719
D 1799 - aged 80 - Buckfield, Me.
M ⓪ bef. Aug. 9, 1773 to Dr. Ezekiel Chase Prob. Hillsboro Co. N.H.

Abraham Jaquith
B
D
M
R Charlestown, Mass.

Ann Jordan
B
D
James Jordan, Chelsea Will 26 April 1655

Abraham Jaquith
B Dec. 19, 1644
M March 13, 1671 - Woburn, Mass.
D 1677 - 1680
R Woburn & Billerica, Mass. (Part now called Wilmington)

Sarah Jaquith
B Sept. 21, 1677
D

Henry Adford (or Adverd)
B
D 1653 - Rehoboth, Mass.
M 6 Oct. 1643
R Scituate & Marshfield Mass.

Mary Adford
B Bap. June 29, 1651 Scituate, Mass.
D
M. ⓪ Jacob 2 Hamblet

Tamson Manson (Came in "Blessing" from London, 1635 - aged 14)
B Abt. 1621
D

B=Born
M=Married
D=Died
R=Resided

CHART X

PATERNAL

Lieut. John Barrett
B Eng.
M bef. 1659
D May 19, 1704
R Chelmsford, Mass.

- (father) B 1619 Eng. M
- D Oct. 6, 1668 - Chelmsford, Mass. R Braintree + Chelmsford, Mass.
- Margaret
- B D July 8, 1681 - Chelmsford, Mass.

Jonathan Barrett
B
M② 1708 (abt.)
D
R Chelmsford, Mass.

Sarah
B
D

- B M
- D R
- B D

John Barrett
B Dec. 13, 1709
M May 24, 1738 - Concord, Mass.
D March 18, 1772
R Chelmsford, Mass.

Roger Wilson
B M
D R
Mary Fuller
B D

John Wilson
B 1631 - Scrooby, Nottinghamshire, Eng.
M
D July 2, 1687
R Woburn, Mass.

Abigail (Wilson) Hildreath, wid.
B Aug. 8, 1666 - Woburn, Mass.
D
M① Joseph Hildreath of Woburn, Mass. 25-12-1683

James
B M
D R
B D

Hannah (James) Palmer
B
D

ANCESTORS OF Cont. from I

MATERNAL

Patty Barrett
B Jan. 20, 1740-1
R Chelmsford, Mass. Buckfield, Me.
M. Benjamin Spaulding
D. Oct. 4, 1819 - Buckfield, Maine

Sergt. John Heald Cont. X a
B bapt. March 1636 Alderly, Eng. M
D June 17, 1689 - Chelmsford, Mass. R
Sarah Dane dau. of Thomas Dane
B D July 22, 1689 - Concord, Mass.

Lieut. John Heald
B Sept. 19, 1666 - Concord, Mass.
M Dec. 18, 1690 - Concord, Mass.
D Nov. 25, 1721 ae. 55 Concord "
R Concord, Mass.

Deacon John Heald
B Aug. 19, 1693 - Concord, Mass.
M
D May 16, 1775 - ae. 82nd yr. Acton, Mass.
R Concord, Chelmsford + Acton, Mass.

Roger Chandler
B abt. 1637 M Apr. 25, 1671 - Concord, Mass.
D R Concord + Billerica, Mass.
Mary Simonds dau. Wm. + Judith (Phippen) Simonds
B D Aug. 25, 1671 - Concord, Mass.

Mary Chandler
B Jan. 6, 1671-2 Concord, Mass.
D Aug. 14, 1759 - 88th yr. Concord, Mass.

Martha Heald
B April 4, 1718 - Concord, Mass.
D Feb. 26, 1795 - Carlisle, Mass.

John Heald (see X a)
B M
D May 24, 1662 R Concord, Roxbury + Cambridge, Mass.
Dorothy Andrews
B D

Israel Heald
B July 30, 1660 - Concord, Mass.
M
D Sept. 8, 1738, ae. abt. 78 - Stow, Mass.
R Concord + Stow, Mass.

Mary Heald (called Hale)
B April 27, 1698 - Concord, Mass.
D Sept. 1, 1758 - 61st yr. Acton, Mass.

Edward Wright Cont. X b
B abt. 1626 - Castle Bromwich Co. Warwick, Eng. M
D Aug. 28, 1691 - Concord, Mass. R
Elizabeth (Mellowes) Barrett, wid. Cont. XI
B bapt. Dec. 10, 1625 Sutterton, Co. Lincoln, Eng. D Feb. 15, 1690-91 Concord, Mass.
M. ① Thomas Barrett, son of Humphrey Barrett

Martha Wright
B June 18, 1659 Concord, Mass.
D June 14, 1746, ae. abt. 87 yr. Stow, Mass.

B=Born
M=Married
D=Died
R=Resided

CHART Xa

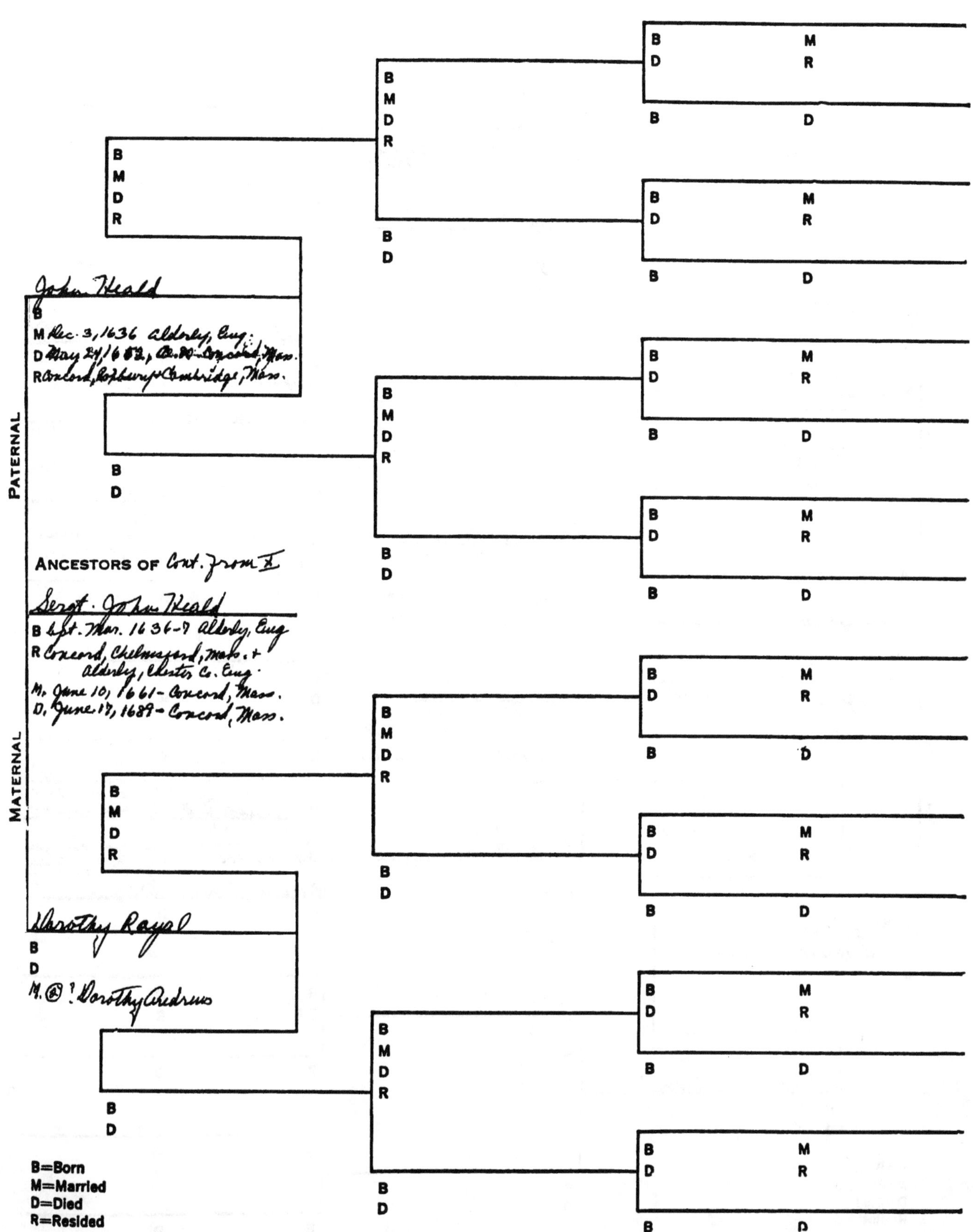

ANCESTORS OF Cont. from X

Sergt. John Heald

B bpt. Mar. 1636-7 Alderly, Eng.
R Concord, Chelmsford, Mass. + Alderly, Chester Co. Eng.
M. June 10, 1661 – Concord, Mass.
D. June 17, 1689 – Concord, Mass.

PATERNAL

John Heald

B
M Dec. 3, 1636 Alderly, Eng.
D May 24, 1662, a. 80 – Concord, Mass.
R Concord, Roxbury & Cambridge, Mass.

MATERNAL

Dorothy Royal

B
D
M. (2)? Dorothy Andrews

B=Born
M=Married
D=Died
R=Resided

CHART XI

Ancestors of Capt. John Warren from I

Capt. John Warren R.S.
B March 5, 1731
R Westbrook + Stroudwater, Me.
D. Jan. 30, 1807, Stroudwater, Me.
M. Jane Johnson, Dec. 25, 1755

PATERNAL

John Warren
B Dec. 16, 1706
M
D Will prov. Feb 24, 1769
R Kittery, Maine

James Warren
B 1658
M November 1, 1692
D Est. adm. July 6, 1725
R Kittery, Maine

James Warren, Prob. a Scotish Prisoner
B abt. 1622 (deposed Sept. 1702 upward of 80.
M
D Will Prob. Dec. 24, 1702
R Berwick, Scotland, So. Berwick + Parish of Unity, Kittery, Maine

B | M
D | R
B | D

Margaret
B Ireland
D Will prob. Oct. 15, 1713

B | M
D | R
B | D

Mary Frost
B By Mar. 11, 1673-4 (date bro. Wm. was born)
D

John Frost (Foss or Froost)
B Jan. 3, 1638 - Ribe Denmark
M *
D Will 17 Dec. 1699 "2. next day"
R Dover, N.H., Portsmouth, N.H.

David Levitsen Foss (or Froost)
B 1604 | M 1637
D Aug. 8, 1659 | R Ribe, Denmark

Anna Hendersdatter
B 1619 | D 1689.

Mary Chadbourne
B 10th mo. 1644 - Boston, Mass.
D By. Jan. 25, 1686-7
* M. (2) Elizabeth, wid. of James Dogge who M. (3) James Emery

William Chadbourne (Wm. Chadbourne)
B | M By. 1644
D | R Kittery + Portsmouth, Boston, Mass.

Mary
B | D

MATERNAL

Mary Heard
B June 10, 1709 - Dover, N.H.
D

Tristram Heard
B March 4, 1666-7
M 1691
D Will Prob. June 3, 1734
R Dover, N.H.

Capt. John Heard
B 1613
M 1643, York, Me.
D Jan. 17, 1688-9, Dover, N.H.
R Dover, N.H.

B | M
D | R
B | D

Elizabeth Hull
B 1626-1628
D Nov. 30, 1706

Rev. Joseph Hull
B 1594 Crewkerne, Co. Somerset | M
D Nov. 19, 1665 | R Weymouth + Hingham, Boston, Barnstable, Yarmouth, Mass. - Yo
(1) Joanna Coffin | (2) Agnes

Thomas Hull
M. Jan. 11, 1572-3
Joan Peson

B | D

Abigail Waldron ?
B By. 1673
D

B
M
D
R

B | M
D | R
B | D

B
D

B | M
D | R
B | D

B=Born
M=Married
D=Died
R=Resided

CHART XII

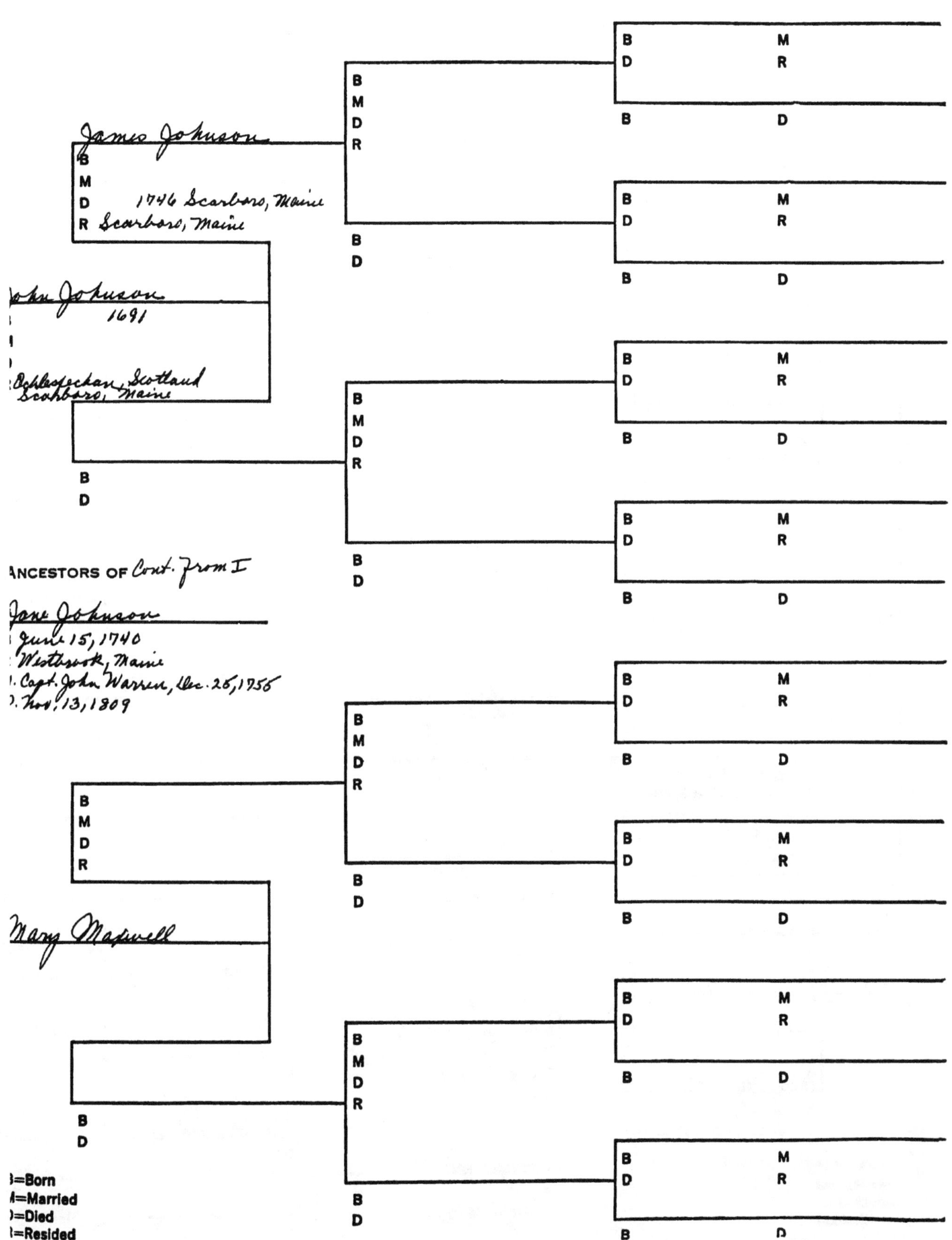

James Johnson
B
M
D 1746 Scarboro, Maine
R Scarboro, Maine

John Johnson
B 1691
M
D
R Ochleofechan, Scotland
Scarboro, Maine

B
D

ANCESTORS OF Cont. from I

Jane Johnson
B June 15, 1740
R Westbrook, Maine
M. Capt. John Warren, Dec. 25, 1756
D. Nov. 13, 1809

B
M
D
R

Mary Maxwell

B
D

B=Born
M=Married
D=Died
R=Resided

B
M
D
R

B
D

B
M
D
R

B
D

B
M
D
R

B
D

B
M
D
R

B
D

B M
D R
B D

B M
D R
B D

B M
D R
B D

B M
D R
B D

B M
D R
B D

B M
D R
B D

B M
D R
B D

B M
D R
B D

CHART XIII

PATERNAL

Thomas Bray
B Oct. 9, 1687, Gloucester, Mass.
M Jan. 29, 1716-17 - Beverly, Mass.
D Est. settled Jan. 14, 1744
R Gloucester, Mass.

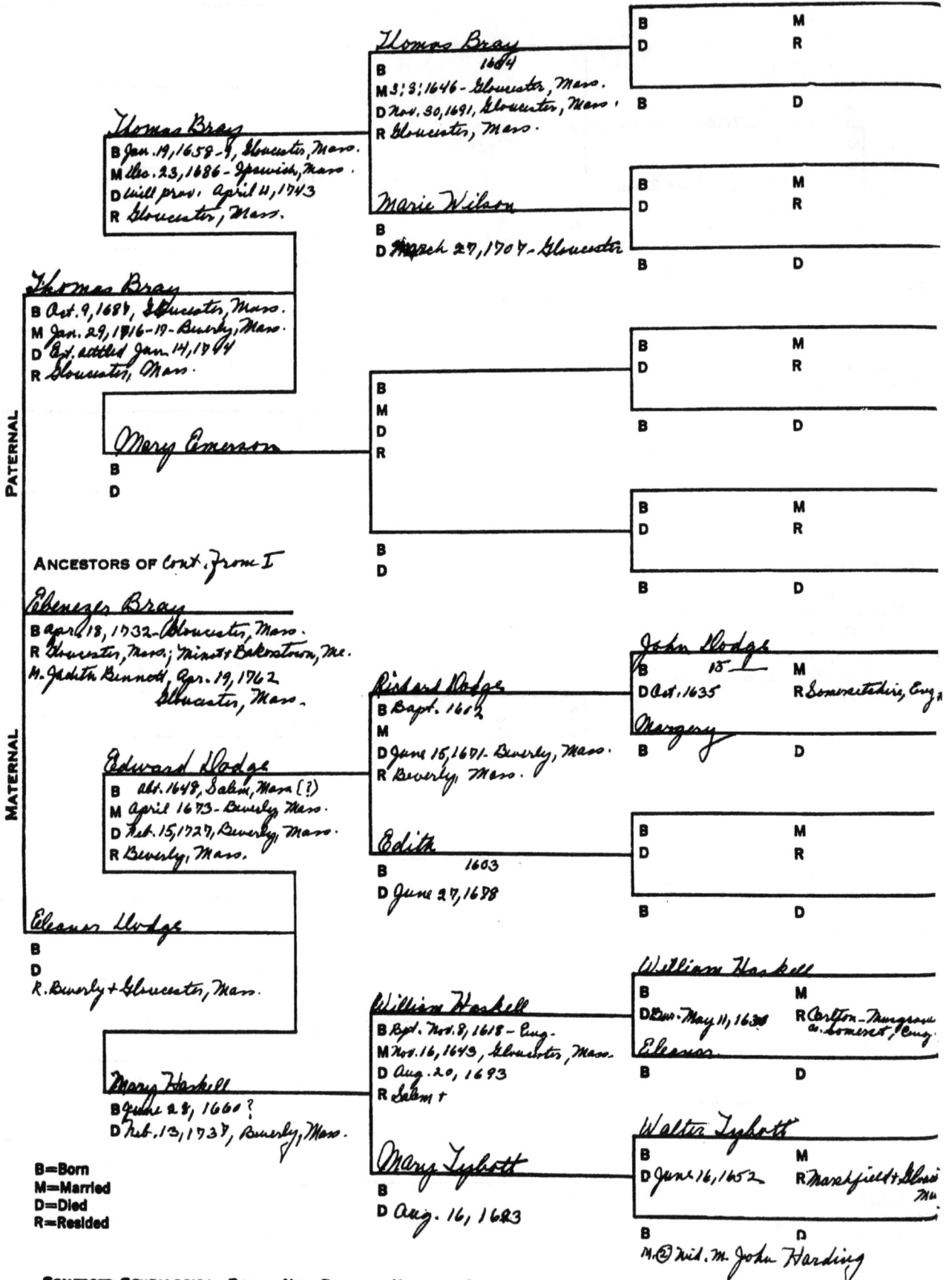

Thomas Bray
B Jan. 19, 1658-9, Gloucester, Mass.
M Dec. 23, 1686 - Ipswich, Mass.
D will prov. April 11, 1743
R Gloucester, Mass.

Thomas Bray
B 1624
M 3; 3; 1646 - Gloucester, Mass.
D Nov. 30, 1691, Gloucester, Mass.
R Gloucester, Mass.

B
D
M
R

B
D

Marie Wilson
B
D March 27, 1707 - Gloucester

B
D
M
R

B
D

Mary Emerson
B
D

B
M
D
R

B
D
M
R

B
D

B
D

B
D
M
R

B
D

ANCESTORS OF cont. from I

MATERNAL

Ebenezer Bray
B Apr. 18, 1732 - Gloucester, Mass.
R Gloucester, Mass.; Minot & Bakerstown, Me.
M. Judith Bennett, Apr. 19, 1762
Gloucester, Mass.

Edward Dodge
B abt. 1648, Salem, Mass (?)
M April 1673 - Beverly, Mass.
D Feb. 15, 1727, Beverly, Mass.
R Beverly, Mass.

Richard Dodge
B Bapt. 1602
M
D June 15, 1671 - Beverly, Mass.
R Beverly, Mass.

John Dodge
B 15
D Oct. 1635
M
R Somersetshire, Eng.

Margery
B
D

Edith
B 1603
D June 27, 1678

B
D
M
R

B
D

Eleanor Dodge
B
D
R. Beverly & Gloucester, Mass.

Mary Haskell
B June 28, 1660?
D Feb. 13, 1737, Beverly, Mass.

William Haskell
B Bapt. Nov. 8, 1618 - Eng.
M Nov. 16, 1643, Gloucester, Mass.
D Aug. 20, 1693
R Salem &

William Haskell
B
D Bur. May 11, 1630
M
R Charlton-Musgrove co. Somerset, Eng.

Eleanor
B
D

Mary Tybbott
B
D Aug. 16, 1683

Walter Tybbott
B
D June 16, 1652
M
R Marshfield & Gloucester, Mass.

B
D
M. (2) wid. m. John Harding

B=Born
M=Married
D=Died
R=Resided

CHART XIV

Ancestors of cont. from I

Paternal

Judith Bennett
B Sept. 2, 1739, Gloucester, Mass.
R Gloucester, Mass.; Minot, Maine
M. Ebenezer Bray, Apr. 19, 1762
D. Jan. 30, 1799.

Stephen Bennett
B Jan. 20, 1707 - Gloucester, Mass.
M Jan. 2, 1728-9 - Salisbury, Mass.
D 1790
R Gloucester + Sandwich, Mass.

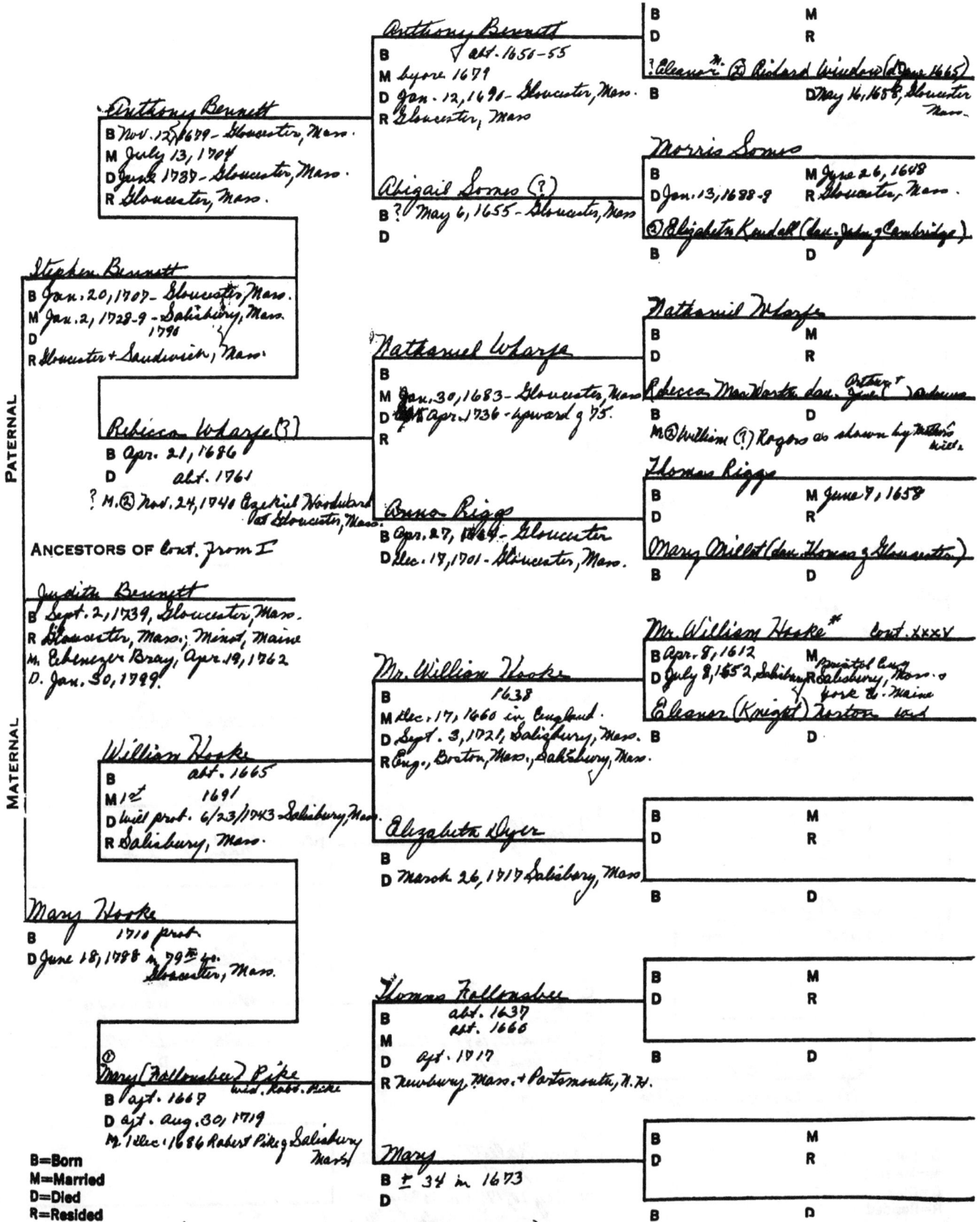

Anthony Bennett
B Nov. 12, 1679 - Gloucester, Mass.
M July 13, 1704
D June 1737 - Gloucester, Mass.
R Gloucester, Mass.

Anthony Bennett
B abt. 1650-55
M before 1679
D Jan. 12, 1691 - Gloucester, Mass.
R Gloucester, Mass.

B
M
D
R

? Eleanor m. (2) Richard Windsor (d. June 1665)
B
D May 16, 1658, Gloucester, Mass.

Abigail Somes (?)
B ? May 6, 1655 - Gloucester, Mass.
D

Morris Somes
B
M June 26, 1648
D Jan. 13, 1688-9
R Gloucester, Mass.

(1) Elizabeth Kendall (dau. John of Cambridge)
B
D

Rebecca Wharfe (?)
B Apr. 21, 1686
D abt. 1761
? M. (2) Nov. 24, 1740 Ezekiel Woodward at Gloucester, Mass.

Nathaniel Wharfe
B
M Jan. 30, 1683 - Gloucester, Mass.
D Apr. 1736 - upward of 75.
R

Nathaniel Wharfe
B
M
D
R

Rebecca MacWorth dau. Arthur + Jane (?) Andrews
B
D
M (2) William (?) Rogers as shown by Mother's will.

Anna Riggs
B Apr. 27, 1664 - Gloucester
D Dec. 17, 1701 - Gloucester, Mass.

Thomas Riggs
B
M June 7, 1658
D
R

Mary Millet (dau. Thomas of Gloucester)
B
D

Maternal

Mary Hooke
B 1710 prob.
D June 18, 1788 in 79th yr. Gloucester, Mass.

William Hooke
B abt. 1665
M 1st 1691
D will prob. 6/23/1743 - Salisbury, Mass.
R Salisbury, Mass.

Mr. William Hooke
B 1638
M Dec. 17, 1660 in England.
D Sept. 3, 1721, Salisbury, Mass.
R Eng., Boston, Mass., Salisbury, Mass.

Mr. William Hooke* Cont. XXXV
B Apr. 8, 1612
M Bristol Eng.
D July 8, 1652, Salisbury
R Salisbury, Mass. + York Co. Maine

Eleanor (Knight) Norton wid.
B
D

Elizabeth Dyer
B
D March 26, 1717 Salisbury, Mass.

B
M
D
R

B
D

(1) Mary (Follansbee) Pike wid. Robt. Pike
B abt. 1667
D abt. Aug. 30, 1719
M 1 Dec. 1686 Robert Pike of Salisbury, Mass.

Thomas Follansbee
B abt. 1637
M abt. 1660
D abt. 1717
R Newbury, Mass. + Portsmouth, N.H.

B
M
D
R

B
D

Mary
B ± 34 in 1673
D

B
M
D
R

B
D

B=Born
M=Married
D=Died
R=Resided

* Gov. of Agamenticus (Now State of Maine)

CHART XV

PATERNAL

Ebenezer Record
B Oct. 8, 1712 Pembroke, Mass.
M March 7, 1744, Pembroke, Mass.
D bef. Feb. 15, 1797
R Pembroke, Mass.

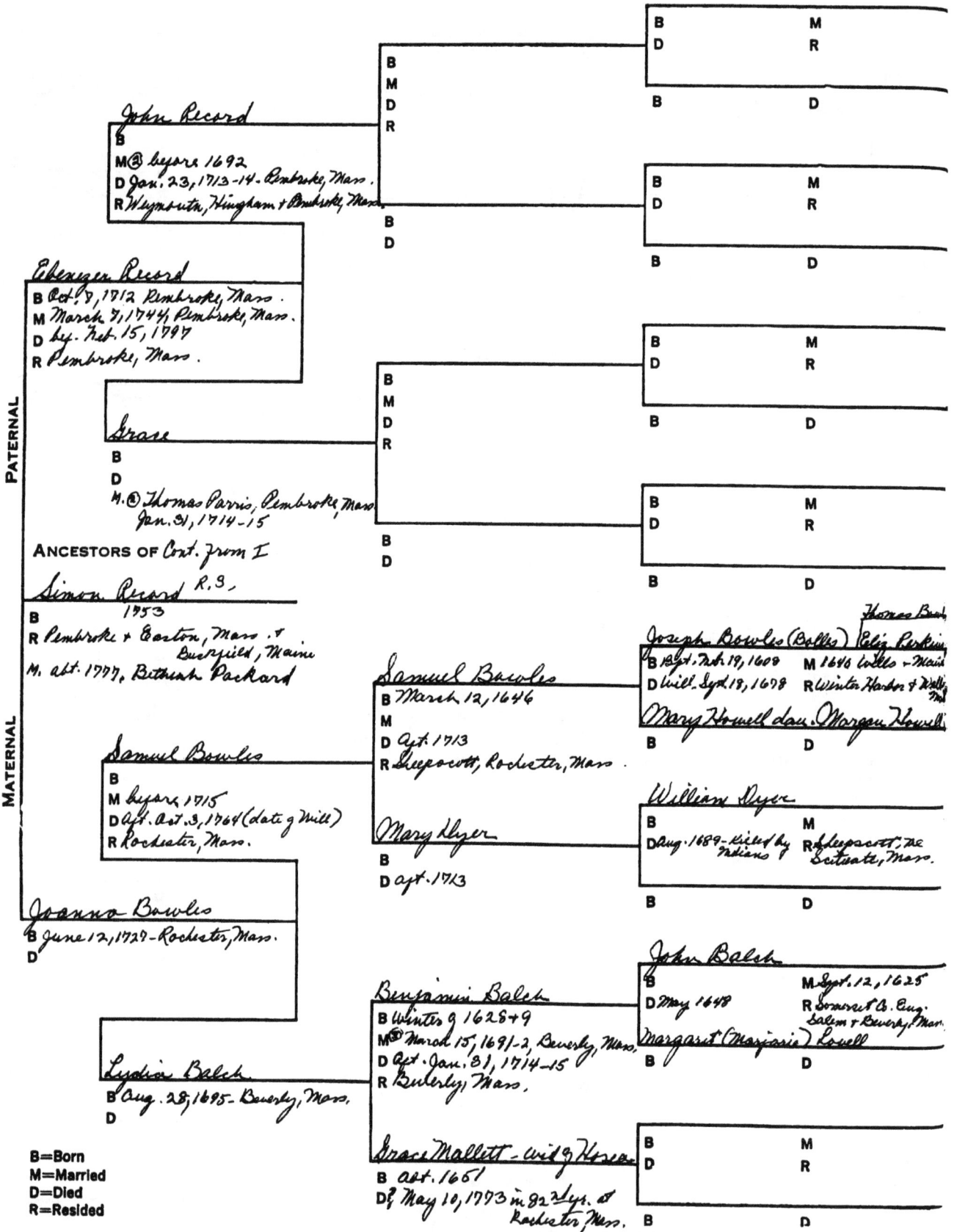

John Record
B
M② before 1692
D Jan. 23, 1713-14 - Pembroke, Mass.
R Weymouth, Hingham + Pembroke, Mass.

B
M
D
R

B
D

B M
D R

B D

B M
D R

B D

Grace
B
D
M.① Thomas Parris, Pembroke, Mass.
Jan. 31, 1714-15

B
M
D
R

B
D

B M
D R

B D

B M
D R

B D

ANCESTORS OF Cont. from I

Simon Record R.S.
B 1753
R Pembroke + Easton, Mass. + Buckfield, Maine
M. abt. 1777, Bethiah Packard

MATERNAL

Joanna Bowles
B June 12, 1727 - Rochester, Mass.
D

Samuel Bowles
B
M before 1715
D aft. Oct. 3, 1764 (date of will)
R Rochester, Mass.

Samuel Bowles
B March 12, 1646
M
D aft. 1713
R Sheepscott, Rochester, Mass.

Joseph Bowles (Bolles) | Thomas Bowles / Eliz. Perkins
B bapt. Feb. 19, 1608
D will. Sept. 18, 1678
M 1640 Wells - Maine
R Winter Harbor + Wells, Me.

Mary Howell dau. of Morgan Howell
B
D

Mary Dyer
B
D aft. 1713

William Dyer
B
D Aug. 1689 - killed by Indians
M
R Sheepscott, Me. Scituate, Mass.

B
D

Lydia Balch
B Aug. 28, 1695 - Beverly, Mass.
D

Benjamin Balch
B Winter of 1628+9
M③ March 15, 1691-2, Beverly, Mass.
D aft. Jan. 31, 1714-15
R Beverly, Mass.

John Balch
B
D May 1648
M Sept. 12, 1625
R Somerset Co. Eng. Salem + Beverly, Mass.

Margaret (Marjorie) Lovell
B
D

Grace Mallett - wid. of Hosea
B abt. 1651
D? May 10, 1773 in 82nd yr. of Rochester, Mass.

B M
D R

B D

B=Born
M=Married
D=Died
R=Resided

CHART XVI

Ancestors of Cont. from I

Bethiah Packard
- B bpt. Sept. 24, 1758 W. Bridgewater, Mass.
- R Bridgewater, Mass. + Buckfield, Maine
- M. Simon Record, abt. 1777

Paternal

**** Joseph Packard**
- B May 30, 1725 W. Bridgewater, Mass. V.R.
- M Dec. 29, 1748 Bridgewater, Mass.
- D
- R Bridgewater, Mass.

Joseph Packard
- B abt. 1697
- M Nov. 28, 1723, W. Bridgewater, Mass.
- D Oct. 19, 1760 in 63rd yr. " "
- R Bridgewater, Mass.

Mary Willis
- B Nov. 27, 1699 Bridgewater, Mass.
- D Dec. 19, 1774 " "

*** Ensign Samuel Packard**
- B
- M
- D Est. settled 1698
- R Bridgewater, Mass.

Elizabeth Lathrop
- B
- D June 19, 1716 - Bridgewater Mass.

John Willis
- B 1671–72
- M 1698
- D Nov. 1, 1732
- R Bridgewater, Mass.

Mary Brett
- B 1678–9
- D Jan. 14, 1756 in 78th yr. West Bridgewater, Mass.

Samuel Packard
- B
- D Nov. 7, 1684 Bridgewater, Mass.
- M
- R Windham, Eng. Bridgewater, Hingham, + Weymouth, Mass.

Elizabeth
- B
- D

Mark Lathrop Cont. XXVII
- B bpt. Sept. 27, 1597
- D Oct. 25, 1688
- M
- R Bridgewater, Salem, Duxbury + Weymouth Mass.

Hannah House
- B
- D

Deacon John Willis Cont. XXI
- B
- D will dated 1712
- M
- R Bridgewater, Mass.

Experience Byram Cont. XXII
- B
- D

Judge Elihu Brett Cont. XXIV
- B by 1650
- D
- M by 1678
- R Duxbury + Bridgewater Mass.

Ann Turner dau. George + Mary (Robbins) Turner
- B
- D

Maternal

Sarah Johnson
- B July 19, 1732 - Bridgewater Mass.
- D Jan. 28, 1775

Capt. David Johnson
- B Oct. 16, 1692
- M Jan. 17, 1719 W. Bridgewater, Mass.
- D Feb. 22, 1773 ae 81 " "
- R Roxbury, Hingham, Scituate + Bridgewater, Mass.

Rebecca Washburn
- B aft. 1688
- D

Hon. Isaac Johnson, Esq.
- B Feb. 18, 1667–8
- M prob. 1691 in Hingham, Mass.
- D May 27, 1738 - 71 yrs. - West Bridgewater, Mass.
- R Bridgewater, Mass.

Abigail, Abiel, Abiah (Leavitt) Lazell
- B Dec. 15, 1667
- D Jan. 4, 1747–8 in 81st yr. West Bridgewater, Mass.

John Washburn
- B 1646 Bridgewater, Mass.
- M April 16, 1679
- D Oct. 1719 ae 73 - Bridgewater Mass.
- R Bridgewater, Mass.

Rebeckar Lapham
- B 1645 Scituate, Mass.
- D abt. 1817 Bridgewater, Mass.

Humphrey Johnson Cont. XXXVII
- B
- D
- M March 20, 1642–3 Roxbury, Mass.
- R Bridgewater, Roxbury + Hingham, Mass.

Elenor Cheney
- B
- D

Deacon John Leavitt Cont. XXIX
- B 1603
- D Nov. 20, 1691
- M Dec. 16, 1645–46 Hingham
- R Dorchester + Hingham Mass.

Sarah Gilman Cont. XXV
- B bpt. Dec. 26, 1617
- D May 26, 1700

John Washburn Cont. XXVI
- B bpt. Nov. 26, 1620
- D Nov. 2, 1686
- M Dec. 6, 1645
- R Bridgewater, Mass.

Elizabeth Mitchell Cont. XXVII
- B 1628 - Plymouth, Mass.
- D by Oct. 1686

Thomas Lapham (David Lapham)
- B Kent Co. Eng.
- D will prov. Oct. 1, 1651
- M March 13, 1636–37
- R Bridgewater, Mass.

Mary Tilden Cont. XXVIII
- B bpt. May 20, 1610
- D

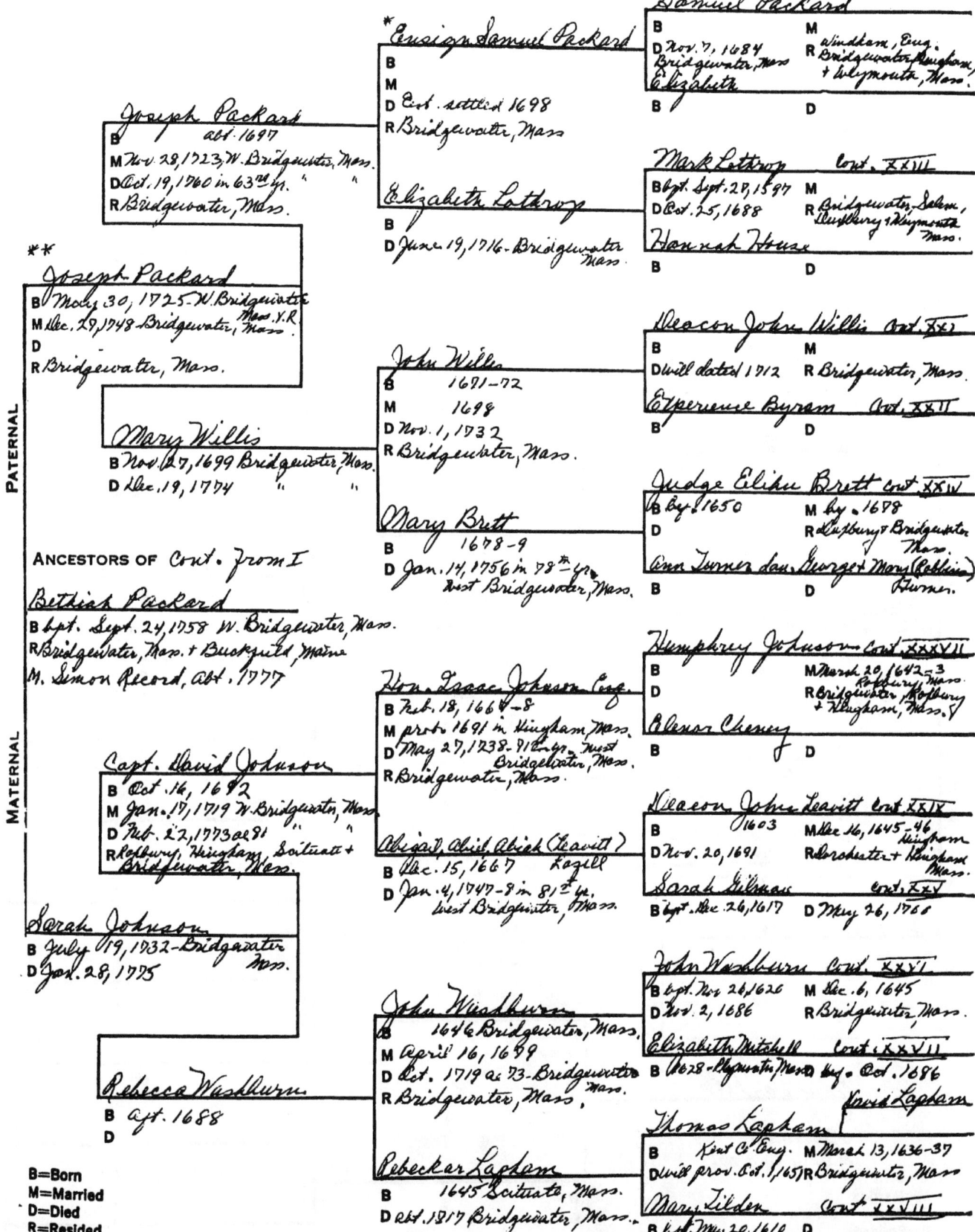

B=Born
M=Married
D=Died
R=Resided

* An officer in King Phillips War in 1676.
** Soldier in French + Indian Wars + served under Gen. Winslow in Nova Scotia in 1755.

CHART XVII

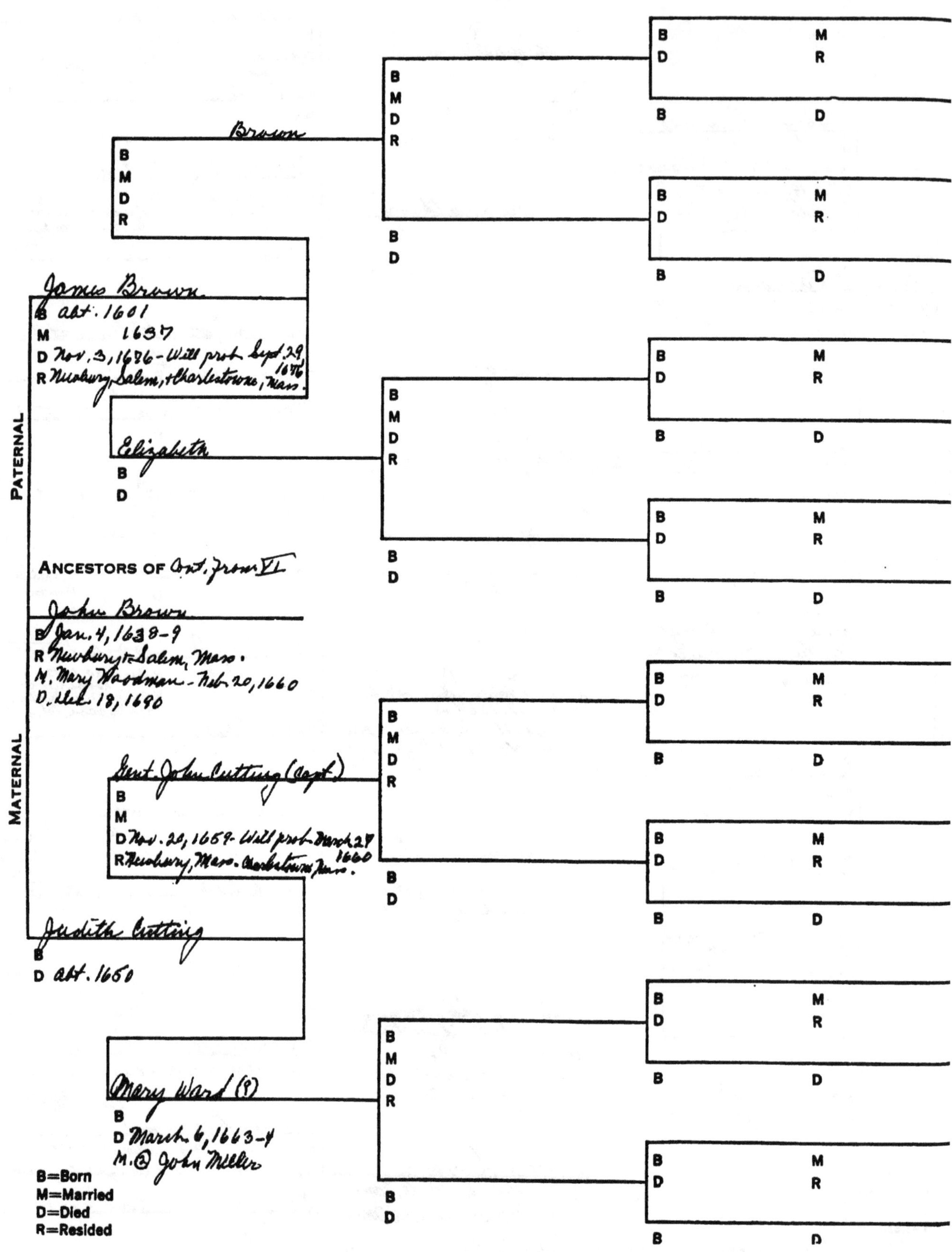

Brown
B
M
D
R

James Brown
B abt. 1601
M 1637
D Nov. 3, 1686 - Will prob. Sept. 29, 1676
R Newbury, Salem, & Charlestown, Mass.

Elizabeth
B
D

PATERNAL

ANCESTORS OF Cont. from VI

John Brown
B Jan. 4, 1638-9
R Newbury & Salem, Mass.
M. Mary Woodman - Feb. 20, 1660
D. Dec. 18, 1690

MATERNAL

Gent. John Cutting (Capt.)
B
M
D Nov. 20, 1659 - Will prob. March 27, 1660
R Newbury, Mass. Charlestown, Mass.

Judith Cutting
B
D abt. 1650

Mary Ward (?)
B
D March 6, 1663-4
M. (2) John Miller

B=Born
M=Married
D=Died
R=Resided

SOMERSET GENEALOGICAL FORM—NEW ENGLAND HISTORIC GENEALOGICAL SOCIETY, 101 NEWBURY STREET, BOSTON, MASS.

CHART XVIII

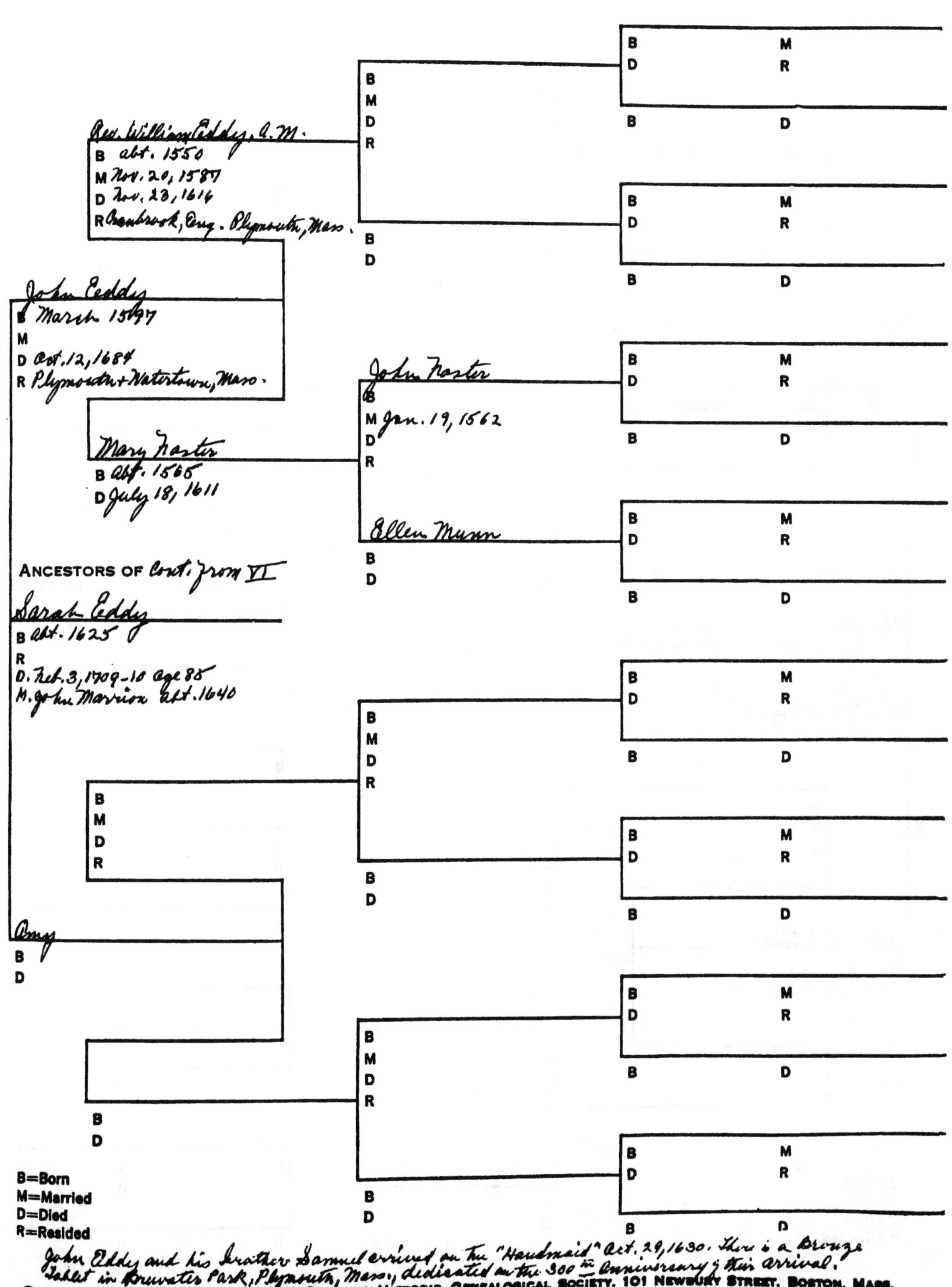

John Eddy and his brother Samuel arrived on the "Handmaid" Oct. 29, 1630. There is a Bronze Tablet in Brewster Park, Plymouth, Mass., dedicated on the 300th Anniversary of their arrival.

Somerset Genealogical Form—New England Historic Genealogical Society, 101 Newbury Street, Boston, Mass.

CHART XIX

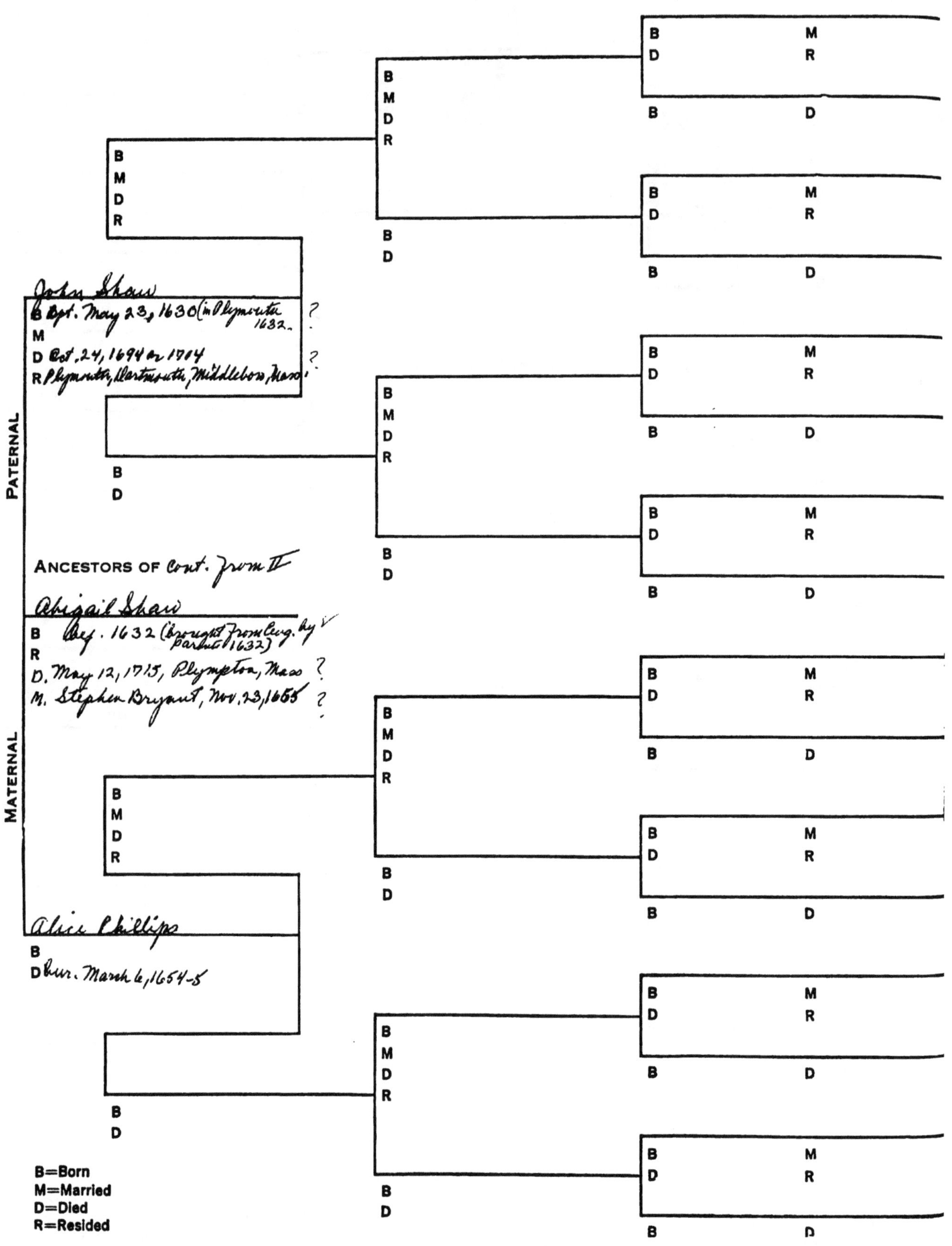

PATERNAL

John Shaw
B Bpt. May 23, 1630 (in Plymouth 1632. ?
M
D Oct. 24, 1694 or 1704 ?
R Plymouth, Dartmouth, Middleboro, Mass.

ANCESTORS OF Cont. from IV

MATERNAL

Abigail Shaw
B Bef. 1632 (brought from Eng. by parents 1632)
R
D. May 12, 1715, Plympton, Mass ?
M. Stephen Bryant, Nov. 23, 1655 ?

Alice Phillips
B
D bur. March 6, 1654-5

B=Born
M=Married
D=Died
R=Resided

Somerset Genealogical Form—New England Historic Genealogical Society, 101 Newbury Street, Boston, Mass.

CHART XX

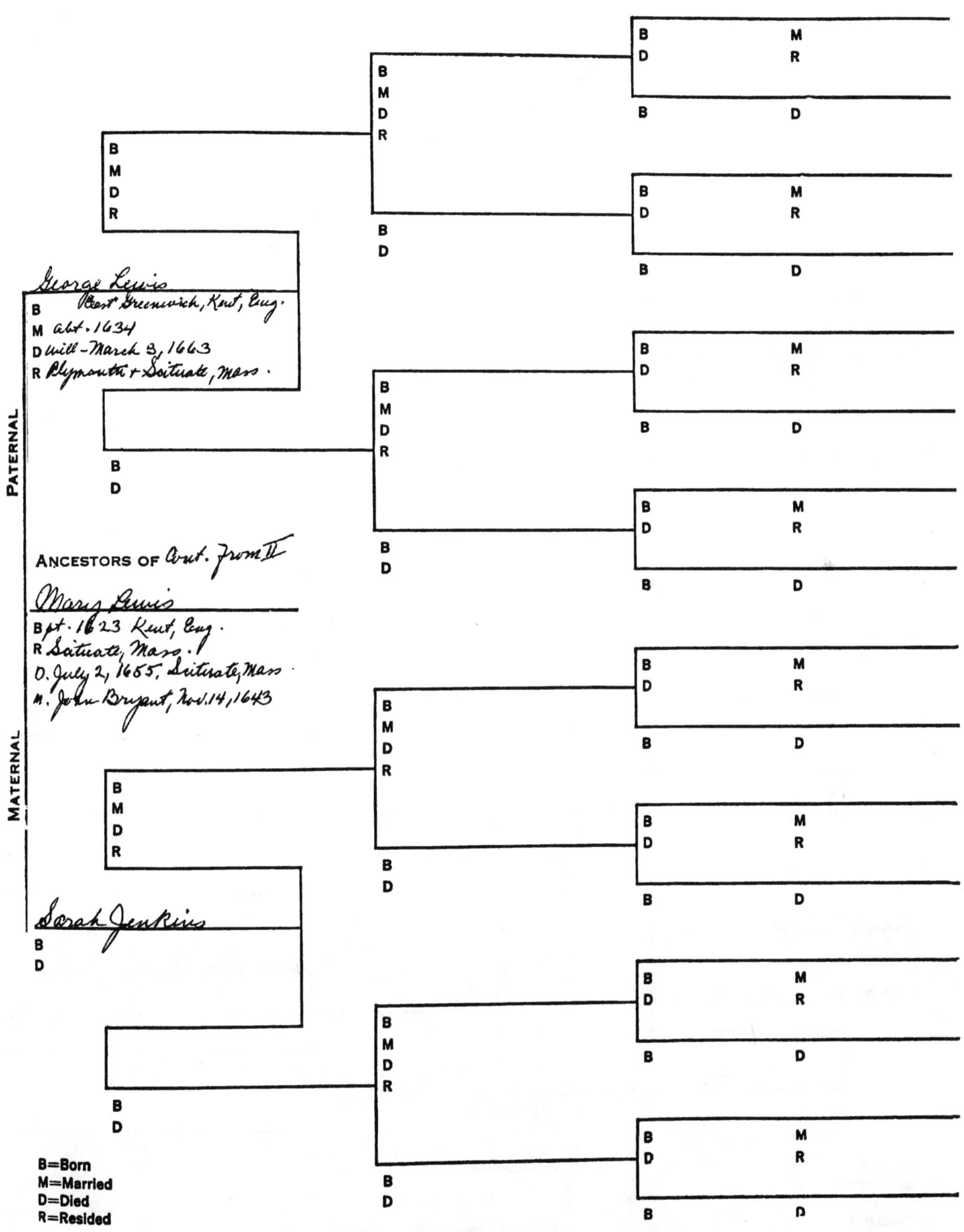

B
M
D
R

George Lewis
B Bapt. Greenwich, Kent, Eng.
M abt. 1634
D will – March 3, 1663
R Plymouth & Scituate, Mass.

B
D

PATERNAL

ANCESTORS OF Cont. from II

Mary Lewis
B pt. 1623 Kent, Eng.
R Scituate, Mass.
D. July 2, 1655, Scituate, Mass.
M. John Bryant, Nov. 14, 1643

MATERNAL

B
M
D
R

Sarah Jenkins
B
D

B
D

B=Born
M=Married
D=Died
R=Resided

CHART XXI

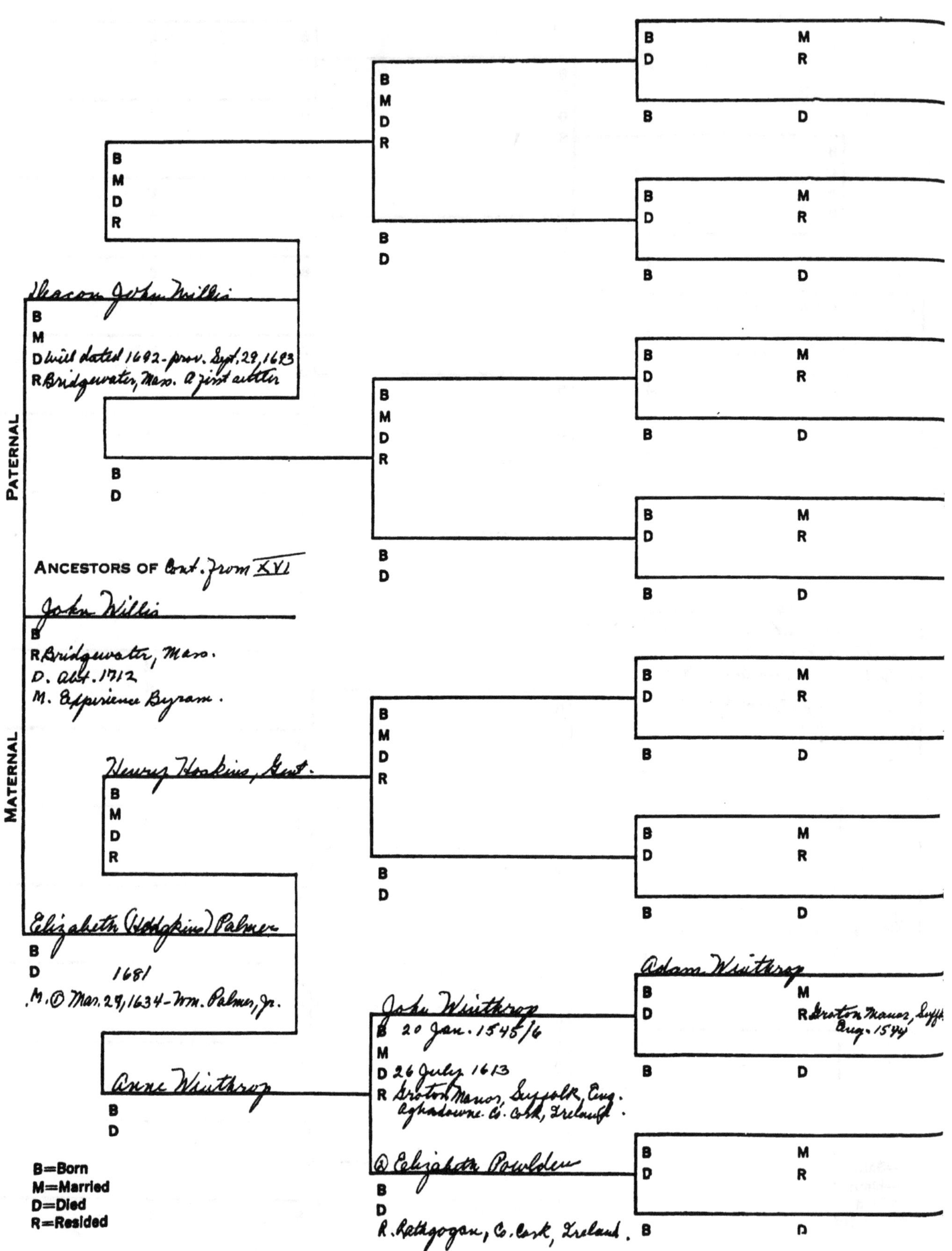

PATERNAL

Deacon John Willis
B
M
D will dated 1692 - prov. Sept. 29, 1693
R Bridgewater, Mass. a first settler

B
M
D
R

B
D

B
M
D
R

B
D

B
M
D
R

B
D

ANCESTORS OF Cont. from XVI

MATERNAL

John Willis
B
R Bridgewater, Mass.
D. abt. 1712
M. Experience Byram.

Elizabeth (Hodgkins) Palmer
B
D 1681
M. ① Mar. 29, 1634 - Wm. Palmer, Jr.

Henry Hoskins, Gent.
B
M
D
R

Anne Winthrop
B
D

B
M
D
R

B
D

John Winthrop
B 20 Jan. 1545/6
M
D 26 July 1613
R Groton Manor, Suffolk, Eng. Aghadowne. Co. Cork, Ireland.

② Elizabeth Powlden
B
D
R. Rathgogan, Co. Cork, Ireland.

B D M R / B D (blank entries)

Adam Winthrop
B
M
D
R Groton Manor, Suff. Aug. 1544
B
D

B
M
D
R
B
D

B=Born
M=Married
D=Died
R=Resided

SOMERSET GENEALOGICAL FORM—NEW ENGLAND HISTORIC GENEALOGICAL SOCIETY, 101 NEWBURY STREET, BOSTON, MASS.

CHART XXII

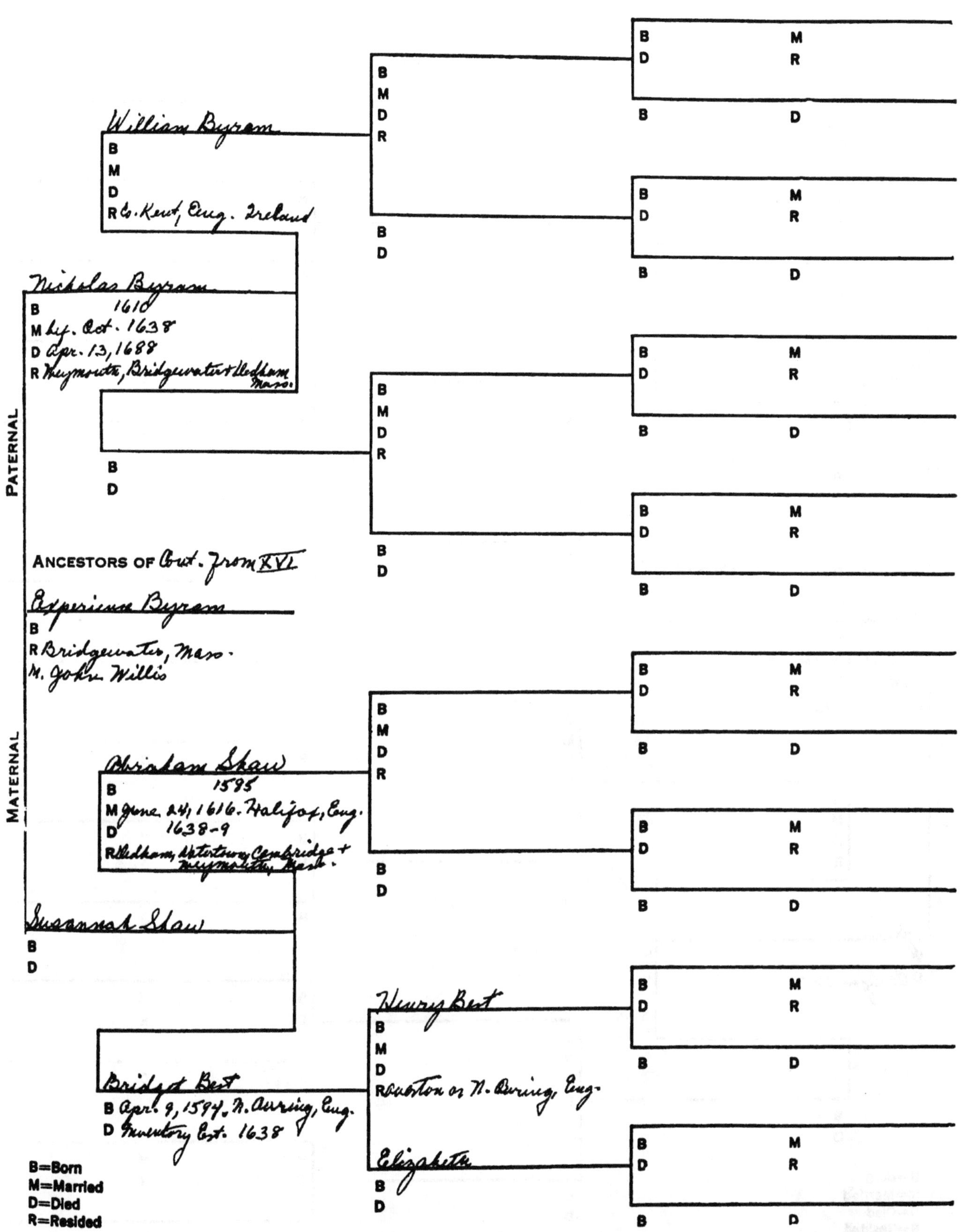

SOMERSET GENEALOGICAL FORM—NEW ENGLAND HISTORIC GENEALOGICAL SOCIETY, 101 NEWBURY STREET, BOSTON, MASS.

CHART XXIII

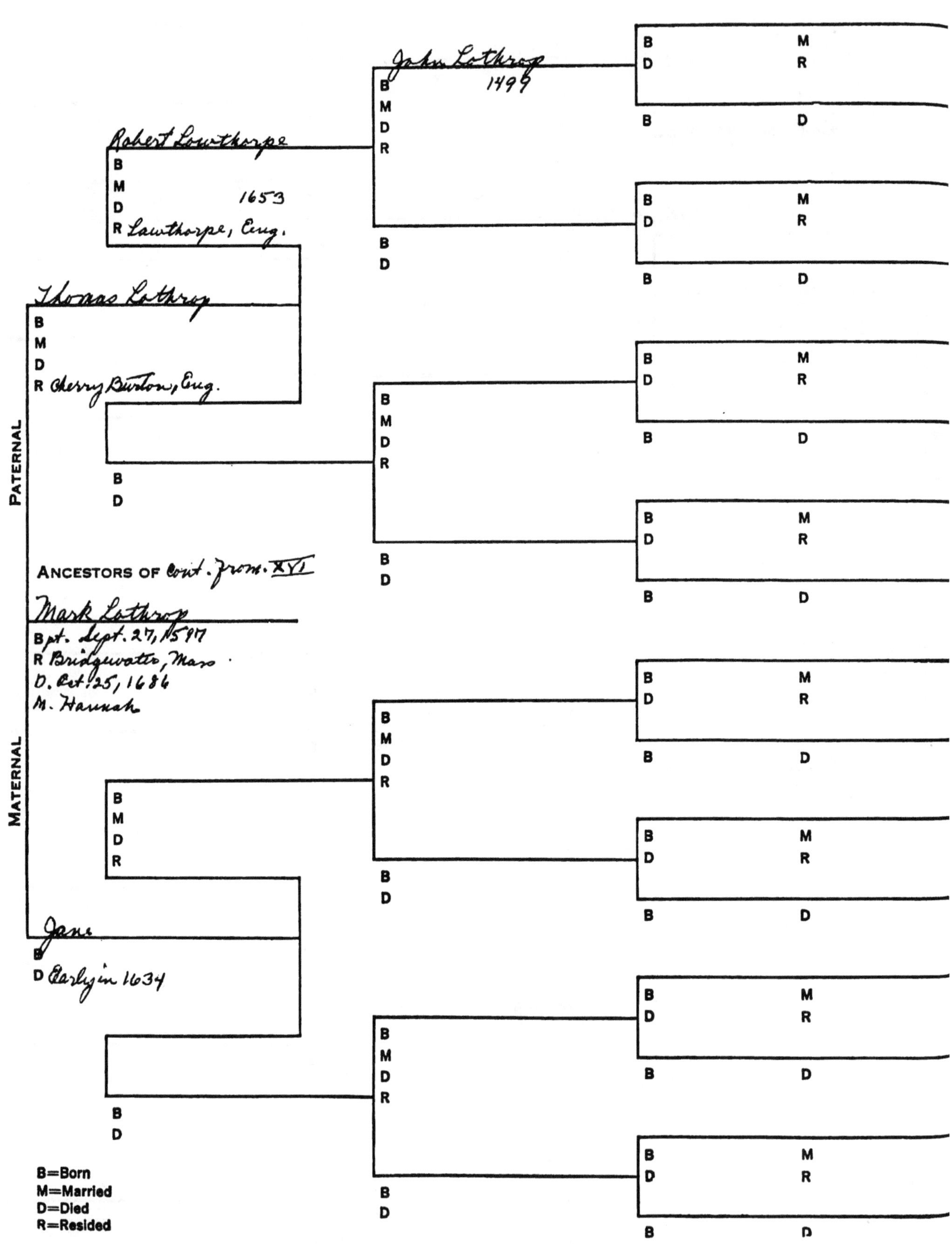

SOMERSET GENEALOGICAL FORM—NEW ENGLAND HISTORIC GENEALOGICAL SOCIETY, 101 NEWBURY STREET, BOSTON, MASS.

CHART XXIV

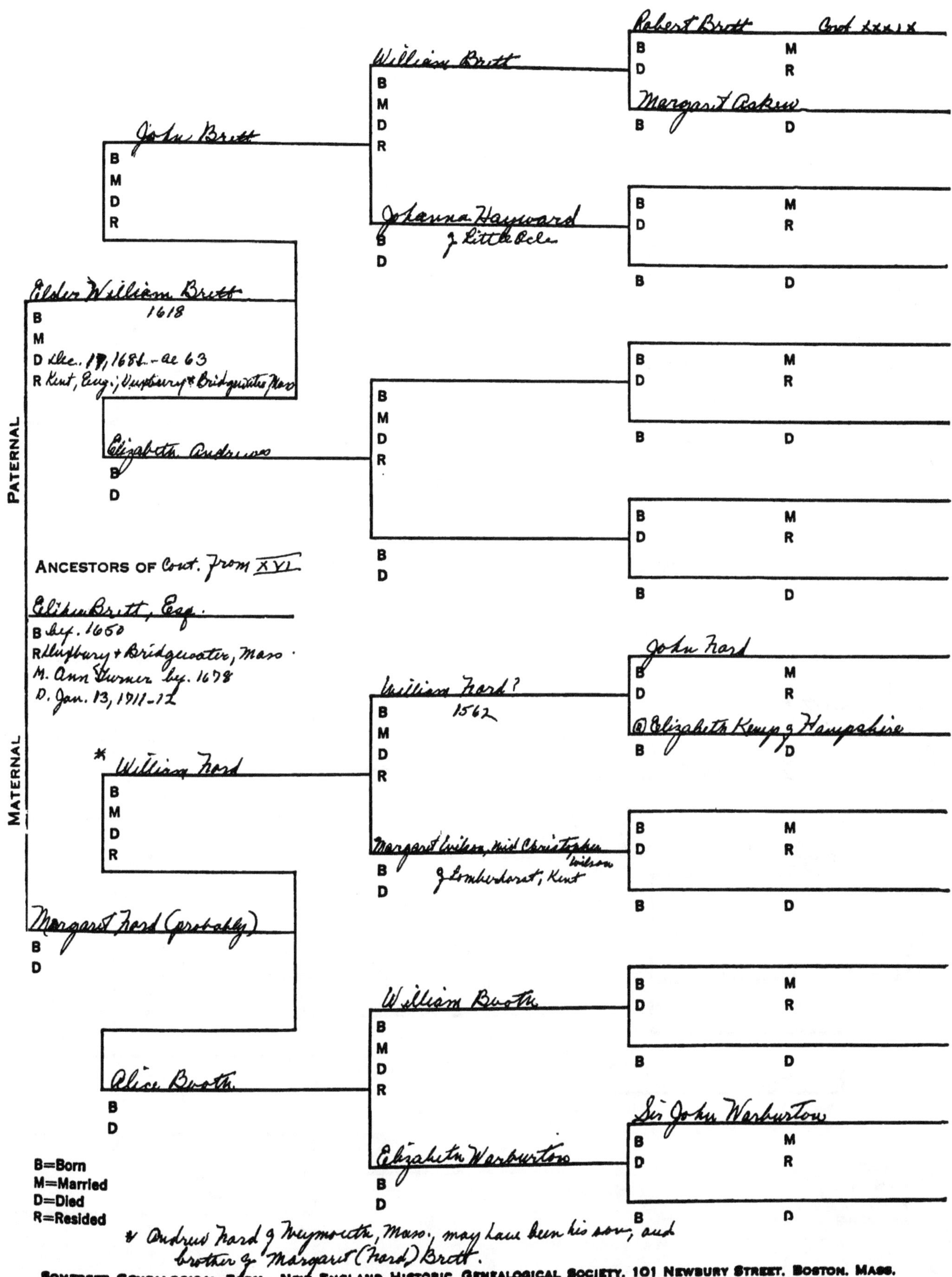

Robert Brett Cont. XXXIX
B M
D R
Margaret Oakew
B D
William Brett
B
M
D
R
Johanna Hayward
of Little Oak
B
D
John Brett
B
M
D
R
Elder William Brett
1618
B
M
D Dec. 17, 1681 - ae 63
R Kent, Eng.; Duxbury & Bridgewater Mass
Elizabeth Andrews
B
D
PATERNAL
ANCESTORS OF Cont. from XVI
Elihu Brett, Esq.
B abt. 1650
R Duxbury & Bridgewater, Mass.
M. Ann Turner bef. 1678
D. Jan. 13, 1711-12
MATERNAL
John Ford
B M
D R
(2) Elizabeth Kemp of Hampshire
B D
William Ford?
1562
B
M
D
R
Margaret Wilson, wid. Christopher Wilson
of Lamberhurst, Kent
B
D
* William Ford
B
M
D
R
Margaret Ford (probably)
B
D
William Booth
B
M
D
R
Sir John Warburton
B M
D R
Elizabeth Warburton
B
D
Alice Booth
B
D
B=Born
M=Married
D=Died
R=Resided
* Andrew Ford of Weymouth, Mass., may have been his son, and brother of Margaret (Ford) Brett.

CHART XXV

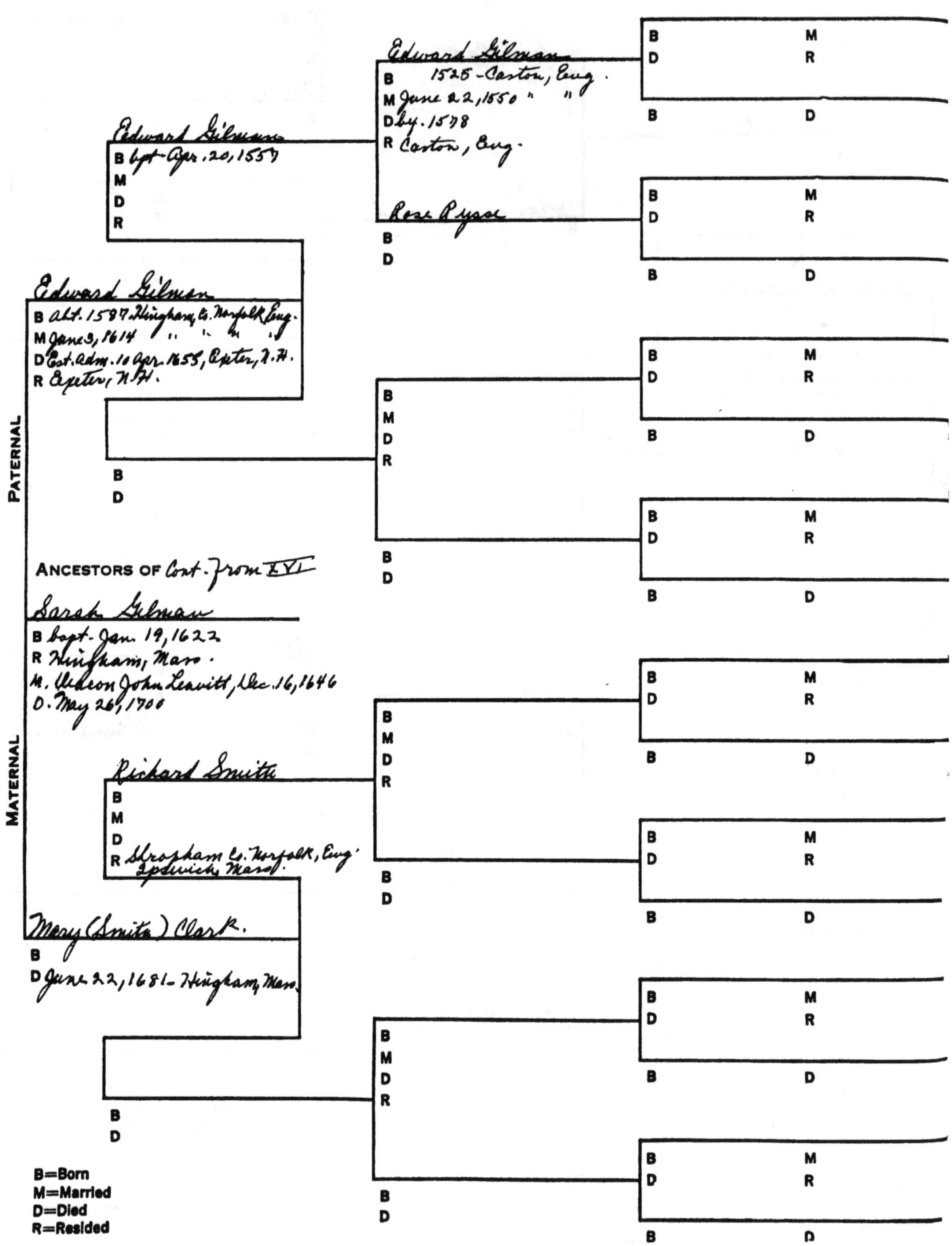

Edward Gilman
B 1525-Caston, Eng.
M June 22, 1550 " "
D by. 1578
R Caston, Eng.
Rose Rysse
B
D
Edward Gilman
B bpt. Apr. 20, 1557
M
D
R
Edward Gilman
B abt. 1587 Hingham, Co. Norfolk Eng.
M June 3, 1614 " " " "
D Est. adm. 10 Apr. 1655, Exeter, N.H.
R Exeter, N.H.
B
D
B
M
D
R
B
D
PATERNAL
ANCESTORS OF Cont. from XVI
Sarah Gilman
B bapt. Jan. 19, 1622
R Hingham, Mass.
M. Deacon John Leavitt, Dec. 16, 1646
D. May 26, 1700
MATERNAL
Richard Smith
B
M
D
R Shropham Co. Norfolk, Eng. Ipswich, Mass.
Mary (Smith) Clark.
B
D June 22, 1681- Hingham, Mass.
B
M
D
R
B
D
B
D
B
M
D
R
B
D
B
D
B=Born
M=Married
D=Died
R=Resided

CHART XXVI

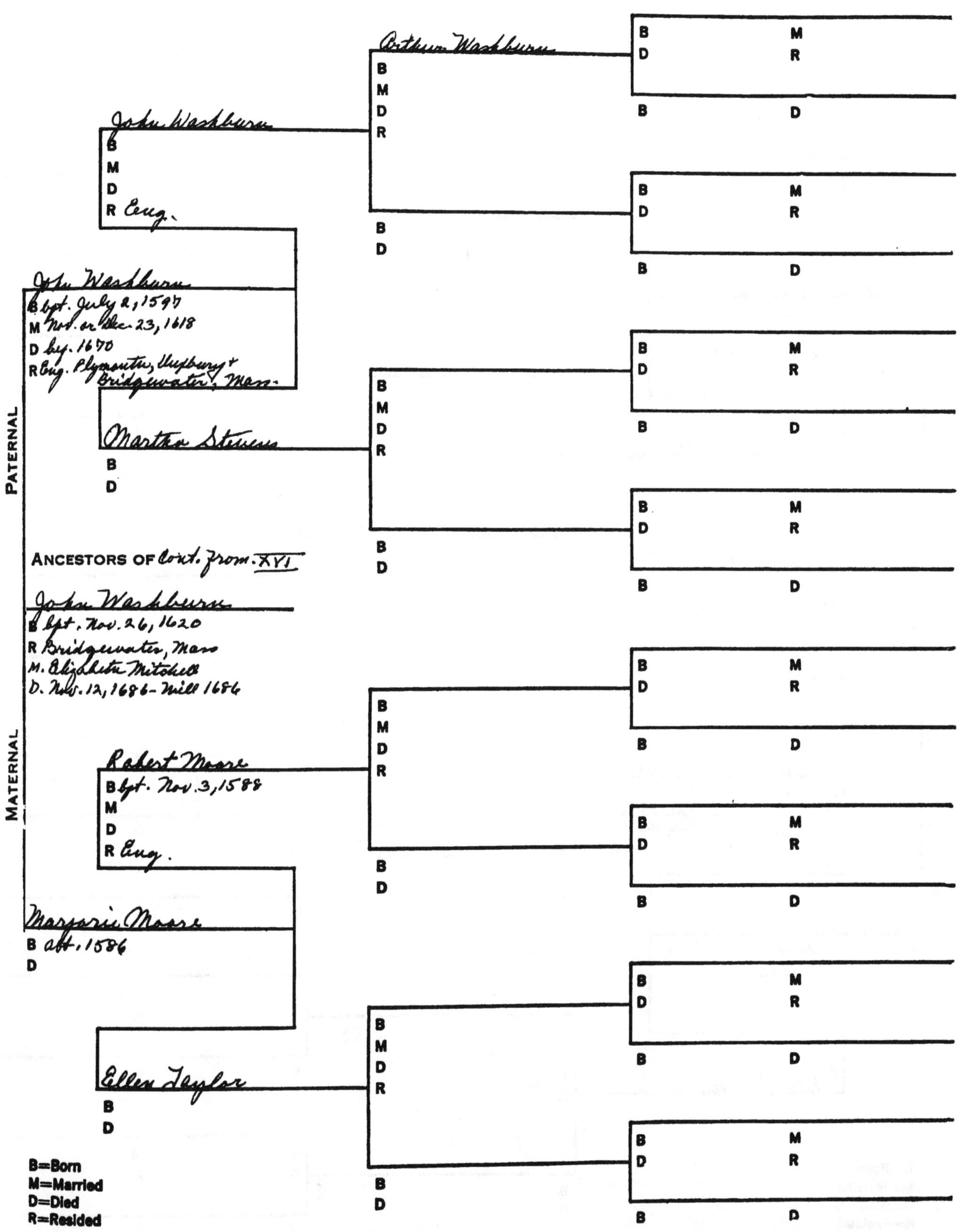

SOMERSET GENEALOGICAL FORM—NEW ENGLAND HISTORIC GENEALOGICAL SOCIETY, 101 NEWBURY STREET, BOSTON, MASS.

CHART XXVII

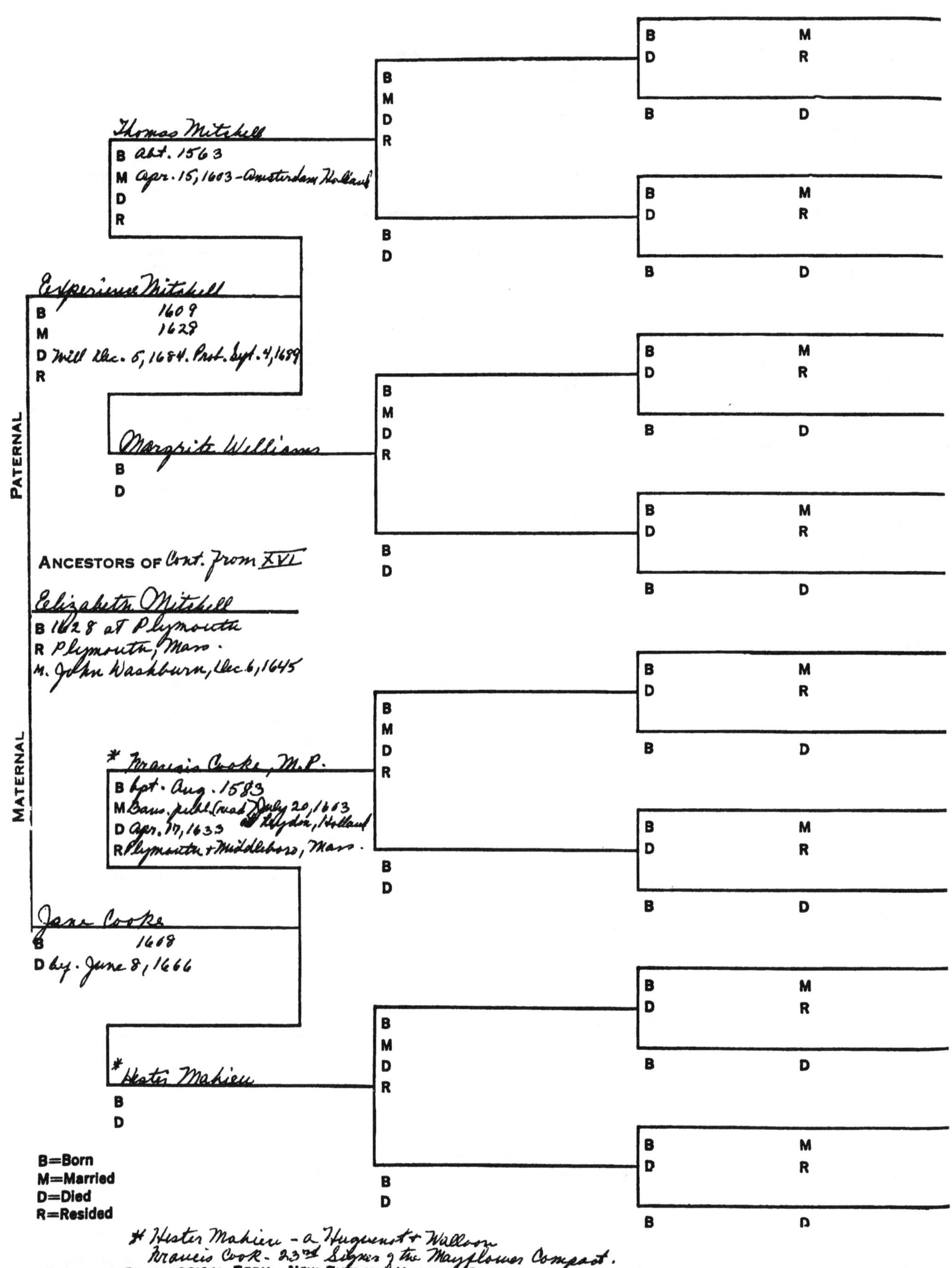

PATERNAL

Thomas Mitchell
B abt. 1563
M Apr. 15, 1603 - Amsterdam Holland
D
R

Experience Mitchell
B 1609
M 1628
D Will Dec. 5, 1684. Prob. Sept. 4, 1689
R

Margrite Williams
B
D

ANCESTORS OF Cont. from XVI

Elizabeth Mitchell
B 1628 at Plymouth
R Plymouth, Mass.
M. John Washburn, Dec. 6, 1645

MATERNAL

* Francis Cooke, M.P.
B bpt. Aug. 1583
M Banns publ. (read) July 20, 1603 at Leyden, Holland
D Apr. 7, 1633
R Plymouth + Middleboro, Mass.

Jane Cooke
B 1608
D by. June 8, 1666

* Hester Mahieu
B
D

B M D R (blank entries for parents and grandparents)

B=Born
M=Married
D=Died
R=Resided

* Hester Mahieu - a Huguenot + Walloon
Francis Cook - 23rd Signer of the Mayflower Compact.

CHART XXVIII

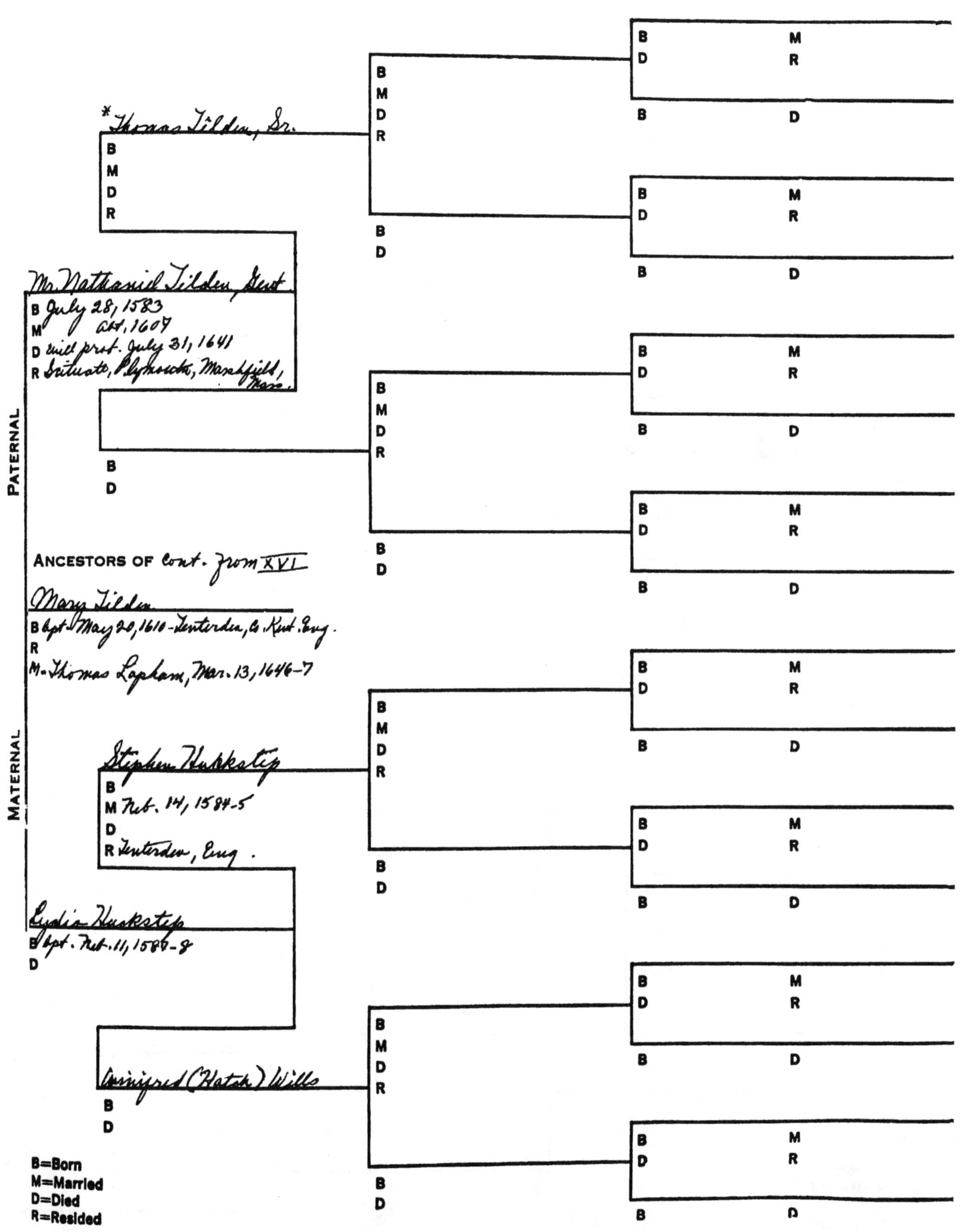

B=Born
M=Married
D=Died
R=Resided

* Thomas Tilden, Sr. had 3 sons: Joseph, Thomas & Nathaniel.

CHART XXIX

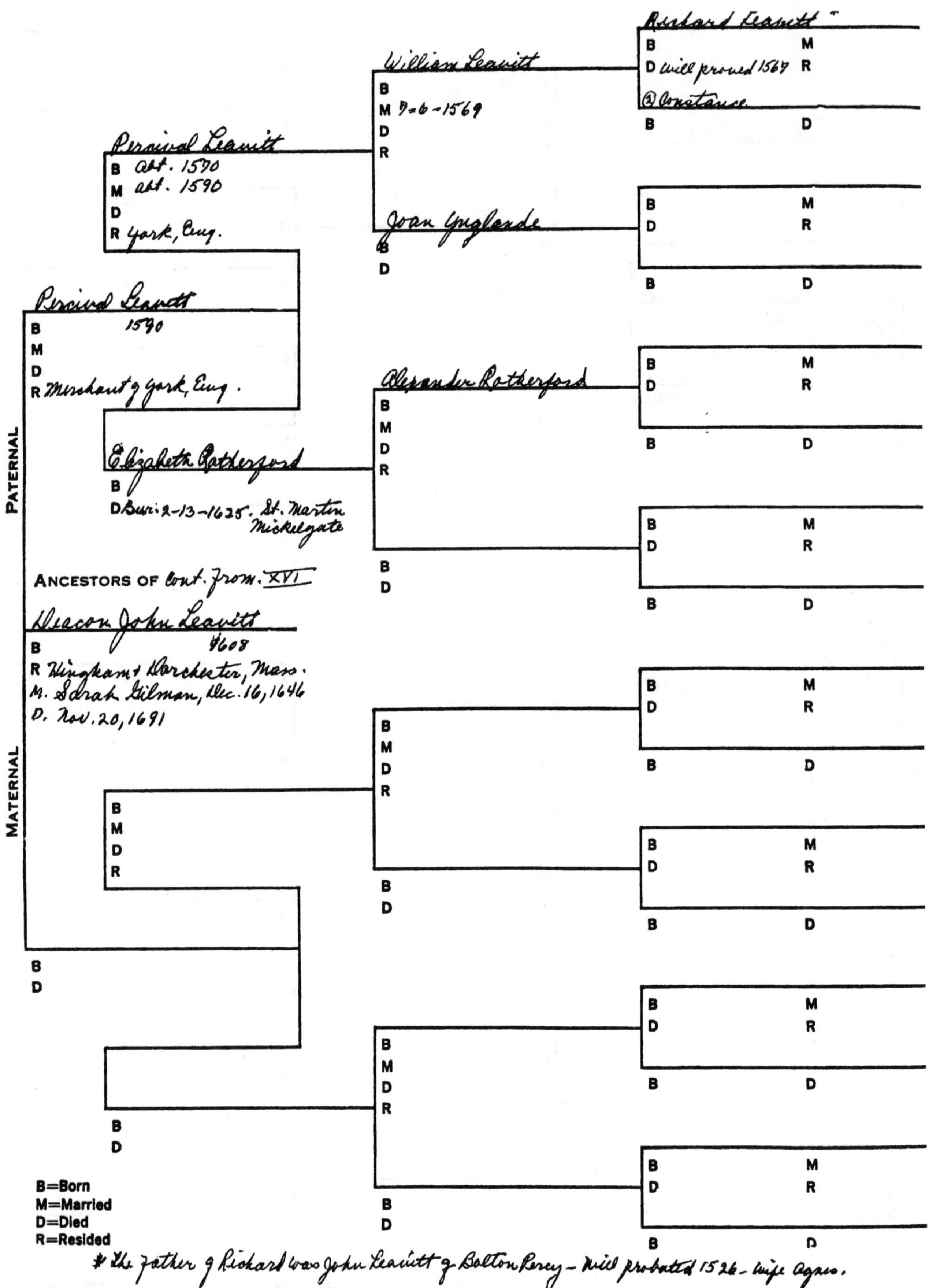

* The father of Richard was John Leavitt of Bolton Percy - will probated 1526 - wife Agnes.

CHART XXX

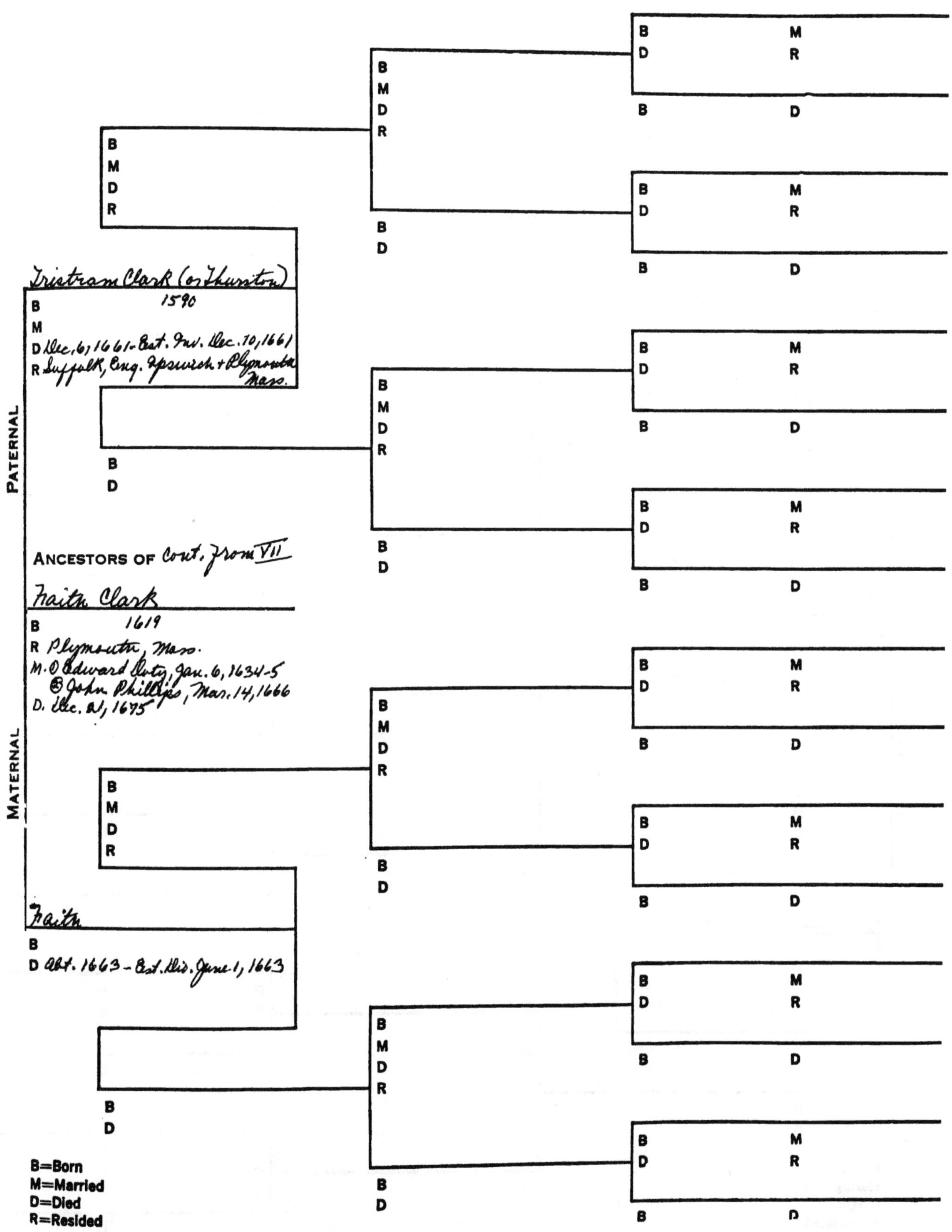

Somerset Genealogical Form—New England Historic Genealogical Society, 101 Newbury Street, Boston, Mass.

CHART XXXI

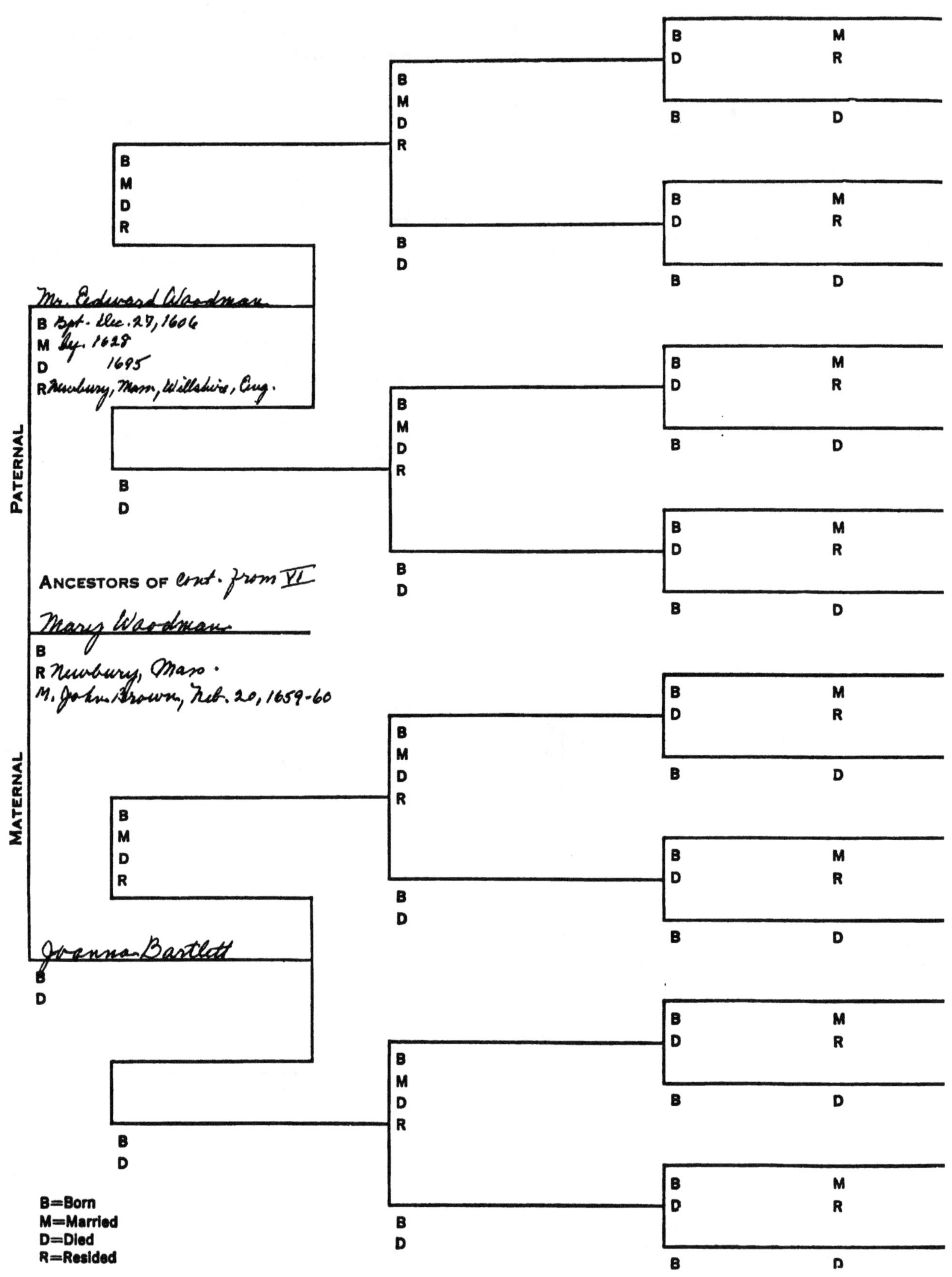

Mr. Edward Woodman
B Bpt. Dec. 27, 1606
M by. 1628
D 1695
R Newbury, Mass, Wiltshire, Eng.
PATERNAL
ANCESTORS OF cont. from VI
Mary Woodman
B
R Newbury, Mass.
M. John Brown, Feb. 20, 1659-60
MATERNAL
Joanna Bartlett
B
D
B=Born
M=Married
D=Died
R=Resided

CHART XXXII

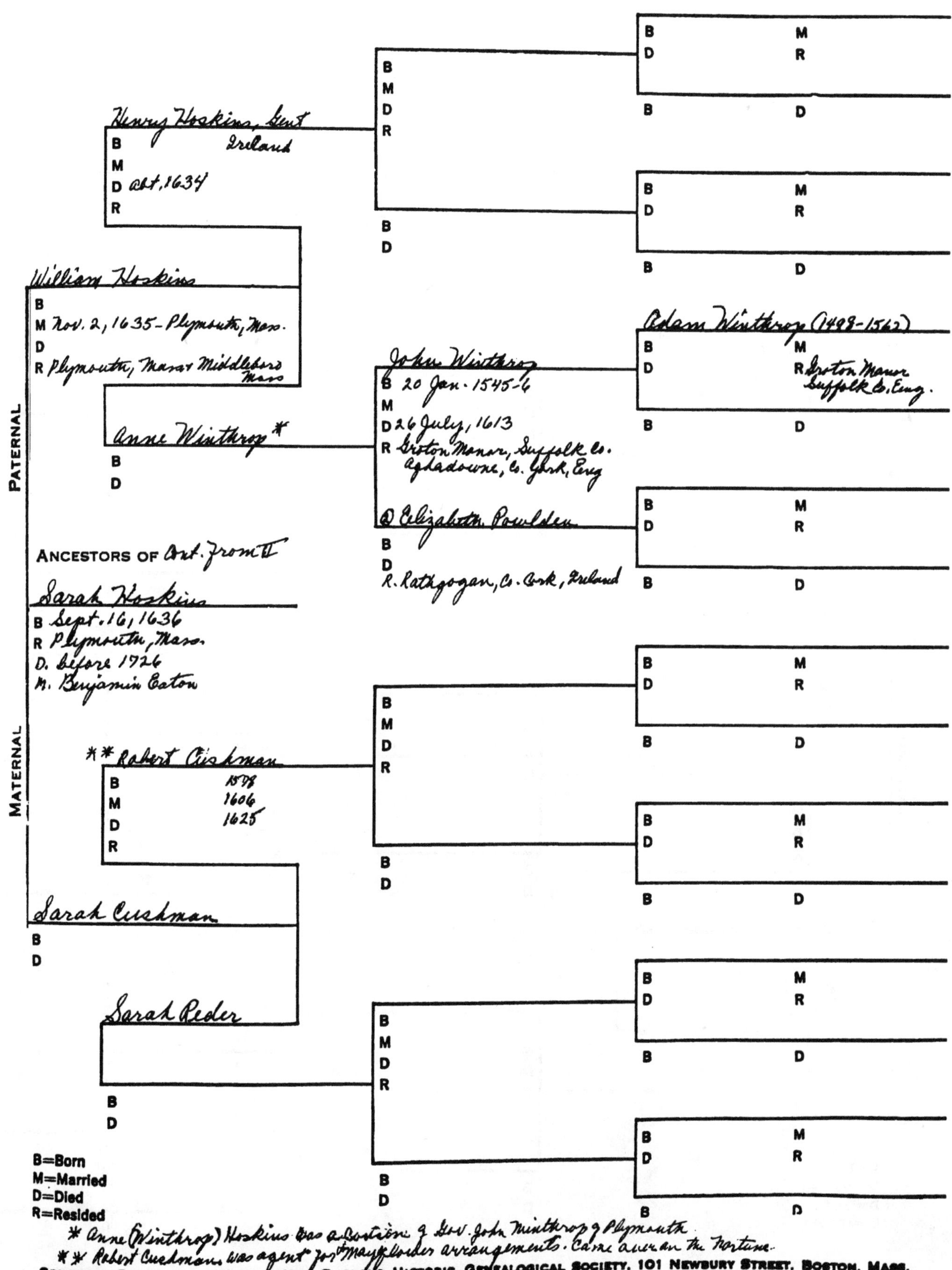

* Anne (Winthrop) Hoskins was a cousin of Gov. John Winthrop of Plymouth.

** Robert Cushman was agent for Mayflower arrangements. Came over on the Fortune.

CHART XXXIII

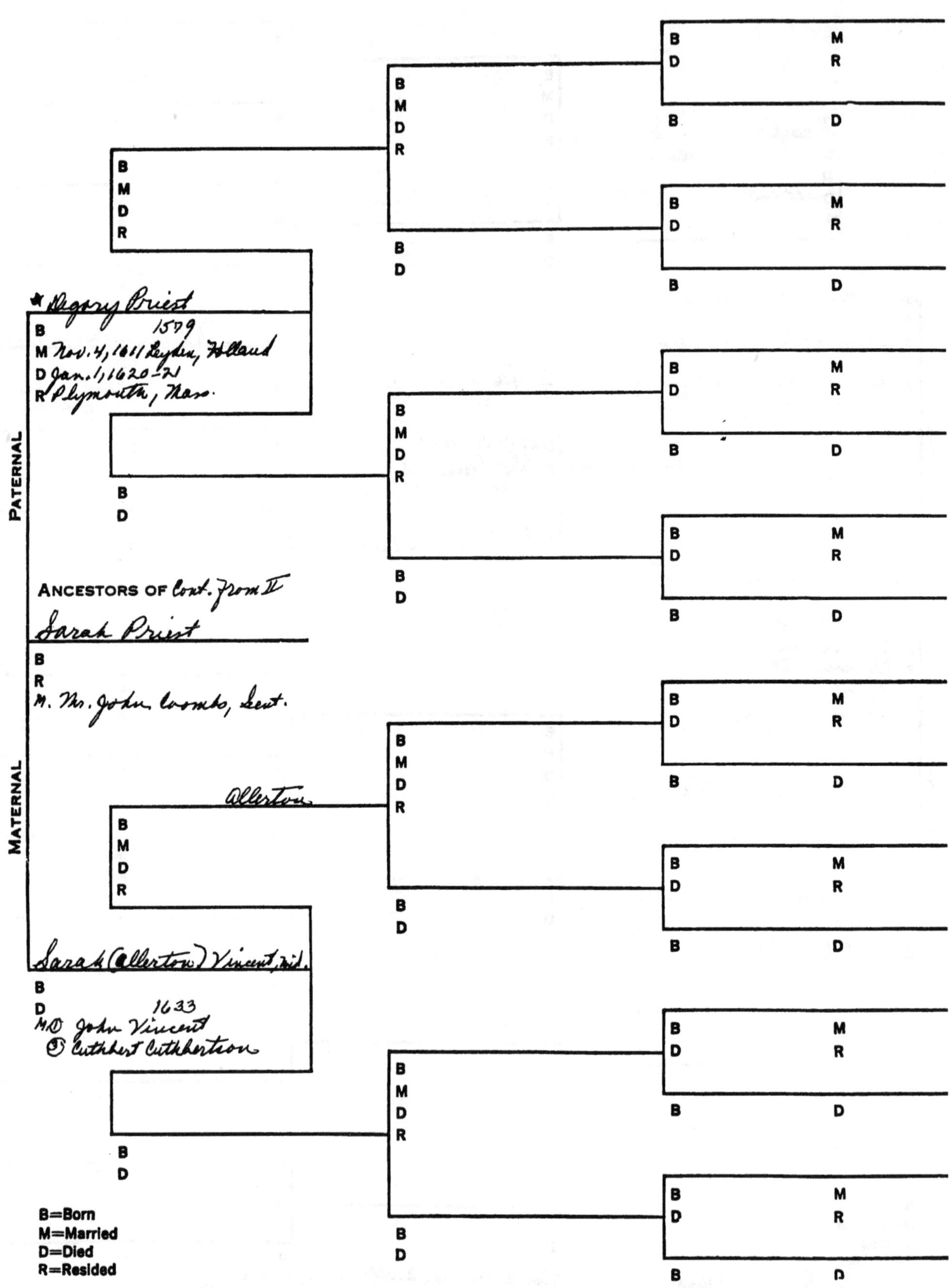

* Degory Priest
B 1579
M Nov. 4, 1611 Leyden, Holland
D Jan. 1, 1620-21
R Plymouth, Mass.

PATERNAL

ANCESTORS OF Cont. from II

Sarah Priest
B
R
M. Mr. John Coombs, Gent.

MATERNAL

Allerton
B
M
D
R

Sarah (Allerton) Vincent, wid.
B
D
M.(1) John Vincent 1633
(3) Cuthbert Cuthbertson

B=Born
M=Married
D=Died
R=Resided

CHART XXXIV

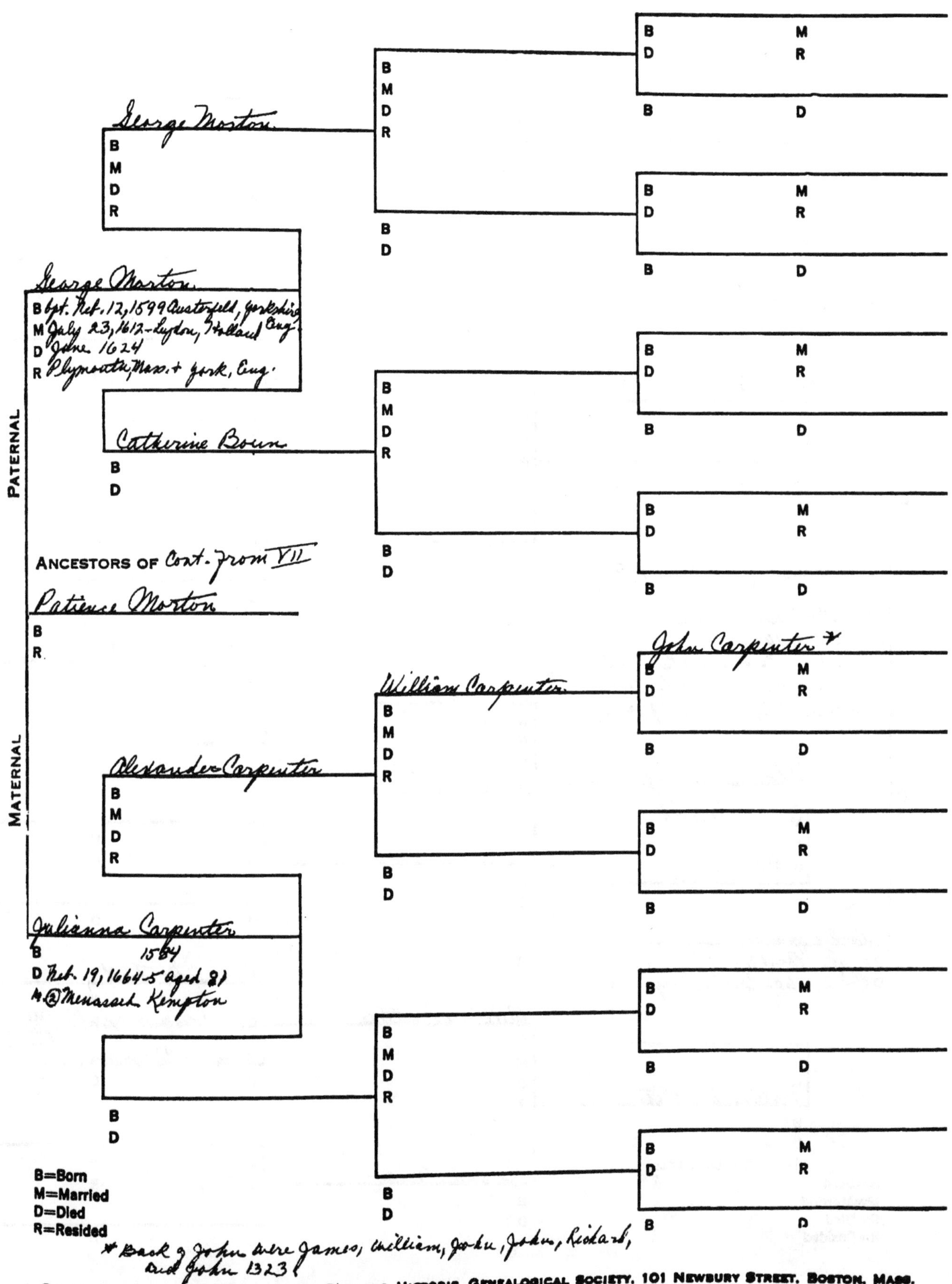

PATERNAL

George Morton
B
M
D
R

Catherine Bown
B
D

George Morton
B bpt. Feb. 12, 1599 Austerfield, Yorkshire Eng.
M July 23, 1612 - Leyden, Holland
D June 1624
R Plymouth, Mass. + York, Eng.

ANCESTORS OF Cont. from VII

Patience Morton
B
R

MATERNAL

John Carpenter *
B M
D R
B D

William Carpenter
B
M
D
R

Alexander Carpenter
B
M
D
R

Julianna Carpenter
B 1584
D Feb. 19, 1664-5 aged 81
M (2) Manasseh Kempton

B=Born
M=Married
D=Died
R=Resided

* Back of John were James, William, John, John, Richard, and John 1323.

CHART XXXV

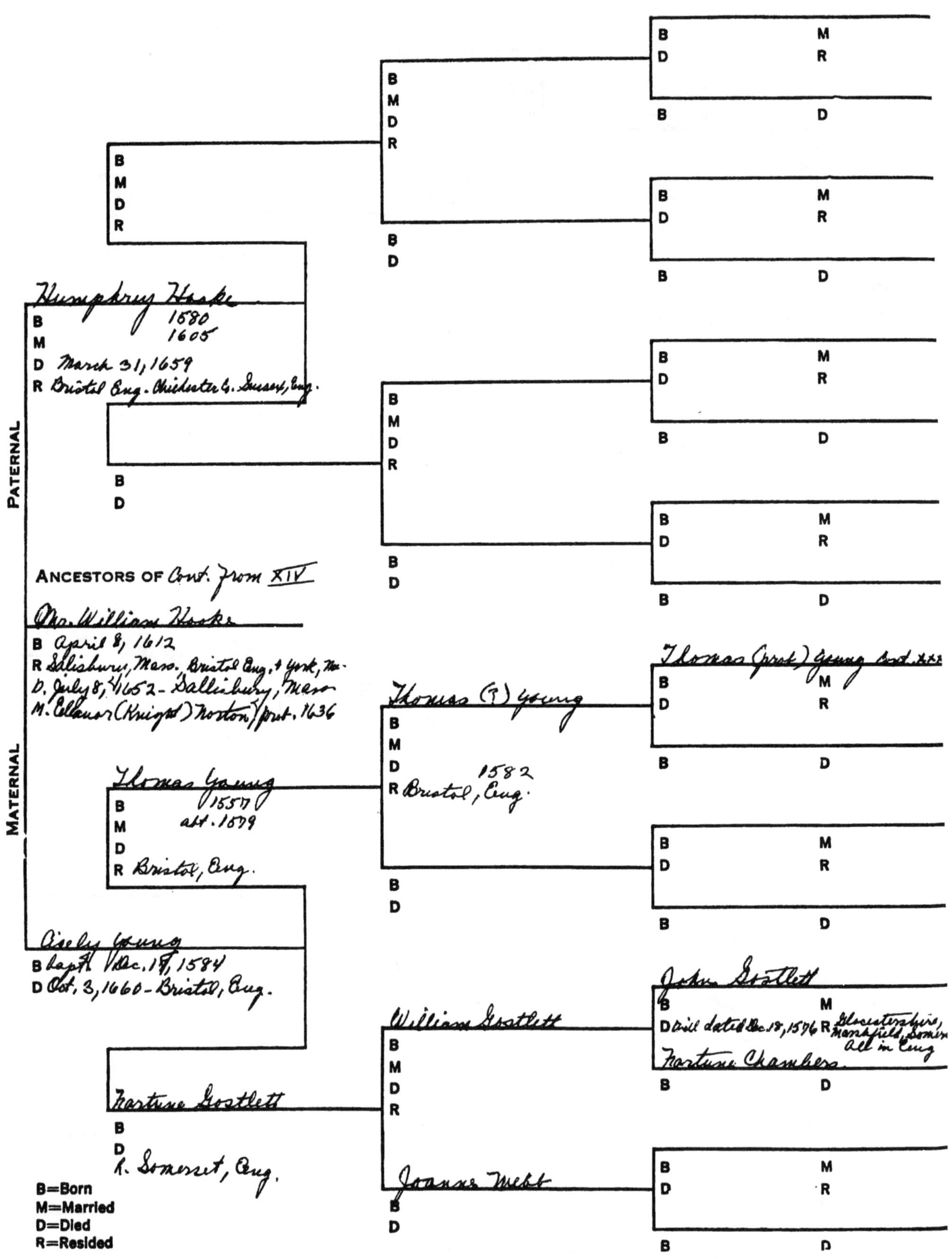

PATERNAL
MATERNAL
Humphrey Hooke
B 1580
M 1605
D March 31, 1659
R Bristol Eng. - Chichester Co. Sussex, Eng.
ANCESTORS OF Cont. from XIV
Mr. William Hooke
B April 8, 1612
R Salisbury, Mass. Bristol Eng. + York, Me.
D. July 8, 1652 - Salisbury, Mass
M. Ellanor (Knight) Norton, prob. 1636
Thomas Young
B 1557
M abt. 1579
R Bristol, Eng.
Aisly Young
B bapt. Dec. 18, 1584
D Oct. 3, 1660 - Bristol, Eng.
Fortune Gostlett
R. Somerset, Eng.
Thomas (?) Young
B 1582
R Bristol, Eng.
William Gostlett
Joanna Webb
Thomas (prob.) Young Cont. XXX
John Gostlett
D will dated Dec. 18, 1576
R Gloucestershire, Mansfield, Somerset All in Eng
Fortune Chambers
B=Born
M=Married
D=Died
R=Resided

CHART XXXVI

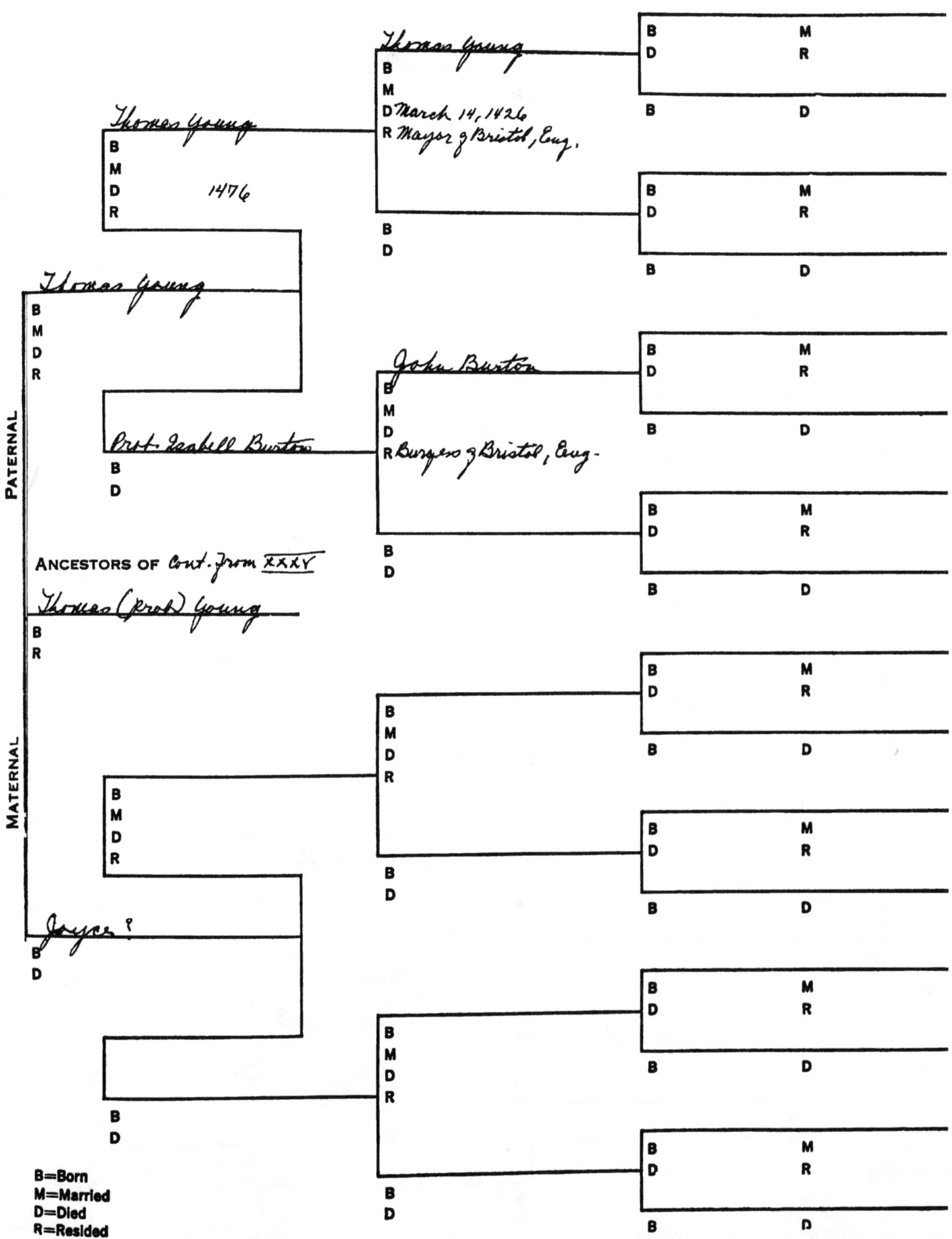
Thomas Young
B
M
D March 14, 1426
R Mayor of Bristol, Eng.
Thomas Young
B
M
D 1476
R
Thomas Young
B
M
D
R
John Burton
B
M
D
R Burgess of Bristol, Eng.
Prob. Isabell Burton
B
D
Paternal
Ancestors of Cont. from XXXV
Thomas (prob) Young
B
R
Maternal
Joyce ?
B
D
B=Born
M=Married
D=Died
R=Resided

CHART XXXVII

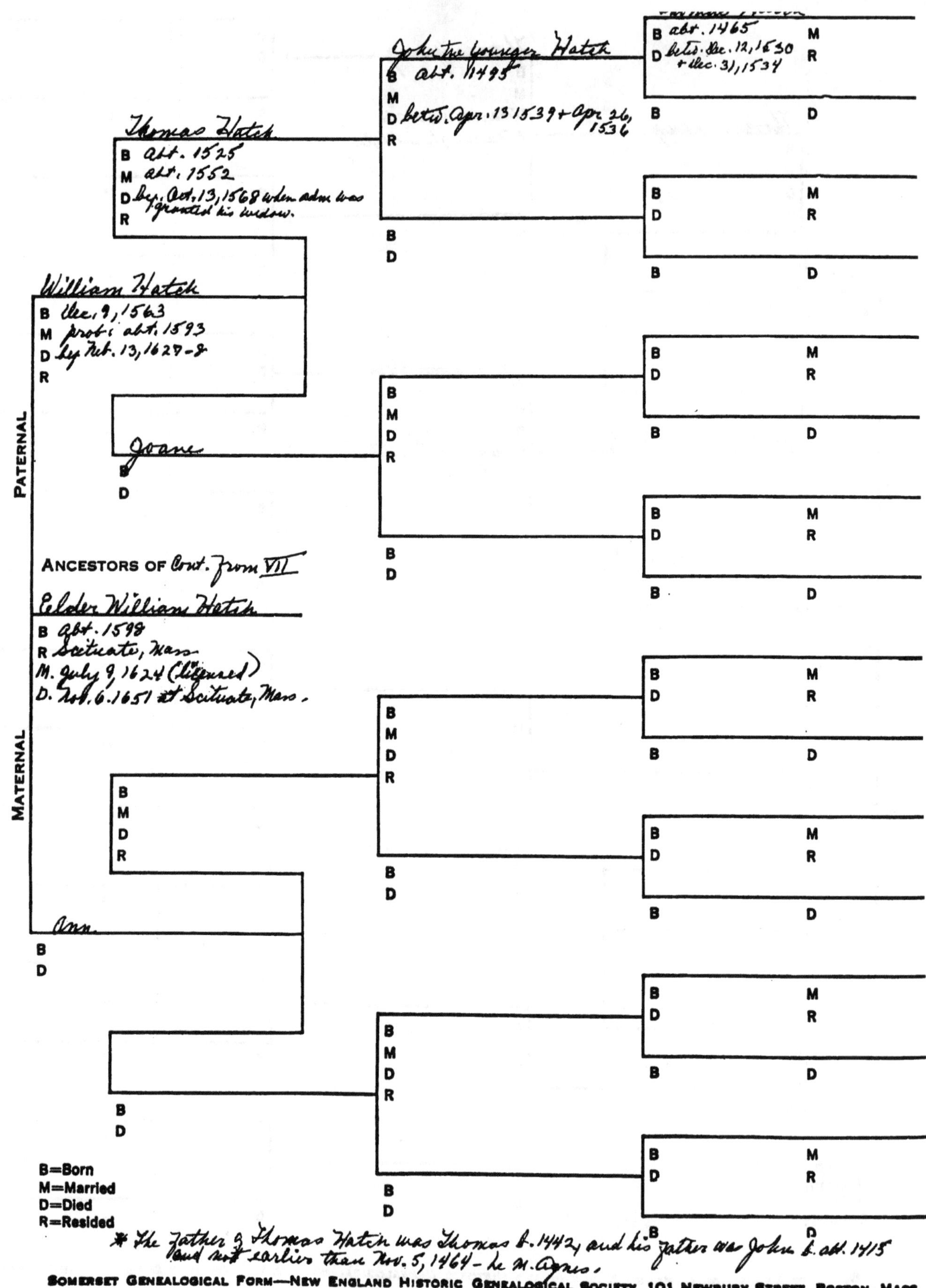

Somerset Genealogical Form—New England Historic Genealogical Society, 101 Newbury Street, Boston, Mass.

CHART XXXVIII

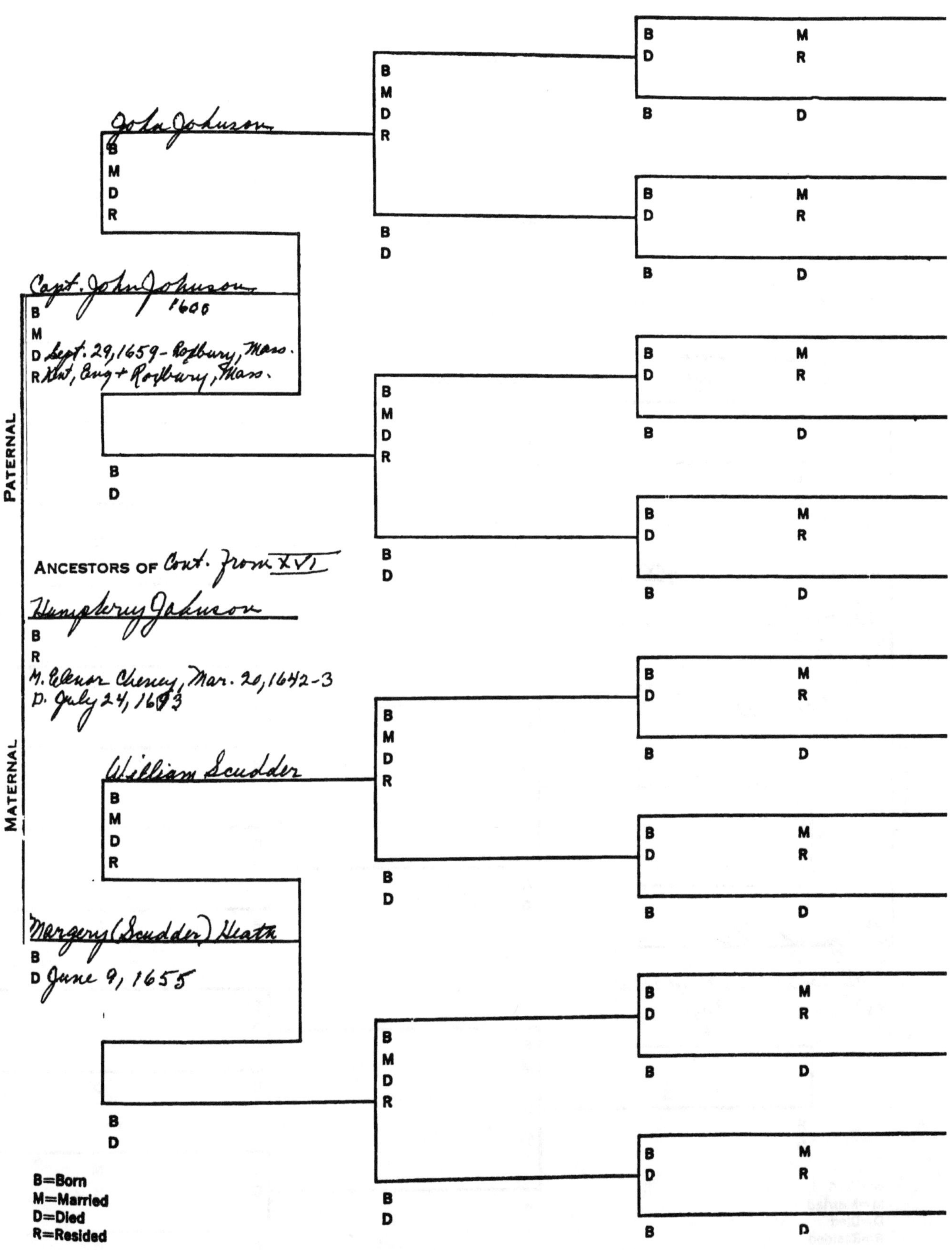

Somerset Genealogical Form—New England Historic Genealogical Society. 101 Newbury Street. Boston. Mass.

CHART XXXIX

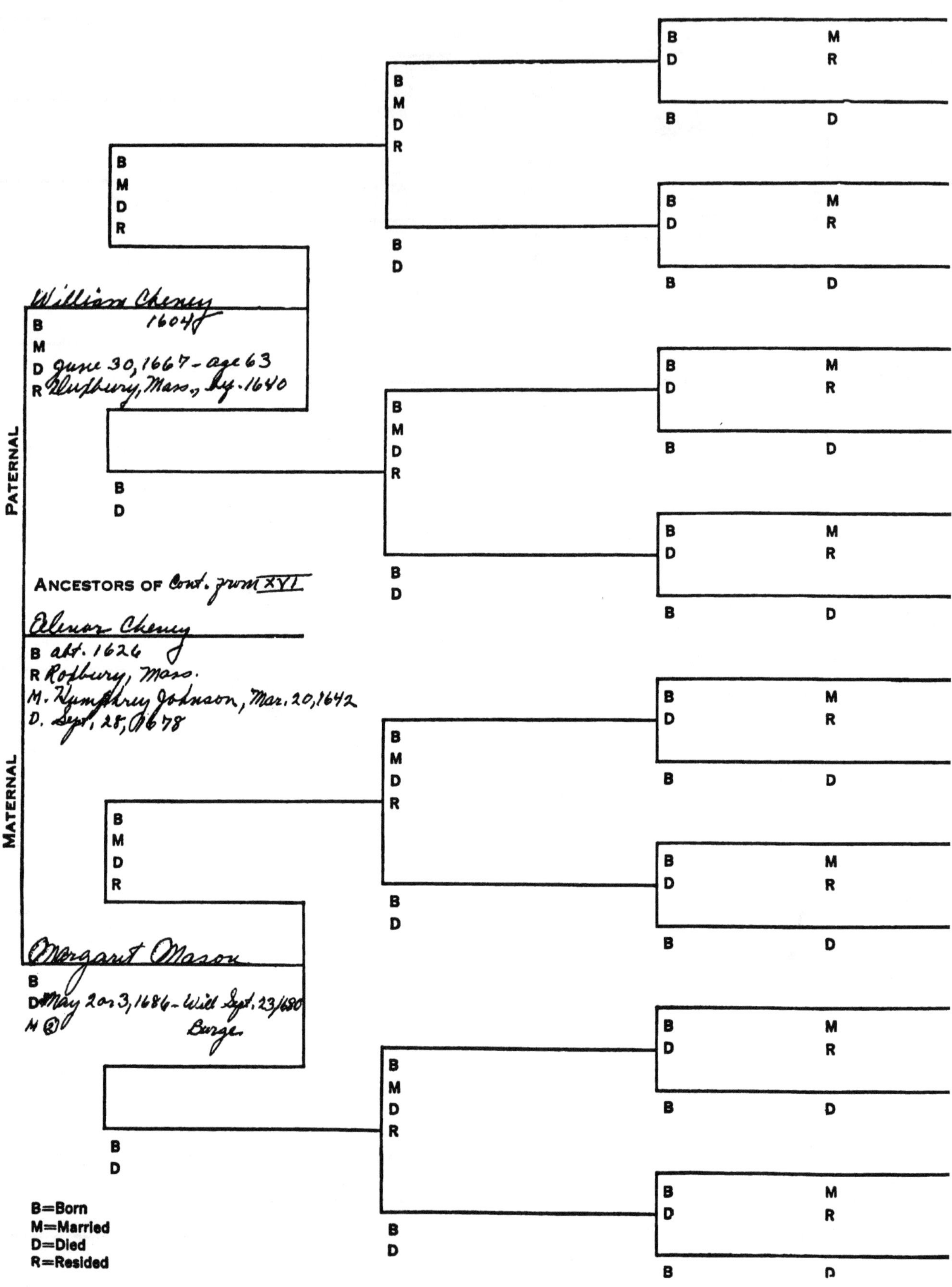
PATERNAL
MATERNAL
William Cheney
B 1604
M
D June 30, 1667 - age 63
R Roxbury, Mass., by 1640
ANCESTORS OF Cont. from XVI
Alinor Cheney
B abt. 1626
R Roxbury, Mass.
M. Humphrey Johnson, Mar. 20, 1642
D. Sept. 28, 1678
Margaret Mason
B
D May 2 or 3, 1686 - Will Sept. 23, 1680
M ②
Burge
B=Born
M=Married
D=Died
R=Resided

CHART XL

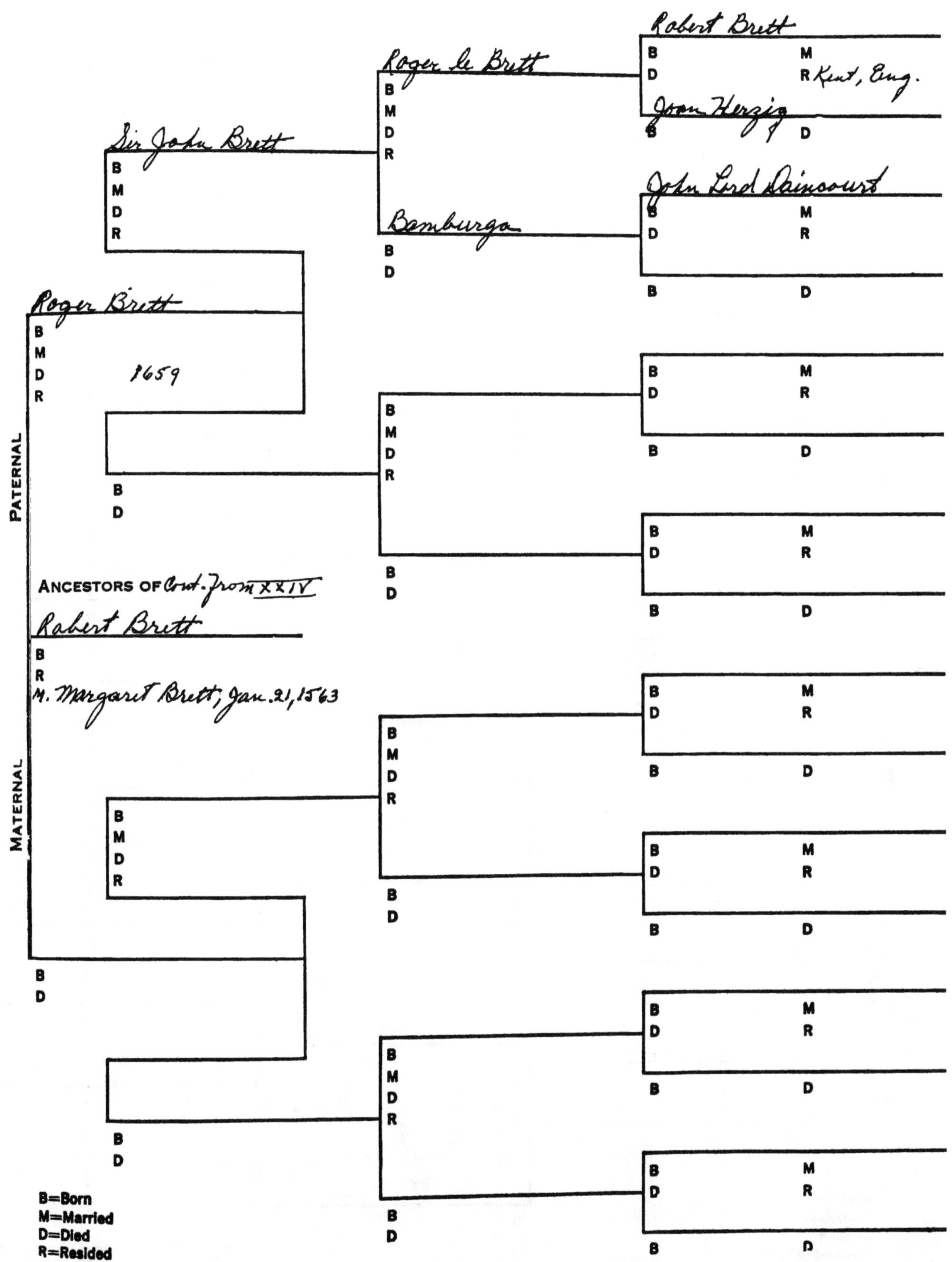
Robert Brett
B
D
M
R Kent, Eng.
Joan Herzig
B
D
Roger le Brett
B
M
D
R
Sir John Brett
B
M
D
R
John Lord Daincourt
B
D
M
R
Bamburga
B
D
B
D
Roger Brett
B
M
D 1659
R
PATERNAL
B
D
ANCESTORS OF Cont. from XXIV
Robert Brett
B
R
M. Margaret Brett, Jan. 21, 1563
MATERNAL
B
D
B=Born
M=Married
D=Died
R=Resided

CHART XLI

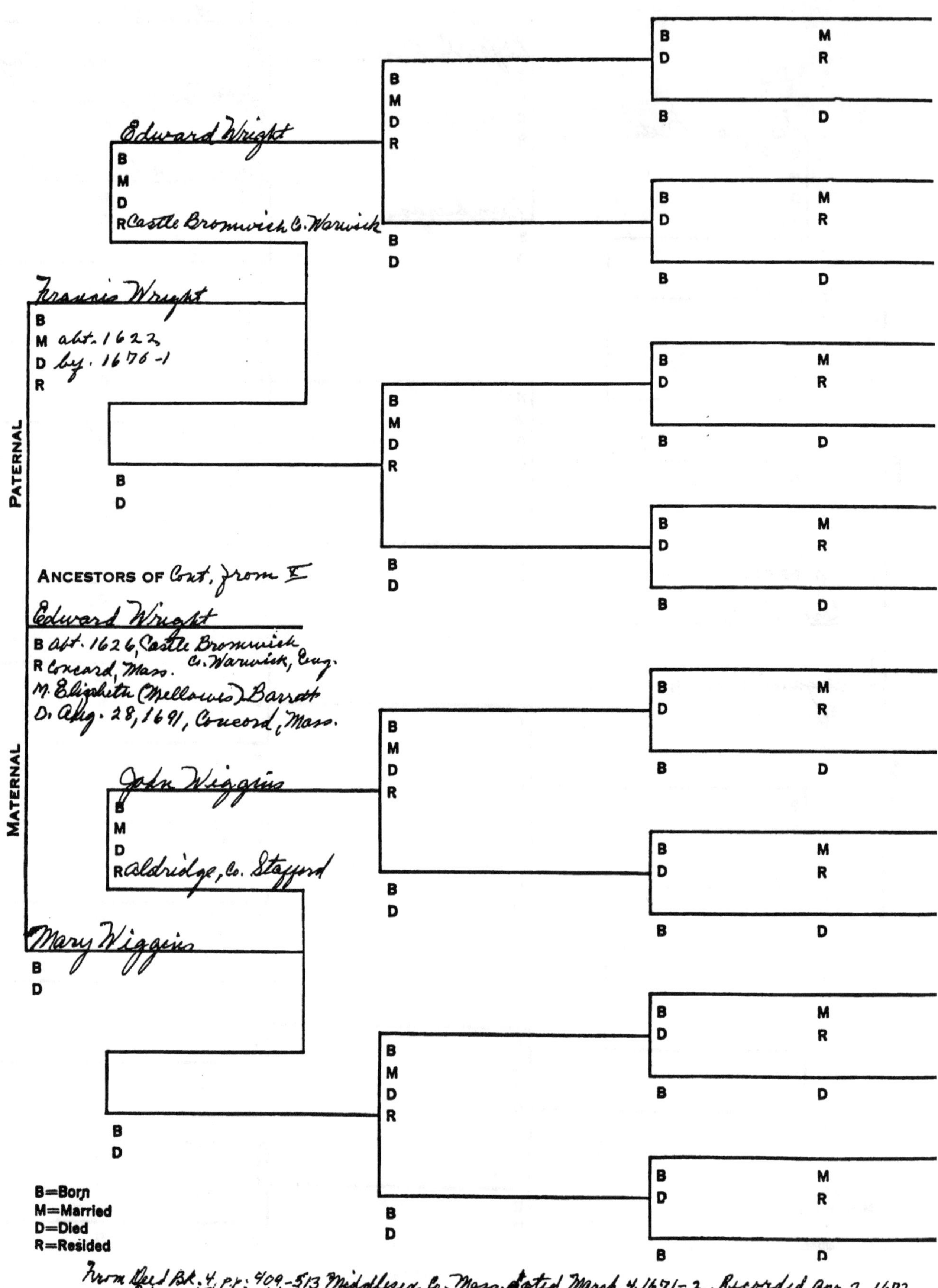

From Deed Bk. 4, pp. 409-513 Middlesex Co. Mass. Dated March 4, 1671-2, Recorded Apr. 2, 1602. Edward Wright & John Horat agreement.

Somerset Genealogical Form—New England Historic Genealogical Society, 101 Newbury Street, Boston, Mass.

CHART XLII

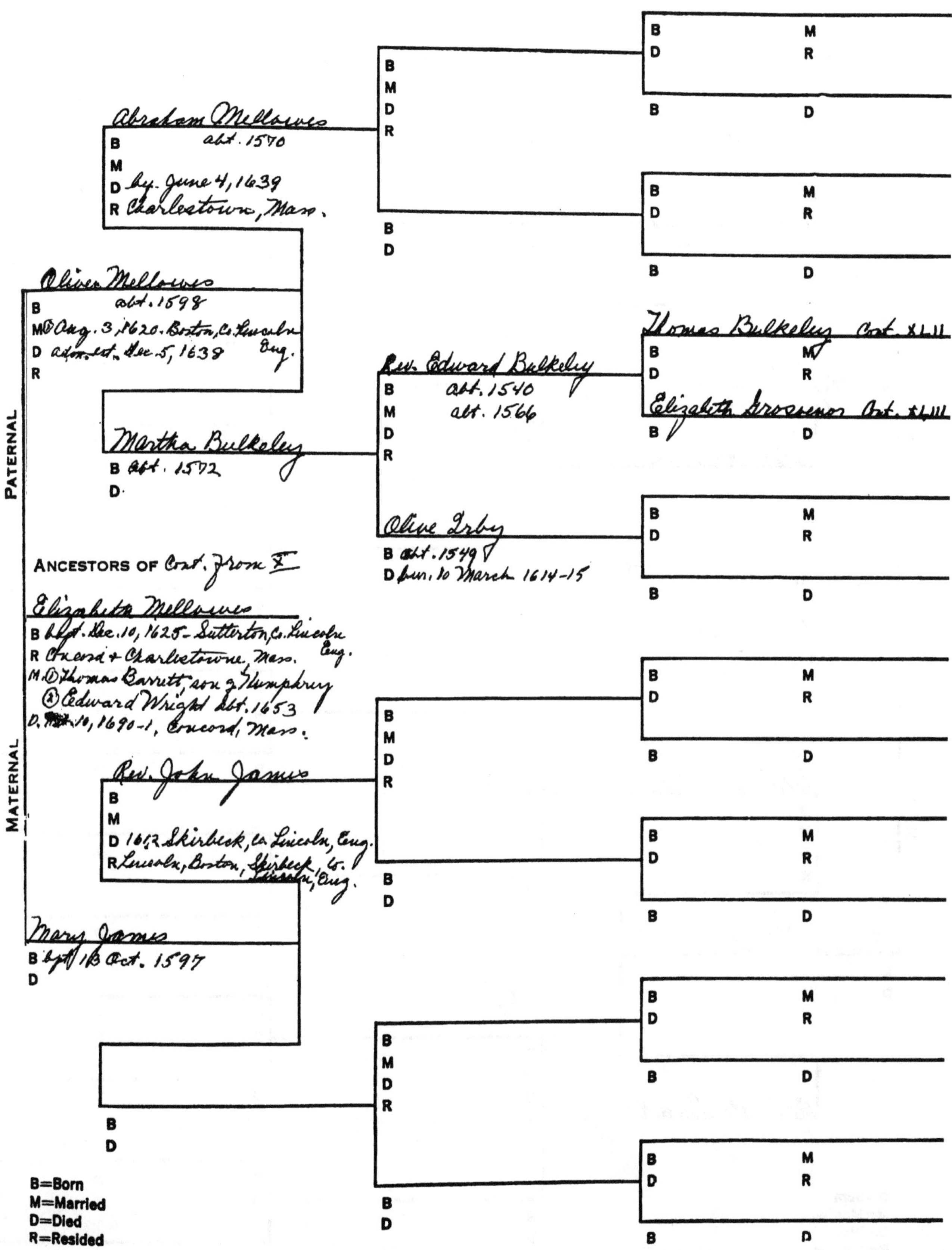
Abraham Mellowes
B abt. 1570
M
D by June 4, 1639
R Charlestown, Mass.
Oliver Mellowes
B abt. 1598
M (1) Aug. 3, 1620. Boston, Co. Lincoln Eng.
D adm. est. Dec. 5, 1638
R
Martha Bulkeley
B abt. 1572
D
Rev. Edward Bulkeley
B abt. 1540
M abt. 1566
D
R
Thomas Bulkeley Cont. XLII
Elizabeth Grosvenor Cont. XLIII
Olive Irby
B abt. 1549
D bur. 10 March 1614-15
PATERNAL
ANCESTORS OF Cont. from X
Elizabeth Mellowes
B bapt. Dec. 10, 1625 - Sutterton, Co. Lincoln Eng.
R Concord & Charlestowne, Mass.
M (1) Thomas Barrett, son of Humphrey
(2) Edward Wright abt. 1653
D. Mar. 10, 1690-1, Concord, Mass.
MATERNAL
Rev. John James
B
M
D 1642 Skirbeck, Co. Lincoln, Eng.
R Lincoln, Boston, Skirbeck, Co. Lincoln, Eng.
Mary James
B bapt 13 Oct. 1597
D
B=Born
M=Married
D=Died
R=Resided

CHART XLIII

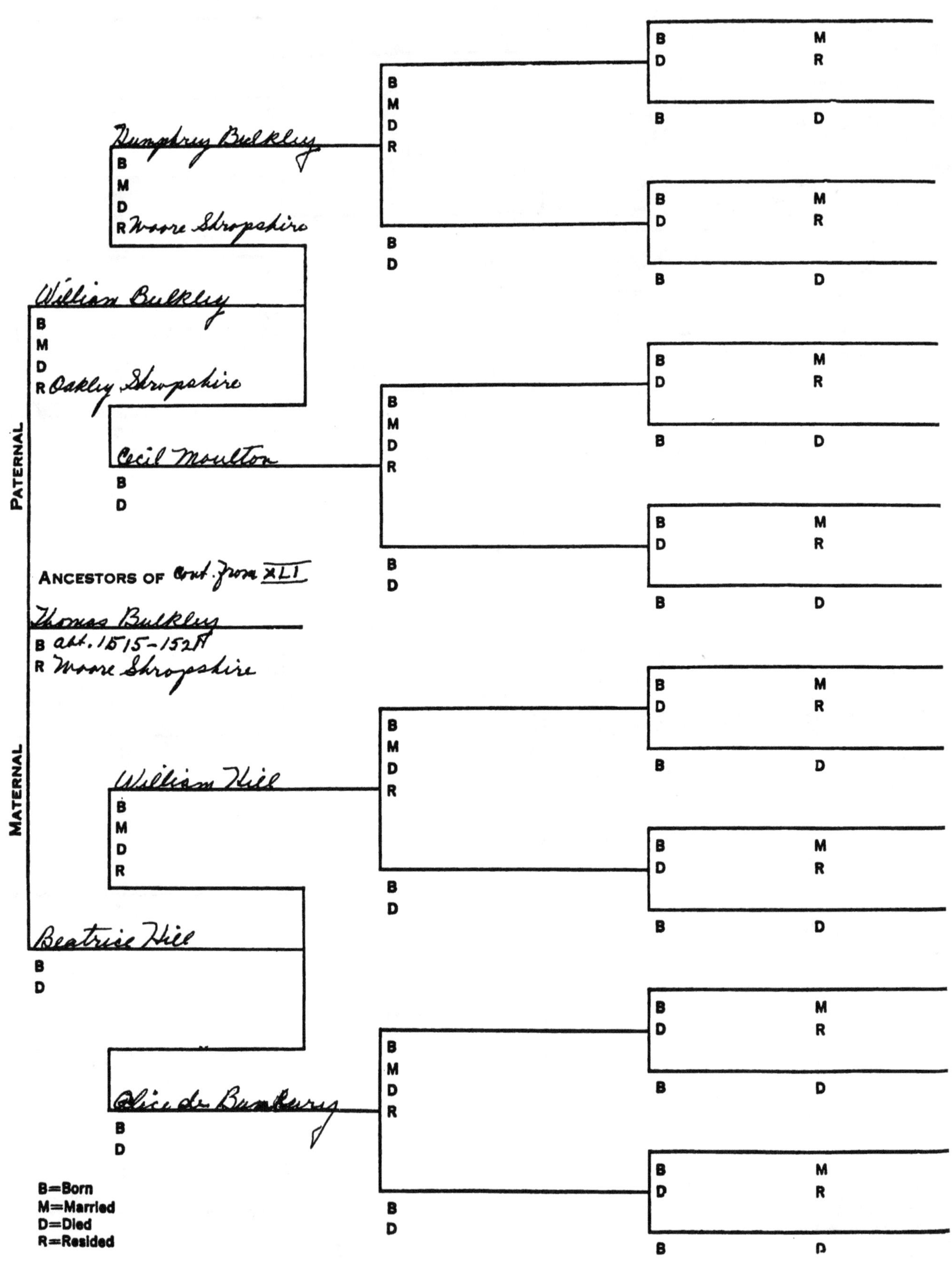
Humphrey Bulkley
B
M
D
R Woore Shropshire
William Bulkley
B
M
D
R Oakley Shropshire
Cecil Moulton
B
D
PATERNAL
ANCESTORS OF cont. from XLI
Thomas Bulkley
B abt. 1515-1524
R Woore Shropshire
MATERNAL
William Hill
B
M
D
R
Beatrice Hill
B
D
Alice de Bunbury
B
D
B=Born
M=Married
D=Died
R=Resided
B
M
D
R
B
D
B D M R
B D

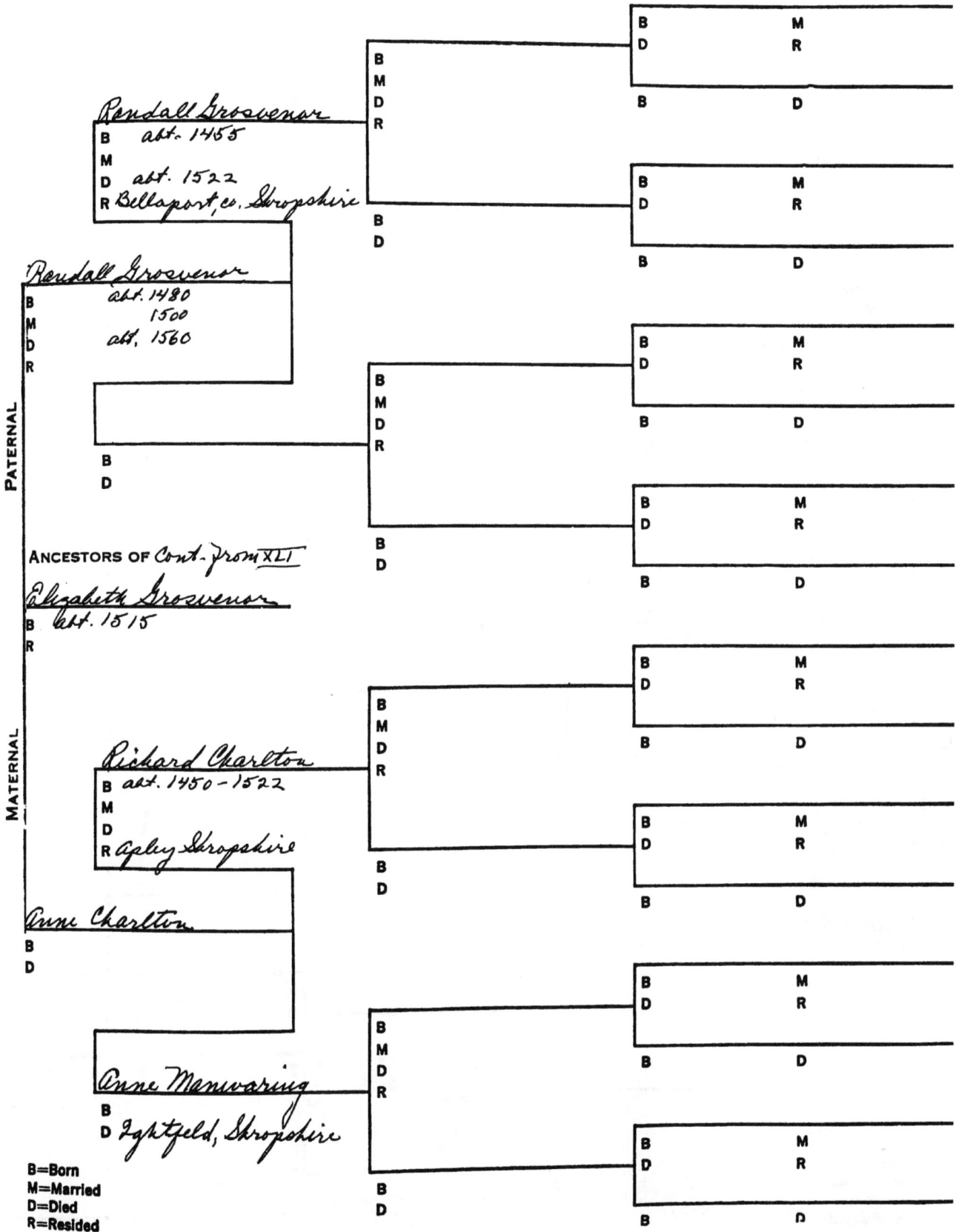

CHART XLIV

Randall Grosvenor
B abt. 1455
M
D abt. 1522
R Bellaport, co. Shropshire

Randall Grosvenor
B abt. 1480
M 1500
D abt. 1560
R

B
D

PATERNAL

ANCESTORS OF Cont. from XLI
Elizabeth Grosvenor
B abt. 1515
R

MATERNAL

Richard Charlton
B abt. 1450-1522
M
D
R Apley Shropshire

Anne Charlton
B
D

Anne Manwaring
B
D Ightfeld, Shropshire

B
M
D
R

B
D

B
M
D
R

B
D

B
M
D
R

B
D

B
M
D
R

B
D

B D M R
B D

B D M R
B D

B D M R
B D

B D M R
B D

B D M R
B D

B D M R
B D

B D M R
B D

B D M R
B D

B=Born
M=Married
D=Died
R=Resided

CHART XLV

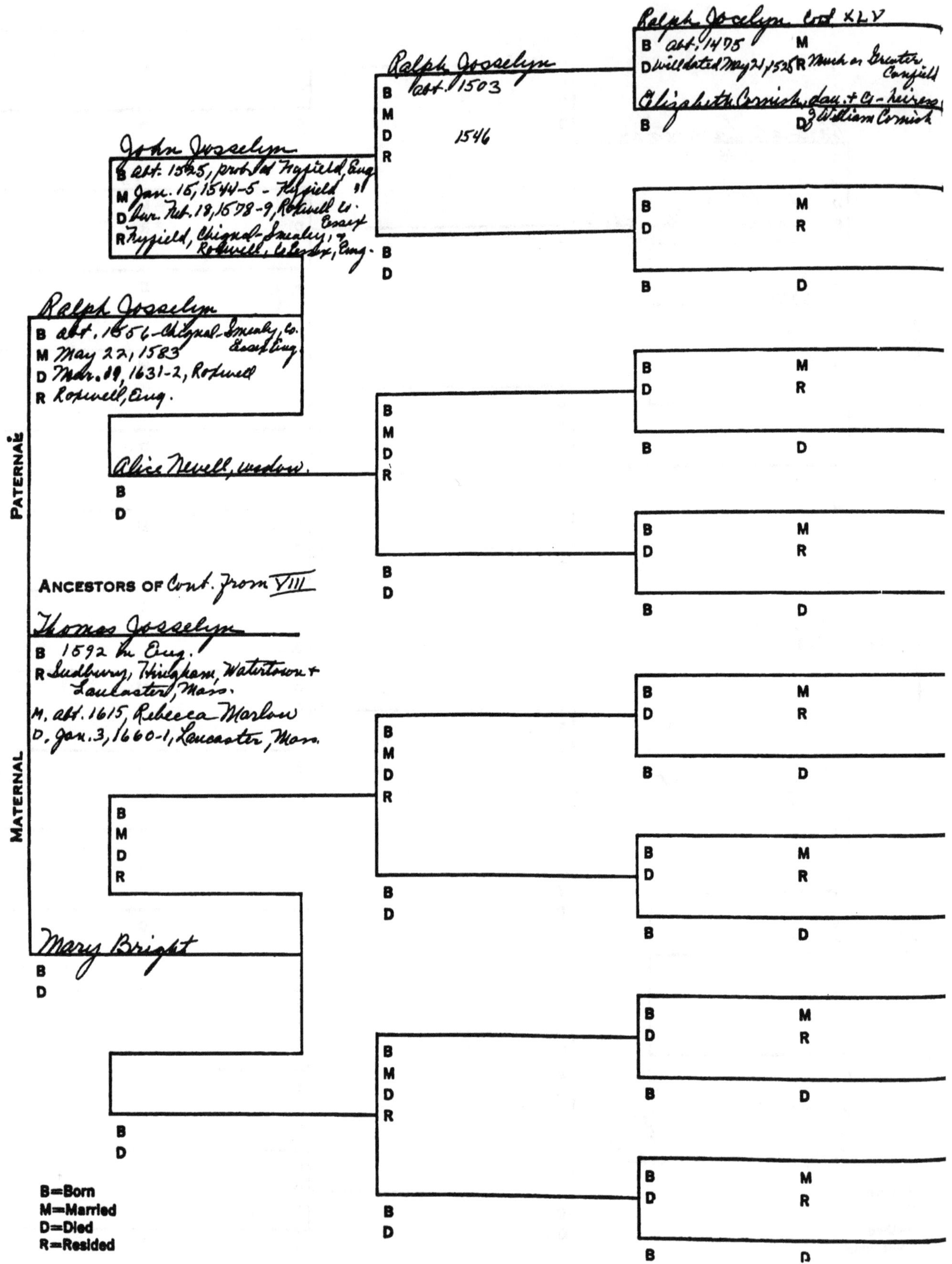

Ralph Joselyn Cont XLV
B abt. 1475
D will dated May 21, 1525
M
R Much or Greater Canfield

Elizabeth Cornish, dau. + Co-heiress of William Cornish
B
D

Ralph Josselyn
B abt. 1503
M
D 1546
R

B
D

John Josselyn
B abt. 1525, prob. at Hatfield, Eng.
M Jan. 15, 1544-5 - Hatfield
D bur. Feb. 18, 1578-9, Roxwell Co. Essex
R Hatfield, Chignal-Smealey, + Roxwell, Co. Essex, Eng.

Ralph Josselyn
B abt. 1556 - Chignal-Smealy, Co. Essex Eng.
M May 22, 1583
D Mar. 19, 1631-2, Roxwell
R Roxwell, Eng.

Alice Newell, widow.
B
D

PATERNAL

ANCESTORS OF Cont. from VIII

Thomas Josselyn
B 1592 in Eng.
R Sudbury, Hingham, Watertown + Lancaster, Mass.
M. abt. 1615, Rebecca Marlow
D. Jan. 3, 1660-1, Lancaster, Mass.

MATERNAL

Mary Bright
B
D

B=Born
M=Married
D=Died
R=Resided

SOMERSET GENEALOGICAL FORM—NEW ENGLAND HISTORIC GENEALOGICAL SOCIETY, 101 NEWBURY STREET, BOSTON, MASS.

CHART XLVI

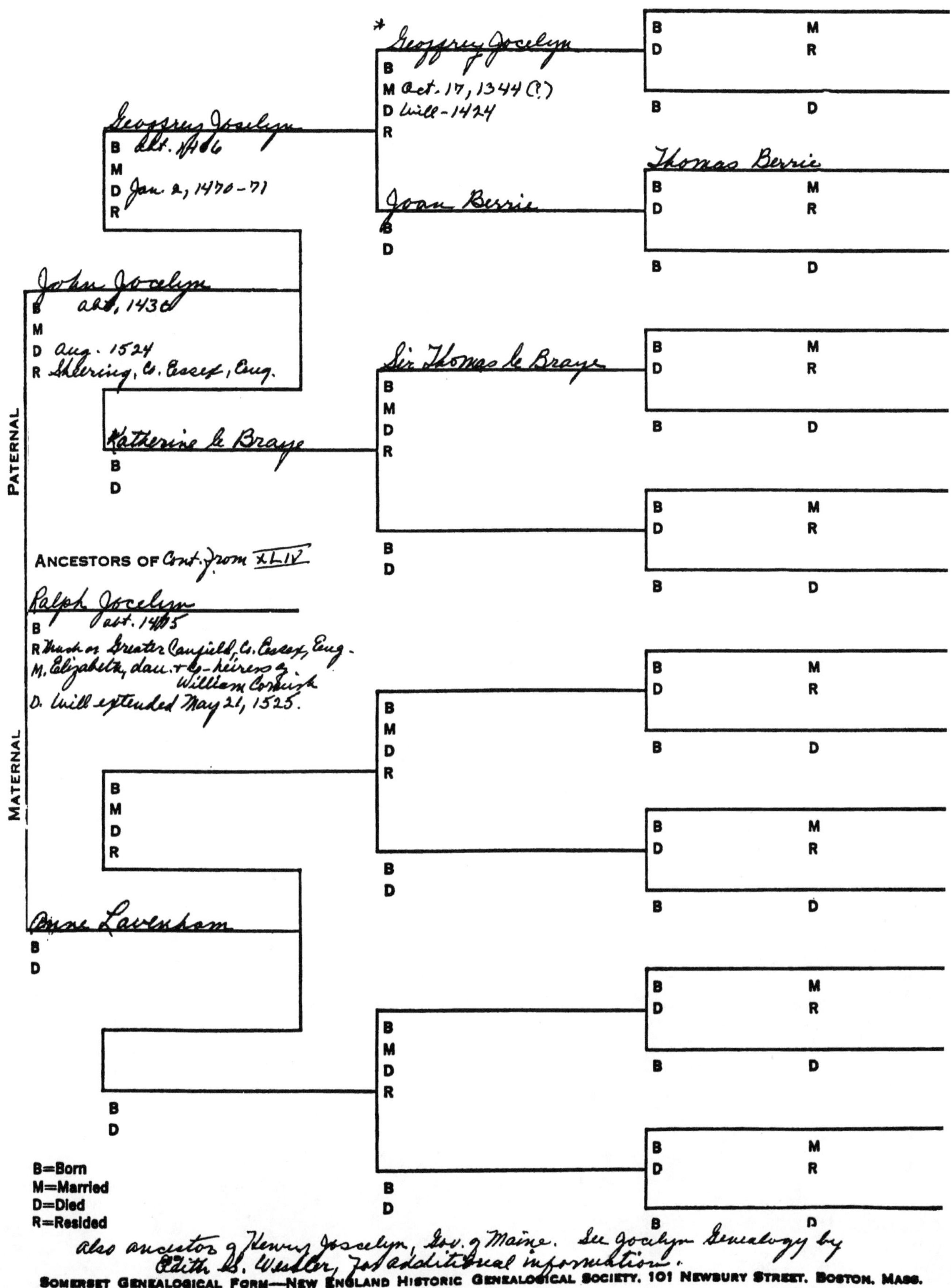

also ancestor of Henry Josselyn, Gov. of Maine. See Jocelyn Genealogy by Edith S. Wessler, for additional information.

ADFORD

Chart IX

Adford, (Advard,) Henry, Scituate, Marshfield, Mass., about 1643, proprietor 1645. He m. 6 Oct. 1643, Tamson Manson, b. abt. 1621; died at Rehoboth Bristol Co. in 1653.

Children:

Mary, bapt. June 29, 1651 at Scituate; m. (1) Abraham[2] Jaquith of Charlestown & Woburn Mass. 13 Mar. 1671 - m. (2) Jacob Hamblet of Woburn, Mass.
Elizabeth, bapt. June 29, 1651 at Scituate
Sarah, bapt. June 29, 1651 at Scituate
Experience, bapt. April 18, 1652 at Scituate; m. Abraham Biam, s. George, June 18, 1672 in Chelmsford. (Scituate & Chelmsford V.R.)

References:

Popes Pioneers of Mass; p. 11 - Scituate, Mass. V.R. Vol. I p. 11, Vol. II p. 11
Chelmsford, Mass. V.R. p. 175
Ntl. Gen. Soc. Quarterly (June 1968) Vol. 56, p. 117 (Jaquith Family)
Ntl. Gen. Soc. Quarterly (March 1962) Vol. 50 pp. 38- (Jaquith Family)
Gen. Guide to Early Settlers of Am. p. 5 & p. 348 (Manson)
Savage's N.E. Dict. (Reprint Ed.) Vol. I p. 19

A Thomas Manson from Gloucester, Gloucestershire, Eng. came to New Haven, Conn. (Banks Topagraphical Index)

BALCH

Chart XV

John[1] Balch, came in 1623 with a colony in charge of Capt. Robert Gorges, son of Sir Fernando. They settled first at Messegusset (now Weymouth). In 1624 the colony removed to Cape Ann. In 1626 they removed with their families, stores & cattle to the Sagamoreship of Naumkeeg (Salem). On Nov. 25, 1635, the town granted a thousand acres in the Bass River District, to be divided between Roger Conant, John Woodbury, John Balch, Capt. Trask and Peter Palfrey. It became known as the "Old Planter's" grant and was included in the town of Beverly, incorporated in 1668.

In 1638 John Balch built a two story frame house upon his land. The home is still standing in Beverly and the Balch family association is known as Balch House Associates of the Beverly Hist. Soc. John Balch had frequent mention in the records as a surveyor of highways and of the bounds of grants made to newcomers in Salem.

John Balch married (1) Margaret Lovell, Sept. 12, 1625, in St. Cuthbert's Church in Wells, Somerset, England. (This information certified from church records in 1935. Certified copy is in the vaults of the Beverly, Mass. Historical Society.) John Balch and his wife Marjorie helped to found the Salem Church in 1629. He was among the first to be made freeman in 1631. John M. (2) Agnes or Annis Patch (no children by this marriage). He made his will 15 May 1648 and the inventory was taken Feb. 2, 1648-9.

Children:

Benjamin, b. winter of 1628-9; m. 1) Sarah Gardner, 2) Abigail Clarke, wid., 3) Grace Mallett, wid. of Hosea, March 15, 1691-2.
John, b. abt. 1630 at Salem m. Mary, daughter of Roger Conant. She m. 2) William Dodge, Jr.; d. June 16, 1662.
Freeborn, b. abt. 1631, said to have gone to England, where he d. 1657.

References: Gen. of the Balch Family by Galusha B. Balch, M.D. 1897; The Old Planters of Beverly in Mass., and The Thousand Acre Grant of 1635, by Beverly Hist. Soc. & The Covant Family Assn. 1930.

Letter from Balch Family Assn.

Benjamin[2] Balch, son of John[1] and Margaret (Lovell) Balch; b. in the winter of 1628-9 at Salem. April 10, 1706 Benjamin gives his age as abt. 77, in a sworn deposition. Family tradition is that Benjamin[2] was the first male child born in the Mass. Bay Colony. He received at his father's death half of the farm. From his brother John[2] he purchased his share in the old homestead on Bass River, and in 1658 secured possession of his brother Freeborn's share of the estate from his adm.

The old home was built when Benjamin was nine years old. He lived there from that time and all his children were born there. Benjamin was free of the puritanisal notions of the times. Once he was arrested and fined for giving a nights lodging to a stranger on foot, and he left the baptism of his children to their own desires. 8 were bapt. Apr. 10, 1670 at the First Parish Unitarian Church. Benjamin deeded most of his land before his death.

Benjamin[2] was married three times and had 11 children by the 1st wife Sarah Gardner, (daughter of Thomas Gardner, overseer of the 1st Cape Ann Plantation) whom he m. about 1650. She d. April 5, 1686. Feb. 5, 1689 he m. (2) Abigail, wid. of Matthew Clark of Marblehead. She d. Jan. 1690, aged 55 years. There were no children by this marriage. Benjamin[2] m. 3) Grace, widow of Hosea Mallett, on March 15, 1691-2 by Simon Bradstreet, Esq. There were two children by this marriage and Grace had one daughter by Hosea Mallett. Grace d. before 1704 since Benjamin signed a deed alone in that year. He d. after Jan. 31, 1714-15 as he deeded land on that date - age over 86 at that time.

Balch

Rochester V.R. Vol. II p. 341. "Balch, Grace, Mrs. d. May 10, 1733 age 82" - buried 1st Parish Cem. Rochester Center. She was b. abt. 1651 and was probably the widow of Benjamin Balch.

Children by 1st wife Sarah (Gardner) Balch

Samuel b. May 1651, bp. Apr. 10, 1670; m. Oct. 27, 1675; Martha Newmarch of Ipswich; d. Oct. 14, 1723
Benjamin, b. 1653; d. spring of 1698
John, b. 1654, bp. Apr. 10, 1670; m. Dec. 23, 1674, Hanah Viring; d. Nov. 19, 1738
Joseph, b. 1658, bp. Apr. 10, 1670; d. Sept. 16, 1675
Freeborn, b. Aug. 9, 1660, bp. Apr. 10, 1670; m. Feb. 20, 1688-9, Mallis ______; d. June 11, 1729
Sarah, b. 1661, bp. Apr. 10, 1670; m. Dec. 29, 1680, James Patch; d. by 1717
Abigail, b. 1663; m. Feb. 8, 1681, Cornelius Larkum; d. Apr. 30, 1706
Ruth, b. 1665, bp. Apr. 10, 1670
Mary b. 1667, bp. Apr. 10, 1670; m. Mar. 26, 1689, Nathaniel Stone, d. Mar. 12, 1737
Jonathan bp. Apr. 10, 1670; probably d. young
David, b. July 9, 1671; d. Apr. 17, 1690 - unmarried

No children by 2nd wife

Children by 3rd wife Grace (   )(Mallett) Balch:

Deborah, b. June 6, 1693; m. Feb. 8, 1710-11 William Rayment; d. May 5, 1717
Lydia, b. Aug. 28, 1695; m. by 1715, Samuel Bowles of Rochester, Mass.

Grace's daughter by Hosea Mallett

Elizabeth Mallett b. at Boston 19 Apr. 1678; m. at Beverly, 15 Oct. 1696, Peter Woodin.

References: Same as for John [1]Balch - also Beverly, Mass. V.R.

BARRETT

Charts I and X

Thomas [1]Barrett, born about 1591 at Norfolk, Norwich Co., Eng., was in Braintree, Mass. 1635-40, was made freeman 1645 (the printed list has Barrill), and was of the number of petitioners for grant of land at Warwick, R.I. He was a proprietor at Chelmsford in 1662. He and his son Thomas purchased a house and 52 acres of land at Chelmsford, April 10, 1663. Thomas [1] Barrett died Oct. 6, 1668 at Chelmsford (will dated 1-1-1662, probated 6 Aug. 1668.(6-8-68) His wife Margaret died July 8, 1681 at Chelmsford, Mass.

Barrett

Issue:

John 2 Barrett m. Sarah _____; d. May 19, 1706
Thomas 2 Barrett m. Frances Waalderson at Braintree, July 7, 1655; died Dec. 8, 1702. She died May 27, 1694
Mary Barrett m. Shadrack Thayer, Feb. 11, 1654; died April 2, 1657
Joseph 2 Barrett died Dec. 17, 1711

References:

Popes Pioneers of Mass.; "Barrett Ancestry" a pamphlet compiled by George Castor Martin; Braintree, Mass. Rec. 1640-1793; Chelmsford V.R.

Lieut. John 2 Barrett, son of Thomas1 and Margaret, born probably about 1620 in Eng.; m. before 1654, Sarah _____; died May 19, 1706 at Chelmsford. Sarah died _____. Lieut. John Barrett, was a mill owner and proprietor of extensive lands, some of which he deeded in 1698. In King Phillips War 1676 - Capt. Thomas Prentice's Co.

Issue:

John3 b. m. Dorothy Proctor Dec. 18, 1679 at Chelmsford
Jonathan3 born about 1654; died March 28, 1743 age 89 yrs.; m. (1) Sarah Learned; d. Jan. 11, 1694-5, (2) Abigail Weston, (3) Abigail (Wilson) Hildreth
Lydia3 b. Sept. 22, 1659; m. James Harwood, April 11, 1678
Samuel3 b. June 16, 1660; m. Sarah Buttrick, daughter of Wm. of Concord, Feb. 21, 1683
Mary3 b. March 13, 1662-3; m. Nathaniel Collar, Oct. 10, 1693
Joseph3 m. Abigail Hildreth, daughter Lt. James, Dec. 15, 1696 at Chelmsford; d. Dec. 17, 1711. She d. Dec. 30, 1729 at Chelmsford; bur. July 22, 1743
Margaret3 b. Nov. 10, 1667; d. 11 mo. 1681
Sarah3 b. ; m. Ambrose Swallow, Dec. 18, 1696; d. Nov. 22, 1756. He d. Apr. 29, 1720

References:

Popes Pioneers of Mass.; "Barrett Ancestry" a pamphlet compiled by George Castor Martin; Chelmsford V.R. Woburn, Mass. V.R.; Hist. of Woburn by Sewell; Gen. Dict of N. E. by Savage.

Jonathan3 Barrett, b. about 1654. Buried March 28, 1743, age 89 yrs.; m. 1st Sarah Learned, b. 2 Oct. 1653 dau. Isaac & Mary (Slearns); she d. Jan. 11, 1695. 2nd Abigail Weston*, June 26, 1696 at Woburn, Mass., who d. Oct. 19, 1706; 3rd about 1708 Abigail (Wilson) Hildreth, wid. of Joseph and dau. of John1 and Hannah (James) (Palmer) Wilson of Woburn, Mass. She was b. Aug. 8, 1666 at Woburn and was buried Nov. 27, 1747 at Chelmsford.

* Was Abigail Weston a Widow? V.R. Vol. I Woburn birth rec. p. 82 Abigail Eames, daughter of Robert, b. Sept. 22, 1666; Woburn Mar. Vol. III p. 298, Abigail Eames m. Samuel Wesson of Reading, Aug. 29, 1688; Abigail Weston m. Jonathan Barrett - June 26, 1696

Barrett

Jonathan^3 Barrett - con't.

Issue: 1st m. Sarah Learned

Hannah^4 Barrett m. Jonathan Bowers, May 17, 1699; d. Oct. 16, 1765
Mary^4 Barrett, b. Nov. 20, 1684; m. Feb. 7, 1705 John Spaulding
Jonathan^4 Barrett b. Oct. 28, 1687
Deliverance^4 Barrett b. Feb. 24, 1690
Experience^4 Barrett b. Jan. 3, 1695; d. Jan. 11, 1695

1st wife d. Jan. 11, 1695

Issue: 2nd m. Abigail Weston

Rachel^4 b. Aug. 9, 1699
Bridget^4 b. Apr. 11, 1701; d. Sept. 7, 1702
Benjamin^4 b. Feb. 14, 1705; d. same day

2nd wife d. Oct. 19, 1706

Issue: 3rd m. Abigail (Wilson) Hildreth, widow of Joseph Hildreth

John^4 b. Dec. 13, 1709; m. Martha Heald of Acton, May 24, 1738

Joseph & Abigail (Wilson) Hildreth - issue b. a Chelmsford

Abigail b. Mar. 8, 1687-8
Abigail, again - Oct. 20, 1691; m. June 10, 1713 Thomas Chamberlain of Concord
Hannah, b. Jan. 19, 1684
Joseph) twins b. May 18, 1686 Joseph d. May 24, 1688
Richard) Richard d. May 26, 1688
Elizabeth b. Oct. 14, 1693-4
Joseph b. Nov. 30, 1695; m. Phebe Fletcher at Chelmsford
John b. 1698; d. March 17, 1714-15
Ephriam b. Aug. 25, 1700; m. Jan. 5, 1722-3 Mary Butterfield
Elizabeth b. July 29, 1703; d. Sept. 4, 1716

Joseph Hildreth d. Jan. 28, 1706 at Chelmsford

John^4 Barrett, son of Jonathan^3 & Abigail (Wilson) (Hildreth) Barrett; b. Dec. 13, 1709 at Chelmsford; d. March 18, 1772 at Chelmsford (will dated March 14, 1772); m. Martha Heald on May 24, 1738 at Concord. She was a daughter of Deacon John & Mary (Hale) Heald. She was b. Apr. 4, 1718 at Concord; d. Feb. 26, 1795 at Carlisle. (agreement of heirs Jan. 12, 1796.) Served in the French & Indian wars, under Capt. Jabeg Fairbanks.

Barrett

Issue: all b. at Chelmsford, Mass.

John[5], b. Feb. 12, 1738-9; d. Oct. 15, 1756, while in Military Service at or near Lake George, N.Y.
Patty[5], b. Jan. 20, 1740-1; d. Oct. 4, 1819 at Buckfield, Maine; m. Nov. 29, 1764, Benjamin[5] Spaulding, son of Leonard[4] & Elizabeth (Durant) Spaulding
Sarah[5] b. Sept. 11, 1741; d. after Jan. 12, 1796; m. at Chelmsford Jan. 22, 1767, Oliver Parker
Rebecca[5] b. Sept. 26, 1744; d. before Jan. 1796; m. Wm. Locke of Ashby, at Chelmsford, Feb. 10, 1773. They settled in Fitzwilliam, N.H. - had 7 children
Jonathan[5] b. Oct. 27, 1746; d. Sept. 11, 1818; m. March 28, 1771, Abigail Rayment. She was b. in Chelmsford May 8, 1752, dau. of Edward & Abigail (Patch) Rayment. They resided at Ashby and had 8 children.
Abigail[5] b. Dec. 29, 1748; d. before her father made his will March 14, 1772
Simeon b. Nov. 2, 1750; d. abt. 1835, age 85 at Sumner, Me.; m. Feb. 16, 1776, Ruth Wright of Westford, Mass; moved to Sumner, Maine.
Stephen b. Oct. 1, 1756; d. before July 1, 1759
Stephen (again) b. July 1, 1759; d. Aug. 16, 1811; m. Apr. 8

Reference:

Popes Pioneers of Mass.; "Barrett Ancestry" a pamphlet compiled by George Castor Martin; Chelmsford V.R.; Woburn, Mass. V.R.; Hist. of Woburn by Sewell; Gen. Dict. of N.E. by Savage; Index of Ancestors, Soc. Col. Wars.

Batchelder

Chart VI

Rev. Stephen[1] Bachiler was b. June 23, 1561 in Eng.; d. 1660 at Hackney, Eng. (2 miles from London in Middlesex); m. (1) Anne Batte, who never came to America; (2) at Abbots - Ann, 2 Mar. 1623-4, Christian Weare, wid.; (3) at Abbots - Ann 26 March, 1627 Helena Mason, wid.; (4) Mary Beedle, widow of Kittery, Maine. This marriage was very unhappy.

Rev. Bachiler's wife Ann, from whom came the Batchelder family in America, may have been a "Bate" a relative of Rev. John Bate, Vicar of Wherwell, who called Stephen Jr., "Cousin".

Rev. Stephen Batcheler matriculated at St. John's College, Oxford Nov. 17, 1581, b. a. 3 Feb. 1586-7, Vicar at Wherwell Hants, 17 July 1587 until deposed in 1605, but living there in 1614. Af. So. Stoveham, Co. Hants in 1631, he was licensed to visit his children in Holland, but having taken up with the co. of Merchant Adventurers called the Plough Co., he came to N.E., arriving at Cambridge in the William and Francis 5 June 1632, age 71.

Batchelder

He preached at Lynn the first year, and was freeman there 1635. Of Ipswich 1633 and Yarmouth 1637, failing settlement at both; Newbury 1638. In 1638, Rev. Stephen Batchelder age 76, traveled the distance from Lynn to the east part of Barnstable on foot. In 1638-39 he was the leader in the settlement of Hampton, N.H. and is said to have named the town. In 1644 he was called to Exeter but was prohibited from preaching there by the Genl. Ct. Apr. 20, 1647 he was later Hampton now of Strawberry Bank. He returned to Eng. after 1650, leaving his 4th wife at Kittery, Me. She asked for a divorce 18 Oct. 1656 alleging he had gone to Eng. many years since and had m. again, which was false.

Children of Rev. Stephen Batchelder and his first wife Ann:

Theodate b. 1588; d. Oct. 16, 1649; m. Christopher Hussey
Nathaniel b. 1590; d. ; m. Hester Mercer b. Aug. 1, 1602; d. before 1636+
Deborah b. 1592; m. Rev. John Wing
Stephen b. 1594; d. 1680 (In 1610 he entered Oxford at age 16)
Samuel b. 1597 or 98; a minister at Gorcum Holland
Ann b. 1601; m. (1) 1619 John Sandburn, (2) before 1640, Henry Atkinson of London

Child by 4th wife (Gen. Dict of Maine & N.H.)

Mary b. abt. 1650; m. bef. 26 Mar. 1673 William Richards whom the court on his petition, after delibaration app. adm. of Stephen Batchelder's estate.

References:

History of Hampton, N.H. by Joseph Daw, Chap. XIX Essex Autiquarian, p. 142; Pickards Life of Whittier Vol. I, p. 12 Morgans Sphere of Gentry (1661); Gen. Register XII:272; Stephen Bachiler & The Plough Co. of 1630 by V.C. Sanborn, Exeter, 1903; Hist. of Bachelder Family pub. by Frederick Piers; Popè's Pioneers of Mass.; Gov. Winthrops Hist. of Mass.; N.E. Hist. Gen. Reg.XVII, XX, XVII, XL, VII; The Hist. of Boston by Samuel Drake, M.A. pub. by Luther Stevens, 1856; N.E. Fam. pub. by Lewis 1913 Vol. I p. 226, Cutlers Gen. of Boston & Eastern, Mass. Lewis Pub. Co.; Gen. Dict. of Maine & N.H., Hist. of Barnstable Co. by Deyo, p. 29

Nathaniel[2] Batchelder born 1590 in Eng.; m. Hester Mercer of Huguenot Descent, daughter of Jan Mercer (or Le Mercier) & Jeanne Le Clere, bapt. Aug. 1, 1602.

Children:

Nathaniel[3] b. 1630; d. Jan. 17, 1710; m. (1) Deborah Smith, Dec. 10, 1656; m. (2) Mary (Carter) Wyman, Oct. 31, 1676; and (3) Elizabeth ( ) Knill, widow of John Knill, Oct. 23, 1689
Stephen, a merchant of London

Batchelder

Anna m. Daniel du Cormet of Middleborough (Eng.)
Francis, resided in Eng.
Benjamin, resided in Eng.

References:

History of Hampton, N.H. by Joseph Daw pp. 580-90; N.E. Families by Lewis Pub. 1913 Vol. I, p. 226; Gen. & Pers. Memoirs by Richard Cutter. A.M. Lewis Pub. Co. 1908, p. 372.

Nathaniel[3] Batchelder b. 1630 in Eng.; d. Jan 17, 1710, at Hampton, N.H. Will dated Feb. 14, 1706-7; m. (1) Deborah Smith daughter of John & Deborah (Parkhurst) Smith Dec. 10, 1656; m. (2) Mary (Carter) Wyman, widow of John Wyman, and daughter of Rev. Thomas and Mary (Parkhurst) Carter of Woburn, Mass. Oct. 31, 1676; m. (3) Elizabeth ( ) Knill, widow of John, Oct. 23, 1689. Mary (Carter) Wyman, his 2nd wife, was b. July 24, 1646 and d. 1688.

Nathaniel[3] Batchelder of Hampton, N.H. was twice, at least, elected Constable, was one of the selectmen for 9 years. When, after the death of his first wife, he determined to marry again, he decided to be governed in his choice by the direction in which his staff, held perpendicularly over the floor should fall when dropped from his hand. The staff fell towards the southwest and in that direction he bent his steps. At Woburn he called on the widow Wyman, offered her his hand, stating that he was going to Boston and would call for his answer on his return. (This is the wife from whom we are descended.) Nathaniel[3] was Representative in General Court (after N.H. was separated from Mass.) Oct. 1694 - May 1695.

Children by 1st wife Deborah Smith:

Deborah b. Oct. 12, 1657; m. Joseph Palmer, 25 Jan. 1677
Nathaniel[4] b. Mar. 24, 1659; d. 1745; m. Elizabeth Foss abt. 1685
Ruth, b. May 9, 1662; d. Jan. 11, 1752; m. Deacon James Blake, 8 July, 1684
Esther, b. Feb. 22, 1665; m. Deacon Samuel Shaw
Abigail, b. Dec. 28, 1667; d. Nov. 13, 1736; m. Deacon John Dearborn
Jane, b. Jan. 8, 1670; m. Benjamin Lamprey, 10 Nov. 1687
Stephen, b. July 31, 1672; d. Dec. 7, 1672
Benjamin, b. Sept. 19, 1673; d. Jan. 12, 1718; m. Susanna Page, 25 Dec. 1696
Stephen, b. Mar. 8, 1676; d. Sept. 17, 1748; m. Mary Dearborn, 25 Aug. 1698

Children by 2nd wife Mary (Carter) Wyman:

Mercy, b. Dec. 11, 1677; m. Samuel Dearborn, July 12, 1694 +
Mary, b. Sept. 18, 1679; died young
Samuel, b. Jan. 10, 1681; m. Elizabeth Davis May 14, 1707 pub. Apr. 1, 1706 +
Jonathan, b. 1683; m. Sarah Blake, 2 Dec. 1708

Batchelder
Children by 2nd wife Mary (Carter) Wyman, con't

Theodate, b. 1684; m. Morris Hobbs, 18 Nov. 1703
Thomas[4], b. 1685; m. (1) Mary Moulton, 14 Mar. 1712; m. (2) Sarah Tuck, 16 Jan. 1718; d. Feb. 10, 1764
Joseph, b. Aug. 9, 1687; d. Oct. 26, 1750; m. Mehitabel Marston
Mary, b. Oct. 17, 1688; d. young

Note: We are doubly descended from Nathaniel[3] Batchelder both from Mercy[4] and Samuel[4] Batchelder

References: History of Hampton, N.H. by Joseph Dow, pp. 590, 566-71; N. E. Hist. Gen. Reg. Vol. 27, p. 364; N.E. Families by Lewis, 1913, Vol. I p. 226; Gen. Dict. of Maine & N.H. Part II p. 81; Index of Ancestors, Soc. Col. Wars, p. 32.

Samuel[4] Batchelder b. Jan 10, 1681-2 at Hampton, N.H.; d. after 1732; m. Elizabeth Davis of Newbury, Mass., May 14, 1707 (publ. Apr. 1, 1706). She was b. Apr. 27, 1687 at Newbury, Mass. daughter of Zachariah and Judith (Brown) Davis; d. after 1732.

Children:

Judith, b. Jan 23, 1708; d. Dec. 4, 1789; m. Nathan Blake
Henry, b. Oct. 30, 1709; m. Mary Marston
Mary, b. Oct. 20, 1711; d. Oct. 30, 1769; m. Nathaniel Dearborn in Hampton, N.H. Dec. 2, 1731 (m. cert. N.H. Bureau V.S.) +
Samuel, b. Aug. 1, 1713; m. Sarah Drake
Elizabeth, b. May 10, 1716; m. Benjamin Brown
Zachariah, b. Dec. 14, 1717;
Hannah, b. Oct. 23, 1720; d. 1809; m. Jedidiah Prescott
Ruth, b. Oct. 29, 1722;
Mercy, b. Sept. 14, 1724; m. John James (?)
Carter, b. Oct. 31, 1726; d. July 16, 1806; m. (1) Huldah Moulto m. (2) Hannah Lane
Patience, bp. Dec. 27, 1729
Nathaniel, b. Mar. 2, 1731; d. Feb. 22, 1802; m. Ruth Sanborn

References:

History of Hampton, N.H. by Joseph Dow, pp. 590-1; m. cert. of Mary B. & Nathaniel D.; N.H. Bureau Vital Statistics; Hist. of Newbury, Mass. by Currier.

BEARCE

Chart III

Augustine (or Austin) Bearce was b. co 1608; came in the confidence Apr. 11, 1638 (age 20) from Longstock, Hampshire, Eng. (Bank's Topographical Dictionary); he joined Lothrops chh. at Barnstable Apr. 29, 1643. His wife (name not known) joined Aug. 7, 1650; Head of family in Barnstable 1640; member Barnstable Military Co., Plymouth Co., 1643 (Service not now accepted for Soc. of Colonial Wars.); d. ante 1697; m. before 1640--name of wife not known by me. (M.Z.G.)

Bearce

Children:

Mary b. 1640
Martha b. 1642
Priscilla, bpt. Mar. 11, 1643; m. 1660 John[2] Hall, son of John[1] and Bethiah (Farmer (?) Hall of Yarmouth, bpt. 13 May 1638 at Charlestown, Mass.; d. Mar. 30, 1712
Sarah, bpt. Mar. 29, 1646; m. Aug. 1667 John Hamlin (Hamblen) of Barnstable
Abigail, bpt. Dec. 19, 1647; m. 12 Apr. 1670 Allen Nichols of Barnstable
Hannah, bpt. Nov. 18, 1649
Joseph, b. Jan. 25, 1651-2; m. 3 Dec. 1675 Martha, daughter of Richard Taylor of Yarmouth
Hester (or Esther), bpt. Oct. 2, 1653
Lydia, b. Sept. 1655
Rebecca, b. Sept. 26, 1657; m. 17 Feb. 1671 William Hunter of Barnstable
James, b. July 1660

References:

Savage's N.E. Dict.; Pope's Pioneers of Mass., Mitchell's Hist. of Bridgwater, Mass., Lapham's Hist. of Woodstock, Me., and of Norway, Me.; Gen. Guide to Eaity Settlers of America by Whittemore; Hist. of Barnstable Co. Mass. by Simeon L. Deyo.

Regarding the wife of Austin Bearce, claim has been made that she was Mary Hyanno, an Indian Princess and daughter of John Hyanno, Sagamore of the Mattachee Indians of Cape Cod, Mass. These Indians were a branch of the Wampannoags or White Indians. (See Utah Gen. Mag. Vol. 26, pp. 99, 100.) An article in the American Genealogists Vol. 15, pp. 111-118, questions the claim that Austin Bearce married the flaming haired Mattachee princess Mary Hyanno--or that Austin Bearce was a Gypsy deported from England for some minor infraction of the law. More work must be done in order to solve the problem as to whether Austin Bearce did, or did not marry Mary Hyanno.

BENNETT

Charts I & XIV

Anthony[1] Bennett, carpenter, had grants of land in Gloucester, Mass., 1679--he settled on one of the grants. One source says the one on the east side of Mill River--another that he may have settled on a six acre grant at Goose Cove.

Anthony[1] came in to possession of the Ancient Mill, with the privilege of the stream; but he found an earnest competitor for the business of the town in John Ring, who had a mill on Sawmill-river Dam. The Mill continued in the Bennett Family and was carried on by them for many years.

Bennett

Anthony[1] Bennett may have been a step son of Richard Window of Gloucester, who died 5 June, 1665, and whose wife Elenor died 16 May, 1658. In his will dated May 2, 1665, Richard Window calls Anthony Bennett his son-in-law, and Elizabeth Bennett his daughter-in-law. This appears not to have been the relationship because Richard Window named Anthony's "Uncle Bennett" as his guardian "if he pleas to except him", if not, he left Anthony in the care of his overseers, William Haskell, Sr. (Note: one of our ancestors-M.Z.G.), James Stevens and Jacob Davis. The Essex Co. Quarterly Court records show that he was committed to the care of the overseers until he chose a guardian. Jacob Davis, one of the overseers, married an Elizabeth Bennett, Jan. 20, 1662, three years before Richard Window, made his will.

Anthony[1] Bennett married Abigail ________ before 1679; died int. Jan. 12, 1690 at Gloucester; and his wife died October 26, 1733, age between 70 and 80, at Gloucester. Bridge St. Cemetery rec. gives her death 1734, age 68. His death was untimely--one item charged against his estate "Sundry charges in getting a Jury _____ to view ye body of Sd. Dead., coming to an untimely end." Although Anthony[1] Bennett died January 12, 1690, his estate was not closed until March 25, 1699. Perhaps this was because the children were minors. His wife Abigail was appointed administratrix; inventory was taken by Famos (?) Stobons (?), Thomas Millett, and John Davis; Sureties were Timothy Somes and John Davis.

Anthony[1] and Abigail (   ) Bennett had:

Anthony[2] b. Nov. 12, 1679; d. June 1737; m. July 13, 1704 Rebecca Wharff (?)
Peter, m. Hannah, dau. Isaac Eueleth in Feb. 1704; in 1706 had a grant of land at Gloucester, between Anthony Bennett's and Widow Somes land,moved to Georgetown, York, Me. by 1718. (My guess is that Peter, whose birth is not recorded at Gloucester, was born between Anthony[2] and John[2] -- say about 1682 or 83 -- M.Z.G.)
John[2] b. April 11, 1686; m. Elizabeth ________; had daughters Jerusha and Ruth and sons Anthony and Jonathan; d. 2-1-1725, age 38
Abigail[2] b. Sept. 7, 1688

References:

Babson's History of Gloucester and Additions to the History of Gloucester by Babson; Gloucester, Mass. Vital Records; Probate of Anthony[2] Bennett's estate.

Anthony[2] Bennett, born Nov. 12, 1679 at Gloucester; died in June 1737; married July 13, 1704 Rebecca, possibly the daughter of Nathaniel[2] and Mary (Riggs) Wharff of Gloucester, born April 21, 1686 at Gloucester.

Bennett

Feb. 9, 1735, being then non compos mentis he, Anthony^2, was placed under the guardianship of his son John. Bond of Guardianship signed by John Bennett, Joseph Albro or Allen, and Ebenezer Kimball.

Sept. 4, 1764, then of Boston, Moses Bennett, son of Anthony^2 and Rebecca, sold to Andrew Millett, the estate of Anthony Bennett, decd. (p. 8 additions to Hist. of Gloucester by Babson). A Rebecca Bennett, widow, m. Ezekill Woodward, Nov. 24, 1740; he d. Sept. 14, 1771 or 74.

Anthony^2 and Rebecca Bennett had the following:

John^3 b. May 20, 1705; m. Experience Haskell, Feb. 11, 1731 and had ch: John, David, Jonathan, Patience, Experience, and Job
Stephen^3 b. Jan. 20, 1706-7; m. Mary Hooke of Salisbury at Salisbury
David^3 b. Dec. 5, 1709; d. Aug. 19, 1728
Jonathan^3 b. Oct. 22, 1711; d. Mar. 21, 1717-18
Nathaniel^3 b. Oct. 26, 1713;
Moses^3 b. Oct. 19, 1715; m. int. Jan. 19, 1745 to Elizabeth Fox of Boston. (The m. of a Moses Bennett and Eleanor Hooke, Mar. 16, 1760 is recorded in Salisbury 2nd Ch. Rec. p. 463 -- Old Fam. Salisbury & Amesbury by Hoyt.)
Sarah b. Aug. 15, 1717;
Job b. July 15, 1719;
Rebecca b. May 5, 1722; m. Benjamin Burdett of Durham, N.H. Oct. 3, 1751
James bo. Apr. 18, 1724;
Peter b. Mar. 16, 1725-6;
Rachel b. Mar. 18, 1727-28; m. int. Jacob Hibbard Oct. 9, 1747
Abigail b. May 19, 1730;

References:

Gloucester, Mass. V.R.; Hist. of Gloucester by Babson; Additions to Hist. of Gloucester by Babson.

Stephen^3 Bennett, son of Anthony^2 and Rebecca (Wharff ?) Bennett, was born Jan. 20, 1706-7 at Gloucester; married Mary Hooke at Salisbury, Mass., Jan. 2, 1728-29. She was born 1710 a daughter of William and Mary (Fallousbee) (Pike) Hooke; and died June 18, 1788 in her 79th year, at Gloucester. Stephen^3 Bennett's death record has not been found. He may have survived his wife.

Issue:

Francis b. 8-18-1729) These from
Mary b. 7-11-1731 m. Noah Davis int. 3-25-1752) Betty Stevens
Anna b. Aug. 21, 1733; m. Jacob Pike of Salisbury - int. 2-3-1753
Betty b. May 18, 1737; m. ? Solomon Stanwood, Nov. 20, 1755; d. Dec. 28, 1760 in her 24th yr.
Judith b. Sept. 2, 1739; m. Ebenezer^4 Bray, Apr. 19, 1762
Stephen b. Dec. 15, 1742;
Job b. June 27, 1745; d. bef. July 12, 1749

Bennett

Abigail b. July 18, 1747; m. ? Job. Knights, int. Aug. 12, 1769; d. Feb. 3, 1803 age 54?
Twins(Job (again) b. July 12, 1749; m. ? Mary Harraden, Nov. 22, 1770
(Francis b. July 12, 1749; m. ? Keturah Fuller, Oct. 29, 1772
William b. Oct. 12, 1751; m. ? Lucy Rust;int. Sept. 18, 1777

Noah Davis b. May 30, 1754 - m. ? Lizzuy Griffin, Apr. 20, 1779 - "prob. the Capt. Noah Bennett who, in a vessel of Gloucester, sailed from the West Indies and was lost in a white squall in about an hour after leaving port." - Additions to Hist. of Gloucester of Babson.

References:

Gloucester, Mass. V.R.; Hist. of Gloucester by Babson; Additions to Hist. of Gloucester by Babson; Old Families of Salisbury and Amesbury by Hoyt.

BOLLES - BOWLES

Chart XV

Joseph Bolles (Bowles) Gentleman, son of Thomas and Elizabeth (Perkins) Bowles, was bapt. at Worksop, Co. Natts, Eng. was bapt. 19 Feb. 1608; married Mary Howell, daughter of Morgan Howell, in 1640; d. 1678 - will dated 18 Sept. 1678, Prob. 29 Nov. 1678. Mary was born in March 1624 and was living at Portsmouth, N.H. in 1684, where she and Joseph had both been members of the church. In his will dated 17 Nov. 1666, prob. 1 Apr. 1667 Morgan Howell bequested to Mrs. Mary Bolles and her children all his estate and property and appointed her executrix of his will. (York Co. Reg. II, 120 and IV 3 & 49.)

In the year 1640 Joseph Bolles was engaged in trade at Winter Harbor, near the mouth of the Saco River in the Province of Maine. He afterwards removed to Wells, Me., where he held the office of Town Clerk from 1654 to 1674, during which period his dwelling house, and the first Volume of the town records were burned by Indians. Mr. Bowles had 100 acres of land next to Mr. Mackworths, 1654. June 1, 1664 Ferdinando Gorgas appointed Joseph Bowles as one of the deputies and Commissioners for the Government of the Province. Joseph Bolles ancestry goes back to Charlemagne and the Three Crusades.

Children, probably all born at Wells, Maine

Mary, b. 7 Aug. 1641; m. Col. Charles Frost of Kittery; d. Nov. 11, 1704
*Thomas, b. 1. Dec. 1644; m. (1) July 1, 1669 Zipparah Wheeler Groton; (2) Rebecca, daughter of Matthew Waller of New London, Conn; (3) Hopestill, widow of Nathaniel Chappell.
Samuel, b. 12 Mar. 1646; m. Mary Dyer, daughter of William Dyer of Sheepscot, Me.
Hannah, b. Nov. 15, 1649; m. (1) Caleb Beck; (2) Nathaniel Wright

Bolles - Bowles

Elizabeth, b. 15 Jan. 1652; m. (1) John Locke; (2) William Pitman
Joseph, b. Mar. 15, 1654; d. Sept. 25, 1683; m. Mary ______
Sarah, b. 20 Jan. 1657; m. Humphrey Chadbourne
Mercy, b. 11 Aug. 1661, never married

*Thomas^2 Bolles, son of Joseph^1 and Mary, was induced by John Winthrop, Governor of Conn., to remove from Wells to New London, Conn., soon after he reached manhood. On the evening of June 6, 1678, while Thomas^2 was absent from home, his wife Zipparah and two of his children were murdered by a boy named John Stoddard. The baby, a son, was in his mother's lap and his life was spared.

References:

Genealogy of the Bolles Family in America, by John A. Bolles, publ. 1865; George E. Williams, 16 Royal Oak Dr. Hartford, Conn., compiler of Bolles Gen.; Libby's Gen. Dict. of Me. & N.H.; Savages, N.E. Dict.; Magna Charta Sureties, 1215, by Adams & Weiss, 2nd edition; Clemins Mar. rec. before 1699

Samuel^2 Bowles, b. March 12, 1646 at Wells, Maine; m. Mary Dyer, daughter of William Dyer of Sheepscot, Me. (New Dartmouth). Samuel^2 and Mary were living in 1713, but the date of their deaths is not known. Samuel^2 received a grant of 300 acres at Wells, Maine in 1668 on condition that he improve it in a year. After being burned out three times in Maine by the Indians, he moved first to Clark's Island in Boston Harbor, and next to Rochester, Mass. In June 1712 Samuel^2 and his wife conveyed to Henry Flint of Cambridge "600 acres of land situated in New Dartmouth, alias Sheepscot commonly known by the name of Dyer's Neck or Massacmac, which said neck of land" says the deed " was formerly granted by Robin Hood, Sagamore of the said Massacmac unto William Dyer" father of Mary (York Co. Reg. of Deeds, Bk. 15 p. 224). In 1713 they conveyed to Samuel Hammond of Rochester, 310 acres of land "lying in the township of Wells." (Bk. 8 p. 120).

William Dyer and his son Christopher (father and brother of Mary (Dyer) Bolles) were killed and scalped by the Indians at Dyer's Neck. (See affidavits in York Reg. B 15 p. 228.)

Children of Samuel^2 and Mary Bolles - the first seven were baptised 4 Sept. 1692.

Mary bp. and owned covenent 4 Sept. 1692
Joanna owned covenent 1st ch., Braintree (rec. at Susanna) m. (1) 23 Jan. 1701-2 Joseph Tilden of Marshfield; m. (2) Charles Turner of Scituate; d. at Boston 1756
Bethiah, bp. 4 Sept. 1692; m. at Plymouth, Helkiah Bosworth
Experience, bp. 4 Sept. 1692; m. at Taunton, Edward Hammett
Joseph, bp. 4 Sept. 1692; m. before 1715, Mary ______
Samuel, bp. 4 Sept. 1692; m. before 1715, Lydia Balch, dau. of Benjamin and Grace (   ) (Mallett) Balch of Beverly; d. after 3 Oct. 1764

Bolles - Bowles

Children of Samuel[2] and Mary Bolles, cont.

Jonathan, bp. 4 Sept. 1692; m. before 1721, Mary ________; d. abt. 1773 in Rochester, Mass. His will (Plymouth Co. Rec.) bears date 1763, adm. to prob. 1773
William, bp. 1 Nov. 1694, may have died young
Deliverance, bp. 27 June 1699, 1st ch. Marshfield; m. Pembroke, Daniel Hayford, 24 May, 1733; prob. d. before 1770

References:

Gen. Dict. of Maine & N.H. by Libby; Gen, of Bolles Family in America, by John A. Bolles, publ. 1865.

Samuel[3] Bowles, bp. 4 Sept. 1692 at Rochester, Mass., d. after Oct. 3, 1764 (date of will); m. before 1715, Lydia Balch, daughter of Benjamin[2] and Grace (   ) (Mallett) Balch of Beverly, Mass. She was b. Aug. 28, 1695. The date of her death is not known.

Children born in Rochester, Mass. (Records of birth from Town Clerk.)

Benjamin b. 29 Nov. 1715; d. abt. 1800 in Rochester; m. Hannah Randall of Rochester, Mass.
Deborah b. Oct. 16, 1717; m. Apr. 5, 1738, Jedidiah Beals at Pembroke
Johannah b. Jan. 28, 1719; d. Apr. 9, 1725
Deliverance, b. May 16, 1722; m. Timothy Clifton of Rochester, Mass.
Lydia, b. Mar. 8, 1723/4; m. July 23, 1744, Rouse Howland at Pembroke
Samuel b. 12 Sept. 1725; d. 1805; m. Molly Walden of Martha's Vineyard. She d. 1817, age 84.
Johannah, b. June 12, 1727; m. Mar. 7, 1744 at Pembroke, Ebenezer Record; d. after Feb. 15, 1797, prob. Buckfield, Me.
David, b. Feb. 27, 1729; m. Lydia Kirby. They removed from Rochester, Mass., to Richmond, N.H.
Ruth, b. Feb. 20, 1731-2; d. Feb. 25, 1800; m. Joshua Snow of Rochester, Mass.

References:

Libby's Gen. Dict. of Me. & N.H.; Vital Records of Beverly, Pembroke, Rochester, Mass.; Genealogy of the Balch Family by Galusha B. Balch, M.D., 1897; Gen. of the Bolles Family in America by John A. Bolles, 1865.

BONNEY

Chart II

Thomas[1] Bonney Shoemaker, came in the Herculise in March 1634, from Sandwich, Kent Co. Eng. He had a certificate from Mr. Tho. Warren, rector of St. Peters in Sandwich, 14 Mar., 1634. Thomas[1] settled first at Charlestown, Mass., "where he had friends." Propr. 1635. He married Mary Terry who died within a year. He removed to Duxbury, Mass., propr. 31 Aug. 1640; freeman 5 March, 1638-9; town officer and civic leader; fought in King Phillips War.

The Bonney's were French, and in the 11th Century from the estate of Bonney near the town of Barry was their start - a branch escaped to Eng. They inter-married with the Washington family. In the 11th Century the knight of the Castle was in the crusade of that age.

Thomas[1] Bonney m. (2) Mary Hunt, daughter of Edmund, in the 1640's. She was the mother of his children. In his will dated Jan. 2, 1688-9 proved May 1, 1693, his widow receives his entire estate during her life. After his mother's decease Thomas[2] is to receive the houses and lands at Duxbury and the moveables are to be divided among "my children as she sees fit." Children:

Thomas[2] probably b. bef. 1660; m. bef. 1684 Dorcas Samson, daughter of Henry of the Mayflower; d. 1735
Mary (or Marcy) m. Dec. 14, 1675 John Mitchell, son of Experience and Jane Cooke Mitchell
Sarah m. Nathaniel Cole
Hannah, bapt. Duxbury - no further record found
John[2] b. Feb. 24, 1664; m. Elizabeth Bishop, daughter of Gov. James Bishop of Conn.; d. Nov. 16, 1745
William[2] b. 1667; m. (1) Ann May (2)
Joseph[2] m. Margaret Phillips
James[2] m. June 12, 1695, Abigail Bishop (sister of William Bonney's wife).

References:

The Bonney Family by Chas. L. Bonney; Bank's Topographical Dict.; Drakes Founders of N.E.; The Gens. & Est. of Charlestown 1629-1818 by Wyman, Vol. I p. 99; Windsor's Hist. of Duxbury; Will of Thomas[1] Bonney, rec. at Plymouth, Mass., abstract of p. 89 Vol. III Genealogical Advertiser; Index of Ancestors, Soc. of Col. Wars p. 53.

Thomas[2] Bonney, Husbandman b. prob. bef. 1660; m. bef. 1684 Dorcas Samson, daughter of Henry of the Mayflower and Ann (Plumer) Samson. Dorcas was b. bef. 1669 and d. after 24 Dec. 1684. Thomas[2] m. 2nd at Duxbury, Sarah Studley, 18 July 1695; d. after July 29, 1735 (date of will) and 8/6/1735 when the will was probated. Sarah, his 2nd wife died before he made his will.

Bonney

Children - all by his 1st wife Dorcas

Ebenezer[3] was drowned as a young fisherman, age 19
Thomas[3] also drowned as a young man
Elizabeth m. Ephriam Norcot at Marshfield, Mass., 30 Jan. 1712-13
Mercy m. (1) Nathaniel Delano; (2) John Curtis

References:

Windsor's Hist. of Duxbury, Mass.; The Bonney Family by Chas. L. Bonney; *Plymouth Co. Wills Bk. 7, pp. 156-157 (Will Thomas[2] Bonney)

BRAY

Charts I & XIII

Thomas[1] Bray, Ship Carpenter, of Gloucester, Mass.; proprietor 1642; was born about 1604 (he deposed 30 (1) 1658, age about 54 yrs.); married Mary Wilson[3] (3) 1646, at Gloucester; died Nov. 30, 1691 at Gloucester. His wife died March 27, 1707, being "aged". His will made 20 Nov., 1672, was probated 29 March, 1692.

Thomas[1] Bray had several grants of land including 6 acres in 1647, at the head of Little River and in 1651, 1/4 acre in the bottom on the north side of Cow-Island Marsh "for a house to be sett on." The first record of land to Thomas[1] Bray is of 3 acres bought of Thomas Smith.

Children born in Gloucester:

Mary b. Jan. 16, 1647; m. John Ring of Ipswich; Nov. 18, 1664; he d. Aug. 21, 1684 at Ipswich
Thomas b. Mar. 31, 1649; d. Aug. 12, 1653
Sarah b. ___________; m. James Sawyer - res. Gloucester
Thomas b. May 16, 1653; d. young
John b. May 14, 1654; m. Margaret Lambert in Gloucester, Nov. 10, 1679; d. Sept. 25, 1714
Nathaniel b. June 21, 1656; m. Martha Wadin, Jan. 22, 1684; d. May 2, 1728 in Gloucester. His wife survived him.
Thomas b. Jan. 19, 1658/9; m. Mary Emerson (?), Dec. 23, 1686; d. 1732
Hannah b. Mar. 21, 1661-2; m. John Roberts of Gloucester, Feb. 14, 1677
Esther b. Apr. 13, 1664; m. Philip Stanwood of Gloucester, Oct. 30, 1683.

References:

The Essex Antiquarian, Vol. II, pp. 101-104. Seven Generations of Brays by Wm. M. Bray; Hist. of Gloucester, Mass. by Babson; Additions to Hist. of Gloucester by Babson; Gloucester, Mass. V.R.; Popes Pioneers of Mass.

Bray

Thomas[2] Bray, born in Gloucester Jan. 19, 1658-9, was a yeoman. He m. Mary Emerson at Ipswich Dec. 23, 1686 (Note: The Ipswich m. rec. gives the groom as Thomas Brag, but most authorities say this is an error...the name should be Thomas Bray). Thomas[2] Bray made his will April 10, 1732, it was proved April 11, 1743.

Children born in Gloucester:

Thomas[3] b. Oct. 9, 1687; m. Eleanor Dodge of Beverly, Jan. 29, 1716-17
John[3] b. Sept. 7, 1689; m. Susanna Woodbury, Dec. 19, 1716
Daniel[3] b. ; d. May 14, 1696
Nathaniel[3] b. May 19, 1694; m. Sarah Haskell, Nov. 22, 1733; d. 1-18-1773
Moses[3] b. Nov. 26, 1696; m. Nov. 21, 1717, Mary Woodberry of Beverly
Aaron[3] b. July 2, 1699; m. (1) Elizabeth Davis, Dec. 28, 1727; m. (2) Ruth Winter, published Nov. 24, 1744
Mary b. Mar. 23, 1702; m. William Ring, Jan. 25, 1719-20
Sarah b. Mar. 31, 1706; d. May 23, 1706
Abigail b. Aug. 3, 1707; m. Humphrey Woodbury, Jan. 13, 1725-6

References:

The Essex Antiquarian, Vol. II, pp. 101-104. Seven Generations of Brays by Wm. M. Bray; Hist. of Gloucester, Mass. by Babson; Additions to Hist. of Gloucester by Babson; Gloucester, Mass. V.R.; Popes Pioneers of Mass.

Thomas[3] Bray b. Oct. 9, 1687 at Gloucester, Mass.; m. Eleanor Dodge of Beverly, Mass., Jan. 29, 1716-17; d. before Jan. 14, 1744-5, when administration was granted on his estate. Eleanor Dodge, was a daughter of Edward and Mary (Haskell) Dodge of Beverly. She was born about 1677, and died about 1763.

Thomas[3] Bray was first, a cardwainer, and then a physician. He practiced medicine in Gloucester for many years until he died.

Children born in Gloucester:

Eleanor b. May 15, 1719; m. Joshua Haskell, Mar. 31, 1741
Thomas[4] b. Mar. 11, 1721; m. Judith Sargent, Jan. 16, 1746
Mary b. Mar. 31, 1723;
Edward b. Mar. 15, 1725; m. Sarah Woodberry in Gloucester, May 25, 1748
Abigail b. July 4, 1727
Ebenezer b. Apr. 18, 1732; m. Judith Bennett, Apr. 19, 1762

References:

The Essex Antiquarian, Vol. II, pp. 101-104. Seven Generations of Brays by Wm. M. Bray; Hist. of Gloucester, Mass. by Babson; Additions to Hist. of Gloucester by Babson; Gloucester, Mass. V.R.; Popes Pioneers of Mass.

Bray

Ebenezer[4] Bray b. Apr. 18, 1732 at Gloucester; d. about 1816, age 84 yrs., at Minot, Me.; m. Judith Bennett, daughter of Stephen and Mary (Hook) Bennett; b. Sept. 2, 1739 at Gloucester, Mass.; d. Jan. 30, 1799, age 66, at Minot, Me.

Ebenezer[4] Bray was a schoolmaster in Gloucester, Mass., for many years. Nov. 6, 1760 he was given seven pounds by the town of Gloucester "towards helping him to the Latting Tongue". In 1777 he moved his family to Bakerstown, Maine, which was afterwards divided up to form Poland, then Minot and finally Mechanic Falls. Ebenezer's family lived in that part afterward called Minot. During his later years he taught in a private school on Bradbury Hill in Minot.

Ebenezer[4] Bray was deformed in hands and feet yet served his country during the American Revolution being employed on the brig "Dolphin" of Conn. His name was on the list of prisoners returned from New York in the Cartel "Rising Empire", commanded by Capt. Godfrey (year not given). One source, which I have been unable to find, so I have been told, states that Ebenezer taught seamanship during the Revolution - a forerunner of Annapolis Naval Academy.

Children born at Gloucester, Mass., except for Thomas[5].

Betty Bennett, b. Apr. 30, 1764
Stephen Bennett, b. Apr. 2, 1766; m. Apr. 7, 1789, Hannah Ring of No. Yarmouth, Me. She m. (2) Mr. Snow Winslow of No. Yarmouth, 1/2/1792; (3) Samuel Gooding, Feb. 19, 1807
Mary Hook bp. Aug. 1768
Mary Hook bp. Sept. 1769
Mary Hook b. Sept. 1770;
Ebenezer, bapt. Dec. 15, 1771; m. July 8, 1793 at Turner, Me., Eleanor Royal - both of Bakerstown
William Bennett b. 1775
Thomas b. Sept. 20, 1779 at Minot, Me.; m. (1) Cynthia Record, Bans Publ. Dec. 30, 1797; d. Mar. 27, 1842. Cynthia d. Jan. 30, 1799. Ebenezer m. (2) Eunice Packard, Sept. 28, 1809; m. (3) Abigail Young, Sept. 28, 1819.

References:

The Essex Antiquarian, Vol. II, pp. 101-104. Seven Generations of Brays by Wm. M. Bray; Hist. of Gloucester, Mass. by Babson; Additions to Hist. of Gloucester by Babson; Gloucester, Mass. V.R.; Popes Pioneers of Mass.; Hist. of Turner, Me., by French; Mass. Soldiers and Sailors in the Am. Rev. Vol. II, p. 446.

Thomas[5] Bray b. Sept. 20, 1779 at Minot, Me., d. Mar. 27, 1842 at Minot, Me.; m. (1) Cynthia Record on Jan. 28, 1798 at Hebron, Me. by John Greenwood, J.P. (Bans. Publ. Dec. 30, 1797). She was a daughter of Simon and Bethiah (Packard) Record, b. Aug. 20, 1778 at Buckfield, Maine; d. Sept. 20, 1819. Thomas[5] Bray m. (2) a first cousin of his first wife, Eunice Packard, daughter of Job and Eunice (Bray) Packard Sept. 28, 1819 (it appears that either this marriage date is wrong, or that Cynthia died before Sept. 20, 1819.) He m. (3) Abigail Young, Dec. 25, 1829.

Bray

Children, by Cynthia, his first wife:

Stephen, b. 1798; d. 1875; m. Nov. 9, 1826, Lois Jones
Eleanor, b. 1799; m. Jan. 26, 1821, Arvin Merrill of Buckfield
Amelia (or Emily) b. 1800; m. June 12, 1822, Capt. Merrill Woodman
Cynthia, b. March 25, 1802; d. Dec. 11, 1864 at Buckfield, Me.; m. Apr. 30, 1825, James Spaulding of Buckfield, Me.
Bennet, b. 1804; d. 1837; m. Sept. 29, 1831, Harriet Long
Bethiah b. 1806; m. Mar. 23, 1828 Barnabas Fuller of Hebron, Me.
Harriett, b. 1807
Armenta, b. 1809; m. Dr. Inglis
Greenlief, b. 1811; m. May 21, 1835, Eliza Reynolds

Children by Eunice his second wife:

Harrison b. 1821; d. 1891; m. Feb. 14, 1850, Keziah Mills Weymouth, daughter of William and Sally Weymouth of New Portland, Me.
Pamelia b. 1823; m. Dec. 7, 1843, David Garland
Frances b. 1825; m. Nov. 15, 1844, Samuel Ryerson of Portland, Me.
Eunice Marie, b. 1827

No children by third marriage.

References: Seven Generations of Brays by William M. Bray; History of Buckfield, Maine by Cole, p. 663.

BRETT

Charts XVI & XXIV & XXXIX

William[1] Brett came from Kent, Eng. to Duxbury, Mass., about 1638-9, and he appears as a purchaser of land early in 1640; Freeman 1646. He left home soon after becoming of age and probably came with his kinsmen the Haywards, although his name does not appear on the passenger list. He at once became a leading man of the Colony, often being associated with John Alden, the Winslows, Constant Southworth and others; is called "of Duxburrow" in deeds of land until he became proprietor of Bridgewater.

In the records of Bridgewater he is often spoken of merely as "The Elder". He early became an Elder of the Church and is called a "Grave and Godly Man". William Brett was one of the Town Council, a Constable, a member of the council of war and Representative to the General Court at Plymouth from June 3, 1656, the date of the incorporation of the town of Bridgewater, to 1661. Served in Capt. Miles Standish Duxbury Co. 1643.

Brett

Between the years 1630 and 1640, according to the Brett Genealogy, "there landed in America from England, two men by the name of William Brett. One went to Virginia and the other to New England. The first was beyond doubt a near relative of Mary, daughter of William Brett of Toddington, and sister of Sir Edward Brett; Mary Brett and Wm. Isham were married Aug. 15, 1625 and were the progenitors of many of the First Families of Virginia". Wm. Brett of Va., so states the Brett Genealogy, probably returned to England or died early, as no trace has been found of him. (Note: Could it be that William Brett of N.E. is the same man as William Brett of Virginia? This might explain why William Brett's name does not appear on lists of passengers for N.E. and William Brett of Va. is not found on records there, giving rise to the thought that he had returned to England or died. --M.Z.G.)

William Brett of Bridgewater, Mass., m. Margaret Ford, before 1648. She was probably a daughter of William and Alice (Booth) Ford, who were m. in Eng. in 1601. Alice was a daughter of William and Elizabeth Warburton (daughter of Sir John Warburton) Booth. William Brett d. Dec. 17, 1681, age 63 years. His will probated 12 March 1681-2, names his wife Margaret and their seven children. The will was witnessed by Thomas Haward and John Howard. An inventory of the estate was taken by Lieut. Thomas Haward and Ensign John Howard. In addition to a sizeable estate, William Brett left his descendents the goodly heritage of an unblemished character, and a godly and industrious life, always foremost in good works.

Children:

William b. about 1648; m. Elizabeth Cary, b. 1649, daughter of John and Elizabeth (Godfrey) Cary of Bridgewater.
Elihu b. about 1650; m. Ann Turner before 1679; d. Jan. 13, 1712 +
Alice b. about 1652; m. Joseph Hayward (his 1st wife), son of Thomas of Bridgewater
Lydia
Hannah b. about 1658; m. about 1676, Francis Cary b. 1647, son of John Cary of Bridgewater
Nathaniel b. about 1661; m. Nov. 21, 1683, Sarah Hayward, (?) daughter of John and Sarah (Mitchell) Hayward.
Margaret

References:

Brett Genealogy by L. B. Goodenow, 1915; Savage N.E. Gen. Dict; Popes Pioneers of Mass.; Bridgewater, Mass. V.R.; Hist. of Bridgewater, Mass.; Duxbury Town Records; Index to Ancestors, Soc. Col. Wars p. 62.

Brett

Elihu[2] Brett was Justice of the Peace and solemnized marriages in Bridgewater and surrounding towns for many years. He was Representative to the General Court from 1691 to 1700; was the next magistrate after Hayward and appointed Judge of the Court of Common Pleas and Sessions 1700. He was one of those entitled to a "Front Seat" nearest the pulpit, an honor reserved only for those in high office. He died Jan. 13, 1712, while sitting in his chair. He had arisen early that Sunday morning, gone to the barn and returned to the house, sat in his chair while waiting for his meal and fell down dead. An agreement of the heirs of Elihu Brett, who died intestate, was made April 11, 1712.

Elihu[2] Brett m. before 1679, Ann (sometimes Hannah in records) Turner, daughter of George and Mary (Robbins) Turner. (Mary Robbins was a daughter of Nicholas and Ann (   ) Robbins of Duxbury.) Ann Brett died after her husband but there does not appear to be a record of her death. She shared in Elihu's estate with their children:

Mary b. 1678-79; d. Jan. 14, 1756 in the 78th year of her life; m. 1698, John[3] Willis, son of John[2] and Experience (Byram) Willis; John[3] Willis d. Nov. 1, 1732
Margaret b. 1680-81; m. Mar. 18, 1715-16 Samuel Wills
Elihu b. 1681-82; m. Dec. 17, 1706, Susanna (Edson) Hayward at Bridgewater, Mass.

References:

Brett Genealogy; Bridgewater V.R.; Hist. of Bridgewater, Mass.; Savage Gen. Dict. of N.E.

BREWSTER

Chart No. III

Elder William Brewster of the Mayflower, was b. about 1567 (42 yrs. of age in 1609); d. Apr. 10, 1644 at Plymouth, Mass.; m. Mary Wentworth about 1591. She was b. about 1569; d. Apr. 17, 1627 at Plymouth.

Elder Brewster was the Fourth Signer of the Mayflower Compact. He was regarded as leader of the Pilgrims at Scrooby, Eng., near Sherwood Forest, where his father became bailiff of the manor of Scrooby in 1575, and in 1588 was appointed post-master by Queen Elizabeth. On his father's death Wm. Brewster was appointed to both posts. He was well schooled in history, philosophy, and religious writings. "The Brewster Book" a very old manuscript containing records relating to Elder Brewster, his wife Mary, son Jonathan and his wife Lucretia, the latters children and many of Jonathan's descendents of the early generations, has been copied and printed in The Mayflower Desc.

Elder Wm. Brewster was Ruling Elder; he wore a violet colored coat, black silk stockings, a ruff, etc.

Brewster

Children:

Jonathan, b. Aug. 12, 1593; d. Aug. 7, 1659; m. Apr. 10, 1624 Lucretia Oldham, at Plymouth, Mass. Jonathan was born at Scrooby, Nottinghamshire, Eng.
Love, d. 1650 at Duxbury, Mass.; m. May 14, 1634 at Plymouth, Sarah Collier. She m. (2) aft. Sept. 1, 1656, Richard Parke.
Patience d. not long bef. Dec. 12, 1634; m. Aug. 5, 1624, Thomas Prence. He m. (2) Apr. 1, 1635, Mary Collier -- he had 2 other wives.
Fear d. Dec. 1634; m. bef. May 22, 1627 Isaac[1] Allerton.
Wrestling d. aft. May 22, 1627, unmarried.
_______ d. bef. June 20, 1609 at Leyden, bur. in St. Pancras June 20, 1609.

References:

Families of the Pilgrims by Shaw, pp. 48-51 incl. The Mayflower Desc., Vols. 1,2,3; Signers of the Mayflower Compact by Annie Armoux Haxtun, part I, pp. 11-14; Popes Pioneers of Mass., p. 67.

BROWNE

Chart V

Christian Browne, widow of George Browne who d. in Salisbury, Eng., in 1633, came to this country in 1640, bringing with her sons Henry, William and George. She came to Salisbury, Mass., with its first company of settlers and received Grants there. Died 28 Dec. 1641 (Savage)

Children:

Henry (Deacon) b. about 1615; m. Abigail bef. 1642; d. Aug. 6, 1701. +
William b. about 1622; m. Elizabeth Murford (? Muneford); June 25, 1645; d. Aug. 24, 1706. William's wife was cancelled on the church list of 1687. She was insane for more than 30 years. See "The New Puritan", pp. 173-5.
George (Capt.) b. about 1623; d. Oct. 31, 1699 at Haverhill; will prob. Nov. 6, 1699; m. (1) June 25, 1645, Ann Eaton, daughter of John[1] of Salsbury and Haverhill; she d. Dec. 16, 1683; m. (2) widow Hannah Hazen of Rowley on Mar. 17, 1683.

References:

Old Families of Salisbury and Amisbury by Hoyt, Vol. I

Deacon Henry[2] Brown, Shoemaker, born in Eng. abt. 1615; d. Aug. 6, 1701 at Salisbury, Mass.; m. abt. 1640, Abigail _______. She d. Aug. 23, 1702 at Salisbury. Deacon Henry Brown received land in Salisbury in 1640,41,42; freeman 1649; commoner in 1650.

Browne
Deacon Henry[2] Brown, con't.

Member Salisbury Church 1677; his name is on most of the early Salisbury lists. He and his wife were members of the Salisbury Church in 1687.

Children of Deacon Henry and Abigail Brown all born Salisbury:

Nathaniel[3], Capt. & Deacon, b. June 30, 1642; d. Oct. 5, 1723, will June 30, 1721; m. Oct. 16 (or 18) 1666, Hannah[2] Fellows (Samuel[1]); she d. Mar. 23, 1727. They resided at Salisbury and a short time at Hampton, N.H. Both d. Salisbury.
Abigail b. Feb. 3, 1643-4; d. Jan. 11, 1678-80; m. June 1, 1664 at Salisbury, Samuel French (Edward[1]). + see French
Jonathan[2] b. Nov. 25, 1646; prob. d. young.
Philip[2], tailor of Salisbury; b. Dec. 1646; d. July 21, 1729; will prob. Aug. 4, 1729; m. Mary[2] Busewell (Isaac). She d. Nov. 27, 1683.
Abraham[2], yeoman, b. Jan. 1, 1649-50; d. Mar. 26, 1723; will prob. Apr. 16, 1732-3; m. June 15, 1675 Elizabeth Shepherd. She is mentioned in Abraham's will.
Sarah b. Dec. 6, 1654; d. June 23, 1727; m. June 12, 1673, Andrew[2] Greely (Andrew[1]); he d. Nov. 26, 1736.
Henry[2] b. Feb. 8, 1658-9; d. Apr. 25, 1708 at Salisbury; m. May 17, 1682, Hannah Putnam of Salem; rem. to Salem about 1693-1700; will of wid. Hannah at Salem May 9, 1730.

References: Old Families of Salisbury and Amesbury, Vol. I.

BROWNE

(Cutting - Brown Family)

Charts VI &XVII

James Browne, Glazier, b. abt. 1604-5; m. (1) bef. 1638, Judith, daughter of Capt. John Cutting of Newbury; Judith d. abt. 1650-59. M. (2) after 1650, Judith's sister Sarah Cutting; d. Nov. 13, 1676 - his will prob. 29 (9) 1676.

James[1] Brown was first of Charlestown. In 1636 he hired Lovells Island of the town. He was disarmed by order of the Court in 1637. Was made Freeman May 17, 1637; Apr. 19, 1638 he was chosen Constable; was proprietor and town officer of Newbury; was freeholder of Newbury; received 150 acre grant before 1645. Removed to Salem about 1668 having bought a house and lot of Christopher Waller. In his will he left to his eldest son John, estate left by Henry Bright of Watertown for money lent him (Bright) many yrs. ago. Estate at Newbury left to wife by her father Capt. John Cutting, was left to wife. His widow Sarah, m. (2) William Healey of Cambridge, Nov. 29, 1677.

Browne

Children by first m. to Judith Cutting:

John b. Jan. 4, 1638; m. Mary Woodman
James b. 1642; d. 1643 - bur. 8-6-1643
James b. 19 (6) 1647; m. 16 (1) 1670 Hannah House (or Huse)
Nathaniel b. 21 (9) 1648;

Children prob. by 2nd m. to Sarah Cutting:

Samuel, b. Jan. 14, 1656-7
Sarah, ; m. ________ Beazley
Hannah, bpt. Sept. 2, 1658
Abraham, bpt. 14 (8) 1660;
Mary, b. May 25, 1663;
Abigail, b. Oct. 24, 1665;
Martha, b. Dec. 22, 1667; m. Sept. 6, 1688 John Tappan

References: Hist. of Salem by Sidney Perley, Vol. II pp. 420, 431; Old Families of Salisbury and Amesbury by Hoyt, Vol. III pp. 888, 948. Neddlesex Files - Popes Pioneers of Mass.; Hist. of Newbury by Currier; Essex Co. Mass., Probate Records Vol. II; Wyman's Charleston Genealogies & Estates Vol. I, p. 136.

John[2] Brown, Glazier, b. Jan. 4, 1638-9 at Charlestown, son of James[1] and Judith (Cutting) Browne; m. Mary Woodman, daughter of Edward[1] and Joanna (Bartlett) Woodman, Feb. 20, 1659/60 at Newbury.

Children:

Judith b. Dec. 3, 1660; m. Feb. 4, 1680 (1) Zachariah Davis; he died June 25, 1692. A widow Judith Davis m. (2) Henry Bradley at Newbury Jan. 7, 1695-6. Judith d. Nov. 14, 1728.
Mary b. Mar. 8, 1661-2; m.?Dec. 1680, William Partridge

BRYANT

Charts I & II

Stephen[1] Bryant, from Eng. to Plymouth, Mass. 1650; Constable at Plymouth June 1, 1663. It appears he was first of Duxbury 1643, Freeman June 6, 1654; chosen Constable of Duxbury June 6, 1654, and surveyor of highways at Plymouth June 1, 1658, juryman March 5, 1660-1. He m. Abigail, daughter of John Shaw of Plymouth and had:

Abigail, m. Nov. 23, 1665, Lieut. John Bryant; d. May 12, 1715 +
John b. Apr. 7, 1650 at Plymouth; m. Sarah
Mary b. May 29, 1654 at Plymouth;
Stephen b. Feb. 2, 1655 at Plymouth; m. Mehitabel
Sarah b. Nov. 28, 1659 at Plymouth;
Lydia b. Oct. 23, 1662 at Plym.; m. William Churchill
Elizabeth b. Oct. 17, 1665 at Plym.; m. Joseph King

Bryant, con't

References: Stephen Bryant & His Desc. N.E.H. Reg. Vol. 24 (1870) p. 315. Popes Pioneers of Mass.; Savage's N.E. Gen. Dict; N.E.H.G. Reg. Vol. 48 (1894) p. 46

BRYANT

Charts I & II

John[1] Bryant, came on the Ann in 1623 (?). Barnstable, Mass., Families by Swift, Vol. I p. 146 gives: "John Bryant, house carpenter, was of Barnstable in 1640. He m. Nov. 14, 1643 Mary, b. at Kent, Eng., daughter of George Lewis, for his first wife. He returned to Scituate and was an active and useful man, much employed in the division of lands, and other public business. In 1657 he married his second wife, Elizabeth, daughter of Rev. William Witherell, and in 1664, Mary, daughter of Thomas Hiland. By his first wife he had 7, and by his third, 10 children."

Name of Bryant can be traced back to Sir Guy deBriant, who lived in time of Edward III and whose descendants had their seat in the Castle of Hereford in the Marches of Wales. Arms: the field is Or, three piles meeting near in the base of the Escutcheon, Azure: Tradition gives that John Bryant, Sr. of Scituate and Stephen Bryant of Plymouth were probably brothers.

John[1] Bryant was a Representative 1677-8. His name appears on the records of Plymouth Colony as early as 1639. His first wife, Mary, was b. about 1623 at Kent, Eng., daughter of George and Sarah (Jenkins) Lewis of Barnstable. She d. July 2, 1655. He m. (2) Elizabeth Witherel Dec. 22, 1657, who d. 1661-2. His 3rd wife was Mary Hiland whom he m. in 1664. John[1] Bryant d. Nov. 20, 1684 at Scituate. His widow Mary (Hiland) Bryant m. (2) Robert Stetson.

John[1] Bryant was Deputy to the Plymouth Colony General Court 1657, 62, 67.

Children of John[1] Bryant and his 1st wife Mary (Lewis)

John, b. 17 Aug. 1644; m. 14 Nov. 1643 Abigail Bryant; d. 20 Nov. 1684.
Hannah, b. 25 Jan. 1645; m. 1665 John Stodder of Hingham.
Joseph, b. 1646 - d. young
Sarah, b. 29 Sept. 1648
CR2 Sarah Mary, b. 24 Feb. 1649; bp. Mar. 23, 1650; d. 8 Apr. 1652
Martha, b. 26 Feb. 1651;
CR2 Samuel, b. 6 Feb. 1653; m. ?Johannah - est. adm. March 1690-1
CR2 Daniel, bp. Feb. 5, 1659; (2nd m.?)
CR2 Mary, bp. Jan. 19, 1661;

Bryant

Children of John[1] Bryant and his 3rd wife Mary (Hiland)

Elizabeth, b. Aug. 1665; d. Dec. 17, 1683 (?)
CR2 Joseph, b. May 1667;
CR2 Benjamin, b. 1669, Dec.
CR 2 Joseph, bp. 1671, Apr. 16
CR2 Jabez, b. 1672, Feb. 18, 1671
CR2 Ruth, b. 1673, Apr. 16
CR2 Thomas, b. 1675, July 15
CR2 Deborah, b. 1677, Jan. 22, 1676
CR2 Agatha, b. 1678, Mar. 12
Ann, b. 1680
Elisha, b. 1682

References:

Barnstable, Mass. Families by Swift - Vol. I p. 146; N.E. Hist. Gen. Reg., Vol. 9 pp. 313, 317; Vol. 48 pp. 46-47; Index of Ancestors, Soc. Col. Wars p. 72; Mayflower Desc. Vol. 5, pp. 2,6,7 - Vol. 17, p. 74; Croziers General Armory; Popes Pioneers of Mass.; Plymouth Vital Records; Scituate, Mass. Records Vols. I, II - Vol. I, pp. 42, 43, 58, 59 - Vol. II pp. 38, 47, 48, 356, 361.

Lieut. John[2] Bryant, b. 17 Aug. 1644 at Scituate, Mass., son of John[1] and Mary (Lewis) Bryant; m. 23 Nov. 1665 at Plympton, Mass. Abigail Bryant, daughter Stephen and Abigail (Shaw) Bryant, b. Nov. 23, 1665 and d. May 12, 1715. John[2] Bryantd. Jan. 26, 1707-8 at Scituate.

Children:

Mary b. Sept. 11, 1666
Hannah b. Dec. 2, 1668
Bethiah b. July 25, 1670
Samuel b. Feb. 3, 1673; m. Joanna _____, d. Dec. 18, 1736 in 65th yr. He d. 1750, Mar. 3, age 76 yrs. - Was deacon of the church in Plympton, d. there.
Jonathan b. Mar. 23, 1677;
Abigail b. Dec. 30, 1682
Benjamin b. Dec. 16, 1688; m. July 31, 1712, Hannah Eaton, daughter Benjamin & Mary (Coombs) Eaton; d. May 4, 1724.
John? b. Mar. 29, 1677-8
David? b. Aug. 17, 1684
Joshua? b. Nov. 14, 1687
Joseph? b. Apr. 16, 1671

References:

N.E.H.G. Reg. Vol. 24 p. 315; May. Desc. Vol. I, pp 209, 210; May. Desc. Vol. 30, p. 70.

Bryant

Benjamin[3] Bryant, son of John[2] (John[1]) and Abigail (Bryant) Bryant, b. Dec. 16, 1688 at Plympton, Mass.; m. July 31, 1712 at Plympton, Hannah, daughter of Benjamin and Mary (Coombs) Eaton; d. May 4, 1724. Hannah was b. Feb. 10, 1692; d. March 4, 1723-4. She was a granddaughter of Francis Eaton and great granddaughter of Degary Priest of the Mayflower.

"Francis Cooke, Jr., Benjamin Bryant, and John Ransom, were all drowned on Plympton shore, May 4, 1724."

Children of Benjamin[3] and Hannah (Eaton) Bryant:

Phoebe, b. Sept. 18, 1713; m. Nov. 29, 1733, David Sears (int. Scers)
Marcy, b. Jan. 3, 1715; m. Nov. 11, 1735, Nehemiah Leech
Hannah, b. Mar. 24, 1716; m. Elishas Bryant Oct. 4, 1737
Micah, b. Apr. 2, 1719; m. int. Apr. 19, 1740 at Kingston, to Elizabeth Norcot
Jerusha, b. Feb. 7, 1721-2; m. Apr. 19, 1739, Solomon Leech of Bridgewater

References:

Plympton, Mass., V.R. pp. 40, 41, 269-272, 451. N.E.H.G. Reg. Vol. 24 p. 315.

Micah[4] Bryant, son of Benjamin[3] and Hannah (Eaton) Bryant, was b. Apr. 2, 1719 at Plympton, Mass.; m. int. Apr. 19, 1740 at Kingston, Mass., to Elizabeth Norcot, daughter of Ephriam and Elizabeth (Bonney) Norcot, b. 19 Feb. 1715 at Marshfield, Mass. She was a great granddaughter of Henry Samson of the Mayflower. Elizabeth d. Jan. 23, 1776 in 60th yr., and Micah d. just five days later on Jan. 28, 1776 in 57th yr. at Middleboro, Mass. They, and their son, Abner, who d. April. 28, 1775 in 22nd yr. are buried in "Grave on Hill" (Nemasket Cemetery), Middleboro, Mass.

Children of Micah[4] and Elizabeth (Norcot) Bryant:

Benjamin b. Oct. 24, 1741
Micah b. Apr. 2, 1744 at Middleboro; m. Nov. 22, 1770, Margaret Paddock; d. abt. 1790 at New Vineyard, Maine
Abner b. abt. 1753; d. Apr. 28, 1775

References:

Plympton, Mass. V.R. p. 41; Taunton, Mass. V.R., Vol. II p. 72; Recs. from Middleboro Town Clerk; Middleboro, Mass. Deaths publ. by Mayflower Soc. 1947, p. 27; Plymouth Co. Prob. Rec. 3176; Plymouth Co. Deeds 58:110.

Micah[5] Bryant, son of Micah[4] and Elizabeth (Norcot) Bryant, b. Apr. 2, 1744 in Middleboro; m. Nov. 22, 1770, Margaret Paddock, b. Dec. 19, 1741 at Yarmouth, Mass., daughter of Joseph and Elizabeth (Mayo) Paddock; d. after 1790 prob. New Vineyard, Maine. Yarmouth Town Records, Bk. 3 p. 120

Bryant

Margaret (Paddock) Bryant d. Dec. 15, 1814 in New Vineyard, Maine and is buried in the Old Burying Ground. Her tombstone inscription:

Sacred to the Memory
Margaret Bryant
Died Dec. 15, 1814
Aged 73 years
Consort of Micah Bryant

Margaret (Paddock) Bryant joined the Middleboro Church June 30, 1776. Removed to Maine. Micah Bryant was a Quaker.

Micah^5 Bryant was a Minute Man during the Rev. War, 1775, 76, 78. He first served as a private under Capt. John Porter on Muster Roll dated Aug. 1, 1775, having enlisted July 7, 1775. Micah Bryant's name again appears as a member of Capt. Porter's Co. on Co. Return dated Oct. 6, 1775 "Camp before Boston" later a member of Capt. William Tupper's Co. 1776, (yet later as a member of ? Capt. Edw. Sparrow's Co. serving as Corporal -- prob. another Micah Bryant.)

Children of Micah^5 and Margaret (Paddock) Bryant, born at Middleboro, Mass.

Elias b. Sept. 8, 1772; m. May 7, 1798, his first cousin, Bathsheba Hackett, daughter Ephriam and Elizabeth (Paddock) Hackett; d. abt. 1833.
Betsy b. Jan. 26, 1773; m. ? Nathaniel Leonard, Jr., Mar. 20, 1788 (Age 15?)
Lucy b. May 5, 1775; m. ? Ephriam W. Vaughan, July 28, 1791 ?Age 16
Sally b. June 14, 1777;
Molly b. Nov. 13, 1779;
Micah b. Feb. 27, 1782; m. abt. 1809, Mary (Polly) Twitchell or Mitchell

References:

Middleboro, Mass. Bk. 4 pp. 136, 138, 184, 243. Hist. of Middleboro, Mass. by Thomas Weston p. 667 # 540; Mass. Soldiers & Sailors in the Rev. War, by Commonwealth of Mass. Vol. 16, p. 16, Vol. 56, p. 195; Vol. 57 file 20, Vol. 3 p. 208, Vol. 23 p. 135, Vol. I p. 112; Vol. 22 p. 195; Cemetery inscription New Vineyard, Maine; Taunton, Mass. V.R. Vol. II pp. 73, 213.

Rev. Elias^6 Bryant, son of Micah^5 and Margaret (Paddock) Bryant, b. Sept. 8, 1772, Middleboro, Mass; m. (1) May 7, 1798, Bathsheba Hackett, daughter of Ephriam and Elizabeth (Paddock) Hackett b. abt. 1776; d. Oct. 1830 in New Vineyard, Maine. Elias and Bathsheba were first cousins, their mothers being sisters.

Bryant

Bathsheba d. Oct. 19, 1816 at New Vineyard, Maine. The inscription on her tombstone in the Old Abandoned Grave Yard in New Vineyard, Maine, is as follows:

Memory of
Mrs. Bathsheba A. Bryant
wife of Rev. Elias Bryant
who died Oct. 19, 1816, aged 40
"Lo the pain of Life is Past,
All the warfare now is oer
Death and Hell behind her cast
Grief and suffering are no more.
Borne by Angels on their wings
Far from Earth the spirit flies
Transferred into Paradise."

Elias Bryant was a farmer, blacksmith and Methodist preacher.

The "Gore" was incorporated as a part of the town of New Vineyard, in 1802 and Mr. Collins was elected Chairman of the Board of Selectmen with Tristram Norton and Rev. Elias Bryant for associates. The early surveyors in laying out townships invariably applied the term "Gore" to any fragment of land remaining after the survey, irrespective of size or shape. New Vineyard was originally part of Industry, Maine.

Rev. Elias Bryant m. (2) March 6, 1817, Mahala Pratt. By his two wives he had seventeen children, all b. at New Vineyard.

By 1st wife Bathsheba (Hackett) Bryant:

(Mayo name prob. from gr. father Thomas^{4} Mayo)

Thomas Jefferson b. Sept. 13, 1799; m. (1) Cordelia Norton,
  (2)   (3)
Epaphrus Kibby b. June 3, 1801; m. Louisa Wells of Augusta, Maine.
Benjamin Franklin, b. Apr. 25, 1803; m. July 23, 1829, Chesterville, Maine, Lucy Ford French; d. Feb. 5, 1870 +
Amassa b. May 12, 1806; m. (1) Salome Snow, (2) Lucy Sylvester
Elias b. May 27, 1809; m. Mehitabel who d. Feb. 18, 1872 aged 57. Elias d. Oct. 23, 1870
Enoch b. Nov. 12, 1811; m. Adeline
Oliver Beale, b. March 16, 1814
Bathsheba, b. Oct. 6, 1816; d. young

Children by 2nd wife Mahala (Pratt) Bryant:

George P., b. Nov. 27, 1817
John Ayer, b. Sept. 22, 1819; m. (1) Sarah Prescott, (2) Mrs. Phoebe Creasey
Cynthia, b. July 10, 1821
Betsey, b. March 18, 1823
Luther Sampson, b. Nov. 12, 1824
Mary Rennick (twin) b. Aug. 24, 1826; m. John Walker
Martha (twin) b. Aug. 24, 1826
Julia, b. abt. 1834; d. July 14, 1924; m. David Bryant
Francis, m. Louise Tarbox

Bryant

References:

Family Papers "The Bryant Family" of Col. John Emory Bryant and Benj. F. Bryant, Jr. (grandsons of Rev. Elias); Record of Births copied from the oldest book of New Vineyard, Town Records (no longer in existance); Taunton, Mass. V.R., Vol. II pp. 213, 72; Hist. of Industry, Maine.

Benjamin[7] Bryant, son of Rev. Elias and Bathsheba (Hackett) Bryant, was b. Apr. 25, 1803 at New Vineyard, Me.; m. July 25, 1829 at Chesterville, Maine, to Lucy Ford French, daughter of Deacon Joseph and Elizabeth (Ford) French; d. Feb. 5, 1870, Age 66 yrs., 9 mo., 7 da., at Wakeman, Ohio. Lucy Ford French was b. July 26 or 27, Chesterville, Maine; d. Sept. 18, 1886, age 81 yrs., 1 mo, 21 days, at the home of a daughter Mary E. Park (Mrs. Joseph), between Murray and Kingsland, Ind. Both Benjamin and Lucy Ford (French) Bryant, are buried at Wakeman, Ohio, as are their daughters Lucy Ann French and Luella S. French (p. 30 Wakeman Twp. Rec. Bk.)

Benjamin Franklin Bryant, was a Methodist Minister and later a physician. He preached in the following towns in Maine; Unity 1836; Vasselboro, 1827; Georgetown 1828; Bath Circuit, 1829; Vasselboro, 1830; Paris, 1832; So. Paris, 1833; Monmouth, 1834; Strong, 1836; Thomaston, 1837; Orono, 1839; Oldtown, 1842; Lincoln 1844; Searsport, 1845; Leasump, 1846; Union, 1848; Bristol, 1850. He joined the Maine Conference 1826. Transferred to East Maine Conf. 1848, Located 1851.

Due to poor health, Benjamin Franklin Bryant, left his native state of Maine and came to Townsend, Ohio in 1855, and the family followed in 1859; in 1862 he came to Wakeman, Ohio; practiced medicine until he died, Feb. 5, 1870. At one time he published a Medical Journal in Minneapolis, Minn.

Children of Benjamin Franklin and Lucy Ford (French) Bryant:

Benjamin French b. Sept. 31, 1837; m. July 12, 1864 at Fayette, Me., Augusta Stevens; d. Warpaka, Minn.
Joseph b. June 25, 1834, Chesterville, Me.; d. Nov. 12, 1834
John Emory b. Oct. 13, 1835; m. June 26, 1864, Emma Frances Spaulding; d. Feb. 27, 1900
Lucy Ann French, b. Oct. 27, 1839, Orono, Me., d. May 25, 1884 Cleveland, Ohio.
Joseph, b. Feb. 28, 1842, Clinton, Me., d. Sept. 25, 1842, Oldtown, Me.
Mary E., b. June 29, 1846; m. Joseph Park of Oleno, Ohio; d. Mar. 17, 1918
Thomas Chalmers, b. Dec. 1843, Oldtown, Me.; m. Apr. 19, 1868, East Townsend, Ohio, Amelia Hansford; d. 1900, Minot, S.D.
Luella S. b. abt. Feb. 19, 1848; d. Wakeman, Ohio Oct. 12, 1870.

Bryant

References:

Leslie's Hist. of the Republi. Party by George O. Seilhamer, Vol. I ; Bryant Bible Record; Notarized copy from Hist. of Wakeman Twp., Huron Co. Ohio, by Dr. F. E. Weeks' (unpublished); Grave record, Wakeman, Ohio, Cemetery;

Col. John Emory Bryant, son of Benjamin Franklin and Lucy Ford (French) Bryant, b. Oct. 13, 1835 at Wayne, Maine; m. June 26, 1864 at Buckfield, Maine, Emma Frances Spaulding, dau. of James and Cynthia (Bray) Spaulding, b. Feb. 16, 1844 at Buckfield, Maine; he d. Feb. 27, 1900 at Hahnermann Hosp. in N.Y.C.; she d. May 2, 1901 at the home of her daughter in Manteno, Ill. They are buried at Woodlawn Cemetery, belonging to New York City.

Col. Bryant was a Lawyer. His education was obtained at Kents Hill (Maine) Seminary and College. In early life Col. Bryant was a school teacher in Maine; his last position being in Buckfield, Me., where he volunteered for service in the army during the Civil War and served with distinction. He was Provost Marshall, Bufort, S.C. on Gen. Sexton's Staff-Captain. Made Lieut. Col. by brivet for bravery in action.

After the war Col. Bryant went to Georgia, in charge of Civil affairs under Gen. Howard, ran for Congress, was defeated; was Postmaster in Augusta, Ga.; member of Constitutional Convention of Ga.; Collector of Customs, Savannah, Ga.; U.S. Marshall Northern Dist. of Ga.; Member National Republican Com. for many years; Delegate to Gen. Conf. Methodist Episcopal Church a number of times; Editor "The Loyal Georgian" and "Georgia Republican" published in Atlanta, Ga.

Col. Bryant's later years were spent in Mt. Vernon, N.Y., where he was manager of the Mt. Vernon Record-Herald, and very active politically. He was engaged in Mission work in New York City with Gen. D. O. Howard, whom he had known almost throughout his entire life. Col. Bryant and his wife also carried on a mission for unemployed men in Mt. Vernon, N.Y.

Mrs. Bryant, a graduate of Kents Hill Seminary and College, was a very conscientious and devoted Christian; an ardent member (once Vice-Pres.) of Woman's Christian Temperance Union; a suffragist and a devoted wife and mother. No one ever doubted her word. During the time that their only child, a daughter Alice, was attending U.S. Grant University in Athens, Tenn., Mrs. Bryant conducted a school for young ladies, in her home.

Issue:

Son b. Mar. 16, 1867 in Atlanta, Ga.; d. Apr. 6, 1867

Emma Alice b. Nov. 16, 1871 in Atlanta, Ga.; m. Jan. 1, 1895 in Mt. Vernon, N.Y., Julius Christian Zeller; d. Apr. 26, 1946 in East Orange, N.J. She graduated from U.S. Grant Univ. Athens, Tenn. at the age of 19. It was here she met her future husband.

Bryant

References:

The Rebellion Record; Maine in the Rebellion; The Adj. Gen's. Report 1865, 1866, State of Maine; Leslie's Hist. of the Republican Party by Geo. Seilhamer 2:351; Spaulding Memorial by C.W. Spaulding, 1897, p. 458.

BYRAM

Charts XXII & XVI

Dr. Nicholas[1], son of William, was born about 1610 in Kent Co. Eng. His father was an English Gentleman of Kent Co. Eng., who, having purchased a landed estate in Ireland, moved his family there. When young Nicholas was 16 years of age his father sent him to Eng., to visit relatives, in charge of an acquaintance who robbed the boy of his money and put him on a ship bound for the West Indies. When he arrived he was sold to service to pay his passage. His master, a physician, taught him medicine. When his years of servitude were ended, Nicholas made his way to N.E. where he practiced medicine at Weymouth, Mass. from 1638-1662. He removed to Bridgewater where he lived until he died Apr. 13, 1688. His will was dated 13 Jan. 1688 and proved 13 June 1688. Soldier in King Philip's War, 1676 - Will names "My brother John Shaw of Weymouth," . not named - wife Susannah exet. Wits: Samuel Allen, sevr., William Brett, John Whitman.

Dr. Byram m. Susannah, daughter Abraham and Bridget (Best) Shaw of Dedham. She made her will 7 Sept. 1698, and it was proved 18 Dec. 1699. Their children all born at Weymouth:

Nicholas[2] m. Mary
Abigail m. 22 Nov. 1656, Thomas Whitman of Weymouth
Deliverence m. 9 Apr. 1660, John Porter of Weymouth
Experience m. John Willis of Bridgewater +
Susannah m. Samuel Edson of Bridgewater
Mary m. Samuel Leach of Weymouth & Bridgewater
Ebenezer

References:

Hist. of Weymouth by Chamberlain, Vol. 3, p. 149; Clipping Lewiston, Me., Journal by C. F. Whitman; Popes Pioneers of Mass.; Mitchell's Hist. of Bridgewater, Mass.; Savage's Gen. Dict. Index to Ancestors, Soc. of Col. Wars, p. 82; Will of Nicholas' Byram dated Jan. 13, 1687 - Abstract p. 20 Vol. I Gen. Advertiser.

CARPENTER

Chart No. XXXIV

Alexander Carpenter of Wington, Co. Somerset, Eng., was a son of William Carpenter. He and his brothers, William and Richard were dissenters and an account of their religious belief and persecution, went to Leyden, Holland.

The family is of great antiquity in England. Alexander, with his wife and five daughters were members of the church at Leyden, where Gov. Bradford knew them.

Children:

Julianna m. (1) George Morton* at Leyden, Holland. She was born abt. 1583; d. 1664, Feb. 19; m. July 23, 1612. Julianna m. (2) Menasseh Kempton.
Agnes, b. 1585 at Wrentham, Eng.; d. bef. 1617; m. Samuel Fuller, 8th signer of the Mayflower Compact.
Alice, b. abt. 1590 ; d. March, 1670; m. (1) Edw. Southworth (2) Gov. William Bradford, as his 2nd wife, on Aug. 14, 1623.
Priscilla, b. ; d. ; m. William Wright.

*From Leyden, Holland Records:

"George Morton, of York, England, accompanied by Thomas Morton, his brother, and Roger Wilson, his acquaintance; with Juliana Carpenter, maid from Bath, England, accompanied by Alexander Carpenter, her father, and Alice Carpenter, her sister, and Anna Robinson, her acquaintance". "The banns published 6-16 July, 1612." "The marriage took place 23-2 July, 1612".

References:

"Abridged Compendium of American Genealogy," by Walter Hammond; "N.E. Families", publ. N.Y. 1913, Lewis Publ. Co. p. 2031; "A Munsey-Hopkins Genealogy" by D.O.S. Lowell, 1920; Signers of the Mayflower Compact by Annie Arnoux Haxtun, Part 3, p. 20.

CARTER

Chart VI

Rev. Thomas Carter, first minister at Woburn, Mass., was born about 1610 in England; son of Peter Carter, educated in St. John's College at University of Cambridge (Eng.) where he received the B.A. Degree in 1629 and M.A. in 1633.

Carter

He came to N.E. from Hinderclay, Suffolk Co. Eng., in 1635, settled first at Dedham after its inc. Sept. 1636 -- removed to Watertown and then to Woburn, where he was invited to preach Nov. 3, 1641. He was ordained Nov. 22, 1642. He was freeman at Watertown May 21, 1638. Rev. Thomas Carter deeded lands to his children before he died Sept. 5, 1684 in his 74th year of age.

Rev. Thomas Carter married Mary Parkhurst before 1640; daughter of George and Phoebe Parkhurst. Mary was bapt. Aug. 28, 1614 and died March 28, 1687. Their children:

Samuel, b. Aug. 8, 1640; m. Eunice Brooks. He grad. from Harvard.
Judith, m. (1) Samuel, son of Deacon Edward Convers, June 8, 1660; m. (2) Giles Fifield in 1672
Theophilus, d. young.
Mary, b. July 24, 1648; m. (1) John Wyman abt. 1671; (2) Nathaniel Bachiler, Oct. 31, 1676.
Abigail, b. Jan. 10, 1649-50; m. John Smith, May 7, 1674; d. bef. 1684.
Deborah, d. young.
Timothy, b. June 12, 1653; m. Ann Fisk, dau. of David Fisk, of Cambridge (Lexington); May 3, 1680; d. July 8, 1727.
Thomas, b. June 8, 1655; m. 1682 Marjorie, dau. of Francis Whitmore.

References:

History of Woburn, Mass.; Desc. of Rev. Thomas Carter by Howard Williston Carter, 1909.

CHADBOURNE

Chart XI

William[1] Chadbourne and his partners James Wall and John Goddard, made an agreement with Capt. John Mason to come to Piscataqua and settle on his lands, and signed a contract 13 Mar. 1633-4, with Capt. John Mason, to build mills in Berwick, Me., and run them on shares. They came in the Pied Cow.

The Chadburns, both in Old and New England, were housewrights, going wherever building was in progress.

Evidently Wm. Chadbourne's wife died in Eng., as she is not mentioned. Children:

William, bapt. 1610 at Winchcombe, Gloucestershire; m. Mary ___.
Patience, bapt. 1612 at Tamworth, Warwickshire; m. Thomas Spencer.
Humphrey, bapt. 1626 (?) at Tamworth, Warwickshire; m. (1) Sarah Bolles (Bowles), dau. of Joseph Bolles of Wells, Maine; m. (2) Lucy Treworgye. She m. (2) Thomas Wills; (3) after 14 March 1687-8 Elias Stileman; d. at Newcastle.

Chadbourne

William[1] Chadbourne may have returned to Eng. No record of his death has been found by me (M.Z.G.). He was still living in 1662 for his name appears on the act of submission to Mass., signed by 41 inhabitants of Kittery, Me. He also resided at South Berwick, Me.

References:

Old Kittery, Me., and Her Families by Stackpole pp. 311, 429; Popes Pioneers of Maine & N.H. p. 34; Gen. Dict. of Maine & N.H. Vol. II p. 134.

William[2] Chadbourne, Housewright, bpt. 1610 at Winchcombe, Gloucestershire; came with his father in 1634; m. Mary _________; resided Berwick, Me., Portsmouth, N.H. 1642, Boston, Mass., 1644, and Kittery, Me. 1652.

Children:

Mary, b. in Boston, Oct. 1644; m. John/Foss or Fost in Dover, N.H.
William[3] b. July 30, 1714 (?)

References:

Old Kittery, Me., and Her Families by Stackpole pp. 311, 429; Popes Pioneers of Maine & N.H. p. 34; Gen. Dict. of Maine & N.H. Vol. II p. 134; Boston Births, Baptisms, Mar. & Deaths 1630-1699, p. 18; Vol. IV p. 2239 Gen. Dict. of Maine & N.H.

CHANDLER

Chart No. X

Roger Chandler, b. abt. 1636; d. Jan. 11, 1716-17, age 80 yrs., at Concord, Mass.; m. Mary Simonds at Concord on April 25, 1671. She was a daughter of William and Judith (Phippen) (Hayward) Simonds. She was b. Aug. 29, 1728 at Woburn, Mass. and d. Aug. 29, 1728 at Concord.

Children, born at Concord, Mass.

Mary, b. Jan. 7, 1671; d. Aug. 14, 1759 in 88th year; m. John Heald at Concord, Dec. 18, 1690.
Samuel, b. Mar. 3, 1673-4; d. Apr. 27, 1743 at Concord; m. Dorcas Bus at Concord, Dec. 11, 1695.
Joseph, b. 7-8-1678; d. 14.9.1679 at Concord.
Abigail, b. 31.3.1681

References: Concord, Mass., V.R.; Hist. of Woburn, Mass., by Sewell

CHAPMAN

Chart II

Ralph[1] Chapman, age 20, certificate from St. Savior's Southwark, Eng., came in the "Elizabeth" in Apr. 1635, from London. He settled at Duxbury; bought land 8 Oct. 1639. He was partner in a ferry at Marshfield, 11 Jan. 1641; Propr. 1644,

Ralph Chapman m. Lydia Wills, Nov. 23, 1642 - the first marriage in the town of Duxbury, Mass. They resided in Marshfield. Ralph made his will Nov. 28, 1671 and was prob. June 4, 1672.

Children:

Mary b. 31 Oct. 1643; m. 4 May 1666, William Throop at Barnstable, Mass. (Clemen's m. bef. 1699)
Sarah b. May 15, 1645
Isaac, b. Aug. 4, 1647; prob. m. 2 Sept. 1678 Rebecca, d. af. James Leonard.
Lydia, b. Oct. 15, 1649; d. 26 Nov. 1649
Ralph, b. 20 June, 1653; d. at 1 month
Sarah, bpt. Sept. 27, 1657; m. William Norcot
John, bpt. Sept. 27, 1657
Ralph, bpt. Sept. 27, 1657; had a son John reported to have lived over 100 yrs.

References:

Reg. VII, 236; Popes Pioneers of Mass. Savage's N.E. Dict.; Will of Ralph Chapman; May. Desc. 19:132; Clemen's Mar. Rec. bef. 1699; May. Desc. Vol. II pp. 4, 5, 6.

CHENEY

Chart XVI & XXXVIII

William[1] Cheney, son of John and Elizabeth Cheney was b. abt. 1604 (Rixford says bapt. Feb. 5, 1598-9 at Burnington); d. June 30, 1667 (age 63). The will of William[1] Cheney of Roxbury, Mass., is found in Suffolk Prob. Register Bk. I p. 528. He m. Margaret Mason before 1626 in Eng. He was a resident and landowner in Roxbury, Mass., before 1640; freeman 1666; member of Roxbury Mass. militia in 1647; served as constable at Roxbury and was a policeman on disagreeable occasions; was messenger of the Selectmen at times but chief care was collecting taxes; Jan. 19, 1656-7 he was elected a member of the board of selectmen. Will of Wm. Cheney of Roxbury found in Suffolk Probate Registry BK. I p. 528. Made in 1667. She m. (2) _____ Burge; d. May 2 or 3, 1686. Will dated Sept. 23, 1680.

Cheney

Children of William[1] Cheney:

Ellen, b. abt 1626; d. Sept. 28, 1678 at Hingham, Mass.; m.
Mar. 20, 1642-3 Humphrey Johnson, son of John of Roxbury.
Margaret b. abt. 1630; m. Apr. 1650, Deacon Thomas Hastings.
John b. Sept. 29, 1639; d. soon.
John (again) b. 25 Sept. 1640; drowned 12-10-1671, ae 31 yrs.
Mehitabel b. June 1, 1643; m. Thomas Wright, Jr.
Joseph b. June 6, 1647; af. Medfield 1678 (rec. Roxbury)
Thomas - not mentioned in father's will.
William Jr. m. Deborah Wiswall bapt. 30-3-1641 (p. 509
Popes Pioneers of Mass.) d. John Wiswall of Dorchester, Mass.

References:

Pope's Pioneers of Mass.; Savages N.E. Dictionary; Desc. Royal Families in Europe by Eliz. M. Leach Rixford; Roxbury, Mass. V.R. Vol. I p. 59, Vol. II pp. 69, 70, 487; Americana, Vol. 21 (1927) p. 460; Hist. of Milford, Mass. by Ballou, Vol. II p. 634 (see Chap. III pt. 1).

CLARKE

Charts VIII & XXX

Thurston (or Tristram) Clarke, was born about 1590 in Eng., died Dec. 6, 1661 at Duxbury, Mass., of cold exposure and an inquest was held. Inventory of his estate was taken Dec. 10, 1661. He married Faith _______ in Eng.

Thurston Clarke, age 44, and his daughter Faith, age 15, of Ipswich, Suffolk, arrived in New England, on the "Francis" of Ipswich, John Cutting, Master, in 1634. They first settled at Plymouth. When Faith, the wife came, appears not to be recorded. She was granted Admin. of his estate 4 March, 1661. Her estate was divided June 1, 1663, between her daughter Faith Dotey and her sons Henry and Thurston Clarke. The two sons, according to Savage's N.E. Dict. (Vol. I, p. 403 reprint edition) were both imbec. put under guardians. Hist. of Duxbury by Winsor, p. 246, these two were unable to take care of themselves and the town, 1682, was ordered to do it; in 1690 "by reason of their age, indescretion and weakness of understanding" they cannot provide for themselves, the court appointed certain individuals to have the management of their estates, which were sufficient for them.

Daughter Faith Clarke, born about 1619; m. (1) Jan. 6, 1634-5 Edward Dotey, a Mayflower Passenger. M. (2) March 14, 1667, John Phillips; died Dec. 31, 1675.

References:

Hist. of Duxbury, Mass. by Winsor, p. 246; Planters of the Commonwealth, Reprint Edition p. 124; Popes Pioneers of Mass. p. 103; Savage's N.E. Dict. Reprint Edition, Vol. I, p. 403 N.E.H.G. Register, Vol. 85 pp. 417-423.

COLLINS

Chart No. V

Benjamin Collins, b. ; d. Dec. 10, 1683 at Salisbury, Mass.; m. Martha Eaton at Salisbury, Nov. 5, 1668. She was a dau. of John[2] (John[1]) and Martha (Rowlandson) Eaton. She was b. Aug. 12, 1648 at Salisbury, Mass., and d. there April 19, 1734. Martha m. (2) Philip Flanders at Salisbury.

Children of Benjamin & Martha (Eaton) Collins:

Mary, b. Jan. 8, 1669
John, b. 1673; m. Elizabeth ____________ a friend.
Samuel, b. Jan. 18, 1676; m. Mar. 1698-9, to Sarah White.
Anna, b. April 1, 1679.
Benjamin, b. May 29, 1681; bapt. June 4, 1699.
Ephriam, b. Sept. 30, 1683; bapt. June 4, 1699; soldier for Salisbury 1703; d. So. Hampton, N.H.; Oct. 20, 1759.

References:

Old Families of Salisbury & Amesbury, Vol. I, 112.
So. Hampton, N. H. V. R. p. 98.

Samuel[2] Collins, b. Jan. 18, 1676; d. April 16, 1762 at Salisbury, Mass.; m. March 16, 1698-99 at Salisbury, Mass., to Sarah White. She may have been a daughter of John White, Jr. of Roxbury, Mass.; b. at Lynn, Mass., 19:6 mo: 1672. Sarah (White) Collins, d. Oct. 19, 1732 at Salisbury, Mass.

Children:

Mary, b. abt. 1700; d. at So. Hampton, N.H., Nov. 11, 1766; m. Samuel French at Salisbury, Mass., Nov. 23, 1721.
Benjamin, b. Dec. 5, 1699; d. ; m. Mehitabel Worcester (Worster) of Andover, at Andover, Mass., May 30, 1722.
Joseph, b. June 27, 1702; d. at So. Hampton, N.H. Mar. 27, 1769.
Miriam, b. May 23, 1706; m. Stephen Lowell of Amesbury, Mass., Dec. 22, 1727.
John, b. Nov. 26, 1708 (another son John was b. Oct. 7, 1704); m. Susanna Morrill.
Hannah, b. Oct. 26, 1710; m. Feb. 1, 1727-28, Joseph Gilman.
Elizabeth, b. prob. 1712; m. Joseph Coffin, May 15, 1729.

Above names as they appear in Salisbury W. Ch. Records -- Old Families S. & A. Vol. 2, p. 428.

Jan. 24 1719/20	Saml. Collins		C.B.
	Sarah Collins		C.B.
Feb. 7 1719/20	Mary	Collins	B.C.
	Benjamin		B.C.
	Joseph		B.C.
	Miriam		B.C.
	John		B.C.
	Hannah		B.
	Elizabeth		B.

Collins

References: Old Families of Salisbury & Amesbury, Vol. I, p. 112, Vol. 2, p. 428. Salisbury, Mass. V.R. pp. 311, 312. So. Hampton, R.I. Vital Records, pp. 99, 100.

COOKE

Chart No. XXVII

Francis[1] Cooke, 17th signer of the Mayflower Compact, came on the Mayflower in 1620 and brought his son John with him. His wife, Hester, came on the Anne in 1623 with the other children.

Francis Cooke was born 1580 to 1583, probably at Blythe near Scrooby, Eng.; died April 7, 1663, "above 80"; married, probably, June 30, 1603 Hester Mahieu, at Leyden, Holland. As a Pilgrim Separatist, Hester reached Holland in 1609 from the southern province of Belgium, and was of the Walloon Contingent worshiping in Pastor Robinson's house. She was an excellent cook, and the receipts of the day prepared under her supervision would suit the gourmet of today.

Francis Cooke, was one of the Pilgrims who immediately occupied a very important place. "His record accumulates and proves that he was behind the throne wielding immense influence. Pursuing the even tenor of his way, his strength grows day by day, until the consciousness comes that he is guiding the 'ship of state' with the rare judgement of his strong personality." (from "Signers of the Mayflower Compact, by Haxtun 1899)

He was one of the 'Purchasers' who bought all the rights of the "adventurers' and in the division of cattle made Tuesday, May 22 - June 1, 1627, the first lot, the smallest of the four black heifers and two she goats fell to his company of thirteen, composed of himself, his wife Hester, his sons John & Jacob, and daughters Jane, Hester & Mary, also Moses Simonson, Philip Delano, Experience Mitchell, John Faunce, Joshua Pratt, and Pheneas Pratt.

Children of Francis & Hester (Mahieu) Cooke:

John, b. after 1603 & before 1610, in Holland; d. at Dartmouth, Mass. Nov. 23, 1695; m. Mar. 28, 1634, Sarah Warren, dau. of Richard Warren.
Jane, b. bef. 1613 in Holland; d. aft. Dec. 5, 1684 & bef. May 14, 1689; m. aft. May 22, 1627, Experience Mitchell.
Jacob, b. abt. 1618 in Holland; d. Dec. 11-18, 1675; m. (1) Damaris Hopkins (2) Elizabeth (Lettice) Shurtleff.
Mary, b. between Mar. 1624 & May 22, 1627 (or Aug. 1626); d. after June 8, 1666; m. Dec. 26, 1645, John Tomson.
Hester, b. bef. May 22, 1627; d. aft. June 8, 1666; m. at Plymouth, 1644, Richard Wright.

Cooke

References:

Families of the Pilgrims by Hubert Kinney Shaw, pp. 65-68; Register VI, 95; Signers of the Mayflower Compact by Anne Arnoux Haxtun, 1899, part 2 p. 3; Popes Pioneers of Mass., p. Savages N.E. Dict. (Reprint Edition) Vol. I, p.

COOMBS

Chart II

Mr. John[1] Coombs, Gent., d. 1646-1648; m. Sarah Priest, about 1630, dau. Degary (of the Mayflower) & Sarah (Allerton) (Vincent) Priest. He was frm. at Plymouth 1630. Aug. 1, 1648 William Spooner was ordered to pay the debts of his master Mr. Coombs, and to take care of his children (William Spooner of Colchester, Eng., apprenticed himself 27 March 1637 to John Holmes, gent. of New Plymouth in America. 1 July 1637 he was transferred to John Coombs of Plymouth, gent. (Plym. Col. Rec.)

Children:

Francis[2], b. ; m. (1) Deborah Morton, (2) in 1678 Mary (Barker) Pratt, widow of Samuel Pratt; d. 3 Dec. 1682 at Middleboro, Mass.
John[2], b. ; m. 24 Feb. 1662 Elizabeth ( ) Barlow, widow of Thomas Barlow. She m. (3) John Warren of Boston. John[2] d. ca Jan. 1672.

References:

Popes Pioneers of Mass.; Savage N.E. Dict.; Families of the Pilgrims by Mass. Mayflower Soc., p. 124.

John[2] Coombs, cooper, b. ; m. at Boston 24 Feb. 1662 Elizabeth, widow of Thomas Barlow; d. ca May 1668. Elizabeth (Royal) (Barlow) Coombs m. (3) John Warren of Boston in 1669, by whom she had a son, Nathaniel, Mar. 27, 1670. Elizabeth's maiden name may have been Royal. After her death in 1671 or 72, two of her children in 1685 chose their "uncle" Joseph Ryall of Charlestown as their guardian.

Children b. at Boston, Mass:

Elizabeth b. Nov. 30, 1662; m. Eleazer Cushman of Plymouth, 12 Jan. 1687.
John b. July 20, 1664; m. Dorothy Davis March 4, 1711; d. May 13, 1716 at Boston
Mary b. Nov. 28, 1666; m. Dec. 18, 1689, Benjamin[3] Eaton; d. July 2, 1728.

Coombs

Elizabeth ( ) (Barlow) Coombs, had by her 1st husband:

Thomas Barlow who d. 23 Oct. 1661
Elizabeth Barlow b. Nov. 13, 1657; d. Apr. 17, 1660
Sarah Barlow b. July 18, 1659

And, by her 3rd husband John Warren:

Nathaniel Warren b. May 27, 1670

Elizabeth ( ) (Barlow) (Coombs) Warren b. poss. abt. 1638 may have been a daughter of William Royal, cooper of North Yarmouth, Maine. William Royal was engaged by Mass. Bay Co., 23 Mar. 1628, to go to New England, and arrived in 1629 at Salem where he gave his name to Royal's Side. By 1636 he settled at Wescustoga on a tract of 250 a. bordering on Royal River, finally granted to him by Thos. Gorgas in 1643. (Gen. Dict. of Maine & N.H. by Nayes & Davis, Part IV p. 599.) William Royal m. Phoebe Greene who d. 16 July 1678; he d. 15 June 1676.

Children of William Royal:

William, [2]John, [3]Samuel, [4]Isaac of Dorchester, [5]Joseph of Boston, sailmaker who had wife Mary who was bur. 8 Mar. 1713-14. He d. 14 Jan. 1728, age 83; will 1727-8. 8 children. Two children of Elizabeth (maiden name not known) wife successively of Thos. Barlow, John Coombs and John Warren, called Joseph Royal Uncle in 1685. A poss. daughter [6]Margaret, wife of Thomas Stevens called William Jr. brother in 1674.

Maine & N.H. Gen. Dict. Vol. II p. 161, gives John Coombs, cooper, Boston; (Note by M.Z.G.: Wm. Royal was also a cooper) m. Elizabeth, wid. of Thomas Barlow, who m. 3rd John Warren from Exeter. Her children by two husbands inherited land and a Warehouse at Saco and called Joseph Royal uncle in 1685. (In Vol. 5, p. 721; John Warren.)

Elizabeth (Royal) Barlow, wid. of Thomas of Boston, m. (2) on 24 Feb. 1662 at Boston, John[2] Coombs. She may have been a daughter of William Royal, North Yarmouth. Elizabeth (Royal)? (Barlow) Coombs, m. (3) John Warren of Boston as his 3rd wife. She had a son Nathaniel Warren by this husband, b. 27 May, 1670, and d. the next year as early in 1672. Nathaniel Warren and Mary[3] Coombs, in 1685 chose for their guardian Joseph Ryall (Royal) of Charleston, who they called uncle. (Savage)

William Royal, cooper, North Yarmouth, Me. & Dorchester, Mass. was engaged by Mass. Bay Co. 23 Mar. 1628 to go to N.E. and arrived in 1629 at Salem where he gave his name to Royals Side. By 1636 he settled at Wescustogo (No. Yarmouth - sometimes called Casco Bay) on a tract of 250 a. bordering on Royal River, finally gr. to him by Thos. Gorgas in 1643. (Gen. Dict. Maine & N.H. by Noyes & Davis Part IV p. 599).

Coombs

m. Phoebe (Green) d. 16 July 1678 - he d. 15 June 1676 -- estate not settled until 1722-3. Children: William, John, Samuel, Isaac of Dorchester, Joseph, Boston, sailmaker, who had wife Mary who was bur. 8 Mar. 1713-4. He d. 14 Jan. 1728, age 83; will 1727-28. 8 children. Two children of Elizabeth (Maiden name unknown) w. successively of Thos. Barlow, John Coombs and John Warren, called Joseph Royal uncle in 1685. A poss. dau. Margaret, wife of Thomas Stevens who called William (Jr.) brother in 1674. (Gen. by E.D. Harris in Reg. XXXIX, 348.)
John Warren
m. (2) Elizabeth Coombs widow of John Coombs. They had one child - Nathaniel Warren. His mother willed to her children: Sarah Barlow, Elizabeth and Mary Coombs and Nathaniel Warren. In 1685 their Uncle Joseph Royal gave bond as guardian of Mary and Nathaniel; the inventory included Winter Harbor land and Warehouse.

References: Gen. Dict. of Maine & N.H. Boston, Mass., Births, Baptisms, Marriages and Deaths 1630-1699 (9th Rep. of the Rec. Comm.) pp. 81, 82, 83, 92, 100; Families of the Pilgrims.

CUTTING

Chart XVII

(Mr.) Capt. John Cutting, Gentleman, b. ; d. Nov. 20, 1659 at Newbury, Mass. (Will prob. March 27, 1660); m. prob. bef. 1620, Mary Ward (?); resided at Watertown, Charlestowne, and Newbury, Mass. Mary (Ward)? Cutting m. (2) John Miller, and with him sold to their son-in-law Nicholas Noyes, land formerly belonging to Stephen Dummer; which tract Dummer had sold to Capt. Cutting, another document tells us. She d. Mar. 6, 1664 at Newbury.

Capt. John Cutting, Shipmaster ofthe "Francis" of Ipswich, Eng. in 1634, and was master of Ship Advent of Boston, 19 (8) 1647 and made many voyages to and from England. Sold his lands in Newbury to John Hull, June 20, 1651. History of Boston gives signature of John Cutting to a petition signed by the most considerable importers to the General Court requesting a reduction of duty on Malt.

Children:

Judith*, b. abt. 1620; m. bef. 1638, James Brown; d. bef. Oct. 22, 1659 when Capt. Cutting made his will. After her death, her widower m. her sister Sarah, who <u>is</u> named in their father's will as Sarah, wife of James Brown.
Mary, b. ; m. abt. 1640 Nicholas Noyes.
Sarah, b. ; m. bef. Oct. 2, 1659, James Brown, her sister's widower.
Thomas, b. ; m. (1) Dorcas ______ (2) Mary ______.
*Judith (?Cutting) Brown was whipt with twenty cruel stripes through the town of Boston (1659). See Chandler's Crimnal Trials Vol. I p. 51; History of Boston, p. 357.

Cutting

John[1] Cutting was attorney of Ferdinando Adams of St. Katherines, shoemaker, to sell to John Frary in Dedham, 1651 (per. Suffolk deeds).

References:

William Aspinwall Notorial Records; Pope's Pioneers of Mass.; Savages Genealogical Dictionary, Vol. I, p. ; The History and Antiquities of Boston from its Settlement in 1630 to the year 1770, by Samuel G. Drake, M.A. of Boston, publ. 1856 - p. 340; Wyman's Charlestown, Vol. I, p. 340; Virkus Compendium, Vol. I, p. 752; Old Families of Salisbury and Amesbury, Mass., Vol. I, p. 197; Probate Records of Essex Co. Mass., Vol. I (1635-1664) pp. 308-9; Newbury V.R. Vol. 2, p. 660.

CUSHMAN

Chart XXXII

Robert Cushman, bapt. Feb. 9, 1577-8; d. 1625 in Eng.; m. Sarah Rider on July 31, 1606 at Canterbury, St. Alphege. She d. before June 3, 1617 at which time he m. (2) Mary Singleton, widow of Thomas Chingleton of Sandwich, Eng., at Leyden, Holland.

Robert Cushman was a woolcarder of Canterbury, Eng.; became a prominent official in the Leyden Church; was one of the most active promoters of the migration from Holland in 1620, of the pilgrims in the Mayflower. He was agent of the Pilgrims in London, 1617-1626. He came the next year in the Fortune, arriving Nov. 10th, the 1st ship after the Mayflower, with son Thomas, age 14. He went home in 1 month on the same ship (Fortune) and took with him the manuscript Journal.

The first sermon preached in N.E. was by Robert Cushman on the highly appropriate subject of self-denial. Hewas constant in service at London for the imigrants and in Dec. 1624 spoke of his hope of coming in the next season; but Gov. Bradford notes that he was dead before receipt of his answer from Plymouth, of June 1625; and his family came soon after to partake in the fortunes of the plantation. By general consent he was assigned a share in the division of land with the comers of the Mayflower. (Davis in Morton's Memo 128; Young's Chronology of the Pilgrim 99 . 249.)

Robert Cushman died in 1625. High Court of Admiralty Records Bk. 44, gives Robert Cushman aged 45, calling himself a yeoman, residing in Rosemary Lane, London. He also resided at Canterbury, Eng.; Leyden, Holland; Revolvendne, Co. Kent; and Plymouth, Mass.

Children of Robert Cushman and Sarah (Reder) Cushman:

Thomas b. abt. 1607; d. Dec. 10, 1691; m. Mary, daughter of Isaac and Mary (Norris) Allerton, in 1636.
Sarah b. ; m. Nov. 2, 1636, William Hoskins of Scituate.

Cushman

References:

Savages N.E. Dict. Vol. I, p. 492 (Reprint Edition); Popes Pioneers of Mass.; The English Ancestry & Homes of the Pilgrim Fathers by Banks, p. 113 (Reprint Edition); Mourt's Relation - A Journal of the Pilgrims at Plymouth; One Small Candle by Thomas J. Fleming; Signers of The Mayflower Compact by Annie Armoux Haxtun; Gen. Guide to Early Settlers of Am., by Whittemore; Minsor's Hist. of Duxbury, Mass.; Cushman Genealogy.

DANE (DEAN)

Chart X

Thomas Dane (Dean) of Concord, Mass., carpenter, came in the Elizabeth and Ann, in May 1635, aged 32. He m. (1) before 1638, Elizabeth ________; (2) Sept. 15, 1673, Mildred ________, who d. Sept. 15, 1673. Thomas Dane d. Feb. 5, 1676 at Concord. His will probated June 24, 1676, bequeathed to son, Joseph, daughters Sarah Heald, Mary Pellett and Hannah Page. All his children were by wife Elizabeth:

Joseph, b. abt. 1638; m. Elizabeth Fuller, 1662 at Concord; d. Mar. 13, 1717-18 age 80th yr.
Sarah, b. ; m. John Heald, June 10, 1661; d. July 22, 1689.
Mary, b. (?) Feb. 24, 1643; m. Mar. 5, 1659, Thomas Pellett (he d. Dec. 1, 1694).
Hannah, b. Mar. 18, 1645; m. Samuel Page bef. 1668; living 1704.
Elizabeth, b. 10-25-1648; d. age 6 mo. 4-20-1649.

References:

Savage's N.E. Dict. (Reprint) Vol. 2, p. 30; Popes Pioneers of Mass., p. 129, 130; Planters of the Commonwealth, by Drake; Gen. Guide to early Settlers of America by Whitmore; Concord Mass., Births, Deaths, & Mar., pp. 2,3,5,6,10,17,19.

DAVIS

Chart VI

John[1] Davis, "Yeoman or Planter" was an early settler of Newbury, Mass.; was admitted Freeman, Mar. 28, 1657. He and his wife were members of the Newbury Church 1674. By his deposition at Salisbury in 1664, he seems to have hired Mr. Hooke's farm in 1662 of Mr. Sam Hall.

Davis

John[1] Davis born abt. 1612; married Elinor before 1642; died Nov. 12, 1675. His will, probated Sept. 26, 1676 bequeaths his son John 4 pounds, the rest to remain in his wife's hands for life, she paying 12 d to each son and daughter and the rest to them at her death.

Issue:

Mary, b. Oct. 6, 1642; died young.
John, b. Jan. 15, 1644; m. Sarah Carter at Newbury Apr. 8, 1681; resided Newbury and Amesbury.
Zachary, b. Feb. 22, 1646; m. Judith Brown (John[2] James[1]) at Newbury Feb. 4, 1681; d. June 25, 1692.
Jeremiah, b. June 21, 1648; m. wid. Mary Joye (daughter of John Huntington) March 5, 1688-9.
Mary, b. Aug. 12, 1650.
Cornelius, b. Apr. 15, 1653; m. (1) Sarah _______, who died at Newbury, Mar. 6, 1695; m. (2) Apr. 24, 1696, Elizabeth Hidden, dau. John Jewitt of Rowley; d. Mar. 16, 1731.
Ephriam, b. Sept. 29, 1655; m. Elizabeth; d. 1721; will dated 1719.

References:

Old Families of Salisbury & Amesbury, Vol. I, p. 129; Popes Pioneers of Mass.; Savages Gen. Dict.; Newbury V.R. Vol. I pp. 136-139; Vol. II pp. 135-139, 579. Rowley V.R. Vol. I, p. 279, Vol. II, p. 11; Essex Co. Probates, Vol. 3, pp. 91, 92.

Zachary[2] Davis, (John[1]) b. Feb. 22, 1646 at Newbury, Mass.; m. Feb. 4, 1680-1 at Newbury, Judith Brown, dau. John[2] and Mary (Woodman) Brown. She was b. Dec. 3, 1660 at Newbury; d. Nov. 14, 1728. Zachary[2] Davis d. June 25, 1692; inventory of estate July 12, 1692; Judith, his widow was appointed administratrix.

Aug. 6, 1675 Zachary[2] Davis was impressed for service in King Philips War, and in French and Indian Wars. He took Oath of Allegiance at Newbury, 1678.

A widow Judith Davis married Henry Bradley at Newbury, Jan. 7, 1695-6.

Children of Zachary and Judith Davis:

Judith, b. Sept. 7, 1684; d. Dec. 9, 1702.
Elizabeth, b. Aug. 26, 1687; m. Samuel Batchelder, May 14, 1707; d. after 1732.
Zachary, b. abt. 1690; d. Dec. 27, 1731 unmarried.

References:

Old Families of Salisbury and Amesbury, Vol. I pp. 129-131; Vol. II p. 720; Newbury, Mass., V.R. Vol. I, pp. 139, 74, 136, 137, Vol. II pp. 139, 579; Hist. of Newbury by John J. Currier.

DEARBORN

Charts I & VII

Godfrey[1] Dearborn, son of William & Agnes (Hay) Dearborn was b. 1599 (bapt. Sept. 24, 1603) at Willoughby, Co. Lincoln; m. Anne bef. 1632; d. Feb. 4, 1686 (will dated Dec. 14, 1680, proved Aug. 26, 1686.) He probably resided at Exeter, Eng., Exeter & Hampton, N.H. (bef. 1659) - from Hanncey, 3 miles from Bilsly, Co. Lincoln.

Godfrey Dearborn was a Weaver. He signed Combination at Exeter, N.H. 5 (4) 1639 and the petition for local court in 1645; Grand Juryman, 1650; Selectman 1648-1650, Exeter, N.H.; Town officer. Removed to Hampton; bought house & land before 12 (1) 1658; Selectman of Hampton 1655, 1663 & 1671.

Anne ( ) Dearborn d. bef. Nov. 25, 1662. Godfrey Dearborn m. (2) Dorothy, widow of Philemon Dalton, Nov. 25, 1662. She outlived him.

Children:

1. Thomas[2], bapt. Nov. 1, 1632; m. Hannah Colcord; d. 1710
2. Henry[2], bapt. Mar. 22, 1633; m. Elizabeth Marrion; d. Jan. 18, 1725.
3. Esther, m. Richard Shortridge
4. Sarah, b. abt 1641; m. Thomas Nudd.
5. John, b. abt. 1642; m. Mary Ward, dau. of Thomas; d. 1731.

References:

Pope's Pioneers of Maine & N.H.; Maine N.H. Dict. Vol. 2, p. 189; N.E.H.G.R. Vol. 68, pp. 68-72; Little's Gen. of Maine Vol. 2, p. 769. Dow's Hist.of Hampton, N.H. Vol. 2.

Henry[2] Dearborn, bapt. Mar. 22, 1633 at Hannay, Co. Lincoln, Eng.; m. Elizabeth Marrion on Jan. 10, 1665-6, dau. of John & Sarah (Eddy) Marrion; d. Jan. 18, 1725, age 92, at Hampton, N.H. Elizabeth was b. about 1644, and d. July 6, 1716 age 72, at Hampton, N.H.

Henry[2] Dearborn was a Selectman of Hampton, N.H. 1676 & 1692; signer of petition to the King in 1683, usually called "Weare's" petition.

Children:

1. John[3] b. Oct. 10, 1666
2. Samuel[3] b. Jan. 27, 1670; m. Mercy Batchelder, July 12, 1694
3. Elizabeth, b. Dec. 13, 1672; d. young.
4. Sarah, b. Nov. 9, 1675; m. Philemon Blake
5. Abigail b. 1679; m. Samuel Palmer
6. Elizabeth, b. Nov. 19, 1681; m. Wm. Sanborn
7. Henry, b. Oct. 28, 1688; m. (1) Hannah Dow, Oct. 28,1708; m. (2) Mary Robie, dau. of Samuel Jan. 12, 1721; (3) Esther, wid. David Fogg.

Dearborn

References:

Gen. Dict. Maine & N.H. Vol. 2 p. 189; Littles Gen. of Maine, Vol. 2, p. 769. Dow's Hist. of Hampton, N.H. Part 2.

Samuel[3] Dearborn, b. Jan. 27, 1670; m. Mercy Batchelder, dau. Nathaniel & Mary (Carter) (Wyman) Batchelder, on July 12, 1694 at Hampton, N.H., liv. 1746. She was b. Dec. 11, 1677; d. Samuel[3] Dearborn was named in Charter of Kingston, N.H., but remained in No. Hampton, N.H.

Children:

1. Mary, b. Apr. 23, 1695; m. John Blake
2. Mercy, b. Feb. 21, 1697; d. young
3. Mehitable, Feb. 21, 1697; m. Jan. 15, 1719 to Thomas Berry
4. Sarah, b. June 27, 1699; m. Nov. 24, 1720 to Edward Tuck; d. Jan. 15, 1756.
5. Mercy, again, b. Feb. 18, 1702;
6. Jeremiah, b. Apr. 1, 1704; m. Dec. 23, 1725 to Sarah, dau. Richard Taylor.
7. Elizabeth, b. Nov. 9, 1706;
8. Nathaniel[4], b. Jan. 21, 1710; m. Mary Batchelder Dec. 2, 1731; d. Nov. 11, 1754.
9. Henry, b. Dec. 27, 1712; m. Jan. 19, 1738 to Margaret Sherbourne, dau. of Lieut. John Sherbourne.
10. Samuel, b. Sept. 1, 1715;
11. Abigail, b. Oct. 19, 1720; m. Abraham Drake as his 2nd wife - no date given.
12. Elizabeth, b. Oct. 11, 1717; m. Robert Drake, Dec. 13, 1739.

References:

Dow's Hist. of Hampton, N.H. Vol. 2.

Nathaniel[4] Dearborn, b. Jan. 21, 1710 at No. Hampton, N.H.; m. Mary Batchelder, dau. Samuel & Elizabeth (Davis) Batchelder, Dec. 2, 1731; d. Nov. 11, 1754.

Nathaniel Dearborn was a Town Officer at Kensington, N.H., 1744; was a Selectman 1740. Resided North Hampton, N.H. & Kingston, N.H.

Children:

Mercy, b. Aug. 21, 1732;
Samuel, b. June 18, 1734;
Henry, b. May 29, 1736;
Mary, b. Jan. 16, 1739/40; m. Dec. 6, 1759 Moses French; d.
Nathaniel, b. Nov. 30, 1741;
Jeremiah, b. Aug. 29, 1743; d. Aug. 16, 1763
Elizabeth, b. May 19, 1745; d. ae 9 - abt. Apr. 17, 1753
Nathan, b. Dec. 12, 1746;
Edward, b. Feb. 1, 1749;
Rebecca, b. Jan. 23, 1751;

References: Dow's Hist. of Hampton, N.H. Vol. 2.

DINGLEY

Chart VIII

John[1] Dingley, was born in Eng., about 1608; d. 16 ; est. adm. March 18, 1689-90; m. Sarah Chillingworth, possibly a daughter of Thomas of Sandwich. John[1] Dingley, resided Lynn, Sandwich 1637, Marshfield abt. 1644 and Duxbury. He was a Smith; of military age Dec. 4, 1638; freeman June 5, 1644, town officer. Removed to Marshfield - Deputy.

Issue:

Jacob, b. ; m. bef. 1667 Elizabeth Newton, dau. of Richard Newton of Marlborough; d. Aug. 18, 1691.
Mary, b. ; m. Dec. 19, 1654, Capt. Josiah Standish at Marshfield; d. 1655.
Sarah, b. ; m. Nov. 4, 1658, William Ford, Jr. at Marshfield; May 7, 1727.
Hannah m. Josiah Keen of Hingham.
John d. July 9, 1655.

References:

Savage's Gen. Dict., Vol. 2 p. 52, Virkus Abr. Comp. Vol. I, p. 249; Marshfield Mass. V.R. pp. 1, 5; Popes Pioneers of Mass.

DODGE

Chart XIII

Richard[1] Dodge, son of John & Marjorie ( ) Dodge, bapt. 1602; m. Edith before 1631; d. June 15, 1671-2 (will dated 14 (9) 1670, inv. June 26, 1671) at Beverly, Mass. Edith ( ) Dodge d. June 27, 1678, age abt. 75 at Beverly.

Richard[1] Dodge came in the "Lyon's Whelp" which sailed from England (Gravesend) Apr. 25, 1629. He was from East Coker, Somersetshire; was received as an inhabitant of Salem, Mass., Oct. 29, 1638; received into the Salem Church, May 5, 1654.

John [oc] Dodge d. in 1635 at Middlechinnock, Eng., - will prov. Oct. 15, 1635. His heirs included his wife Marjorie, and sons Michael, Richard and William.

Children of Richard[1] and Edith ( ) Dodge:

1. John, bapt. Dec. 29, 1631 (in Eng.); m. d. Oct. 11,1711.
2. Richard, b. Feb. 1643; m. Feb. 23, 1668 at Winham, Marah Eaton.
3. Samuel, b. 1643; m. ; d.
4. Edward, b. ; m. Apr. 1673, at Beverly, Mary Haskell.
5. Joseph, b. 1651; m. Feb. 21, 1716 at Beverly, Sarah Eaton; d. Aug. 10, 1716.
6. Mary, b. 1632; m. Zachariah Herrick, 1653; d. Aug. 18, 1710.
7. Sarah, b. 1644; m. July 1667 at Beverly, Mass., Peter Woodberry; d. 1726.

Dodge

References:

Dodge Family; Popes Pioneers of Mass.; Hist. of Salem by Perley, Vol. 2, pp. 39-42, Planters of the Commonwealth by Banks, p. 61; Gen. Gleanings in Eng. by Waters pp. 448, 449; Will of Richard and Edith Dodge - Probate Rec. of Essex Co. Mass., Vol. 3, pp. 230 - 233 & Vol. 3 pp. 198, 199.

Edward[2] Dodge b. ; m. April 30, 1673, Mary Haskell, dau. of William & Mary (Tybott) Haskell; d. Feb. 13, 1727 (will dat. Feb. 17, 1714-15, filed Mar. 20, 1727. Mary (Haskell) Dodge was b. June 28, 1650 (?) at Gloucester, Mass.; d. Feb. 13, 1737 at Beverly, Mass.

Children:

1. Mary b. Apr. 12, 1675; m. Peter Woodbury ; d. Nov. 20, 1763 - ae 90th yr.
2. Elinor b. Jan. 29, 1677; m. Thomas Bray of Gloucester, in Beverly, Jan. 29, 1716-17; d. aft. 1763.
3. Jonathan, b. July 3, 1678; m. Jerusha Rayment (?) May 15, 1705 at Beverly; d. 1756 ? at Beverly.
4. Edith, b. Jan. 3, 1681; m. Israel Wood, March 9, 1708-9 at Beverly; d. Nov. 3, 1743, ae. 62 yrs. at Beverly.
5. Ruth, b. Aug. 15, 1685.
6. Edward, bpt. Nov. 6, 1687; m. ? Abigail Hayward of Salem, Mar. 14, 1716-17; d.
7. Hannah, b. 1692; m. ; d.
8. Mark, bpt. Oct. 21, 1694; m. (1) Sarah Dodge of Wenham, Nov. 29, 1717, (she d. Dec. 14, 1718), m. (2) Elizabeth Woodberry at Beverly, Jan. 25 , 1721-2; d.

References: Wenham, Mass. V.R.; Beverly, Mass. V.R.

DOTY

Chart VII

Edward[1] Doty (Dotey, Dote, Doten), Mayflower Passenger, b. abt. 1599 in England; m. Faith Clark, dau. of Tristram and Faith ( ) Clark, Jan. 6, 1634-5. Edward Doty is believed to have been married before, but the name of wife is unknown. He was admitted Freeman before March 7, 1636-7; was 40th Signer of the Mayflower Compact.

Edward[1] Doty and Edward Lister, both of whom came over with Stephen Hopkins, fought the only duel in the colony. His will made in Plymouth and found in Plymouth Colony Records of Wills, Vol. 2, p. 4, was signed by John Howland, James Hurst, John Cooke, William Hopkins. Will dated May 20, 1655; proved Aug. 23, 1655, at Plymouth, Mass.

Doty

Faith (Clark) Doty, widow of Edward[1], m. March 14, 1666, John Phillips of Marshfield, Mass. She was b. about 1619, and d. in 1675.

Children of Edward[1] and Faith (Clark) Doty:

Edward[2] Doty b. 1637; m. Feb. 25 or 26, 1662 to Sarah Faunce, dau. of John Faunce and Patience, his wife; d. Feb. 8, 1689-90.
John[2], b. 1639-40; m. (1) in 1667 to Elizabeth Cooke, dau. John Cooke and Damaris Hopkins; m. (2) Sarah, dau. of Giles Rickard.
Thomas[2], b. 1641 (prob.); d. 1679; m. Mary Churchill, was a seaman, lived on Cape Cod, then removed to Piscataway, N.J.
Samuel[2] (Capt.), b. 1643; d. 1715 at Piscataway,NJ.; m. 1678 to Jane Harmon at Piscataway, N.J.
Desire, b. 1645; d. Dec. 1731, ae. 86; m. (1) Xmas 1667 to William Sherman, Jr. of Marshfield, son of Wm. & Prudence (Hill) Sherman; m. (2) Israel Holmes, a fisherman who was drowned 1685 in Plymouth Harbor; m. (3) Alexander Standish, son of Miles, as his 3rd wife.
Elizabeth, b. 1647; m. Jan. 13, 1675, at Marshfield, John, son of John & Annis (Peabody) Rouse.
Isaac[2], b. Feb. 8, 1648-9; m. Elizabeth, dau. of William & Elizabeth England of Portsmouth, R.I.
Joseph[2] Doty b. Apr. 30, 1651; m. (1) Elizabeth Warren, dau. of Nathaniel & Sarah (Walker) Warren; m. (2) Deborah, dau. Walter Hatch & Elizabeth Holbrook; m. (3) Sarah Edwards.
Mary, b. 1653; m. Samuel Hatch, between July 10-20, 1677, and Feb. 28 to March 10, 1679-80.

References:

The Doty-Doten Family in America, compiled by Ethan Allen Doty, Brooklyn, N.Y. Publ. for the Author 1897. Savage's Gen. Dict. Vol. I, p. 584; Signers of the Mayflower compact by Annie Arnoux Haxtun, 1899, part 2, pp. 32-36. Old Plymouth Records, N.E.H.G.R., 9:317. N.E. Families by Lewis Publ. Co. N.Y. 1913, p. 1271. Mayflower Desc. & Other Marriages.

Edward[2] Doty, b. 1637; d. Feb. 8, 1690 - was drowned with his son and Elkanah Watson, in Plymouth Harbor; m. Feb. 25, 1663 to Sarah Faunce, dau. of John & Patience (Morton) Faunce, she was b. 1645.

Children, all born at Plymouth, Mass.

Edward[3], b. May 20, 1664; d. unmarried betw. Mar. 1689 & Dec. 1696.
Sarah, b. June 9, 1666; d. bef. Aug. 16, 1749; m. June 21, 1687, at Plymouth, James[3] Warren (Nathaniel[2], Richard[1])
John[3], b. Aug. 4, 1668; d. Feb. 8, 1689-90 - unmarried.
Mary, b. July 9, 1671; d. bef. Apr. 6, 1642; m. Dec. 21, 1699, to Joseph Allen (Allyn) at Barnstable; d. at Withersfield, Conn.
Martha, b. July 9, 1661; d. aft. Aug. 26, 1741; m. Dec. 23, 1696, Thomas Morton, at Plymouth.

Doty

Children of Edward[2] Doty:

Elizabeth, b. Dec. 22, 1673; d. at Marshfield, Dec. 16 or 17, 1745; m. Tobias Oakman.
Patience, b. July 7, 1676; d. Feb. 26, 1690-1.
Mercy, b. Feb. 6, 1678; d. Nov. 30, 1682.
Samuel[3], b. May 17, 1681; d. Jan. 26, 1750 at Saybrook, Conn.; m. Dec. 3, 1706, Anne Buckingham.

Edward[2] Doty, was a man of many virtues, having the Doty "intelligence, integrity and thrift".

Sarah (Faunce) Doty m. (2) in Plymouth, March 2, 1693, to John Buck, and d. at Scituate, Mass. June 27, 1695.

References:

The Doty-Doten Family in America, compiled by Ethan Allen Doty, Brooklyn, N.Y. Publ. for the Author 1897. Savage's Gen. Dict. Vol. I, p. 584. Signers of the Mayflower Compact by Annie Arnoux Haxtun, 1899, part 2, pp. 32-36. Old Plymouth Records, N.E.H.G.R., 9:317. N.E. Families by Lewis Publ. Co. N.Y. 1913, p. 1271. Mayflower Desc. & Other Marriages. Families of the Pilgrims publ. by Mass. Soc. of Mayflower Desc.; also "The Faunce Family" by James Freer Faunce, a publ. in N.E.H.G.R. for July 1960, p. 119.

DURANT

Chart IX

John[1] Durant received a grant of land at Billerica, Mass., in Nov. 1659. He died in prison at Cambridge, Mass., during the Witchcraft delusion, of which he was probably a victim. The birth date of John Durant is not known, however, he was at least 21 in 1659, so was born 1638 or before; d. Oct. 27, 1692; m. Susanna Dutton, at Billerica on Nov. 16, 1670. She was a dau. of Thomas and Susanna (   ) Dutton of Reading, Mass., born Feb. 27, 1654; died _________. She m. (2) Justinian Holden of Cambridge, Mass., at Billerica Dec. 6, 1693, by whom she had a dau. b. Oct. 16, 1694 at Billerica.

Children of John[1] and Susanna (Dutton) Durant:

John[2] b. July 31, 1672; d. Feb. 25, 1757 at Billerica; m. Aug. 10, 1695 to Elizabeth Jaquith
Thomas[2] b. Jan. 7, 1674; d.   ; m. June 12, 1702, at Billerica, Mass., to Sarah Jaquith (sister of the wife of John[2] Durant). Elizabeth and Sarah Jaquith, were daus. of Abraham and Mary (Adford) Jaquith. Sarah was b. Sept. 21,167
Abigail, b. Sept. 24, 1681; d.   ; m. Aug. 9, 1697 at Cambridge, Mass., to Abraham Ireland
Mehitable, b. Apr. 20, 1687; d.   ; m. Dec. 16, 1708 to Thomas Skinner (both of Malden) at Charleston, Mass.

Durant

References:

Hist. of Billerica, Mass., by Hazen; Billerica, V.R. pp. 65, 66, 67, 248, 249, 356. Reading, Mass. V.R. p. 71; Cambridge, Mass. V.R. Early Mass. Mar. by Baily, Part 3, p. 9.

Thomas[2] Durant, b. Jan. 7, 1674 at Billerica, Mass.; d. m. Sarah Jaquith on June 12, 1702 at Billerica. She was a dau. of Abraham & Mary (Adford) Jaquith; b. at Woburn, Mass., Sept. 21, 1677. The date and place of her death, or that of Thomas[2] Durant, is not known.

Children of Thomas[2] and Sarah (Jaquith) Durant:

Sarah, b. Jan. 1, 1703-4 at Billerica, Mass.; m. May 17, 1728 at Billerica, James Farley - dismissed to Hollis in 1765.
Thomas, b. June 2, 1705.
Susanna, b. Aug. 18, 1707; m. Joseph Hamblett, Jr., of Nottingham, N.H. (now Hull);
Benjamin, b. Aug. 19, 1709; m. May 9, 1738 at Bellerica, Mary Butler of Nottingham, N.H., dau. John & Eliz. (Wilson) Butler.
John, b. May 2, 1712; m. Phebe Butler, sister of Benjamin's wife.
Elizabeth (probably) b. abt. 1719; m. (1) (int) Dec. 18, 1737, Leonard Spaulding of Chelmsford; m. (2) Dr. Ezekiel Chase.

DUTTON

Chart IX

Thomas Dutton, probably a son of John[1] Dutton of Reading, Mass., was b. abt. 1621; resided at Woburn, Billerica, and Reading, Mass. He was accepted as an inhabitant of Billerica Nov. 22, 1669. He m. (1) Susannah __________; b. abt. 1626; d. Aug. 27, 1684 at Billerica; (2) Mrs. Ruth Hooper, on Nov. 10, 1684, prob. wid. of William Hooper of Reading.

Children of Thomas & Susannah Dutton:

Thomas, b. Sept. 14, 1648; m. Jan. 11, 1678, Mrs. Ruth Draper, widow, of Concord, Mass.; m. (2) Nov. 1721 Sarah Convers.
Mary, b. Nov. 14, 1651; d. July 9, 1678; m. Dec. 21, 1669, to Jacob Hamblet. (Mary d. of smallpox).
Susanna b. Feb. 27, 1654; m. (1) Nov. 16, 1670 at Billerica, John[1] Durant; (2) Justinian Holden.
John, b. Mar. 2, 1656; d. Apr. 7, 1735; m. (1) Sept. 20, 1681 to Sarah Shedd, dau. of Daniel, at Billerica; m. (2) May 1721, Ruth Frost, prob. wid. Samuel Frost.

Dutton

Children of Thomas & Susannah Dutton:

Elizabeth, b. Jan. 28, 1659; m. 5-3-1681 at Concord, Wm. Baker.
Joseph, b. Jan. 25, 1661; m. Aug. 19, 1685 at Reading, Mass., Rebecca Fitch.
Sarah, b. Mar. 5, 1662; m. Apr. 3, 1623, to Samuel Lewis at Billerica.
James, b. Aug. 22, 1665.
Benjamin, b. Feb. 19, 1669; m. (1) July 1, 1690 to Johanna Dunkin, widow of John Duncan. She was killed, with Benjamin and Mary, by the Indians Aug. 1, 1692 at Billerica; m. (2) Susanna __________.

References:

Hist. of Billerica, Mass., by Hazen, p. 45; Billerica V.R. pp. 249, 357, 366; Reading, Mass. V.R. pp. 71, 323, 357; Concord, Mass. Births, Deaths & Mar. pp. 21, 24.

DYER

Chart XIV

William Dyer, was an early settler of Sheepscot, Maine, in 1665. He and his son Christopher, were killed and scalped by Indians at Dyer's Neck in Aug. 1689. (See affidavits in York, Reg. 13, p. 228). In June, 1712, Samuel and Mary (Dyer) Bowles, conveyed to Henry Flint of Cambridge, 600 acres of land conveyed to a William Dyer Feb. 11, 1662, situated in New Dartmouth, alias Sheepscot, commonly known by the name of Dyer's Neck, or Nassacmac, which said neck of land "says the deed" was formerly granted to Robin Hood. Sagamore of the said Nassacmac, with William Dyer, father of the said Mary. (York Co. Reg. of Deeds, Bk. 15, p. 224)

William Dyer was an Associate, Court of Genl. Sess., and Wealthy and prominent, until Indian attacks in 1676, drove all away; that year he was in Scituate, all left behind including 56 head of cattle, and 30 swine. Although only his sons signed the petition in 1682, records show he did return to Sheepscot and was killed by Indians in Aug. 1689.

Children of William[1] Dyer (wife's name not known):

John, b. abt. 1648; d. (bur.) Apr. 23, 1733; m. (1) name of wife not known; m. (2) Anna
Christopher, b. abt. 1640; d. Dec. 1689 - killed & scalped by Indians.
Mary, m. Samuel[2] Bowles.

References:

Maine, N.H. Gen. Dict. Vol. 2, p. 213; Bowles Gen. by John A. Bolls, 1865.

EATON

Chart II

Francis Eaton was a Mayflower Passenger. He came over with "Sarah, his wife and Samuel, their son, a young child." In Gov. Bradford's report, 30 years later, he says "Francis Eaton, his first wife died in the general sickness and he married again and his 2nd wife died and he married the 3rd and had by her three children. One of them is married and hath a child, the others are living but one of them is an Ideate. He died about 16 years ago."

Francis Eaton was the 23rd signer of the Mayflower Compact. Vol. 4, p. 186 gives Francis Eaton's name among Purchasers of Dartmouth.

Christopher Cary of the city of Bristol, Eng., parish of St. Stevens, in his will speaks of a lodge in the parish of St. Philips, as occupied by Francis Eaton, house carpenter. The will was made in 1615, proved 1625.

Francis Eaton's first wife was Sarah, who died in 1621 and his second wife was probably Gov. Carver's maid servant. His third wife was Christian Penn. After his death the widow Christian married Francis^{2} Billington (John^{1}) in 1634 and had eight children by him.

Children by Sarah Eaton:

Samuel^{2} b. 1620; d. abt. 1684, at Middleboro; m. (1) ________; m. (2) Jan. 10, 1660, Martha^{3} Billington (Francis^{2}, John^{1}) - She m. (2) Robert Crossman.

Children by Christian (Penn) Eaton:

Rachel^{2} b. abt. 1625; d. bef. Oct. 1661; m. Mar. 2, 1645, at Plymouth, Joseph Ramsden. He m. (2) Oct. 16, 1661, at Plymouth, Mary Savery.

Benjamin^{2} b. aft. June 1, 1627; d. Jan. 16, 1711-12, at Plympton; m. Dec. 4, 1660, at Plymouth, Sarah Hoskins ________^{2}, b. ________; d. aft. 1650.

References:

Mayflower Descendents - Vol. 2, pp. 115-117 (V.S. of Mayflower Passengers, compiled from Original sources, by George Ernest Bowman; Gov. Bradford's list of Mayflower Passengers, Vol. 1, p. 9. Mayf. Desc. Savage's Gen. Dict., Hist. of Eaton Family, compiled by Nellie Zoda Rice Malyneux, Syracuse, N.Y. C.W. Bordied, Publ. 1911. Families of the Pilgrims, Publ. Mass. Soc. Mayf. Desc.

Eaton

Benjamin[2] Eaton, b. 1627; d. Jan. 16, 1711-12 at Plympton, Mass.; m. Dec. 4, 1660 at Plympton, Mass., to Sarah Hoskins, dau. of William and Sarah (Cushman) Hoskins. She was b. abt. 1636 and d. __________.

Children:

William b. abt. 1662; d. bef. Mar. 18, 1690-1 - unm.
Benjamin b. 1664; d. bef. Dec. 20, 1745; m. Dec. 18, 1689 at Plymouth, Mass. to Mary Coombs; m. (2) Mar. 11, 1728-9 at Hingham, Mass. to Susanna (Lewis) Beal.
Rebecca,b. 1675; m. Nov. 21, 1699 to Joseph (or Josiah) Rickard; d. Jan. 22, 1765 at Plympton, Mass.

References:

Mayf. Desc. Vol. II, p. 78 (Plymouth Births, Mar. & Deaths p. 28). Savage's Gen. Dict. Mayf. Desc. Vol. II, p. 140 (Early Records of Plympton). His. of Eaton Family.

Benjamin[3] Eaton, b. 1664 at Plymouth; d. 1745 at (will dated Apr. 23, 1745; proved Dec. 20, 1745); m. Dec. 18, 1689 to Mary Coombs, dau. of John and Elizabeth (   ) (Barlow Coombs, b. Nov. 28, 1666 at Boston, Mass.; d. July 2, 1728, age 63. Benjamin[3] Eaton, m. (2) Susannah Beal, who d. Apr. 13, 1730, aged 70.

Benjamin[3] Eaton was a Housewright in Kingston, Mass.

Children of Benjamin & Mary (Coombs) Eaton:

Francis, b. 1690 m. Thankful Alden, int. June 10, 1727 at Kingston, Mass.
William b. June 1, 1691;
Hannah b. Feb. 10, 1692; m. July 31, 1712, Benjamin Bryant, at Plympton, Mass.; d. Mar. 4, 1723 at Plympton, Mass.
Jabez b. Feb. 8, 1693; d. May 19, 1724
Sarah b. Oct. 20, 1695; m. Jan. 8, 1712 to Benjamin Cushman
John b. Oct. 6, 1697;
Benjamin, b. 1698; m. Mercy
David, b. 1698; m. Deborah Fuller
Mary, b.   ; m. Zachariah Soule
Elizabeth, b.   ; m. Cornelius Sturtevant
Daniel, b.   ;

References:

Savage's Gen. Dict.; Mayflower Descendents, Vol. II, pp. 78, 140; Vital Statistics of Plympton, Mass.; Dave's Landmarks of Ancient Plymouth, p. 100; N.E. Families by Lewis Publ. Co., 1913, Vol. I, p. 148.

EATON

Chart No. V

John Eaton, proprietor of Salisbury, Mass., 1639-46; Removed to Haverhill, proprietor 1648; town officer. The earliest Eaton grants of land at Salisbury, were for John[1] Eaton. He m. (1) Martha ________. She d. aft. 20 (2) 1655. He m. (2) Ann ________, who d. Feb. 5, 1660; m. (3) Phebe, widow of Thomas Dow, Nov. 20, 1661. John[1] Eaton d. Oct. 29, 1668; will probated April 13, 1669.

Children:

John[2], b. abt. 1619; m. Martha[2] Rowlandson
Ann[2], b. ________; m. June 25, 1645 at Salisbury, George Brown, brother of Henry and William and son of Christian.
Elizabeth[2], b. ________; m. Dec. 1, 1648 at Haverhill, James[2] Davis.
Thomas[2] b. bef. 1630; m. (1) Aug. 14, 1656, Martha Kent; (2) Jan. 6, 1658-9, Eunice Singletary.
Ruth[2], b. ___________; m. Dec. 9, 1656, Samuel Ingalls of Ipsiwich.
Hester[2], b. _________; d. unmarried.

References:

Pope's Pioneers of Mass.; Haverhill, Mass. V.R. Vol. 2 p. 101; Probate Records of Essex Co. Mass., Vol. II, pp. 155-158; Old Families of Salisbury and Amesbury, Vol. I, p. 147.

John[2] Eaton of Salisbury, planter; b. abt. 1619; d. Nov. 1, 1682 - will dated Sept. 12, Nov. 28, Dec. 26; m. Martha[2] Rowlandson (Thomas[1]). She d. July 1712 in Salisbury. Both were members of the Salisbury Church.

Children:

Esther d. 1649
John, d. Jan. 17, 1717-18; m. Mary ______________.
Thomas, b. Jan. 17, 1646-7 at Salisbury; m. Nov. 14, 1679, Hannah Hubbard.
Martha[3], b. Aug. 12, 1648 at Salisbury; m. (1) Nov. 5, 1668; to Benjamin Collins; (2) Nov. 4, 1686 at Salisbury, to Philip[2] Flanders (Stephen[1]).
Elizabeth[3], b. Dec. 12, 1650 at Salisbury; m. Jan. 7, 1673-4, John Groth.
Ann[3], b. Dec. 17, 1652 at Salisbury; d. June 12, 1658 at Salisbury.
Sarah[3], b. Dec. 28, 1654 at Salisbury; m. May 6, 1675 at Salisbury, Robert Downer.
Mary[3], b. Dec. 9, 1656 at Salisbury; d. Jan. 1, 1656-7, at Salisbury.
Samuel[3], b. Feb. 14, 1658-9 at Salisbury; a "Seaman"; oath of allegiance & Fidelity at Salisbury 1678; liv. 1683.
Joseph[3], b. March 6, 1660 at Salisbury; m. Dec. 14, 1683, Mary[3] French (John[2], Edward[1]).
Ephriam[3], b. April 12, 1663 at Salisbury; m. Feb. 5, 1688-9, Mary[3] True.

Eaton

References: Old Families of Salisbury and Amesbury - Vol. I p. 148.

EDDY

Charts No. VI & XVIII

Rev. William Eddy, A.M., b. abt. 1550 at Bristol, Eng. d. Nov. 23, 1616 at Cranbrook, Co. Kent, Eng.; m. (1) Mary Foster of Cranbrook, Eng., on Nov. 20, 1587. She was a daughter of John and Ellen (Munn) Foster; was born about 1565; died July 18, 1611. Rev. Eddy m. (2) Sarah Taylor, widow, Feb. 22, 1614.

Rev. William Eddy was educated at University of Cambridge, St. John's & Trinity College, with degree of M.A. He was Vicar of St. Dunston's, Cranbrook 1591-1616. Rev. Eddy was very Methodical, a strict Episcopalian, judician, humane & reprover of immortality. There is a tablet in Brewster Park, Plymouth, Mass., to his memory & that of his two sons John & Samuel who arrived at Plymouth, Mass., on the "Handmaid" Oct. 29, 1630.

Children of Rev. William & Mary (Foster) Eddy, all born in Cranbrook, Co. Kent, England.

John, b. 1597; d. Oct. 12, 1684; m. (1) Amy (2) Joanna.
Abigail, b. Oct. 1601; d. 1687; m. 1619 John Benjamin of Cambridge, Mass.
Samuel, b. May, 1608; d. 1688; m. Elizabeth
Mary, b. Sept. 1591.
Phineas, b. Sept. 1593.
John, (2nd) b. March 1597-8.
Ellen, b. Aug. 1599.
Anna, b. May 1603.
Elizabeth, b. Dec. 1606.
Zachariah, b. March, 1610.
Nathaniel, b. July 1611; d. July 1611.
Priscilla, a daughter by his 2nd wife was b. 1614, bpt. Dec. 10, 1614.

References:

Virkus p. 390, 397, Vol. II & Vol. I, p. 968; Eddy Genealogy by Charles Eddy 1881; Freeman Gen.; The Eddy Family in America, Eddy Family Assn. 1930.

John[1] Eddy and his brother Samuel, came on the "Handmaid" which sailed Aug. 10, 1630 and arrived at Plymouth, Mass. Oct. 29, 1630. John[1] Eddy resided at Cranbrook, Co. Kent, Eng.; Baxted, Suffolk Co., Eng.; Plymouth, Mass; and Watertown, Mass. (1633). John Eddy was admitted Freeman, Sept. 3, 1634; was first Town Clerk and was a Selectman of Watertown, Mass.

Eddy

John[1] Eddy was baptized March 1597, at Cranbrook, Co. Kent, Eng. in his father's Church. The records written by his father Rev. William Eddy. He died Oct. 12, 1684, aged 90 at Watertown, Mass.; married (1) Amie Doget, daughter of John & Dorothy Doget of Groton, bapt. July 16, 1597 at Groton, Co. Suffolk, Eng.; m. (2) Joanna, probably the widow of Gabriel Meade who died 12 (3) 1666. She was born about 1603; died at Watertown, Mass., 1683, Oct. 25, aged 80.

Children:

John[2], bapt. at Nayland, Co. Suffolk, Eng. June 9, 1622; bur. Feb. 8, 1622-3. (Church register at Nayland)
John[2], bapt. Mar. 29, 1624;
Mary, bapt. Mar. 10, 1625 at Nayland, Eng.; d. Sept. 13, 1693; m. Thomas Orton of Charleston, Mass.
Sarah, b. in Eng.; d. Feb. 3, 1709-10 at Boston in her 85th yr; m. John Marion abt. 1640, at Watertown.
Pilgrim b. Aug. 25, 1634 at Watertown, Mass.; d. young; m. 3 times; Steadman; William Baker, and Eveleth.
John[2] (again), b. Feb. 16, 1636-37 at Watertown;
Benjamin bur. at Watertown, 1639.
Samuel, b. Sept. 30, 1640 at Watertown; d. Nov. 22, 1711; m. Sept. or Nov. 30, 1664, Sarah Meade, dau. Gabriel & Joanna Meade.
Ruth, b. prob. at Watertown; m. Ezekiel Gardner of Boston, who d. bef. Feb. 9, 1703.
Abigail, b. Oct. 11, 1643; d. before 1677, not mentioned in her father's will.

FAUNCE

Chart VII

John[1] Faunce, b. abt. 1602; d. Nov. 29, 1653 at Plymouth, Mass., (Inventory of Est. Dec. 15, 1653); m. Patience Morton, 1633-4, at Plymouth, Mass. She was a dau. of George and Julianna (Carpenter) Morton, b. 1615 at Leyden, Holland; d. Aug. 16, 1691, age 77.

John[1] Faunce came to Plymouth in the "Ann" 1623. In the same vessel came George Morton, the author of "Mourts Relation". In 1633 he became a "Freeman" having taken the oath to defend the church and State.

Patience Morton came on the Anne, with her mother Julianna (Carpenter) Morton of Wrington, near Bath, Somersetshire, dau. of Alexander Carpenter, a member of the Ancient Brethern. Patience Morton, m. (2) Feb. 1, 1661, Thomas Whitney.

Faunce

Children of John and Patience (Morton) Faunce, b. in Plymouth.

Sarah, b. abt. 1645; d. June 27, 1695 in Scituate; m. Feb. 26, 1663 Edward[1] Doty; m. (2) March 2, 1693, John Buck of Scituate.
Thomas, b. abt. 1647; d. Feb. 27, 1745-6 at Plymouth, age 99 - bur. on Burial Hill; m. Dec. 23, 1672, Jean Nelson, dau. Wm. and Martha (Ford) Nelson.
Joseph, b. May 14, 1653; d. Jan. 18, 1687; m. Jan. 3, 1672, Judith Rickard, dau. of Giles and Hannah (Dunham) Rickard.
Priscilla, b. 1634; d. May 15, 1707; m. 1652, Joseph Warren, son of Richard & Elizabeth Warren.
Mary, d. Oct. 4, 1664; m. Aug. 15, 1664, Sgt. William Harlow as his 2nd wife.
Patience, m. Nov. 20, 1661, John Holmes in Plymouth. He d. in 1697.
Elizabeth, b. March 23, 1648; d. March 3, 1649.
Mercy, b. Apr. 10, 1651; d. Feb. 11, 1732; m. Dec. 29, 1667, Nathaniel Holmes, brother of her sister Patience's husband. He d. July 27, 1727, aged 84 yrs.
John, b. and d. Nov. 29, 1654.

References:

The Faunce Family by James Freer Faunce, N.E.H.G.R. July 1960 p. 115; Popes Pioneers of Mass., Planters of the Commonwealth by Banks; The English Ancestry & Homes of the Pilgrim Fathers by Banks; Mayflower Descendents 11:159, 17:143; The Faunce Family History & Gen., by James Freer Faunce, pp. 1-14.

FOLLONSBEE

Chart XIV

Thomas[1] Follonsbee, b. abt. 1637; d. aft. 1713 and prob. 1726; m. (1) Mary __________, as early as 1660; m. (2) Sarah; 1st wife was alive in 1673; m. (3) int. Apr. 4, 1713, Jane Moseman of Boston, Mass.

Thomas[1] Follonsbee, Joiner, of Portsmouth, N.H. 1665-71, and Newbury, Mass. 1677. He finished the Portsmouth Church and schoolhouse. In 1671 he had moved from Great Island and hired Abraham Corbett house near the meetinghouse, when Mr. Harry Deering, also removed to Strawberry Bank, hired the same house under a better title, whereupon the sheriff turned Thomas Follonsbee out, without notice, in the depth of winter with no habitation provided for his wife and many small children. Signed oath at Newbury, Mass., 1678, age 41.

Follonsbee

Children:

Rebecca, b. abt. 1660; d. bef. 1713; m. Nov. 22, 1677, at Newbury, Thomas Chase.
Annie, b. abt. 1668; d. Apr. 18, 1708; m. Nov. 10, 1684, Moses Chase.
Mary, b. abt. 1667; m. (1) Dec. 1, 1686, Robert Pike; (2) 1691, William Hooke.
Thomas (Capt.) b. abt. 1670; d. 1755; m. (1) June 19, 1694, Abigail Rolfe (Prob. Abigail Bond, wid. of Ezra Rolfe); m. (2) Feb. 18, 1734-5, Mary Bancroft of Reading, Mass.
Francis, b. Oct. 22, 1677, at Newbury, Mass.
Hannah, b. Apr. 10, 1680 at Newbury, Mass.
Jane, m. 1688, to Lieut. John Hubbard of Salisbury, at Kingston, Mass.

References:

Old Families of Salisbury & Amesbury by Holt, Vol. II, p. 569, 570. Gen. Dict. of Maine & N.H. by Libby, Vol. II, p. 236.

FORD

Charts I & VII

William (?) Ford, died in the ship "Fortune" on the way over in 1621. He was a Leather Dresser of Southwark, Eng. His wife Martha ( ) Ford, gave birth to a son the night she landed. Eighteen months later she married, Peter Brown, 23rd Signer of the Mayflower Compact. She had two children by him.

Children of William (?) & Martha Ford:

William, b. 1604; d. Sept. 28, 1676; m. bef. 1640, Anna Winslow (?).
Martha (?)
John, b. Nov. 1621; d. 1693; m. Hannah ____________.

References:

The English Ancestry & Homes of the Pilgrim Fathers by Banks (Revised ed.) p. 117; Signers of the Mayflower Compact by Annie Arnoux Haxtun (Brown) p. 27, part 2; Saints and Strangers by Willison, p. 445; One Small Candle by Fleming, p. 216.

William[1] Ford, settled early in Marshfield, Mass. He was a miller - established the mill on the site at Marshfield, known at "Dunham's Mill" near Brown's Blacksmith Shop. He was also a Miller at Duxbury, Mass. He was Constable at Marshfield in 1658; Selectman 1666, 1670 & 1675. (Vital Records of Duxbury, gives William Ford as b. 1594 - private record from Nathaniel Ford Bible in possession of Jonathan Ford of Duxbury in 1911).

Ford

William Ford d. Sept. 23, 1676, age 72, at Marshfield, Mass.; m. before 1633, Ann Winslow (?) She was buried Sept. 1, 1684, at Marshfield, Mass.; buried in the old Winslow Cemetery beside her husband.

Children:

William, Jr., b. 1633-4; d. Feb. 7, 1721, age 88; m. Nov. 4, 1658 to Sarah Dingley, dau. John & Sarah Dingley.
Michael, b. ; d. Mar. 28, 1789; m. (1) Dec. 12, 1667, Abigail Snow; m. (2) 1683 Bethiah Hatch.
Margaret, b. ; m. Zachariah Soule bef. 1640.
Millicent, m. (1) Nov. 4, 1658 to John Carver; (2) March 9, 1681 at Marshfield, to Thomas Drake.

References:

Wm. Ford of the Fortune, compiled by Hanibal C. Ford; 233 King's Point Rd. Great Neck, N.Y.; Mayflower Desc. Vol. 2, p. 181; Hist. of Marshfield, Mass., Vol. 2, p. 102; Duxbury, Mass. V.R. p. 254; Marshfield, Mass., V.R., pp. 14 & 9; Popes Pioneers of Mass. p. 228; N.E.H.G.R. Vol. 8, p. 192; Clemens Mar. Rec. before 1699, p. 55; Pierce's Colonial Lists, 1621 to 1700, pp. 45, 46; Signers of the Mayflower Compact by Annie Arnoux Haxtun, pp. 27 & 28 Part II and p. 16 Part III.

Michael[2] Ford, of Duxbury, Marshfield and Scituate, was born in 1643; d. March 27, 1729 at Marshfield, Mass.; m. (1) Abigail, dau. of Anthony and Abigail (Warren) Snow, Dec. 12, 1667; m. (2) Bethiah Hatch, dau. of Walter and Elizabeth (Holbrooke) Hatch, in 1683. She was b. March 31, 1661 at Scituate, Mass.; d. Nov. 22, 1728, aged 67 at Marshfield; bur. in the Old Burial Ground at the Congregational Church at Marshfield.

Michael[2] Ford, was Constable of Marshfield in 1674; and on the Grand Jury in 1683.

Children by 1st wife:

Lydia, b. 1668
Hannah, b. 1670
William, b. Dec. 26, 1672
James, b. Apr. 4, 1675
Abigail, b. 1679
Patience & twin b. Apr. 2, 1682; Patience d. June 26, 1682 - same day as the 1st wife.

Children by 2nd wife Bethiah Hatch:

Twin daughters b. and d. Nov. 17, 1683.
Thomas, b. Apr. 30, 1685; d. Oct. 22, 1769 age 85th yr; m. Apr. 5, 1711, at Cambridge, Mass. to Ruth Bradish.

Ford

Children by 2nd wife Bethiah Hatch:

Deborah, b. Oct. 24, 1686.
Susanna, b. July 26, 1689; m. Jan. 13, 1714 to John Tilden; d. Oct. 8, 1743.
Bathsheba, b. Mar. 1, 1691; m. (?) Ebenezer Sherman in 1730.
Ephriam, b. July 18, 1693; d. Sept. 28, 1785; m. Jane Delano.
Elizabeth, b. Mar. 3, 1694; m. (?) Richard Lowden, Dec. 11, 1718.
Elisha, b. Jan. 19, 1696; d. Nov. 4, 1758 at Marshfield; m. Jan. 11, 1719 to Elizabeth Oakman.
Mehitable, b. Sept. 18, 1698; m. Caleb Sampson, Feb. 12, 1729.
Martha, b. Oct. 29, 1700; d. Apr. 5, 1768 in 65th yr; m. J oshua Carver.
Bethiah, b. Mar. 16, 1687-8.

References:

Marshfield, Mass. V.R., pp. 8, 10, 12, 13, 14, 15, 16, 18, 20, 21, 42, 85, 401, 408; Hist. of Marshfield by Richards - Vol. 2, p. 102 - Ford Family; Pierces Colonial Lists, pp. 45, 55. Scituate, Mass. V.R. pp. 74 & 181. Mayflower Desc. Vol. 17, p. 202.

Elisha[3] Ford b. Jan. 19, 1696 at Marshfield, Mass.; d. Nov. 14, 1758 at Marshfield, Mass.; m. Jan. 14, 1719-20, at Marshfield, to Elizabeth,dau. Tobias & Elizabeth (Doty) Oakman. She was b. May 10, 1701, prob. in Maine; d. Nov. 5, 1768 - aged 68 - at Marshfield, Mass.

Children:

Lemuel, b. Jan. 20, 1720-1 at Marshfield, Mass.; d. Feb. 20, 1752 at Marshfield; m. Priscilla Turner Feb. 20, 1752.
Patience, b. Jan. 1, 1722-3 at Marshfield, Mass.; d. Apr. 7, 1800 in 78th yr.; m. James Sprague, Jr., Feb. 24, 1742-3.
Jerusha, b. Dec. 7, 1727; m. Arthur Howland, Dec. 7, 1727 at Marshfield.
Priscilla, b. July 20, 1730; d. Aug. 3, 1801, aged 70; never married.
Elisha, b. Nov. 16, 1734; at Marshfield; d. 1788; m. Dec. 6, 1759, Elizabeth Tilden.
Isaac, b. July 19, 1738 at Marshfield; d. in Maine after Mar. 1806 or Jan. 27, 1807; m. Lucy Josselyn, Oct. 1, 1761, Pembroke, Mass.
Tabitha, b. Aug. 13, 1742; m. Feb. 13, 1766, Seth Ford. Moved to Maine; d. May 11, 1785 in her 43rd yr. Seth Ford d. Sept. 3, 1807 in his 69th yr.
Bethiah (?) m. Apr. 11, 1751 to Simeon Turner;
William (?) m. Sarah Hayden.

Ford

References: Hist. of Marshfield, by Richards, Vol. 2, p. 102-; Ford Family; Mayflower Index, Vols. 1 & 2 (together) p. 566 #24962; p. 288 #13407; p. 289 #13465; Scituate V.R. to 1850, Vol. 2, p. 122; Marshfield, Mass. V.R. pp. 12, 34, 91, 92, 149, 172, 401, 409.

Isaac[4] Ford, b. June 19, 1738 at Marshfield, Mass., d. after Jan. 27, 1807, in Maine; m. Lucy Josselyn, dau. of Henry and Hannah (Oldham) Josselyn. She was b. Oct. 1741 at Pembroke, Mass.; date of death not known, but after March 1806.

Isaac[4] Ford, was a private in Capt. Abijales Rowlee Company and the Company (Mass.). Return was endorsed "July 6, 1775."

Children:

Lucy, b. Oct. 14, 1762; m. Constant Southard, Oct. 27, 1785 at Marshfield.
Bethiah, b. Dec. 1, 1764; m. Matthiew Pettingill, Sept. 22, 1785 at Marshfield.
Isaac, b. Feb. 7, 1767;
Henry, b. Nov. 14, 1768; d. Sept. 3, 1843; m. Jan. 15, 1797, to Priscilla Records. She was b. 1770; d. Oct. 15, 1840.
Elizabeth, b. Jan. 30, 1771; d. Nov. 17, 1855; m. int. Filed, March 7, 1794 to Joseph French, resided Chesterville, Maine.
Tabitha, b. Jan. 27, 1776; m. Nathaniel Jennings.

The first five children were born at Marshfield, Mass.

References: Hist. of Fayette, Me., by Underwood, pp. 107, 157; Marshfield, Mass. V.R.

FOSS - FOST

Chart XI

David Lewitseen Foss, b. 1604 in Norway; d. Aug. 8, 1659 at Rebe, Denmark; m. Anna Hundevard in 1637. She was b. 1619; d. 1684 at Rebe, Denmark; m. at Rebe, Denmark. He was magistrate, Provost, and Minister of the Gospel.

The Secretary of the Genealogical Institute of Copenhagen, Denmark, sent the following information: "The Foss Family belonged to the Norwegian Nobility. The first one of the name coming to Denmark, was David Lewitseen Foss."

Children:

Johann, b. Rebe, Denmark, Jan. 3, 1638; d. Dec. 19, 1699 at Dover, N.H.; m. Mary Chadbourne.
Laurita Davidson b. Jan. 8, 1643 at Rebe, Denmark.
Antonius, b. May 8, 1646, at Rebe, Denmark.

Foss - Fost

References: Gen. of the Foss Family of America, compiled by Guy S. Rix, Concord, N.H.

John[1] Foss, b. Jan. 3, 1638 at Rebe, Denmark; d. Dec. 19, 1699, at Dover, N.H.; m. Mary Chadbourne, dau. of William & Mary ( ) Chadbourne. She was b. 10th mo. 1644 at Boston, Mass.; d. bef. 1686.

John[1] Foss arrived in Boston, Mass. on a British War Vessel on which he was employed as a calker. He jumped overboard to escape further service and went to Portsmouth, N.H., after thinking of settling at Reid's Temple. He was granted lands in Portsmouth, N.H., Feb. 24, 1657. Was admitted an inhabitant of Dover, N.H., Jan. 1, 1665-6, and took oath of allegiance Jan. 21, 1669.

John[1] Foss m. (2) Jan. 25, 1686, Elizabeth (Furnicide) Goss, widow of James Goss (an error in the records gives her name as Sarah). The marriage was performed by John Wincool. He m. (3) Elizabeth Berry, dau. of William & Jane Berry, and widow of John Locke, who was killed by Indians on Dover Plains Aug. 26, 1696.

Children of John[1] and Mary (Chadbourne) Foss:

Mary, b. ; d. ; m. about 1692, James Warren.
Humphrey
William, b. Mar. 11, 1673-4;
Jemima
Elizabeth, b. 1666; m. (1) Nov. 8, 1698, Daniel Dill; (2) Henry Beedle.
Hinkson, b. abt. 1679; d. June 26, 1696 - Killed on Dover Plains, age 17 years.
John
Samuel
Joshua
Walter
Hannah
Thomas

Children by 2nd wife Elizabeth (Fernicide) Goss:

Samuel (again), Mariner of Boston, m. (1) July 9, 1714, Mehitable Lincoln; m. (2) 15 Sept. 1726, Mary White.
Lydia, m. Feb. 24, 1717, Capt. Peter Grant of Berwick.

References: Gen. of the Foss Family of America, compiled by Guy S. Rix, of Concord, N.H.; Gen. Dict. of Maine & N.H.

FRENCH

Chart I & V

Thomas French, Sr. The Elder resided Arksden, Essex Co. Eng., will proved 1551; m. Elizabeth __________. Her will proved 1556.

Children:

Elizabeth
Joane
Agnes
Thomas

Thomas French, Jr., resided Wethersfield, Essex Co., Eng., inherited the Manor Pitley from his father. His will proved 1599; m. (1) Elizabeth __________; (2) Bridget __________.

Children:

Mary
Elizabeth
Thomas

Thomas French III, was bur. at Halstead, Nov. 20, 1613. Will proved at Court of Canterbury, Jan. 27, 1614, mentions his wife Anne, sons Thomas, John, Edward, William,Robert & Francis. He left each son £ 400 and to each dau. £ 300. They had 14 children.

Thomas French III m. Anne Olmstead, dau. of John Olmstead, Gent., of Stanstead Hall, which she inherited, or got as a marriage portion. She was bur. Feb. 11, 1624-5. Her Estate Adm. by her son Edward and dau. Margaret. (Vide Reg. LXV, p. 285.)

Children:

Thomas, d. Mar. 2, 1620-1; m. Palladia Wood.
John, bur. Mar. 11, 1638; in Halstead, England.
Edward, b. Aug. 13, 1598; m. Anne Goodale; d. Dec. 28, 1674.
Lt. William, bpt. Mar. 15, 1603; will proved 1639.
Robert, d. 1660; m. (1) Edith; (2) Elizabeth Man.
Francis, b. 1606.
Mary, b. 1592; m. bef. 1621 __________ Bacon.
Anne, b. 1592
Eleanor, b. 1597; m. abt. 1630 George Gunter.
Elizabeth, b. 1600
Margaret, b. 1601; m. July 16, 1627, Samuel Dike.
Jemima, b. 1607
Judith, b. 1609; m. Edward Wyatt
Dorothy, b. 1611; m. Thomas Lewyn

The three generations above were compiled by Mabel Gertrude French Taylor, mother of Robert French Taylor, 27 Warner Rd.; Grosse Pointe Farms, Mich. 48236.

French

Edward[1] French, came from England, with his wife and children in 1636. He was founder of Ipswich, Mass., where he was a large landowner. He later removed to Salisbury, Mass. Bought land in Salisbury in 1642; selectman 1646-8. He was a "Tailor".

Edward[1] French was b. Aug. 13, 1598 at Halstead, Eng., d. Dec. 28, 1674 at Salisbury, Mass.; m. Ann Goodale in Eng. bef. 1635. She d. March 9, 1682/3 at Salisbury, Mass.; inventory of the estate April 10, 1683.

Children, all probably born in England.

Hannah, m. (1) Nov. 25, 1662 to John White of Haverill, Mass.; m. (2) Thomas Philbrook of Hampton, N.H.
Joseph, m. Susanna
John, m. March 23, 1659, Mary Noyes
Samuel, m. (1) June 1, 1664, Abigail Brown; m. (2) Esther _________. d. July 26, 1692.

References:

N.E.H.G.R. Vol. 8, p. 82; Old Families of Salisbury & Amesbury, Vol. I, p. 166; Salisbury V.R. pp. 366, 563, 564.

Samuel[2] French b. in Eng.; d. July 26, 1692 at Salisbury, Mass.; estate adm. June 28, 1693; m. June 1, 1664 to Abigail Brown. She was b. Feb. 23, 1643-4, at Salisbury, Mass., dau. of Deacon Henry & Abigail (   ) Brown. Samuel[2] French signed Salisbury petition in 1658; member of Salisbury Church 1677-87.

Abigail (Brown) French, d. Jan. 11, 1679-80. Samuel[2] French m. (2) Esther _________ (or Hester), who survived him. His estate was adm. June 28, 1693, and guardians appointed for minor children.

Children of 1st marriage:

Abigail, b. May 17, 1666.
Hannah, b. Jan. 15, 1668; m. Thomas Nelson of Rowley, Mass. d. aft. 1693.
Samuel[3], b. Jan. 24, 1670-1; d. before his father (1693)
Henry[3], b. 1673; m. Nov. 8, 1695, Elizabeth Collins - Phillip Brown appt. guardian.
Joseph[3], b. abt. 1676; d. Aug. 27, 1749 at Salisbury; m. Hannah ?
Nathaniel[3], b. Dec. 8, 1678; m. Sarah   res. Kingston, N.H.; John French of Hampton, N.H. appt. guardian for Joseph & Nathaniel.

French

Children by 2nd marriage:

Joanna, b. Dec. 16, 1683 - James Jackman appt. guardian
John[3], b. June 9, 1686; d. aft. 1693 - Richard Jackman appt. guardian.
Esther, b. Sept. 22, 1688 - Joseph Palmer (or Holmar) appt. guardian.

References:

Old Families of Salisbury, Mass., Vol. I, p. 167; Adm. estate of Samuel French, Essex Co., Mass.; Salisbury, Mass. V.R.

Joseph[3] French (Deacon) cordwainer, was b. abt. 1676; d. Aug. 27, 1749 at Salisbury, Mass., (will dated Mar. 20, 1744-5); m. Hannah ________; her maiden name and birth and death dates not known.

Children:

Abigail, b. Aug. 16, 1698;
Samuel, b. Dec. 11, 1699; d. aft. 1749; m. Nov. 23, 1721, to Mary Collins at Salisbury.
Elizabeth, b. Aug. 31, 1708.
Nathaniel, b. Aug. 2, 1702; d. Oct. 20, 1720.
Joseph, b. Sept. 15, 1713.

References:

Old Families of Salisbury & Amesbury, Vol. I, pp. 169, 170; Salisbury, Mass., V.R.; Will of Joseph[3] French, proved Sept. 18, 1749, Essex Co. Mass.

Samuel[4] French, b. Dec. 11, 1699 at Salisbury, Mass.; d. - Will proved Apr. 29, 1767 (agreement of sons & daus. Apr. 23, 1767); d. at South Hampton, N.H.; m. Mary Collins, Nov. 23, 1721 at Salisbury, Mass. She was a dau. of Samuel and Sarah (White) Collins; b. abt. 1698; d. (?) Nov. 11, 1766 at So. Hampton, N.H.

Children named in will of Samuel French:

Nathaniel[5], b. Jan. 13, 1723-4, at Salisbury, Mass.
Hezekiah[5], b. Feb. 26, 1725; d. Aug. 8, 1730; b. & d. Salisbury.
Miriam, b. Jan. 11, 1727-8 at Salisbury; m. (2) Sept. 24, 1751 at So. Hampton, N.H., Benania Dow; m. (1) ________ Gove (had son Ebenezer Gove).
Offen[5] (son) b. Mar. 28, 1729-30 at Salisbury; m. Nov. 7, 1751 at So. Hampton, N.H., Abigail French.
Mary, b. June 22, 1732 at Salisbury; m. (?) July 11, 1763, David Perkins at Kingston, N.H.

French

Children named in will of Samuel French:

Samuel[5], b. Aug. 14, 1734 at Salisbury.
Moses[5], b. Dec. 20, 1736 at Salisbury, Mass.; d. Feb. 10, 1819; m. Dec. 6, 1759 at Kensington, N.H., Mary Dearborn.
Sarah, b. Aug. 31, 1739 at Salisbury, Mass.
Levie[5], b. June 14, 1741 at Salisbury, Mass.; m. Oct. 25, 1764, at Kingston, Mass., Hannah French.
Deborah, b. March 2, 1741-2 at Salisbury; d. bef. 1767.

References:

Salisbury, Mass. V.R. to 1850; Marriage Record of Moses French & Mary Dearborn - N.H.; Birth Certificate of Mary Dearborn; Other records from N.H. Bureau of Vital Statistics.

Moses[5] French, b. Dec. 20, 1736 at So. Hampton, N.H.; d. Feb. 10, 1819; m. Dec. 6, 1759 at Kensington, N.H. by Jerimiah Fogg, Clergyman, to Mary Dearborn, dau. of Nathaniel and Mary (Batchelder) Dearborn. She was b. Jan. 16, 1739 at Kensington, N.H. (Birth reported from Hampton, N.H.); d. Jan. 9, 1818 at South Hampton, N.H.

A Moses French was in the N.H. Militia, Capt. Nathan Brown's Co., Col. David Gillman's A gt.

Children of Moses[5] and Mary (Dearborn) French, b. in So. Hampton. N.H.

Nathaniel, b. Oct. 26, 1760; d. Nov. 19, 1760.
Molly, b. June 5, 1766; m. (1) Oct. 9, 1788 at So. Hampton, N.H., Ezekiel French.
Moses, b. July 14, 1769; m. Jan. 8, 1795 at So. Hampton, to Elsey Cole.
Joseph, b. Oct. 4, 1770; m. abt. 1794 (m. int. filed March 7, 1794) at Fayette, Me., Elizabeth Ford; d. Nov. 6, 1841, age 72 at Chesterville, Maine.
Elizabeth (Liza), b. Sept. 26, 1772; m. Nov. 25, 1790 at South Hampton, N.H., to Ephriam Dow.
Sarah, b. July 25, 1774; m. Nov. 28, 1799 at So. Hampton, Thomas Fitts.
Samuel, b. Sept. 5, 1776; m. Sept. 12, 1798 at So. Hampton, Miriam French.
Dearborn, b. Jan. 16, 1779; m. Feb. 3, 1801 at So. Hampton, N.H., Anna Carr of Kensington, N.H.
John, b. July 9, 1780.
Nathan, b. May 14, 1783; m. Sept. 11, 1822 at So. Hampton, N.H. to (?) Polly Brown.

References:

So. Hampton, R.I. Vital Records; Hist. of Fayette, Me. by Underwood.

French

Joseph[6] French, b. Oct. 4, 1770 at So. Hampton, N.H.; d. Nov. 6, 1841, age 72, at Chesterville, Maine, bur. in No. Fayette Cemetery; m. (int. filed) March 7, 1794 prob. at Fayette, Me.; she was b. Jan. 30, 1771 at Marshfield, Mass., dau. of Isaac and Lucy (Josselyn) Ford; d. Nov. 17, 1855, age 84, at Chesterville, Maine; bur. No. Fayette Cemetery.

Children of Joseph and Elizabeth (Ford) French, born at Chesterville, Maine:

Nathaniel, b. March 22, 1795; d. May 27, 1814 at Chesterville.
Moses, b. Nov. 27, 1796; d. Feb. 15, 1882 at Chesterville.
Joseph, b. Nov. 20, 1799; d. Nov. 15, 1800 at Chesterville.
Isaac, b. Oct. 20, 1801; d. Feb. 28, 1879 at Chesterville; m. (1) Elizabeth _______; m. (2) Abigail _________.
Seth, b. Feb. 25, 1804; d. Apr. 8, 1806.
Lucy, b. July 26, 1805; d. Sept. 18, 1886 at Murray, Ind., m. Benjamin Franklin Bryant, July 3, 1832.
Sarah, b. Jan. 25, 1808; d. Dec. 9, 1858 at Chesterville; m. __________ Bryant.
Harriet, b. July 10, 1809; m. ___________ Stevens.
Nancy, b. Sept. 27, 1813; d. May 2, 1859 at Chesterville, Me.

References:

Town Records from C.A. Thomas, Town Clerk, Chesterville, Me., June 24, 1964; Will of Joseph French dated Dec. 20, 1839, Chesterville, Franklin Co., Me.; Hist. of Fayette, Me., by Underwood, p. 108; Unpublished Manuscript by Dr. Frank E. Weeks, Huron Co., Ohio.

GILMAN

Charts XVI & XXV

Edward[1] Gilman, b. abt. 1587, near Hingham, Co. Norfolk, Eng.; d. Estate Adm. Apr. 10, 1655 at Exeter, N.H.; m. Mary Clarke on June 3, 1614 at Hingham, Eng. She d. June 22, 1681 at Hingham, Mass.

Edward[1] Gilman came from Gravesend, Eng., in the Deligent of Ipswich, Aug. 10, 1638, with a large party led by Rev. Robert Peck, with wife, 3 sons, 2 daus., and 3 servants. Freeman, Mar. 13, 1638-9. Partner with Hingham men in large grant at Rehoboth 1641, by 1650 he had sold there to Joseph Peck, the younger, whom his sons John & Moses called 'cozen' in 1663.

Edward[1] Gilman, resided at Hingham, Mass.; Ipswich, Mass., and Exeter, N.H. He was Selectman at Ipswich, 1649.

Gilman

He deeded his entire estate, with the exception of £30 each to sons John and Moses, to wife Mary, 14 Jan. 1654-5, effective at his death. Adm. to her 10 Apr. 1655, the sons and sons-in-law agreeing to distribute according to his deed. Widow Mary signed a q.c. deed, 7 Mar. 1663, apparently at Hingham, Mass.

Children:

Mary, bpt. Aug. 6, 1615, at Hingham, Eng.; m. John Folson.
Edward, bpt. Dec. 26, 1617; d. abt 1653; m. bef. Sept. 28, 1647, Elizabeth Smith, dau. of Richard Smith of Ipswich, Mass.
Sarah, bpt. Dec. 26, 1617.
Moses, bpt. Sept. 15, 1619; d. Sept. 19, 1619.
Joshua, bpt. Sept. 15, 1619; d. Sept. 19, 1619.
Lydia, d. Mar. 12, 1688-9; m. Jan. 19, 1644-5, at Hingham, Mass., Daniel Cushman.
John, b. Jan. 10, 1624; d. July 24, 1708; m. June 30, 1657, Elizabeth Treworgy, dau. of James Treworgy, at Exeter, N.H.
Jeremy, bpt. Nov. 27, 1628; bur. 1635.
Moses (again), bpt. Mar. 11, 1630; d. abt. 1702; m. Elizabeth Hershey.
Sarah, bpt. Jan. 19, 1632-3; d. May 26, 1700; m. Dec. 16, 1646, Deacon John Leavitt.
Daniel, bur. Apr. 21, 1634.

The Plymouth Company granted Edward[1] Gilman, a parcel of land near the R.I. state line. A tract of land eight miles square called "Seekonk", granted to him in 1641.

Edward[1] Gilman was a gr. son of Edward and Rose (Rysse) Gilman of Caston, Eng., through their son Edward b. Apr. 20, 1557. This is a very ancient family.

References:

The Story of Gilmans, by Constance LeNeve Gilman Ames; Gen. Dict. of Maine & N.H. Vol. 3, p. 262; Mayflower Desc., 25:65; 26:103.

HACKETT

Chart I & IV

Jabez Hackett, b. abt. 1623 or 24 in Eng., d. Nov. 4, 1686 at Taunton, Mass.; m. Frances ________, bef. 1654. She was b. abt. 1632; d. after Mar. 21, 1695-6. Jabez Hackett, was in Lynn, Mass., in 1644.

Children, b. at Taunton:

1. John, b. Dec. 26, 1654 at Taunton, Mass; d. 1712; m. Sept. 10, 1688 to Elenor Gardner at Taunton, Mass.
2. Jabez, b. Sept. 12, 1656;
3. Mary, b. Jan. 9, 1659;
4. Sarah, b. July 13, 1661; m. Dec. 18, 1689, Edward Cobb, at Taunton, Mass.

Hackett

Children, b. at Taunton:

5. Samuel, b. July 29, 1664; m. Mar. 18, 1690 to Mary Crane, at Taunton, Mass.
6. Hannah, b. Jan. 25, 1666; m. Jan. 14, 1684/5 to Robert Godfrey, at Taunton, Mass.

References:

Mayflower Desc. Vol. 18, p. 166; Taunton, Mass. V.R. Vol. I, p. 191; Vol. 2, p. 213; Vol. 3, p. 94; Gen. Dict. of N.E. Vol. 2, p. 326; Ancient Taunton, p. 7; Essex Co. Mass. Quarterly Court Files 1:61;70;82;83; 107; 136; 229; Suffolk Co. Deeds 1:54; Emery's Hist. of Taunton, pp. 93, 330; Plymouth Co. Court Recs. 5:228; Proprietors Records of Taunton, Oct. 14, 1684 and Aug. 18, 1686.

John[2] Hackett, b. in Taunton, Mass., Dec. 26, 1654; d. prob. Oct. 1703 - a John Hackett of Middleboro was found in a grist mill at Taunton. He had fallen through a hole in the stair, was carried to the next house and died soon after. A jury said John Hackett was "killed or came to his death by misfortune". The inquest was held at Taunton Oct. 25, 1703. (Suffolk Co. Court Records #5919.)

Administration of his estate Aug. 27, 1712. His son John[3] Hackett was appointed administrator.

John[2] Hackett m. in Taunton, Sept. 10, 1688, Eleanor Gardner. She was probably the Eleanor Hackett of Middleboro whose marriage to William Cleaves of Sandwich, Mass., took place Dec. 1, 1707 at Bridgewater, Mass. Hist. of Middleboro, Mass., by Weston, p. 656 - 1st Church Records, shows that Eleanor Cleaves had a grandchild baptized there in 1721 "bro't by her". Inasmuch as John[2] and Eleanor (Gardner) Hackett were married in 1688 it doesn't appear that a daughter Eleanor, even if they had one, could have had a grandchild baptized in 1721. Yet Eleanor (Gardner) Hackett, could easily have had a grandchild by 1721 (See John[3] Hackett).

Children of John[2] and Eleanor Gardner Hackett:

John[3] Hackett, b. abt. 1689.
Perhaps others.

References:

Plymouth Co. Probate, 8839; Suffolk Co. Court Records #5919; Taunton, Mass. V.R.   ; Bridgewater, Mass, V.R.   ; Hist. of Middleboro, Mass. by Weston, p. 656.

Hackett

Deacon John^3 Hackett was a selectman of Middleboro, Mass. He was b. Sept. 12, 1689; m. (1) Elizabeth Elliott, May 18, 1711; m. (2) Mrs. Elizabeth Richmond, Sept. 5, 1728; m. (3) Priscilla Richmond abt. 1636, daughter of Capt. Edward Richmond who m. (2) Rebecca Thurston.

Children by 1st wife:

John, b. Apr. 17, 1712; d. May 31, 1712 at Middleboro, Mass.
Edmond, b. May 5, 1713;
Alice, b. Jan. 17, 1714-15; m. Nov. 2, 1732 to (1) Nathaniel Richmond; (2) _____________ Finney.
Hannah, b. Apr. 1, 1716; m. Nov. 7, 1734 to Benjamin Waldron.
Elijah, b. Feb. 13, 1718/19; m. bef. 1745, Prudence^5 Richmond (Edw.^{4,3} John^{2,1}); d. at Middleboro, Apr. 11, 1802.
Elizabeth, b. May 19, 1720; m. Oct. 6, 1743, Joseph Richmond, Jr. (Joseph^{4,3} John^{2,1}).
(?) Elinor, b. abt. 1721-2; m. Jacob Borden, Apr. 1, 1742, both of Middleboro.
Thankful, b. Jan. 26, 1724-5; d. Feb. 5, 1724-5 at Middleboro.
John (again) b. March 1, 1725-6.
Benjamin, b. March 1, 1725-6; m. Dec. 5, 1747 to Mercy^5 Richmond (Josiah^4, Edw.^{3}, John^{2,1})
A daughter, b. Jan. 15, 1727-8; d. Jan. 16, 1727-8.

No children by 2nd wife.

Children by 3rd wife Priscilla Richmond:

Ephriam, b. abt. 1737-8; m. (1) Abigail Leonard, on June 18, 1761; she d. March 19, 1762; m. (2) May 14, 1764, at Middleboro, Elizabeth Paddock, dau. Joseph and Elizabeth (Mayo) Paddock; d. 1820 at New Vineyard, Maine.

References:

Richmond Family Gen., by Joshua Baily Richmond, pp. 27-28; Mayflower Desc. V. 5, p. 38, V. 8, pp. 226, 228, 241; Will of John Hackett, Yeoman - dated Nov. 2, 1763, proved Jan. 4, 1768 - Plymouth Co., Mass.

Epriam^4 Hackett, b. abt. 1737-8; m. (1) Abigail Leonard, June 18, 1761; she d. March 19, 1762; m. (2) May 14, 1764, at Middleboro, Mass., Elizabeth Paddock, dau. of Joseph and Elizabeth (Mayo) Paddock; d. 1820 at New Vineyard, Maine. She d. abt. 1812, age 72 at Middleboro.

Children of Epriam & Elizabeth (Paddock) Hackett:

Child stillborn, bur. May 8, 1771.
Simeon, b. abt. 1772; m. Dec. 3, 1793, Nabby (Abigail) Leonard; d. Apr. 15, 1846 at New Vineyard, Maine.
Edmond, b. Jan. 15, 1766.
Bathsheba, b. 1776; d. Oct. 19, 1816 at New Vineyard, Maine; m. May 7, 1798 at Middleboro, Mass., to her first cousin, Rev. Elias Bryant. He was a son of Micah and Margaret (Paddock) Bryant.

Hackett

Children of Epriam & Elizabeth (Paddock) Hackett: (con't)

Elizabeth, b. abt. 1781; d. Sept. 25, 1854 at New Vineyard, Maine; m. David Pratt.

References:

Taunton, Mass., Vital Records, Vol. II p. 213; Richmond Family by Joshua B. Richmond, pp. 27, 28; New Vineyard, Maine, Grave Records - typed copy - Me. Hist. Gen. Soc. pp. 132; Mayflower Desc., V. 24; p. 132, 56; V. 30, p. 6; V. 25, p. 88; Family Records; Hackett by Dr. Lewis Wendell Hackett, Mss.

HALL

Chart III

John[1] Hall came in 1630 from Coventry, probably with Winthrop Fleet; No. 19 on the list of members of Boston Church and one of the founders; in Charlestown, with wife Bethiah in 1632; freeman May 14, 1634; removed to Barnstable where he was Constable; later removed to Yarmouth. He was Surveyor of Highways and a member of the Grand Inquest of Yarmouth.

John[1] Hall was b. 1609; d. July 23, 1696 at Yarmouth, Mass.; m. Bethiah _________ before 1637.

Children:

Samuel; m. Eliz Pollard.
John, bapt. May 13, 1638; d. Oct. 24, 1710; m. 1660, Priscilla Bearce.
Shebar, b. Jan. 9, 1640.
Joseph,
William,
Benjamin,
Elisha,
Nathaniel,
Gershom,

References:

Hist. of Yarmouth, Mass., by Swift, p. 61; The Winthrop Fleet of 1630 by Banks, p. 73.

John[2] Hall b. 1637 at Charlestown, Mass.; d. at Yarmouth Oct. 14, 1710, aged 73 yrs.; bur. on old homestead at Dennis, Mass.; m. 1660, Priscilla Bearce. She was b. March 10, 1643 at at Barnstable; d. March 30, 1712 at Yarmouth, Mass. She was a daughter of Austin and Mary Bearce.

Hall

Mary Bearce is said to have been a flaming haired Indian Princess and Austin Bearce, a gypsy.

Children of John[2] and Priscilla (Bearce) Hall:

John, b. 1661; d. in infancy.
Deacon Joseph, b. Sept. 29, 1663 at Yarmouth; d. Jan. 29, 1737; m. (1) Feb. 12, 1689, Hannah Miller; m. (2) Mary (Faunce) Morton, widow of John Morton.
John, b. 1666 at Yarmouth; d. March 21, 1734-5; m. Apr. 30, 1694, Margaret Miller.
twins (Priscilla, b. Nov. 15, 1668; d. in infancy - at Yarmouth.
(Bethiah, b. Nov. 15, 1668 in Yarmouth; d. Mar. 8, 1708-9; m. Zachariah Paddock, son of Zachariah and Deborah (Sears) Paddock.
Priscilla, b. at Yarmouth Feb. 1671; d. at Yarmouth, Jan. 2, 1725; m. 1694 to Capt. John Paddock, son of Zachariah and Deborah (Sears) Paddock.
Esther, b. at Yarmouth, Apr. 1672; m. 1691 John Rider.
Mary, b. Mar. 1, 1674.
Martha, b. Mar. 24, 1676; m. Mar. 6, 1701-2, Robert Paddock, son of Zachariah and Deborah (Sears) Paddock.
Nathaniel, b. Sept. 15, 1678; m. Aug. 29, 1710 Jane Moore, widow; removed to Lewistown, Penn.
Experience, b. Dec. 1683 at Yarmouth; m. Mar. 22, 1705 Ebenezer Rider.
Barshua, b. at Yarmouth Apr. 1685; m. Oct. 29, 1709, Joseph Crowell of Nobschussett, son of John and Bethiah (Sears) Crowell.

References:

Bearce Genealogy by Meadows & Ames, in N.E.H.G. Library, Boston, pp. 1-10 Inclu.;

HAMPSON

Chart XIII

Philip Hampson, Clothier of London, Eng., made his will June 2, 1654; will proved July 4, 1654; he was buried at the Parish Church of St. Michael Queenhithe, London. He m. Ann _______.

Children:

Beatrice, b. abt. 1623; m. (1) Abraham Josselyn; m. (2) Serg. Benjamin Bosworth of Hull, Mass.
Hannah, m. Hugh Phillips.

References:

Josselyn Fam. Gen. by Edith S. Wessler; Gen. Gleanings of Eng. by Waters, Vol. I, p. 765.

HASKELL

Chart XIII

William Haskell of Salem and Gloucester, Mass., was bapt. Nov. 8, 1618 in Eng., d. Aug. 20, 1693 at Gloucester, Mass. - will dated July 3, 1692; proved Sept. 4, 1693; m. Nov. 6, 1643 at Gloucester, Mass. to Mary Tybott, dau. of Walter and _______ Tybott. She d. Aug. 16, 1693 at Gloucester.

William Haskell was a Selectman at Gloucester for several years, and representative to the General Court six times, in the course of twenty years. In 1681 he was appointed the General Court, lieutenant to the train band, of which he was afterwards appointed Captain. He was also a deacon of the First Church, -one of the first two known Deacons.

William Haskell came with his brothers Roger and Mark. The family is said to be descended from a companion of William the Conqueror, and to be of Norman French stock. William Haskell was a Mariner engaged in fishing.

Children of William and Mary (Tybott) Haskell:

1. William, b. Aug. 26, 1644 at Gloucester; d. June 5, 1708 at Gloucester; m. Mary Walker, dau. of William Brown, but she took the name of her step-father Henry Walker.
2. Joseph, b. June 2, 1646 at Gloucester; d. Nov. 12, 1727 in his 82nd yr. at Gloucester; m. Dec. 2, 1674 to Mary Graves, dau. of Marke Graves of Andover.
3. Benjamin, b. abt. 1648; m. (?) Nov. 21, 1677 to Mary Riggs.
4. John, b. abt. 1648; m. (?) May 20, 1665, Mary Baker, d. (?) Feb. 2, 1717-18.
5. Ruth, b. abt. 1654; m. 2-10m-1676, Nehemiah Grover
6. Mark, b. Apr. 8, 1658 at Gloucester; d. Sept. 8, 1691, at Gloucester; m. Dec. 16, 1685 at Gloucester, Mass. to Elizabeth Giddings.
7. Sarah, b. June 28, 1660 at Gloucester; d. (?) Mar. 4, 1690-1, at Gloucester; m. (?) Feb. 5, 1684 at Gloucester, Edward Haraden.
8. Mary, b. June 28, 1660; d. Feb. 13, 1737 at Beverly, Mass., m. Feb. 13, 1737 at Beverly, Edward Dodge, son of Richard and Edith (   ) Dodge.
9. Elenor, b. May 28, 1663 at Gloucester; m. Jacob Griggs of Beverly, Mass., Nov. 12, 1685.

References:

Hist. of Gloucester, Mass., by Babson; Notes & Additions to Hist. of Gloucester, by Babson; American Gen. Vol. 21, p. 436; N.E.H.G.R. Vol. 4, p. 363; Gloucester, Mass. V.R. Vol. 1, pp. 329, 330 - Vol. 2 pp. 265, 266 - Vol. 3, p. 162; Beverly, Mass. V.R., Vol. 2, p. 423.

HATCH

Charts VII & XXXVI

John the younger Hatch (Thomas b. 1465, d. betw. Dec. 12, 1530 and Dec. 31, 1534; Thomas b. 1442; John b. abt. 1415 m. Agnes, d. not earlier than Nov. 15, 1464), b. abt. 1495; died betw. Apr. 13, 1535 & Apr. 26, 1536.

Child:

Thomas, b. abt. 1525; d. bef. Oct. 13, 1568; m. Joan abt. 1552; adm. of estate to widow Oct. 13, 1568. His widow Joan, m. (2) bef. Oct. 25, 1574, Richard Brissendon.

Child:

William, b. Dec. 9, 1563; d. bef. Feb. 13, 1627-8; m. Ann, abt. 1593.

Child:

Elder William[1] Hatch b. abt. 1598 at Sandwich, Co. Kent, Eng.; d. Nov. 6, 1651 at Scituate, Mass.; m. (2) Jane Young, License to Marry July 9, 1624, Thorington, Eng. She m. (2) March 6, 1651 Elder William King of Scituate, Mass. She was b. abt. 1596.

The Hatch family is of Anglo Saxon origin and has been traced back to John at Heeche of Salinge in the hundred of Street, Co. Kent, Eng. 1464.

Elder William[1] Hatch came over in the "Hercules" 1635, brought 5 children and 6 servants. He came to America, first, before 1633, stayed two years then returned to Eng. to get his family. He was the first ruling Elder of the Second Church of Scituate founded in 1644; Representative from Scituate 1645. William Hatch was a Merchant Planter.

Children:

Walter[2], b. abt. 1625 in Eng.; d. May 24, 1699; m. Elizabeth Holbrook May 6, 1650, at Scituate, Mass.
Jane, m. John Lovell.
Ann, m. Lieut. James Torrey, Nov. 2, 1643 at Scituate, Mass.
Hannah, m. Samuel Utley, Dec. 29, 1657 (Scituate V.R. Dec. 6, 1658)
Jerimiah[2], d. 1713; m. Mary Hewes, Dec. 29, 1657 at Scituate, Mass.

References:

Scituate V.R. Vol. 1:174, 177; Vol. 2, pp. 141-145, 396; N.E.H.G.R. Vol. 25, pp. 124, 388 ; N.E. Families, Vo. I, p. 299; N.E.H.G.R. 70:245 & 160; 75: 219; May. Desc. 2:33, 34, 171; N.E.H.G.R. 4:320 (Plymouth, Mass. Wills)

Hatch

Walter[2] Hatch, b. abt. 1625 in Eng.; d. May 24, 1699, at Scituate, Mass.; m. (1) Elizabeth Holbrooke, May 6, 1650 at Scituate, Mass. She was a daughter of Thomas and Jane ( ) Holbrooke of Weymouth, Mass.; b. 1634 at Broadway Dorsetshire, Eng.; d. 1674 at Scituate, Mass.

Walter[2] Hatch, was a Shipwright. With his brother Jeremiah, he bought land in what is now Hanover, Mass. Most of the Hatch families in Hanover, are descended from Walter[2] Hatch. He was Constable at Scituate in 1653; m. (2) Aug. 5, 1675, Mary Stable at Marshfield, Mass.

Children born in Scituate, Mass.

Hannah, b. March 13, 1651-2.
Samuel, b. Dec. 22, 1653; d. June 1735; m. aft. July 10, 1677, Mary Doty, daughter of Edward Dotey.
Jane, b. March 7, 1655-6; m. 1677 to John Sherman of Marshfield.
Antipas, b. Oct. 26, 1658; d. Dec. 7, 1705 at Scituate, Mass.
John, b. July 8, 1664; d. July 20, 1737, age 73, at Scituate.
Bethiah, b. Mar. 31, 1661; d. Aug. 1737; m. Dec. 30, 1696, Michael Ford of Marshfield, Mass.
Israel, b. March 25, 1667; d. Oct. 1740 at Marshfield; m. Elizabeth Hatch, a 2nd cousin, July 27, 1699 at Scituate.
Joseph, b. Dec. 9, 1669; m. (?) ; d. July 20, 1737 at Marshfield, Mass.

References:

Scituate, V.R. Vol. I, pp. 171-177; Vol. 2, pp. 142-145; N.E.H.G.R. Vol. V, pp. 111, 112, 113; N.E. Families Vol. 1, p. 299.

HEALD

Chart X & X a

John[1] Heald, b. in Eng.; d. May 24, 1662, Concord, Mass. (Will dated Apr. 19 - Prob. June 16, 1662); m. (1) Dec. 3, 1636 at Alderly, Cheshire Parish, Eng., Dorothy Royal; m. (2) Dorothy Andrews, prob. abt. 1644-45. She d. Oct. 29, 1694 at Dedham, Mass.

In his will, John[1] Heald, mentions his three "eldest children that is to say John my eldest son and Timothy and my daughter Hannah", also "to my five younger children ------------ said children by my loving wife Dorothy".

John[1] Heald was freeman June 2, 1641.

Heald

Children of John[1] Heald:

John[2], bpt. Mar. 1637 at Alderly, Eng.; d. June 17, 1689 at Concord, Mass.; m. June 10, 1661 at Concord, to Sarah Dane.
Timothy[2], b. abt. 1638; d. July 26, 1689; m. Sarah Barber (?), abt. 1663 (Timothy Hale of Windsor Conn. to Suffield, Conn.) Mentioned in his father's will.
Hannah, b. 1640; d. Aug. 14, 1689; m. John Spaulding of Chelmsford, Mass., May 1658 (m. rec. Hannah Hale).
Doras, b. Mar. 22, 1645; d. Mar. 1, 1650; b. & d. Concord, Mass.
Gershom[2], b. Jan. 23, 1647; d. May 13, 1717, Springfield, Mass.; m. May 6, 1673, Ann Vinton, at Concord, Mass.
Dorothy, b. Aug. 16, 1649.
Thomas[2], b. Jan. 19, 1651; d. Apr. 22, 1725; m. (1) abt. 1675, Priscilla Markham of Hadley, Mass., m. (2) Sarah (Patch) Osborn, dau. of John Patch of Salem.
Isaac[2], b. 1656; d. June 1, 1717; m. Elizabeth ________.
Israel[2], b. July 30, 1660 at Concord; d. Sept. 8, 1738 at Stow, Mass.; m. Martha Wright, dau. of Edward[1] & Elizabeth (Mellowes) (Barrett) Wright, abt. 1685 or 86.

References:

Pope's Pioneers of Mass.; Concord, Mass. V.R. pp. 4, 5, 9, 10, 55; The American Genealogist, Vol. 10, p. 15; Stow, Mass., V.R.

John[2] Heald, bapt. Mar. 1636/37 at Alderly, Eng.; d. June 17, 1689 at Concord, Mass.; m. June 10, 1661 at Concord, Mass., Sarah Dane, dau. Thomas and Elizabeth (   ) Dane. She was born (prob.) 24 (12) 1642 at Concord, Mass.; d. July 22, 1689 at Concord.

John[2] Heald was freeman 1680; termed Sarg^{nt} in death record.

Children b. at Concord:

Elizabeth, b. Apr. 15, 1664; d. June 13, 1699; m. June 9, 1690 Thomas Chamberlain.
John[3], b. Sept. 19, 1666; d. Nov. 25, 1721 at Concord; m. Dec. 18, 1690 at Concord, Mary Chandler.
Gershom[3], b. Mar. 1, 1667-8; d. May 13, 1717 at Springfield, Mass.; m. Hannah Parlin.
Sarah, b. Dec. 18, 1670;
Eunis, b. Mar. 15, 1673; m. Joseph Butterfield of Chelmsford.
Hannah, b. Oct. 10, 1676; d. Nov. 11, 1755; m. Nov. 15, 1699, Richard Stevens at Chelmsford.
Dorothy, b. May 10, 1679; m. Mar. 3, 1701, Joseph Fletcher, at Chelmsford.

References:

Concord, Mass. V.R., pp. 10,11,12,14,15,17,55.; Heald Manuscript by Clarence Torrey - N.E.H.G.R.

Heald

Lieut. John[3] Heald, b. Sept. 19, 1666 at Concord, Mass.; d. Nov. 25, 1721, age 55, at Concord; m. Dec. 18, 1690 at Concord, Mary Chandler, dau. Roger and Mary (Simonds) Chandler. She was b. Jan. 7, 1671-2 at Concord; d. Aug. 14, 1759, age 88th yr. She is buried in the Old Burying Ground at Concord.

April 19, 1689, the Concord Co., under Lieut. John Heald, marched to Boston and helped execute the order of the Representatives, signed by Ebenezer Prout, for removal of Andros to the Castle.

Children of Lieut. John[3] & Mary (Chandler) Heald, b. at Concord.

Mary, b. Aug. 18, 1691; m. May 12, 1718, John Parling.
John[4], b. Aug. 18, 1693; d. May 16, 1775 at Acton, Mass.; m. (1) Mary Hale (or Heald) in 1716; m. (2) Elizabeth (Jones) Wright at Acton.
Timothy, b. June 7, 1696; d. Mar. 28, 1736 at Concord; m. 1721, to Hannah _________.
Josiah, b. Feb. 28, 1698-9; m. Sarah Remington.
Elizabeth, b. Dec. 12, 1701; m. Zachariah Emery.
Sam[ll], b. May 4, 1705; d. Apr. 17, 1784.
Amos, b. May 13, 1708; d. Jan. 4, 1775; m. Elizabeth Billings.
Ephriam, b. Feb. 19, 1710-11; m. Elenor Robbins of Chelmsford int. Feb. 25, 1732-3 (he is given as of Townsend). They went to Maine in 1765.
Dorcas, b. Aug. 22, 1713; m. (1) William Fletcher of Townsend, at Concord, June 28, 1734; m. (2) Jonathan Fisk, May 18,1763.
Eunice, b. 1717; d. Jan. 17, 1795; m. July 16, 1735 Deacon Samuel Fellows of Concord, Mass.

References:

Concord, Mass. V.R. pp. 34,35,38,42,47,52,63,71,77,82,205,104;
Middlesex Co., Hist. of by D. Hamilton Hurd, 1890 - p. 577;
Heald Manuscript, N.E.H.G.S., Boston - by Clarence Torrey.

Deacon John[4] Heald, b. Aug. 18, 1693 at Concord, Mass.; d. May 16, 1775, in 82nd yr., at Acton, Mass.; m. (1) Mary Hale abt. 1716. She was b. April 27, 1698 at Concord, dau. of Israel[2] and Martha (Wright) Heald; d. at Acton Sept. 1, 1758. Mary Hale was a first cousin of Lieut. John[3] Heald, father of John[4] Heald.

Deacon John[4] Heald was first Selectman of Acton, after its incorporation (July 21, 1735); chosen Deacon of the 1st Church , Dec. 15, 1738; was a member of committee to contract for a minister.

Deacon John[4] Heald, m. (2) at Acton, Elizabeth (Jones) Wright of Concord, int. Nov. 10, 1759.

Heald

Children of John[4] and Mary (Heald) Heald, b. at Concord.

Martha, b. Apr. 4, 1718; d. Feb. 26, 1795, age 77, at Carlisle, Mass.; m. May 24, 1738, John Barrett of Chelmsford, Mass., at Concord.
John[5], b. Feb. 14, 1720-21; d. Oct. 10, 1810; m. July 18, 1745, Elizabeth Barrett at Chelmsford, Mass.
Mary, b. June 14, 1719; d. April 6, 1794; m. May 24, 1738 at Chelmsford, Mass., Jonas Robbins.
Sarah, b. Nov. 2, 1722; d. Nov. 11, 1746; m. Jan. 1, 1744, Jonas Hildreth of Chelmsford, Mass.
Joseph, b. Sept. 12, 1724; d. unmarried in Indian War.
Lydia, b. Nov. 12, 1726; m. ?Jacob Robbins of Westford, at Acton, Nov. 25, 1749.
Oliver, b. July 24, 1729; d. Sept. 23, 1733 at Concord.
Dorothy, b. Nov. 25, 1731; m. (int.) Apr. 28, 1753, Nehemiah Davis of Concord, at Acton, Mass.
Oliver (again) b. Apr. 6, 1734; d. Jan. 21, 1790; m. Dec. 2 1760, Lydia Spaulding of Townsend, Mass. (Oliver was given as "of Sliptown", now Sharon, N.H.
Israel, b. Aug. 16, 1736; d. 1815; m. Dec. 30, 1760, Susannah Robbins.
Ruth, b. Mar. 1, 1739; d. Jan. 4, 1801;m. Sept. 1, 1759, James Faulkner.
Asa, died young.

References:

Concord, Mass. V.R. pp. 33,103,112,118, 122,127; Acton, Mass. V.R. p. 276; 182. Heald Manuscript in N.E.H.G.S. Library, Boston, by Clarence A. Torrey.

HEALD

Chart X

Israel[2] Heald, son of John[1] and Dorothy Andrews Heald, b. July 30, 1660 at Concord, Mass.; d. Sept. 8, 1738 at Stow, Mass., bur. at Stow, Mass.; m. Martha Wright, dau. Edward & Elizabeth (Mellowes) (Barrett) Wright. She was b. June 18, 1659 at Concord, Mass.; d. June 14, 1746 at Stow, Mass.

Several of the children of Israel[2] Heald adopted the name "Hale". His son Benjamin[3] Heald is buried in Stow, Mass., in the same lot as his father, under the name of Hale. Mary Heald, his daughter, m. her father's great nephew as "Mary Hale."

Children:

Oliver, b. Sept. 8, 1686 at Stow, Mass.; m. Hannah Gates.
Israel, b. Dec. 2, 1687; m. Rachel Buttrick.
Joseph, b. 1689; m. Mercy Brown.
Dorothy, b. 1692; m.
Mary, b. Apr. 27, 1698 at Concord, Mass.; m. abt. 1716, John[4] Heald, her father's great nephew; d. at Acton, Mass., Sept. 1, 1758.
Benjamin, b. 1704; m. Keziah Whitney; d. Nov. 16, 1776, age 72 yrs. 3 mo. 21 days.

Heald

References:

Mdx. Co. Mass. Gen. & Pers. Memoirs by Cutler 1:172; Concord, V.R.; Stow, Mass. V.R.; Bulkeley Genealogy by Donald Lines Jacobus; Heald Genealogy by Clarence A. Torrey at N.E.H.G.S. Library.

HEARD

Chart XI

John[1] Heard, b. 1613; d. Jan. 17, 1688-9 at Dover, N.H. (will dated Apr. 2, 1687 - proved 1692); m. 1643 at York, Me.; Elizabeth Hull, dau. Rev. Joseph and Joanna (Coffin (?)) Hull. She was b. 1626 at North Leigh, Devonshire, Eng.; d. Nov. 30, 1706, prob. at Dover.

John[1] Heard was a commander of ships in the foreign trade of Dover, N.H., while in business connection with Capt. Richard Waldron. He was a Proprietor & Selectman; joined in petition of Dover inhabitants to Gen. Court, Oct. 10, 1665.

John[1] Heard had a Garrison House at Dover, N.H. Of the five Garrisons there, his was the only one saved in the massacre of June 28, 1689, being successfully defended by his widow Elizabeth (Hull) Heard. Although urged to secure safety in Portsmouth after the massacre, she continued stoutly to hold her frontier Garrison all through the War. She d. Nov. 30, 1706. Pike's Journal says "Old Widow Heard (commonly called Dame Heard) deceased after a short illness with fever. She was a grave and pious woman, even the mother of virtue and piety."

Children, prob. all born at Dover, N.H.

Benjamin, b. Feb. 20, 1643-4; d. Feb. 1710; m. Elizabeth Roberts, dau. of Gov. Thomas Roberts of Dovers Neck, N.H.
William, b. bef. 1655; d. abt. 1675; left widow but no child.
Mary, b. Jan. 26, 1649-50; m. May 6, 1669, John Ham of Dover.
Abigail, b. Aug. 2, 1651; m. Jenkin Jones of Dover.
Elizabeth, b. Sept. 15, 1653; m. (1) James Nute, Jr.; (2) Wm. Furbur, Jr.
Hannah, b. Nov. 22, or 25, 1655; m. Nov. 6, 1674, John Nason.
John[2], b. Feb. 24, 1658-9; d. bef. April 2, 1687 as he is not mentioned in his father's will, however, he was on the tax list in 1675.
Joseph[2], b. Jan. 4, 1660-1; d. before Apr. 2, 1687 as he is not mentioned in his father's will.
Samuel[2], b. Aug. 4, 1663; d. Feb. 20, 1695-6; m. 1686 Experience Otis, dau. Richard & Rachel Otis; widow Experience (Otis) Heard, scalped by Indians July 26, 1696.

Heard

Children of John[1] Heard (con't)

Tristram[2], b. Mar. 4, 1666-7; d. 1734; m. 1691 Abigail (possibly Waldron).
Nathaniel[2], b. Sept. 20, 1668; d. Apr. 3, 1700; m. Sarah _____. She m. (2) April 26, 1703, William Foss.
Dorcas, b. 1670; m. Jabez Garland.

References:

Old Families of Salisbury & Amesbury by Hoyt, Vol. I p. 199; Hist. of Dover, N.H. pp. 446 to 450; Pope's Pioneers of Maine & N.H. pp. 92,93; Gen. Dict. of Maine & N.H. by Noyes, Libby & Davis, Part 3, p. 322.

Lieut. Tristram[2] Heard, b. March 4, 1666-7 at Dover, N.H.; d. - made his will Apr. 18, 1734 - will prob. June 3, 1734; m. 1690, Abigail Waldron (?). She d. after her husband.

Tristram[2] Heard, was Lieut., N.H. Militia 1725, and was Capt. in Command of"Heard's Garrison" at Dover, N.H. (Soc. Col. Wars). He was Constable at Dover 1698, and Selectman 1700-1.

In 1711, on a Sabbath day, several people were ambushed as they were returning from meeting, and John Horn was wounded and Humphrey Foss was taken Captive "but by the determined bravery of Tristram Heard he was recovered out of the hands of the enemy".

Children of Tristram[2] Heard:

Joseph[3] of Dover & Rochester, b. Feb. 15, 1692-3; m. Aug. 9, 1722, Rebecca Richards of Newington.
Tristram[3], b. Mar. 26, 1695; was killed by Indians, Summer of 1723; m. Jane Snell. She m. (2) Benjamin Hayes.
Nathaniel[3], b. Jan. 26, 1676-7; d. Oct. 1733; m. Dec. 18, 1718, Margaret Warren of Berwick.
John[3], b. Jan. 1, 1700; d. 1765; m. bef. 1735, Charity Day.
Abigail, b. Apr. 15, 1702; d. by Apr. 1734 - not mentioned in father's will.
Samuel[3], b. Feb. 28, 1703-4; d. June 1, 1756; m. bef. 1729, Dorcas _________.
Elizabeth, b. Feb. 8, 1706-7; m. 1729, Robert Knight.
Mary, b. June 10, 1709; m. John Warren.
Keziah, b. Dec. 1, 1712; m. (1) Spencer Wentworth of Dover; (2) Capt. Thomas Pierce of Portsmouth, N.H.

References:

Hist. of Dover, N.H. by Scales Vol. I pp. 451, 453; Gen. Dict. Maine & N.H. Part III, p. 323.

HIGGINS

Chart III

Richard[1] Higgins d. bef. June 5, 1677 at Piscataway, N.J.; m. (1) Dec. 11, 1634 (or Nov. 23) at Eastham, Mass., Lydia Chandler, dau. of Edmund Chandler of Duxbury & Scituate. She d. by 1650; m. (2) Mary, wid. of John Yates, Oct. 1651.

Richard[1] Higgins was one of the seven original settlers of Eastham, Mass. 1654; Juryman Aug. 7, 1638 at Plymouth; was a Tailor; settled in N.J. before 1668.

Children by 1st wife:

Benjamin b. July 1640; m. Dec. 24, 1661 at Eastham, Lydia Bangs.
Jonathan b. at Plymouth, July 1637; m. (1) Elizabeth Rogers, dau. Joseph Rogers (Thomas[1]); m. (2) Hannah Rogers, sister of his 1st wife.

Children by 2nd wife:

Thomas, b. Jan. 1651;
Eliakim, b. Oct. 20, 1654;
William, b. Dec. 15, 1655;
Jediaiah, b. Mar. 1656; m. Mary Newbold of Burlington, N.J.
Ezra, b. June 1658 at Eastham.
Zerah, b. at Eastham; m. 1680 Elizabeth Oliver at Piscataway, N.J.
Thomas, b. at Eastham, Jan. 1661-62; m. Elizabeth Hull.
Lydia, b. July 1664.
Rebecca, b. at Eastham (or poss. Piscataway, N.J.) 1666; m. Thomas Martin at Piscataway, N.J. abt. 1683.
Ruth, b. at Eastham (or poss. Piscataway, N.J.) 1668; m. (1) Isaac Fitz Randolph; (2) Stephen Tuttle.
Sarah, b. abt. 1670 at Piscataway, N.J.; m. Samuel[2] Moore.

References:

Higgins Gen. by Katherine Higgins, Vol. I pp 26-42; Clemens Mar. Rec. bef. 1699, p. 114; Reg. Vol. XXX, p. 242.

Jonathan[2] Higgins, b. July 1637; living in 1715; m. (1) Jan. 9, 1660-61 at Eastham, Elizabeth Rogers, dau. of Joseph and Hannah ( ) Rogers. She was b. Sept. 29, 1639 and d. abt. 1678 at Eastham; m. (2) Hannah Rogers, sister of his list wife.

Jonathan[2] Higgins was Ensign of the Military Co. of Eastham. Elected May 12, 1675; held office 4 years. Adm. freeman 1683-84.

Children by 1st wife: (Elizabeth Rogers)

Beriah b. Sept. 29, 1661.
Jonathan b. Aug. 1664; m. Lydia (Sparrow) Freeman.
Joseph, b. Feb. 14, 1666-7; m. Ruth __________.

Higgins

Children by 2nd wife: (Hannah Rogers)

Elisha b. abt. 1677-9
Elizabeth, b. Feb. 11, 1680-1; d. Nov. 4, 1721; m. Apr. 3, 1701, Thomas[4] Mayo of Eastham.
Mary, b. Jan. 22, 1682-3; m. at Treveo, Feb. 12, 1706, James Young, son of Joseph & Sarah (Davis) Young.
Rebecca, b. Nov. 30, 1686; d. Dec. 25, 1776; m. Aug. 11, 1715 Jacob Hurd. She d. at Colchester, Conn.
James, b. July 22, 1688; m. (1) Sarah Mayo; (2) Sarah Bixbie.
Sarah, b. Oct. 18, 1690; m. (2) Apr. 10, 1717, William Mitchell.

References:

Higgins Gen. by Katherine Higgins, Vol. I, pp. 42-50; May. Desc. Vol. III p. 67 (will of Joseph Rogers Jan. 2, 1677-8). Joseph came on the Mayflower with his father Thomas Rogers.

HOLBROOKE

Chart VII

William Holbrooke, b. abt. 1560-1; d. at Glastonbury, Somersetshire, Eng. betw. Dec. 11, 1625 and Feb. 21, 1626.

Thomas[1] Holbrooke, b. abt. 1589 prob. at Glastonbury, Eng.; d. early in 1677 at Weymouth, Mass. - will prob. Apr. 24, 1677, Inv. of est. March 10, 1677,; m. (1) Jane Powyes on Sept. 12, 1616 at St. John's, Glastonbury, Eng. She was b. abt. 1601 (was 34 in 1635); d. bef. Apr. 24, 1677. (Some authorities say that Thomas Holbrook m. in Eng. Experience Leland, dau. of Hopestill & Experience ( ) Leland. However, this appears to have been Thomas Jr. Good authorities differ. The Powyes athorities claim later and indisputable evidence.)

Thomas[1] Holbrook, embarked from Weymouth, Dorsetshire, Eng., March 20, 1635-6, aged 34, with wife Jane, aged 34; John 11; Thomas, Jr. 10; Ann 5; Elizabeth 1. They came with Rev. Joseph Hull's Co., and settled at Weymouth, Mass.

Thomas[1] Holbrook was freeman of the Mass. Bay Col. in 1643; Selectman 1645, 1646, 1651, 1652 & 1654; Representative to the General Court.

The family was ancient and distinguished in Eng. Ancient Coat of Arms is a Chevron between three Martletts.

Holbrooke

Children of Thomas[1] Holbrooke:

Elizabeth, b. abt. 1633-4; d. 1674; m. May 6, 1650 to Walter Hatch of Scituate, Mass.
John, b. 1617; m. 1699; m. (1) Sarah ______; (2) Elizabeth Stern; (3) Widow Sarah Loring.
Thomas, b. abt. 1625; d. Apr. 11, 1705; m. (1) Experience Leland; (2) Hannah Shepherd; (3) Margaret Baker; (4) Mary Rogers.
William, Capt., b. July 12, 1620; d. July 3, 1699; m. Elizabeth Pitts.
Ann, b. abt. 1629-30; m. John Reynolds of Weymouth, Mass.
Jane, b. Sept. 13, 1635; d. bef. 1681; m. abt. 1655-6, Thomas Drake. He m. (2) Millicent, widow of John Carver and dau. of William Ford.

References:

Middlesex Co. Hist., by Hurd, Vol. 1, pp. 681, 682; Hist of Weymouth, Mass. Vol. 3, pp. 267, 268; Scituate, Mass. V.R., Vol. 2 pp. 150, 397; The Planters of the Commonwealth, by Banks; Hottens Emigrants to America 1660-1700, p. 285; N.E. Families by Lewis Publ. Co. N.Y. 1913, p. 29.

HOOKE

Charts XIV & XXXV

Humphrey Hooke, b. 1580; d. 1659; m. abt. 1605 Cecily Young, dau. of Thomas and Fortune (Gostlett) Young. She was bapt. Dec. 17, 1584 and died 1661, probably at Bristol, Eng.

Humphrey Hooke was Alderman and Mayor of the city of Bristol, Eng. Thomas Young (his father-in-law) was also Mayor of Bristol, Eng. Humphrey Hooke was a merchant of great wealth.

Children:

Francis, b. ; d. Jan. 10, 1695, prob. at Kittery, Maine, where he was Justice of the Peace, County Treasurer, Member of the Council and Judge of Probate of the Court of Common Pleas. He m. Sept. 20, 1662 to Mary (Maverick) Palgrave.
Thomas, m. Mary Hele, dau. of Nicholas Hele.
William, bapt. Apr. 8, 1612 at St. Stephens, Bristol, Eng.; d. July 8, 1652 at Salisbury, Mass. (prob.); m. March 25, 1636, Elenor (Knight) Norton, widow of Capt. Walter Norton.
Humphrey,
Mary,
Sarah, m. __________ Hellier
Elizabeth, m. __________ Crestwick
Jackson

Hooke

References: Humphrey Hooke of Bristol and His Family by Frederick W. Todd, publ. by The Tuttle, Morehouse & Taylor Co., New Haven, Conn. 1938; James Hooke & Virginia Eller, publ. 1925, New Haven, Conn., The Tuttle, Morehouse and Taylor Co. pp. 29, 31, 32; Old Families of Salisbury & Amesbury.

Mr. William Hooke, bapt. Apr. 8, 1612 at St. Stephens, Bistol, Eng.; d. July 8, 1652, Bristol, Eng., where he returned in 1650; m. Mar. 25, 1636, Elenor (Knight) Norton, widow of Capt. Walter Norton. She d. aft. 1611.

Mr. William[1] Hooke, went to Kittery, Maine, in 1633, to look after the Agamentecus Land Patent of his father; laid out land in York, Maine, 1637; was one of the attorneys of Gorgas, 1641; Merchant & Citizen of Bristol, Eng.; later of Salisbury, Mass., (1643-1650); First Governor of New Somersetshire, now the State of Maine. He was Freeman in Mass., Oct. 1640; Repr. 1643, 1647.

Children:

Humphrey, b. abt. 1636-7.
William, b. 1638; d. Sept. 3, 1721 at Salisbury, Mass.; m. Elizabeth Dyer in Eng.; Dec. 17, 1660. She d. Mar. 26, 1717.
Jacob, b. Sept. 15, 1640 at Salisbury, Mass.
Josias, d. 1683.

References: Old Families of Salisbury & Amesbury; Hist. of York, Maine; Humphrey Hooke of Bristol & His Family - preface p. VIII, pp. 100-104.

Mr. William[2] Hooke, b. 1638; d. 1721 in Salisbury, Mass.; m. Dec. 17, 1660 in Eng., to Elizabeth Dyer. She d. Mar. 26, 1717 at Salisbury, Mass.

When "a pretty big lad" William Hooke, went to Eng. with his mother, married there and had at least two children; returned to New England about 1667 and "came to his mother who then lived in Boston. He was attorney for Henry Deering, of Boston, Merchant William and Elizabeth (Dyer) Hooke, signed the Bradbury petition 1692.

Children: all but Florence & William, b. in Salisbury, Mass.

Florence, b. in Eng.; m. Nov. 16, 1685 James Coffin at Newbury, Mass. (p. 238 V.R.)
William, b. in Eng.; m. Mary (Follonsbee) Pike abt. 1691.
Elizabeth, b. "22, 12th mo., 1671" at Salisbury; m. Ezekiel Cravath of Boston, June 14, 1698.
Jacob, b. Jan. 7, 1677 at Salisbury; m. Mary March of Newbury, Apr. 17, 1717.
Martha, b. June 18, 1681; m. Apr. 7, 1715, to Wm. Buswell.
Josiah, b. 1683; d. 1683.

Hooke

References:

Gen. Dict., Maine & N.H. pp. 347-8; Vital Records of Newbury, Mass., p. 238; V.R. Salisbury, Mass. pp. 135-137, 391, 577; Humphrey Hooke of Bristol, pp. 126, 127; Old Families of Salisbury & Amesbury by Hoyt, Vol. 1, p. 204, Vol. II p. 756.

William[3] Hooke, b. abt. 1665 in Eng.; d. Dec. 26, 1743; m. (1) Mary (Follonsbee) Pike in 1691; m. (2) Sarah Carr, widow, May 17, 1738. Mary was b. abt. 1667; d. Oct. 25, 1736. She m. (1) Robert Pike; (2) William Hooke.

William[3] Hooke was with Capt. Francis Hooke in Kittery, Maine, at times 1686-1690, and was there adm. as an attorney in Sept. 1687, tho of Boston Mar. 14, 1687-8. William[3] Hooke was admitted to the Salisbury Church, July 26, 1713, and Mary, his wife, was admitted Aug. 30, 1719.

Children, prob. all b. at Salisbury, Mass.

Mary, b. Jan. 31, 1694-5; d. Nov. 24, 1697.
Elizabeth, b. Feb. 14, 1692-3; m. July 2, 1728; to John[4] Eaton.
Ann, b. Mar. 16, 1696-7; d. Dec. 7, 1697.
Jacob, b. Nov. 1698;
Josiah, b. Mar. 15, 1700-1;
Francis, b. Mar. 22, 1705-6;
Mary (again), b. abt. 1710; d. June 18, 1788, age 78; m. Jan. 2, 1728-9, to Stephen Bennett of Gloucester.
William, liv. in 1743.

References:

Salisbury, Mass. V.R., pp. 135, 137; Old Families of Salisbury & Amesbury, by Hoyt, p. 203; Essex Antiquarians, Vol. 8, pp. 89-90;

HOSKINS

Charts II & XXXII

Mr. William Hoskins, son of Henry & Anne (Winthrop) Hoskins, was b. abt. 1613-14; d. Sept. 7, 1695; m. (1) Sarah Cushman on Nov. 2, 1635. She was b. before June 1617, dau. of Robert & Sarah (Rider) Cushman; d. bef. Dec. 1638 as William Hoskins m. (2) Ann Hynes, widow, Dec. 21, 1638. William Hoskin's mother was a first cousin of Gov. John Winthrop's.

Mr. William Hoskins was Freeman of Plymouth Colony, Jan. 1, 1634-35; Juryman 1636 and numerous other times; on the Grand Inquest, June 4, 16[illegible] June 6, 1643, June 6, 1645, June 5, 1672 and June 6, 1682. Proprietor; one of the 26 Mens Purchase at Middleboro, Mass., upon incorporation as a town in 1669, he was chosen town clerk.

Hoskins

The town records were burned by the Indians as there is no record of his appointment, however May 24, 1681 he was unanimously elected town clerk, which post he held until 1693. June 1662 William Hoskins, with several others, had a grant of land in Taunton on behalf of their children "being the first borne children of this government" as the record expresses it.

Mr. Hoskins stood well in the community and was a man of superior education.

Children:

Sarah, b. Sept. 16, 1636; m. Dec. 4, 1660, Benjamin[2] Eaton. She was the only child by the first wife. Mr. William Hoskins placed his dau. Sarah with Thomas and Winifred Whitney, Jan. 2, 1643, to remain till 20 years of age.

Of second marriage:

Mary, b. prob. 1640; m. Nov. 28, 1660 Edward Cobb.
Rebecca, b. 1642; m. Aug. 15, 1662, Richard Briggs at Taunton.
Elizabeth, b. 1644; m. July 7, 1666, Ephriam Tilson.
William, b. Nov. 30, 1647; m. July 3, 1677 to Sarah Caswell at Taunton, Mass.; d. abt. 1730.
John, b. 1650; m. (2) June 1716, Amee ________; d. abt. Aug. 1716 at Dighton.
Samuel, b. Aug. 8, 1654; m. (1) Abigail Stacey; (2) Nov. 5, 1684 or 85, Mary Austin; (3) May 12, 1692 Rebecca Brooks, dau. of Gilbert & Elizabeth (Symons) Brooks.
Richard, b. 1660; m. (1) at Taunton, Aug. 2, 1686, Jane Feuster (or Fluster); m. (2) Mary[3] Tisdale, dau. of James[2] and Mary (Avery) Tisdale.

References:

Clemen's Mar. bef. 1699; pp. 120, 244; Hist. of Middleboro, Mass. by Weston pp. 45, 46, 530 & numerous others; Signers of the Mayflower Compact by Huxtun, Part II, p. 23; Pope's Pioneers of Mass., p. 234. The Granberry Family and Allied Families by Donald Lines Jacobus, pp. 240-248.

HOWELL

Chart XV

Morgan Howell came with Vines; had lawsuit in Maine Court March 6, 1636-7; bought 100 acres of land of Gorgas, July 18, 1643; took oath of allegiance to Mass. Gov't., July 5, 1653; will dated Nov. 17, 1666 bequeathed to Mrs. Mary Bolles and her children.

Morgan Howell of Cape Porpus, Maine, was a Planter. The date and place of his birth are not known, nor the name of his wife or date of marriage. It appears that Mary, wife of Joseph[1] Bolles (Bowles) was a daughter of Morgan Howell who died between Nov. 17, 1666 and April 1, 1667 (the date his will was probated).

Howell

References:

Maine Wills 1640-1760, pp. 30, 31; American Marriages before 1699 by Clemens, p. 42, (Revised edition); Maine, N.H., Pioneers of by Pope (Revised edition), p. 103; Bolles Gen. by John A. Bolles, publ. 1865, p. 3.

HULL

Chapter XI

Rev. Joseph Hull, son of Thomas & Joanna (Peson) Hull, was b. near 1595 at Crewkerne, Co. Somerset, Eng.; d. Nov. 19, 1665 at Isle of Shoals, N.H.; m. (1) Joanna Coffin, (2) Agnes ________. Agnes was b. abt. 1608 (she was 25 in 1633); d. aft. Nov. 19, 1665. She was the mother of the children born in America.

Joseph Hull matriculated at St. Mary Hall, Oxford, Eng., May 12, 1612, age 17, B.A. Nov. 14, 1614; teacher & curate at Colyton, Co. Devon, then Rector at Northleigh, diocese of Exter, 1621-32.

In the vicinity of Crewkerne, Joseph Hull gathered a company of 106 souls, who, under his leadership, sailed from Weymouth to Dorset, on or near Mar. 20, 1634-5. They landed at Dorchester, June 7, 1635, then went to Weymouth, Mass. His family included his wife Agnes, age 25, 7 children and 7 servants. Joseph Hull was Freeman Sept. 2, 1635; minister at Barnstable before Mr. Lothrop; invited to preach in Yarmouth and did so without permission of the Barnstable Church so was excommunicated. Apparently leaving all but the smallest children behind, he was in Launseston, Co. Cornwell in 1652, called Mr. Joseph Hull, minister; 10 years later was ejected from the rectory of Buran, Co. Cornwall. He returned to his children at Oyster River; later at the Shoals, where he died.

Children of 1st marriage:

Joanna, b. abt. 1619; m. (1) Nov. 28, 1639, John Burseley, one of the Gorgas Co.; (2) Dolor Davis of Barnstable & Concord.
Joseph, b. abt. 1621; was at York, Me., in Dec. 1644.
Tristram, b. abt. 1623; m. Blanche _______; settled at Barnstable.
Temperance, b. abt. 1625; m. John Bickford of Oyster River.

Children, prob. by 2nd wife:

Elizabeth, b. abt. 1627; 1643 to John Heard of Dover, N.H.
Griselda, b. abt. 1629.
Dorothy, b. abt. 1631; m. (1) Oliver Kent, (2) Benj. Mathews.
Hopewell, b. 1635, probably in Weymouth, Mass.; m. Mary Martin in Quaker ceremony, dau. of John & Esther (Roberts) Martin; removed to Piscataway, N.J. (was a founder). N.J. authorities did not recognize the Quaker marriage, who ordered them to be remarried, which took place Dec. 29, 1669.

Hull

Children (con't) by 2nd wife:

Benjamin, bpt. Mar. 22, 1639, at Hingham, Mass.; m. abt. 1668, Rachel York. In 1678 moved to Piscataway, N.J. where he had signed agreement, May 1, 1668, and previously bought land.
Naomi, bpt. at Barnstable Mar. 23, 1639-40; m. Davy Daniel and pos. (2) Richard Sylvester.
Ruth, bpt. May 9, 1641.
Dedovah, d. 1682; m. Mary Seward.
Samuel (Piscataway, N.J.); m. (1) Oct. 1677 to Mary Manning of N.J.; (2) bef. 1702, Margaret ________.
Phineas, b. abt. 1647.
Reuben, b. abt. 1649.
Priscilla, bur. at Launceston, Cornwall 1652.
Sarah (possibly) b. 1636; d. 1647.

References:

Maine, N.H. Gen. Dict., by Noyes, Libby & Davis, Part III pp. 357, 358; Hist. of Yarmouth, Mass. by Swift, 1884; Hist. of Weymouth, Mass. Vol. I, Chap. XV pp. 72-75, Vol. III pp. 300, 301; N.E.H.G. Reg. 25:13; Stackpolis Hist. of Durham, N.H. 2:221-5.

HUNT

Chart II

Edmund[1] Hunt was in Cambridge, Mass., 1634; Duxbury, 1637; proprietor Bridgewater, 1645; was on Military list at Duxbury, Aug. 1643. Inventory of his estate was taken March 2, 1656.

Edmund[1] Hunt was settler in the first company at Cambridge; was surveyor of highways at Duxbury, 1645 and Constable, 1656.

Children:

Mary, m. Thomas[1] Bonney, 1640.
Christian (?) m. Richard Moore at Duxbury.
Thomas (?) killed at Pawtucket 1676.
Samuel (?) Lieut. of Duxbury Co. 1681.

References:

Hist. of Cambridge, Mass., pp. 33 & 592; Hist. of Duxbury, by Winsor, pp. 22, 81, 92; Popes Pioneers of Mass., p. 248; Pierces Colonial Lists p. 53.

JAQUITH

Chart IX

Abraham[1] Jaquith, was in Charleston, Mass. bef. 1643; member of the Church 1643; Freeman, May 14, 1643; d. 1676 (will dated 16 (9) 1675, prob. Dec. 19, 1676); m. Ann (or Hannah) Jordan, dau. of James Jordan of Dedham. She d. bef. 29 (1) 1655.

Children:

Abraham, b. Dec. 19, 1644; 1677-80; m. Mar. 13, 1671 to Mary Adford, dau. of Henry & Tamson (Manson) Adford.
Mary, b. 1646.
Lydia, named in father's will.
Sarah, named in father's will.
Deborah, named in father's will.

References:

Ntl. Gen. Soc. Quarterly, Vol. 50 #1, p. 38; Pope's Pioneers of Mass., p. 256.

Abraham[2] Jaquith, b. Dec. 19, 1644; d. betw. 1677-1680; m. Mary Adford at Woburn, Mass., March 13, 1671. She was a dau. of Henry and Thomasine (Manson) Adford; bapt. June 29, 1651 at Scituate, Mass. She m. (2) Jacob Hamblet as his 3rd wife.

Children: (Jaquith)

Abraham[3] b. Feb. 17, 1673; d. Dec. 18, 1753; m. Dec. 26, 1700, to Sarah Jones; res. Billerica.
Elizabeth, b. May 19, 1675; m. John Durant Aug. 10, 1695; res. Billerica, Mass.
Sarah, b. Sept. 21, 1677; m. Thomas Durant June 12, 1702; res. Billerica, Mass.

Mary (Adford) (Jaquith) Hamblet had:

Jacob, b. Aug. 1, 1680; d. within a week.
Joseph, b. Aug. 31, 1681; m. Apr. 14, 1607, Susanna Cutler.
William, b. Sept. 8, 1683; m. Dec. 8, 1720, Rebecca Butters.
Jacob (again), b. Jan. 4, 1686.
Henry, b. Feb. 6, 1688; d. very soon.
Abigail, b. Mar. 25, 1689; d. Oct. 23, 1755; m. 1716 James Thompson.

References:

Ntl. Gen. Soc. Quarterly, Vol. 50, #1, p. 38; Billerica V.R. p. 248; Hist. of Billerica, p. ; Hist. of Woburn, Mass., by Sewell, p. 618; Woburn, Mass. V.R. (Mar.) pp. 10, 127.

JEFTS

Chart IX

Henry[1] Jefts, resided Woburn & Billerica, Mass.; d. May 24, 1700 abt. 94 yrs. (was b. abt. 1604); m. at Woburn, Mass. as his 2nd wife, Hannah Births, on May 21, 1649. She d. Sept. 15, 1662.

Henry[1] Jefts was a subscriber to the "Town Orders" for Woburn, Mass., in 1640; taxed in the Country rate of Sept. 1645; had grants of land made to him at Woburn. In 1653 he became an inhabitant of Billerica, Mass. His 1st wife was Ann Stowers, m. Sept. 13, 1647 at Woburn. He m. (3) Oct. 3, 1666, Mary Bird, widow of Simon Bird, at Woburn; and (4) May 5, 1681, Mary Baker, widow of Concord, Mass.

Hannah Births sister Christian Births, m. George Farley, Apr. 9, 1641. The Farley's moved to Billerica. Christian d. Mar. 22, 1702.

Children:

John, b. May 11, 1651; m. Lydia.
Hannah, d. May 1653 - 1st death in Billerica.
Hannah (again), b. Feb. 4, 1654 - 1st female born in Billerica; d. Jan. 21, 1730 at Chelmsford, Mass.; m. Apr. 30, 1674, Andrew[2] Spaulding at Chelmsford, Mass.

References:

Hist. of Billerica, Mass., by Hazen, p. 78; Hist. of Woburn, Mass., by Sewell, p. 618.

JOHNSON

Charts I & XII

James[1] Johnson, resided at Scarborough, Maine; died there 1746; m. before 1691 to Mary __________. Their son John[2] Johnson was b. abt. 1691.

John[2] Johnson, b. 1691; resided Echelfsfechan, Scotland and Scarboro, Maine; m. Mary Maxwell. Their daughter; Jane, b. June 15, 1740; m. Capt. John Warren of Kittery, Maine; d. Nov. 13, 1809, possibly Stroudwater, Maine.

References:

Old Kittery, Maine and Her Families by Stackpole, p. 31;

JOHNSON
Chart XVI & XXXVII

Capt. John[1] Johnson, b. abt. 1600, probably in Co. Kent, Eng.; d. Sept. 29, 1659 at Roxbury, Mass. (Will prob. Oct. 15th following); m. Marjorie; she d. June 9, 1655 at Roxbury, Mass. (Marjorie may have been a daughter of William Scudder or of George Humphrey.)

Capt. John Johnson, resided in Herne, Co. Kent, Eng., and Roxbury, Mass. He came over with the Winthrop Fleet; was Freeman May 18, 1631; Constable; Representative of the first Gen. Court 1634 and many years following; Town Officer; deputy; Surveyor Gen. of Arms & Ammunition from 1641 to 1649; a member of Ancient and Honorable Artillery Co., when the charter was granted, and its first Clerk from 1638 to 1640. His house was burned Aug. 2, 1645, with 17 barrels of his country's powder and many arms in his charge. At the same time the town records were destroyed. Late in his life, John Johnson was granted one thousand acres of land in consideration of his great service to the Colony.

Capt. John Johnson m. (2) Grace (Naugus) Fawer, widow of Barnabas.

Children:

Isaac, m. Jan. 20, 1637 to Elizabeth Porter; d. Dec. 19, 1675 - killed in the Narragauset fight in King Phillip's War.
Humphrey, m. (1) May 20, 1643, to Elenor Cheney, (2) Abigail __________; d. Sept. 24, 1692 at Hingham, Mass.
Mary, m. Roger Mowry; bur. Jan. 27, 1678.
Elizabeth, m. Mar. 14, 1643, to Robert Pepper at Roxbury, Mass.; d. Jan. 5, 1684.
Sarah, b. abt. 1627.

References:

Popes Pioneers of Mass.; Winthrop Fleet by Banks; Banks Topographical Index; Planters of the Commonwealth by Banks; Little's Gen. of Maine, Vol. 3, p. 1465; Savage's N.E. Dict.; Johnson Gen. by Paul F. Johnson.

Serj Humphrey[2] Johnson, was b. in Eng.; d. at Hingham, Mass., July 24, 1693; m. (1) Elenor Cheney on March 20, 1642-3, at Roxbury, Mass. She was a daughter of William and Margaret (Mason) Cheney of Roxbury, Mass., b. abt. 1626; d. Sept. 28, 1678 at Hingham, Mass. Hobarts Journal in N.E.H.G. Register, Vol. CXXI (July 1967), p. 202 "Humphrey Johnson's wife died in bed in the night by him." Humphrey Johnson m. (2) Abigail May, Dec. 6, 1678.

Humphrey Johnson was a capable man in public affairs and often employed in Town business. He was Constable at Scituate 1658 and surveyor of highways there in 1661.

Johnson

Children by 1st marriage:

Mehitable, bpt. 29 1 mo. 1646 at Roxbury, Mass.; m. (1) Samuel Hinsdale; (2) Rob't Root. Both husbands killed by Indians.
Martha, b. Sept. 12, 1647 at Roxbury, Mass.
Deborah, bp. 20, 11 mo., 1649-50 at Roxbury, Mass.; d. Apr. 1, 1669 at Hingham, Mass.
John, b. Mar. 1653 at Scituate, Mass.; drowned at Hingham, Mass. June 12, 1674; m. Rebecca Hershey, June 11, 1683.
Benjamin, b. Aug. 27, 1657 at Scituate, Mass.
Margaret, b. Dec. 22, 1659 at Scituate, Mass.; m. Oct. 20, 1676 at Hingham, Mass., to Joseph Leavitt.
Mary, b. at Scituate, Apr. 19, 1662.
Nathaniel, bpt. July 1666; bpt. at Hingham.
Isaac, b. Feb. 18, 1667-68 in Hingham, Mass.; m. Abiah (Leavitt) Lazell, wid. of Isaac Lazell & dau. of John Leavitt of Hingham, Mass.
Joseph, b. _________; d. Sept. 6, 1676 at Hingham.

Children of Abigail:

John,b. Nov. 17, 1679 (?)
John, b. June 8, 1680
Deborah, b. Feb. 19, 1682/3, Scituate, Mass.

References:

Dean's Hist. of Scituate, Mass., p. 296; Little's Gen. of Maine, Vol. 3; Savage's N.E. Dict., Vol. ; Hist. of Hingham, Mass., Vol. 2, p. 384; Scituate, Mass. V.R., Vol. I, p. 206; Roxbury, Mass. V.R. Vol. I, pp. 194, 195, Vol. 2, p. 224; Hobarts Journal, N.E.H.G. Reg. (July 1967) Vol. CXXI, pp. 202, 123; Capt. John Johnson, by Paul Franklin Johnson.

Isaac[3] Johnson, b. Feb. 18, 1667-8 at Hingham, Mass.; b. Feb. 18, 1667-8 at Hingham, Mass.; d. May 27, 1738 in 71st yr., at West Bridgewater, Mass., bur. Old Graveyard, So. St., West Bridgewater, Mass.; m. abt. 1690 Abiah (Leavitt) Lazell, widow of Isaac Lazell. She was a dau. of Deacon John & Sarah (Gilman) Leavitt; b. Dec. 15, 1667 at Hingham, Mass.; d. Jan. 4, 1747-8, in 81st yr., at West Bridgewater, Mass.; bur. in Old Graveyard, at West Bridgewater, Mass.

Isaac[3] Johnson was a Captain; Civil Magistrate; and a member of the General Court 1729-1731. He resided at Hingham and West Bridgewater, Mass.

Johnson

Children: First 5 born in Hingham, Mass., and the others at West Bridgewater, Mass.

Abigail, b. Apr. 28, 1689.
David, b. Oct. 16, 1692; m. Rebecca Washburn at Bridgewater, Mass., Jan. 7, 1719.
Hannah, b. Jan. 17, 1694-5.
Solomon, b. Mar. 9, 1696-7; m. Susanna Edson, at Bridgewater, Apr. 2, 1723.
Daniel, b. Apr. 20, 1700; m. Bettie Latham, Jan. 5, 1725.
James, m. Jane Harris, dau. of Isaac Harris.
Deborah, m. Benjamin Perry of Sandwich at Bridgewater, May 27, 1723.
Rebecca, m. Jonathan Washburn in Boston, Dec. 17, 1719.
Sarah, b. 1702; m. Solomon Pratt at Bridgewater, Mass. Jan. 27, 1719.
John, b. 1705; m. (1) Peggy, dau. of Col. John Holman, at Bridgewater, Oct. 21, 1731; m. (2) Esther _________; d. 1770.
Joseph, b. 1707; d. 1730.
Benjamin, b. 1711; m. Ruth Holman at Bridgewater, Feb. 8, 1731-2; d. Nov. 22, 1768.
Mary, b. 1716; m. James Hooper at Bridgewater Feb. 10, 1737; d. Dec. 28, 1757.

References:

Hist. of Bridgewater , Mass., by Mitchell, pp. 210, 211; Little's Gen. of Maine, Vol. 3, p. 1465; Bridgewater, V.R., Vol. 2, pp. 203, 204; West Bridgewater, Mass. V.R. p. 205. Capt. John Johnson, by Paul Franklin Johnson.

Capt. David[4] Johnson, b. Oct. 16, 1692 at Hingham, Mass.; d. Feb. 22, 1773, age 81, at West Bridgewater, Mass.; m. Jan. 7, 1719, at Bridgewater, Mass., Rebecca Washburn, dau. of John and Rebecca (Lapham) Washburn. They resided at Roxbury, Hingham, Scituate and Bridgewater, Mass.

Children, b. at Bridgewater, Mass.

Isaac, b. Aug. 9, 1721; m. Jan. 21, 1744 at Bridgewater, Mass., Mary Willis; d. 5-2-1807.
David, b. Aug. 8, 1724; m. May 26, 1743 at Bridgewater, Mass., Susanna Willis.
Mary, b. Aug. 29, 1729.
Sarah, b. July 19, 1732; m. Dec. 27, 1748 at Bridgewater, Mass., Joseph Packard, Jr.
Rebecca, b. June 22, 1734; m. Nov. 18, 1756 at Bridgewater, Mass., Ezra Edson, son of Samuel.

References:

Bridgewater, Mass., V.R. Vol. 1, pp. 177, 178; Vol. 2, pp. 203, 204.

JORDAN

Chart IX

James[1] Jordan was at Dedham, Mass., before 1655; died there 29 (1) 1655; will probated Aug. 1, 1655.

Children:

Thomas
Mary, who was blind, d. 12-8-1681.
Anne, m. (1) Abraham[2] Jaquith of Charleston.

References:

N.E.H.G. Reg. Vol. 5:441; Gen. Dict. of N.E. Vol. II p. 48; Pope's Pioneers of Mass., p. 263.

JOSSELYN

Charts I, VIII & XLIV

Thomas[1] Josselyn, son of Ralph and Mary (Bright) Jocelyn, was b. 1591/2 at Bollinghatch, Co. Essex, Eng.; d. Jan. 3, 1660-1, at Lancaster, Mass.; resided at Watertown, Sudbury, Hingham and Lancaster, Mass.; m. Rebecca Marlow, 1615 in Eng. She was b. 1592 in Eng.; m. (2) at Lancaster, Mass., 16.3.1664, William Kerley (one of the founders of Lancaster, Mass.)

Thomas[1] Josselyn, arrived at Boston, Mass., on the Increase, the end of July 1635, with his wife age 43, five of their children and one servant (Elizabeth Ward age 38). He was one of the selectman of Hingham, Mass., 1645.

Children:

Rebecca, b. 1616; m. 1638 Thomas Nichols of Scituate; d. Sept. 2, 1675 at Hingham, Mass.
Abraham, b. 1619; m. Beatrice Hampson, dau. of Philip Hampson of London, Eng.; d. April 1670.
Joseph, b. abt. 1621.
Dorothy, b. abt. 1624; d. at Roxbury, Mass. Dec. 2, 1645.
Nathaniel, b. June 12, 1627;
Elizabeth, b. 1629; m. at Boston, June 21, 1652 to (1) Edward Emmons (or Yeomans) of Charlestown; (2) John Kelby, tailor.
Mary, bapt. Mar. 16, 1633-4, at Barham, Eng.; m. at Lancaster, Mass., 1656, to Deacon Roger Sumner; d. Aug. 21, 1711, at Milton, Mass.

References:

Josselyn Genealogy by Edith S. Wessler; Pope's Pioneers of Mass.; Hist. of Hingham, Mass. Vol. II; Town Clerk of Hingham; Annals of Lancaster by Henry S. Nourse; Lancaster Births, Mar. and Deaths 1643-1850.

Josselyn

Abraham[2] Josselyn, was b. 1619 in London, Eng.; d. June 13, 1670 at Sea; m. Beatrice Hampson in London, Eng., before 1649. She was a daughter of Philip and Ann Hampson of London, Eng.; b. about 1624; d. Jan. 1712, age 88, at Boston, Mass. She m. (2) Serg. Benjamin Bosworth, of Hull, Mass., on Nov. 16, 1671.

Abraham[2] Josselyn, attended Corpus Christi School in London; m. before 1644, one child d. before Sept. 1, 1644 and his wife probably d. soon after. He resided at Hingham (in 1647), Boston, Lancaster, Stow and Salisbury, Mass., and Scarborough, Mass. He was a Mariner and probably owned several ships sailing between Plymouth, Mass. and London, Eng.

Children of Abraham and Beatrice (Hampson) Josselyn:

Abraham, bpt. at Hingham Apr. 8, 1649; d. Feb. 10, 1676 a victim of massacres; m. Ann Hudson, dau. of Daniel Hudson, Sept. 9, 1672.
Philip, bpt. in Hingham, Mass., Dec. 15, 1650; d. at Boston, Aug. 2, 1652.
Henry[3], b. at Scarborough, Me., 1652; d. Oct. 30, 1730 at Hanover, Mass.; m. Abigail Stockbridge, on Nov. 4, 1676.
Rebecca, b. 1655; m. (1) John Croakham of Boston; (2) Thomas Harris in 1679; (3) Edward Stevens of Boston, Oct. 8, 1700; d. Mar. 1713.
Thomas, b. at Scarborough, 1658/9.
Nathaniel, b. July 4, 1660 at Boston; m. (1) Mary
Joseph, b. at Lancaster, May 26, 1663; d. Sept. 1726; m. (1) Hannah, dau. of John Farrow Mar. 17, 1688; (2) Sarah Ford, dau. Andrew & Abiah (Whitman) Ford.
Marie, b. at Lancaster, Oct. 14, 1666; killed by Indians in Peter Joslin's house July 18, 1692; m. 1689 to Jonathan Whitcomb.

References:

Hist. of Hingham, Vol. II Gen.; Town Clerk of Hingham; Annals of Lancaster, Mass., by Henry S. Nourse; Town Clerk, Lancaster; Josselyn Family by Edith Wessler; Gen. Adv. Vol. IV p. 41.

Henry[3] Josselyn, b. abt. 1652 at Scarborough, Maine; d. Oct. 30, 1730 at Hanover, Mass., age 90 "The Oldest Man in that part of town"; m. Abigail Stockbridge on Nov. 4, 1676, at Scituate, Mass. She was a dau. of Deacon Charles and Abigail (Pierce) Stockbridge; b. Feb. 24, 1660/1 at Charlestown, Mass.; d. July 15, 1743.

Children:

Abigail, bpt. Apr. 12, 1677; m. Benjamin Harmer (Hanmer) Dec. 15, 1718.
Abraham, b. Jan. 14, 1678-9.
Anne, b. Feb. 22, 1680-1; d. Nov. 17, 1683.
Charles, b. Mar. 15, 1682-3; m. Dorothy Paul, Oct. 24, 1711.
Mary, b. Jan. 22, 1684-5; m. Benjamin Munrow of Swanzie, Dec. 3, 1713.

Josselyn

Children of Henry³ Josselyn, con't.

Nathaniel, b. Feb. 10, 1686-7; m. Frances Yellings, Dec. 27, 1711.
Rebeckah, b. Mar. 25, 1689; d. Apr. 20, 1689.
Jabez, b. Feb. 5, 1690-1; m. Sarah Turner, Jan. 3, 1722.
Rebeckah, b. May 14, 1693; m. Joseph Perry of Hanover, Apr. 24, 1728.
(Jemima, b. Dec. 17, 1695; d. Feb. 14, 1695-6.
(Keziah, b. Dec. 17, 1695; m. Samuel Linze of Bristol, Nov. 19, 1718; d. Jan. 27.
Henry, b. Mar. 24, 1696-7 at Scituate; m. Hannah Oldham, Sept. 23, 1718; d. (will prob.) June 26, 1787.
Joseph, b. Dec. 16, 1699; m. (1) Ruth Bates of Scituate, Dec. 19, 1726; m. (2) Mrs. Sylvester Barker of Pembroke, Oct. 3, 1751; d. Jan. 6, 1742.
Thomas, b. Sept. 1702; m. Anne Stockbridge, Jan. 1, 1732-3.

References:

Josselyn Gen. by Edith Wessler; Scituate, Mass., V.R. Vol. I, pp. 209-210; Vol. II, pp. 169, 407.

Henry⁴ Josselyn, b. Mar. 24, 1696-7, at Scituate, Mass., bpt. 2nd Church of Scituate, Jan. 27, 1716-17 age 20; d. (will proved) June 26, 1787 at Pembroke, Mass.; m. Hannah Oldham, Sept. 23, 1718 at Pembroke, Mass. She was a daughter of Isaac and Hannah (Keene) Oldham, b. June 23, 1700 at Pembroke, Mass.; d.

Children:

Hannah, b. Oct. 1, 1719; m. Nov. 16, 1738, Henry Munroe of Swanzey.
Lydia, b. Aug. 25, 1722.
Mary, b. 1724; m. Nov. 10, 1742, Shubael Munro, son of Benj.
Henry, b. June 11, 1727; d. Mar. 1, 1818; m. Ann Palmer.
Margaret, b. Dec. 9, 1729; m. Jan. 7, 1747-8, Seth Foord at Pembroke.
Joseph, b. Jan. 2, 1731-2; d. Feb. 27, 1733-4.
Joseph, b. June 22, 1734; m. (2) Marcy Waterman.
Charles, b. May 7, 1739; m. Rebecca Keen, July 10, 1760.
Lucy, b. Oct. 5, 1741; m. Isaac Foord of Marshfield, at Pembroke, Oct. 1, 1761. They moved to Fayette, Maine.
Isaac, b. Nov. 4, 1743; m. Lois Ramsdell in Hanover, Mass., Sept. 12, 1773.

References:

Josselyn Gen., by Edith Wessler; Scituate, Mass. V.R., Vol. I p. 209; Vol. II p. 170; Pembroke, Mass., V.R. pp. 118, 123, 298, 302.

KEEN

Chart VIII

Josiah Keene came in the Confidence April 11, 1638, with Martha 60, John 17, Eliza 13, Martha (prob. 11). Josiah was possibly 9 years of age when he came, so was b. abt. 1628 or 9; made his will May 28, 1695 (probated Sept. 15, 1710).

Josiah Keene, m. (2) Hannah Dingley, dau. of John & Sarah (Chillingworth) Dingley. His first wife was Abigail Little, dau. of Thoman & Anna (Warren) Little of Marshfield; he was surveyor of highways at Marshfield, Mass. 1666.

Children of 1st marriage:

Josiah, m. bef. 1692, Lydia Baker.
A dau. who d. young.

Children of 2nd marriage:

John
Matthew, m. Dec. 20, 1698, Martha Mackfarlin, dau. of Purth of Hingham.
Hannah, m. Nov. 21, 1695, Isaac Oldham.

References:

Hist. of Duxbury, Mass. by Windsor, p. 273; Duxbury V.R. pp. 229, 281; Mayflower Desc. Vol. 8, pp. 191, 192 & Vol. 19, p. 128; Drake's Founders of N.E. p. 59; Bank's Planters of the Commonwealth, p. 197; Pierce's Colonial Lists, p. 55.

KNOWLES

Chart III

Richard[1] Knowles was at Plymouth 1639 or before, removed to Eastham; Proprietor at Plymouth 1638-9. He m. Aug. 15, 1639, Ruth Bower, at Plymouth (prob.)

Children:

Samuel, b. Sept. 17, 1651; d. June 19, 1737; m. Dec. 1679, Mary Freeman, dau. Hon. John Freeman.
Mehitabel, b. at Eastham May 20, 1652; d. May 20, 1653.
Mehitabel, (again) b. May 20, 1653; d. young.
Barbara, b. at Eastham Sept. 28, 1656; d. at Eastham Apr. 23, 1729; m. June 13, 1677 Thomas[3] Mayo.
Mercy, m. Feb. 5, 1668, Ephriam Doane.

References:

Mar. Rec. bef. 1699 by Clemmons, p. 137; Savage's N.E. Dict. Vol. III, p. 42; May. Desc. 15 p. 53; Pope's Pioneers of Mass., p. 275.

LAPHAM

Chart XVI

Thomas[1] Lapham, son of David; made his will June 15, 1644; will probated Oct. 1, 1652; Inventory Jan. 23, 1648. He resided at Scituate, Mass.

Thomas Lapham was from Tenterden, Co. Kent; came over on the Herculese, 1634, as a servant to Nathaniel Tilden. He joined Lothrop's Church Apr. 24, 1636; freeman Mar. 5, 1638-9. He sold his house and one-half acre of land in Tenterden, Eng., near to Sir Edward Hale's place called Bures Ile, to Thomas Hiland; confirmed by widow June 22, 1650.

He m. Mary Tilden, dau. of Nathaniel and Lydia (Huckstep) Tilden, on March 13, 1637. She was born (bapt.) May 20, 1610 at Tenterden, Co. Kent, Eng. She m. (2) William Bassett.

Children of Thomas and Mary (Tilden) Lapham:

Elizabeth, bapt. May 6, 1638.
Mary
Lydia, b. abt. 1644; m. Samuel Bates of Hingham at Scituate, Feb. 20, 1666.
Rebecca, bapt. Mar. 15, 1645; m. John[3] Washburn, Apr. 16, 1679; d. abt. 1717 at Bridgewater, Mass.
Joseph, bpt. Sept. 24, 1648.
Thomas, b. abt. 1643, resided Marshfield, Mass.

References:

N.E.H.G. Reg. IV, p. 319; Popes Pioneers of Mass. p. 279; Bridgewater, Mass. V.R. Vol. II, pp. 574, 226.

LEAVITT

Charts XVI & XXIX

John[1] Leavitt (Deacon), son of Percival Leavitt of York, Eng.; b. 1608; d. Nov. 20, 1691 age 83 yrs.; will Nov. 30, 1689; prov. Jan. 27, 1691-2 at Hingham, Mass. He resided at Dorchester and Hingham, Mass. His first wife d. July 3, 1646 at Hingham, Mass. He m. (2) Sarah Gilman on Dec. 16, 1646 at Hingham, Mass. She was a dau. of Edward and Mary (Clark) Gilman; b. 1-19-1622 at Caston, Eng., and d. May 26, 1700.

John[1] Leavitt was Freeman 1636; Deacon of the church for many years; Representative at the Gen. Court; employed in business of the town; proprietor.

Children by 1st wife; b. in Hingham, Mass.

John[2], b. 1637; d. Nov. 19, 1674; m. Bathsheba, dau. of Rev. Peter Hobart, June 27, 1664. His widow (John[2] Leavitt's) m. (2) Joseph Turner, Nov. 19, 1674.
Hannah, bpt. Apr. 7, 1639; d. Apr. 23, 1662 at Hull, Mass.; m. July 19, 1659, to Joseph Lobdill.

Leavitt

Children by 1st wife, con't.

Samuel[2] bpt. Apr. 1641; m. (2) Mary in Exeter, Mass., where he had moved; d. Aug. 6, 1707.
Elizabeth, bpt. Apr. 8, 1644; d. Feb. 4, 1688-9; m. at Hingham, Mass., Apr. 25, 1667 to Samuel Judkins.
Jeremiah[2], bpt. Mar. 1, 1645-6; removed to Exeter, N.H., then to Rochester, N.H.

Children by Sarah (Gilman) Leavitt:

Israel, bpt. Apr. 22, 1648; m. Lydia Jackson at Plymouth, Jan. 10, 1676-7; removed to Exeter, N.H.
Moses, b. Aug. 1650; m. Dorothy Dudley, Oct. 26, 1681; removed to Exeter, N.H.; d. 1731.
Josiah, b. May 4, 1653; m. Oct. 20, 1676 to Margaret Johnson at Hingham.
Nehemiah, b. Jan. 22, 1655-56; removed to Exeter, N.H. m. Alice, wid. Daniel Gilman, removed to Hingham, Mass., Boston and Exeter, N.H.
Sarah, b. Feb. 25, 1658-9; m. (1) Apr. 17, 1678 to Nehemiah Clapp of Dorchester, at Hingham; m. (2) Samuel Howe.
Mary, b. June 12, 1661; m. Oct. 10, 1682, to Benjamin Bates at New London, Conn.
Hannah, b. Mar. 20, 1663-4; m. Oct. 25, 1683 to Joseph Loring at Hingham.
Abigail, b. Dec. 9, 1667; d. Jan. 4, 1747-8 in 81st yr., at West Bridgewater, Mass.; m. (1) Isaac Lazell; m. (2) Isaac Johnson abt. 1690.

References:

Pope's Pioneers of Mass., p. 282; Hist. of Hingham, Mass., Vol. 2, p. 428; Maine & N.H. Dict., Vol. 3; N.E.H.G. Reg. (Hobart's Journal) Vol. CXXI.

LEWIS

Chart II & XX

George[1] Lewis d. abt. 1663; will probated March 3, 1663; m. Sarah Jenkins in Eng. He probably m. (2) Mary as he named wife "Mary" in his will.

George[1] Lewis came from East Greenwich in Kent, Eng.; came over before 1633; Resided Plymouth bef. 1633, Scituate, Barnstable, Mass.; joined the Church Sept. 20, 1635; Frm. June 3, 1657; was a Clothier.

Lewis

Children:

Mary, m. John[1] Bryant, Nov. 4, 1643.
George[2], m. Dec. 1654 (prob.) Mary, dau. of Bernard Lumbard; d. Mar. 20, 1710.
Thomas[2], m. Jan. 15, 1653, Mary Davis d. (pos.) of Dolor[1] Davis.
Edward[2], m. Hannah, dau. of Henry[1] Cobb, May 9, 1661.
Jabez[2] d. unmarried.
----(these 5 prob. b. in Eng.)
John[2] b. in Scituate, Mass.; bpt. Mar. 11, 1638.
Ephriam[2] b. at Barnstable, Mass.; bpt. July 25, 1641.
Sarah, b. at Barnstable, Mass.; bpt. Feb. 11, 1644.
James, b. abt. 1632; d. Oct. 4, 1713 in 82nd yr.; m. Sarah Lane, dau. of George Lane of Hingham, Oct. 31, 1655.

References:

Pope's Pioneers of Mass.; N.E.H.G. Reg. VI, p. 185; Savage's N.E. Dict., Vol. 3.

LOTHROP

Charts XVI & XXIII

Mark Lothrop, son of Thomas and Jane Lothrop (Lowthorppe) of Cherry Burton, Eng. was bapt. Sept. 27, 1597 at East Reding, Yorkshire, Eng.; d. Oct. 25, 1686 at West Bridgewater, Mass. (son Samuel adm. his estate). He resided at Duxbury, Salem, Weymouth and West Bridgewater, Mass. The name of his wife is not known.

Mark Lothrop was a half-brother of Rev. John Lothrop, the eminent Clergyman who came to Mass., in the Griffin in 1634; elected Constable of Bridgewater and for 25 years held a prominent place in the town, serving as trial and grand juror; surveyor of highways.

Children:

Elizabeth m. Samuel[2] Packard.
Mark[2] d. in the Canadian Expedition against the French and Indians in 1690.
Samuel[2], b. 1660; d. abt. 1724; m. abt. 1681, Sarah Downer.
Edward, d. abt. 1696 without issue.

References:

Gen. of Maine, Vol. 1, p. 374; "The Lo-Lothrop Family" by Rev. E.B. Huntington, A.M.; Hist of Duxbury by Winsor; "The Packard & Lothrop Families & Connections" written for the Lewiston, Me. Journal by C. F. Whitman (co-author Hist. of Buckfield, Me.)

LUND

Chart IX

Thomas[1] Lund, d. bef. Feb. 5, 1677 (date estate adm.). He resided in Boston, Mass., and was a Trader.

March 16, 1672, Thomas Lunn was a witness to a deed of Samuel Bennett to Benjamin Muzzey of Rumney Marsh, conveying land in Boston. He d. bef. Feb. 5, 1677 when adm. on the estate of Thomas Lunn, late of Boston, seaman, was granted to Benjamin Muzzey, Senior, of Rumney Marsh, in the right of Thomas the only child of said deceased.

The name of his wife is not known.

Child:

Thomas[2] Lund, b. abt. 1660; living in 1721 (no death record found); m. Eleanor __________, before 1682.

References: Dunstable Families by Stearns;

Thomas[2] Lund, b. abt. 1660; living in 1721 (no death record found); m. Eleanor ________, bef. 1682 (date of her death not known); resided at Dunstable, Mass.

Thomas[2] Lund came to Dunstable about 1680. His was one of two families who remained in Dunstable during the troublous time of King William's War. John Solendine and Thomas Lunn Garrisons were near each other. For many years, during seasons of alarm the Thomas Lunn place was one of the fortified Garrisons of the settlement. He was a selectman and useful citizen.

Children:

Thomas[3], b. Sept. 9, 1682; d. Sept. 5, 1724. He was killed by Indians near Thorton's Ferry; m. Jan. 16, 1711-12, at Concord, Mass., to Elizabeth Taylor, dau. of Abraham & Mary (Whitaker) Taylor.

Elizabeth, b. Sept. 29, 1684; d. April 17, 1781; m. (1) abt. 1703 to Henry[3] Spaulding of Chelmsford, Mass.; m. (2) int. Feb. 6, 1723 at Chelmsford, to Samuel Scripture of Groton, Mass.

William, b. Jan. 25, 1686-7; d. abt. 1758; m. Dec. 20, 1716 to Rachel Holden, dau. Stephen & Hannah (Lawrence) Holden of Groton.

Margaret, b. ; d. June 13, 1764 at Groton, Mass.; m. (1) in Concord, Mass., Lieut. Jonathan Robbins, on Jan. 16, 1711-12; m. (2) in 1729, to William Shattuck of Groton.

References:

Dunstable Families by Stearns; Hist. of the Old Township of Dunstable by Charles J. Fox, 1846; Hist. of Groton by Caleb Butler, 1848.

MACKWORTH

Chart XIV

Arthur Mackworth, Gentleman, d. bef. Mar. 28, 1658; m. wid. Jane Andrews, wid. of Samuel Andrews; She was b. abt. 1605 (age 30 in 1635 - came in the "Increase" Apr. 14, 1635, age 30); d. - will dated May 20, 1676 at Boston, Mass.

Arthur Mackworth may have been the same as son of Thomas and Day (House) Mackworth in the Village of Newton, parish of Meole Bruce. This Arthur Mackworth was b. ± 1598.

He was one of the most respected settlers of the early times; received a grant from Sir F. Gorgas for 500 a, "for many years in his possession", "at the mouth of Presumpscot River on Casco Bay, known as Menickoe, but hereafter to be known as Newton - together with a small island (still known as Mackworth's Isl.) on Mar. 30, 1635. He probably came over in 1630 with Vines or in 1631 with Lewis and had an early, unrecognized grant, from Vines at Saco. An outstanding member of the Gorgas party, he acted for Sir. Ferdinando in giving possession to Cleeve; was magistrate in 1645 and often employed as arbitrator.

The Mackworth's were lords of the Manor, in Shropshire, (in the 15th Century they came from Co. Derby) of the Manor of Meole Brace, now a suburb of Shrewsbury.

Children (Mackworth)

Rebecca, m. (1) bef. 1666, Nathaniel Wharfe; m. (2) William Rogers after 1673.
Sarah, m. bef. 1665, Abraham Adams.
Arthur
John

Children (Andrews)

Jane, b. 1632; m. _______ Neal.
Elizabeth, b. 1633; m. ________ Purchase.
James, b. 1635.
Philippe m. George Felt, Jr.

References:

Gen. Dict. Maine & N.H. Part 5, p. 451; Maine Wills 1640-1760, p. 44; Pioneers on Maine Rivers pp. 186, 233 & others; Maine Hist. & Gen. Reg. Vol. I, p. 88; Pope's Pioneers of Maine & N.H. p. 131;

MARION

Chart VI

John[1] Marion (Isaac, John) was a son of Isaac Marion of Stebbe, Co. Essex, Eng. He was b. abt. 1619; d. Jan. 27, 1705 (aged 86) at Boston, Mass.; m. abt. 1640 at Watertown, Mass., to Sarah Eddy, dau. of John[1] and Joanna Eddy. She was b. in Eng. abt. 1625; d. at Boston, Mass. Feb. 3, 1709/10 in her 85th year. Both John and Sarah are buried in King's Chapel Burying Ground, Boston, Mass.

John[1] Marion was a cordwainer. He and his wife were adm. to the First Church at Boston Feb. 15, 1651/52. Both were active in Church affairs. John was adm. Freeman in 1652; was a Selectman in Boston, 1693.

Children, b. at Watertown & Boston:

Mary, b. 1641; d. 1641.
John, b. 1643; d. 1643.
Elizabeth, b. abt. 1644; d. July 6, 1716; m. Jan. 10, 1665, Henry Dearborn.
John, b. Dec. 22, 1651; m. Anna
Isaac, b. Jan. 1, 1652-3; d. June 25, 1724; m. Phoebe. Both Isaac & Phoebe bur. King's Chapel Burying Ground.
Samuel, b. Dec. 14, 1655; m. Hannah.
Sarah, b. Apr. 24, 1659.
Thomasin, b. 23rd d. 7 m. 1660; m. James Pennyman.
Mary, b. May 13, 1663.
Joseph, b. Oct. 14, 1666.
Benjamin, b. Aug. 25, 1671.

Tombstone Inscriptions

Here Lyes
Ye Body of
John Marion
Died Janua
Ye 27 - 1705
In Ye 86 Year
Of His Age

Here Lyes Ye
Body of Mrs.
Sarah Marion
Wife of Ye Late
Mr. John Marion
Died Febry Ye 30
1709/10 in 85th
Year of Her Age

References:

Hist. of Hampton, N.H. by Joseph Dow, p. 834; Eddy Family in America by the Eddy Family Assn., pp. 29, 30; Report of the Records Com. 1883 (Births etc. Boston); Pope's Pioneers of Mass., p. 300.

MAYO

Chart III

John[1] Mayo, was b. abt. 1598 in Eng.; d. May 3, 1676, at Yarmouth, Mass.; m. Tamson (prob. a second wife). She d. Feb. 26, 1682 at Yarmouth, Mass.

John[1] Mayo came to N.E. 1638, and settled in Barnstable; ordained a teaching Elder in connection with Rev. John Lothrop, April 15, 1640. Adm. as Freeman March 13, 1645. In 1646 he removed to Eastham and was pastor there until 1654. Nov. 9, 1655 he became pastor of the "Old North Church" (second Church) at Boston. In 1658 he preached the annual sermon before the General Court. On April 15, 1670, he removed to Barnstable and resided with his daughter.

Children:

Hannah, m. Dec. 4, 1642; m. Nathaniel[1] Bacon. She m. (2) John Sunderland of Boston. (see Sam'l wid. below)
Samuel[2], b. abt. 1625 in Eng.; d. 1663/4; m. abt. 1643 Tamson Lumpkin, dau. Wm. & Thomasine Lumpkin of Yarmouth.
Nathaniel[2], b. abt. 1627; m. Feb. 13, 1650 Hannah Prence, dau. of Gov. Thomas Prence and Patience (Brewster) Prence; m. (2) Capt. Jonathan Sparrow.
John[2], b. abt. 1630; d. 1706; m. Jan. 2, 1651, Hannah Lecraft of Yarmouth, Mass.
Elizabeth, d. Mar. 16, 1701; m. Joseph[2] Howes (Thomas[1]) of Yarmouth, Mass.

References:

Mayo Gen. by Jean Mayo, pp. 2-23 incl.; Pope's Pioneers of Mass. p. 308;

Nathaniel[2] Mayo (John[1]), was b. 1627 in Eng.; d. 1662 - will prov. March 4, 1661/2 - at Eastham, Mass.; m. Hannah Prence on Feb. 13, 1650 at Eastham, Mass. She was a dau. of Gov. Thomas and Patience (Brewster) Prence; b. 1627/8 at Plymouth, Mass.; d. at Eastham, Mass.; m. (2) Capt. Jonathan[2] Sparrow as his 2nd wife.

Nathaniel[2] Mayo was able to bear arms for the first time in Barnstable, in 1643.

Children:

Thomas[3], b. Dec. 7, 1650; d. Apr. 23, 1729; m. June 13, 1677 to Barbara Knowles, dau. Richard & Ruth (Bower) Knowles of Plymouth.
Nathaniel[3], b. Nov. 16, 1652; d. Nov. 30, 1709; m. (1) Elizabeth Wixan, dau. Robt. Wixon; m. (2) June 10, 1708, Mercy (   ) Young.
Samuel[3], b. Oct. 12, 1655; d. Oct. 29, 1738; m. Ruth Hopkins, dau. Giles & Katherine (Weldon) Hopkins; m. (2) Mrs. Mary Sweat.

Mayo

Children, con't.

Hannah, b. Oct. 17, 1657; d. ; m. (mentioned in will of John[1] Mayo)
Theophilus[3] b. Dec. 17, 1659; d. without issue.
Bathsheba, b. abt. 1662; (not Mentioned in will of her father, but mentioned in will of gr. father John[1] Mayo.

References:

Mayo Gen. by Jean Mayo (mimeographed) in N.E.H.G.S. Library, Boston, pp. 23, 24, 35, 39, 48.

Thomas[3] Mayo (Nathaniel[2] John[1]) was b. Dec. 7, 1650 at Eastham, Mass.; d. April 23, 1729 at Eastham; m. June 13, 1677 at Eastham, Barbara Knowles, dau. of Richard & Ruth (Bower) Knowles, b. Sept. 28, 1656 at Eastham and d. Feb. 23, 1714/15 at Eastham.

Children:

Thomas[4], b. Apr. 3, 1678; d. June 1769; m. (1) Apr. 3, 1701 to Elizabeth Higgins (Jonathan[2] Richard[1]); (2) Oct. 6, 1722 at Eastham, Mass., to Elizabeth Rogers.
Theophilus[4], b. Oct. 31, 1680; d. Oct. 6, 1763; m. (1) Aug. 16, 1705 Rebecca Smith; (2) Rachel (Hopkins) Higgins.
Mary, b. Aug. 6, 1683; d. 1777; m. Mar. 16, 1715, Samuel[3] Arey (Richard[2,1])
Mercy, b. Jan. 10, 1685; m. Oct. 30, 1707 Jonathan Godfrey.
Ruth, b. Jan. 20, 1688; d. Jan. 14, 1720; m. Mar. 5, 1718/19, William Norcot.
Judah[4], b. Sept. 25, 1691; d. 1761; m. Jan. 27, 1722, Mary Hamilton of Chatham, Mass., dau. Daniel & Mary (Smith) Hamilton.
Lydia, b. June 12, 1694; m. June 14, 1714, Joshua Myrick.
Richard[4], m. Rebecca Sparrow, dau. Richard Sparrow, Dec. 26, 1728. Richard was b. Jan. 13, 1696; d. May 8, 1744.
A son b. Aug. 1, 1699; d. Aug. 18, 1699.
Israel[4], b. Aug. 12, 1706; d. 1760; m. Apr. 2, 1724 Mercy Rector.

References: Mayo Gen. by Jean Mayo, pp. 24, 26, 31-34.

Thomas[4] Mayo (Thomas[3], Nathaniel[2], John[1]) b. April 3, 1678 at Eastham, Mass.; d. June 1769 at Eastham; m. (1) Elizabeth Higgins, dau. Jonathan[2] & Elizabeth (or Ann) Rogers (both daus. of Joseph[2] Rogers, Thomas[1]). She was b. Feb. 11, 1681; d. Nov. 4, 1721 at Eastham, Mass.; m. April 3, 1701; Thomas m. (2) Oct. 6, 1722 at Eastham, Mass., to Elizabeth Rogers who d. May 10, 1772 at Eastham.

Mayo

Children by 1st wife:

Elizabeth, b. May 1, 1702 at Eastham; d. Dec. 19, 1761 at Lakeville, Mass.; m.? Joseph[4] Paddock, Nov. 29, 1739 as his 3rd wife. (see strong circumstantial evidence below.)
Thankful, b. Jan. 10, 1704; m. (1) Oct. 7, 1725, Eastham, Thomas Rich, Jr. (Thomas[2], Richard[1]); m. (2) Nov. 2, 1752, Middletown, Conn., Lemuel Lee.
Bathsheba, b. Apr. 27, 1705 at Eastham; m. 1732 to James Allen of Boston.
Eliakin[5], b. April 1, 1707 at Eastham; d. 1636 in Boston; m. May 7, 1735 at Hingham, Mass. to Elizabeth Kent. She m. (2) __________ Pitcher.
Sarah, b. June 12, 1710 at Eastham; d. July 27, 1711.
Joshua[5], b. May 28, 1712 at Eastham.
Mercy, b. Feb. 27, 1718/19 at Eastham; m. Oct. 28, 1736 at Eastham, to Elkanah Young.

Child by 2nd wife:

Hannah, b. Nov. 8, 1724; m. Aug. 21, 1766, at Eastham, Mass. to Benjamin[5] Higgins (Thomas[4] Benjamin[3,2], Richard[1].)

Reference: Mayo Gen. by Jean Mayo pp. 24, 25, 26.

There is very strong circumstancial evidence that Elizabeth[5] Mayo, b. 1 May 1702, dau. of Thomas[4] Mayo (Thomas[3], Nathaniel[2], John[1]) and Elizabeth Higgins, granddaughter of Joseph Rogers, married Joseph Paddock on 29 Nov. 1739 at Eastham.

1. See attached Elizabeth Mayos and Mayos who married Elizabeth's. The above Elizabeth is the only one who could have married Joseph Paddock.

2. The only Bathsheba Mayos are those descended from Nathaniel[2] Mayo. Joseph and Elizabeth (Mayo) Paddock had a daughter Bathsheba (see Yarmouth Birth Records attached), also their daughter Elizabeth (Paddock) Hackett, had a daughter Bathsheba. See list of Bathshebas from "Rev. John Mayo and His Descendents" by E. Jean Mayo (mimeographed). A copy is in the N.E.H.G.S. Library in Boston.

Margaret Zeller Garrett

Further information reveals that Ephriam and Elizabeth (Paddock) Hackett's daughter Elizabeth, married David Pratt and that they had a daughter Bathsheba.

Elizabeth Mayo

Mayos who m. Elizabeths, 1714-1739

1. Jeremiah Mayo and Elizabeth Mulford, int. May 21, 1725, Eastham - m. June 17, 1725 (Truro). Elizabeth w. Jeremiah Mayo d. June 14, 1761 aged about 66 yrs. (Wellfleet Cemetery Records)
2. James Mayo and Elizabeth Higgins, int. Dec. 21, 1734 m. Jan. 16, 1735/6.
   James, son of James & Elizabeth, b. Eastham, Oct. 12, 1745.

3. Thomas Mayo and Elizabeth Higgins m. Apr. 3, 1701 (M.D. 9:4,10) Elizabeth Mayo, w. of Thomas Mayo, Jr., d. Nov. 4, 1721 (M.D. 9:10)

   Thomas Mayo, Jr. and Elizabeth Rogers, int. Oct. 6, 1722, Eastham (M.D. 28:112)

   This Thomas and Elizabeth were alive in 1740, as shown by a deed. (M.D. 15:203)

Note: Thomas and Elizabeth (Rogers) Mayo, had one child - a daughter Hannah b. Nov. 8, 1724 at Eastham, Mass.; m. Benjamin Higgins Aug. 21, 1766 at Eastham. Barnstable Co. Mass., Probate Record Vol. 17 p. 253, is an Insolvency Comm. Report in the Estate of Thomas Mayo. Benjamin Higgins, Administrator, presented a bill for the care of his "Father-in-law Thomas Mayo" and his "wife Elizabeth", from: Sept. 19, 1766 - Sept. 19, 1767
More for the following yr.
More for the next 9 months following in his last illness (Thomas Mayo d. about June 1769).
For the care of his widow to her decease 10 May 1772.

Elizabeth Mayos, born 1698-1706

1. Elizabeth[4] Mayo, dau. John[3] (Samuel[2], John[1]) & Hannah, b. July 16, 1706 at Harwich, Mass., mentioned in will of her father John Mayo, Jr. probated Feb. 15, 1725/6.
   Elizabeth Mayo of Harwich and Ebenezer Nickerson of Harwich, int. of m. Sept. 24, 1726 (Harwich Vital Recs. in M.D. 8:218), m. Oct. 18, 1726.

2. Elizabeth Mayo, Sen., Eastham and Elisha Hamlin of Harwich, int. Jan. 25, 1721/2 (M.D. 28:112), mentioned in estate of her father Samuel[3] Mayo (John[2,1]) probated 1731/2 (Barnstable, Mass. Probates Vol. 4, p. 598).

3. Elizabeth Mayo, of Eastham, dau. Nathaniel[4] Mayo (Nathaniel[3,2], John[1]) and David Nickerson of Chatham, int. Aug. 7, 1731; m. Sept. 30, 1731; m. (2) Aug. 29, 1751, Judah Rogers, as his 4th wife. (See p. 638, Vol. 3, Mayflower Index). She was born Sept. 29, 1712.

Elizabeth Mayos, con't.

4. Elizabeth^{5} Mayo (Thomas^{4,3} Nathaniel^{2}, John^{1}) b. March 1, 1702 at Eastham.

5. Elizabeth^{4} Mayo (Daniel^{3} John^{2,1}) b. abt. 1700 m. March 15, 1716, John Lewis. (Plymouth County Deed - Bk. 29, p. 97 proves this marriage.)

From
"Rev. John Mayo and His Descendents"
by
E. Jean Mayo

1. Bathsheba^{3} Mayo (Nathaniel^{2}, John^{1}) b. 1662, Eastham, Mass. (not mentioned in her father's will of 1661/2, but mentioned in grandfather John^{1} Mayos estate settlement in 1676) p. 48.

2. Bathsheba^{5} Mayo (Thomas^{4,3} Nathaniel^{2}, John^{1}) b. Apr. 27, 1705, Eastham, Mass., m. 1732 James Allen of Boston. p. 26.

3. Bathsheba^{4} Mayo (Nathaniel^{3,2} John^{1}) b. Sept. 23, 1683, Eastham, Mass., d. Jan. 9, 1707; m. Aug. 22, 1706, Eastham, Mass., to Thomas^{4} Freeman (Thomas^{3} John^{2} Edmund^{1}) p. 36.

4. Bathsheba Rich, dau. Thomas^{3} Rich, Jr. (Thomas^{2}, Richard^{1}) and Thankful^{5} Mayo (Thomas^{4,3}, Nathaniel^{2}, John^{1}) b. Jan. 7, 1738, Eastham, Mass.; m. Feb. 7, 1766 to John Haling. p. 25.

5. Bathsheba Smith b. Nov. 30, 1766, dau. George Smith of Chatham and Barbara^{5} Mayo (Judah^{4}, Thomas^{3}, Nathaniel^{2}, John^{1}). p. 32.

6. Bathsheba^{5} Higgins b. June 13, 1718, Eastham, Mass., dau. John^{4} Higgins (Ichabod^{3} Benjamin^{2}, Richard^{1}) and Hannah^{4} Mayo. (Nathaniel^{3,2}, John^{1}). p. 37.

MELLOWES

Chart X & XLI

Abraham Mellowes was b. abt. 1570; d. bef. 4 June, 1639 at Charlestown, Mass., when will mentioned in General Court; m. abt. 1597 in Eng., to Martha Bulkeley, dau. of Rev. Edward & Olive (Irby) Bulkely. She was b. abt. 1572; d. after 11 mo. 1652 when she was remembered in the will of Rev. John Cotton as a "Kinswoman".

Before coming to N.E. Abraham Mellowes invested £ 50 in the stock of the Mass. Bay Co. He owned an interest in property in Cambridge, Eng. parish of All Saints, which he sold shortly before 1607 (owned jointly with Edmond Brendish, Gent. sold to Thomas Crapley of Cambridge, Eng.) Abraham Mellowes, his wife Martha & son Edward, adm. to Church at Charlestown, Mass., 19 Aug. 1633. He received a grant of 200 acres, Sept. 1638.

Mellowes

Children:

Oliver, b. abt. 1598; m. (1) 3 Aug. 1620 at Boston Co. Lincoln to Mary James; (2) at Boston, Eng., Elizabeth (Hawkredd) Coney on Jan. 1, 1633/4; d. 1638.
Elizabeth, bur. at Boston, Eng. 8 Feb. 1618/19; desc. as spinster.
Anne, m. 26 Nov. 1631 at Boston, Eng. to John Smith.
Abraham, bur. at Boston, Eng. 29 Jan. 1615/16.
Catherine, m. at Boston, Eng. 17 Jan. 1627/8 to William Newland.
Edward, bpt. 10 Sept. 1610; d. May 10, 1650; m. (1) Hannah Smith. She m. (2) Joseph Hills.

References:

Pope's Pioneers of Mass., p. 310; Bank's Topographical Index, p. 2; Savage's N.E. Dict. Vol. III p. 195; Hist. of Charlestown by Frothingham, p. 51; Charlestown, Mass. Estates, p. 665; "Family of Rev. Peter Bulkley" by Donald Lines Jacobus pp. 24, 25.

Oliver[2] Mellowes, son of Abraham & Martha (Bulkeley) Mellowes, was b. abt. 1598 at (prob.) Boston, Co. Lincoln, Eng., d. 1638 at Braintree, Mass., adm. to est. granted 5 Dec. 1638; resided Boston & Braintree, Mass.; m. (1) 3 Aug. 1620 at Boston, Co. Lincoln, to Mary James, dau. Rev. John James. She was bpt. 13 Oct. 1597 & d. bef. 1633/34. Oliver[2] Mellowes m. (2) 1 Jan. 1633/34 at Boston, Eng. Elizabeth (Hawkredd) Coney (wid. of John Coney). She m. (3) Thomas Makepeace.

Children by 1st wife:

John, bapt. at Sutterton Co. Lincoln 6 June, 1622; d. bef. 29 Jan. 1674/75; m. Martha _________. She m. (2) Dean Winthrop, son of Gov. Winthrop.
Elizabeth, bapt. 10 Dec. 1625 at Sutterton, Co. Lincoln, d. Feb. 15, 1690/91 at Concord, Mass.; m. (1) Thomas Barrett, son of Humphrey Barrett, of Concord; m. (2) Edward Wright of Concord.
Abraham, bapt. 6 Apr. 1628 at Boston, Co. Lincoln; d. at Boston, Mass., abt. 1652.
Elisha, bapt. at Boston, Eng. 8 Mar. 1631/32; Capt. at Barbados, where he was a large slave holder in 1679.

Children by 2nd wife, born in Boston, Mass.

Samuel, bapt. 7 Dec. 1639; d. young.
Martha, bapt. 6 Mar. 1635/6; m. 13 Sept. 1655, to Joseph Waters at Boston, Mass.
Mary, bapt. 26 Aug. 1638; m. 13 Sept. 1655 at Boston, Mass., to Emanuel Springfield. They lived in Eng. 1666.

Mellowes

References:

Pope's Pioneers of Mass. p. 310; Savage's N.E. Dict. Vol. III, p. 195; Hist. of Braintree & Quincy by W. S. Pattee, M. D. p. 187; Boston, Mass. V.R. pp. 3, 4, 7, 53; Family of Rev. Peter Bulkley by Jacobus, pp. 25, 26; Concord, Mass. V.R. p. 55; Banks Topographical Index, p. 55.

MERCER

Chart VI

Jan Mercer (Le Mercier) was b. Tournas Belgium, of Huguenot descent; resided Ypres in 1566; m. Oct. 18, 1579, Jeanne Le Clere of Valenciennes, France.

Children:

Marie, bpt. Sept. 2, 1582; m. (1) Martin Vander Best of Rochelle, France; (2) _________ Coquell.
Elizabeth, b. June 9, 1586; m. (1) _________ Straac; (2) _________ Blanchard.
Judith, b. May 30, 1587; m. ________ Johnson.
Pierre, b. Aug. 29, 1588; d. after 1667.
Phillipe. b. Dec. 14, 1589; d. young.
Esther, b. May 23, 1591; d. young.
Phillipe, (again) b. Mar. 3, 1593;
Samuel b. Sept. 4, 1594.
Ann, b. July 2, 1600; m. Peter Hublon.
Daniel, b. July 24, 1601; m. Sarah Hublon (probably a sister of Peter Hublon.)
Esther (or Hester) b. Aug. 1, 1602; m. Nathaniel Batchelder; d. bef. June 6, 1661.

References:

N. E. Family History Vol. III, pp. 379-381, Vol. IV pp. 589, 590; N.E.H.G. Reg. Vol. XXVII p. 368, Vol. XLVII pp. 510-513; English Ancestry of the American Sandborns, p. 21; Huguenot Soc. of London publications; Gen. Gleanings of Eng., by Waters, Vol. I, pp. 785-787, will of Paul Mercer of Southampton, June 6, 1661 wills to niece Ann du Cornet, dau. of late Nathaniel & Hester Bachiler & to her 3 younger bros. nephews Francis, Nathaniel, and Benjamin Bachiler; Vol. II pp. 985-988; Will of Mary Coquell, Feb. 27, 1608, wills sister Hester a diamond ring.

MILLETT

Thomas[1] Millett, b. abt. 1605 in Eng.; d. 1676 at Brookfield, Mass.; m. Mary ________, in Eng., before 1633. She was b. abt. 1606 & d. Sept. 22, 1682.

Millett

Thomas[1] Millett, age 30, his wife Mary age 29, and son Thomas, age 2, came to N.E. in the "Elizabeth" of London, in' 1635. He was certified by minister of St. Saviours, Southwick, Co. Surry. He and his family went to Dorchester, Mass.; moved to Gloucester; In 1655 he bought of William Perkins, who had been teaching elder in the Church, all the property he owned in the town. Thomas Millett came to Gloucester with the rare title of "Mr." He was the successor to William Perkins in the Church as teaching elder. He became a citizen of Brookfield, several years before his death.

Children: 5 born at Dorchester.

Thomas[2], b. in Eng. abt. 1633; d. June 18, 1707 at Manchester, bur. at Gloucester; m. (1) Mary Eveligh, dau. Sylvester, at Gloucester; m. (2) Abigail,wid. Isaac Eveleth.
John[2], b. 1635; d. Jan. 21, 1730 at (?) Falmouth, Maine; m. July 3, 1663, Sarah Leach.
Jonathan[2], b. 1638; d. 1638.
Mary, b. 1639; d. Jan. 23, 1694-5; m. June 7, 1658, Thomas Riggs.
Mehitabel, b. 1641.
Nathaniel, b. 1647; d. Nov. 7, 1719 age 72; m. May 3, 1670, Ann Lester at Gloucester.

References:

Hist. of Gloucester by Babson, p. 116; Gloucester V.R. Vol. II pp. 374-376; Vol. III pp.214, 216; Savage's N. E. Dict. Vol. III pp. 211, 212.

MITCHELL

Chart XVI & XXVII

Experience Mitchell, son of Margriete (Williams) and Thomas Mitchell (m. Apr. 15, 1603 at Amsterdam, Holland), was b. 1609; will dated 5 Dec. 1689; inv. taken 14 May 1689, prob. Sept. 4, 1689; m. Jane Cooke, dau. Francis and Hester (Mahieu) Cooke, before 22 May 1627. She was b. bef. 1613, in Holland; d. 1666.

Experience Mitchell came to Plymouth in 1623, removed to Duxbury; was juryman, town officer, and proprietor in 1623 with George Morton. Removed to Bridgewater, Mass.

Children:

Sarah, b. abt. 1641; d. aft. 1731; m. abt. 1662, John Hayward.
Edward, b. bef. 1650; d. 15 Mar. 1716/17; m. (2) 26 Aug. 1708, Alice Bradford; (1) Mary Hayward.
Jacob, b. bef. 1650; d. 1675 at Dartmouth, Mass.; m. at Plymouth, 7 Nov. 1666, Susanna Pope.

Mitchell

Children, con't.

Elizabeth, d. aft. Nov. 1, 1681; m. 6 Dec. 1645, at Plymouth, John Washburn. He m. (2) Elizabeth, wid. of Samuel Packard.
Hannah, b. aft. 1656; m. Joseph Hayward.
John, d. aft. 1701; m. (1) 14 Dec. 1675 at Duxbury, Mary Bonney; (2) Mary Lathrop; (3) Mary Prior.
Mary, m. 24 Dec. 1652, at Plymouth, James Shaw.
Thomas, b. bef. 1651; d. aft. Aug. 1672 & bef. Dec. 1688.

References:

Families of the Pilgrims by Shaw, pp. 68, 69; Pope's Pioneers of Mass., p.   ; Gen. Adv. Vol. I, pp. 73, 74 (Experience Mitchell's Will).

MORTON

Charts No. VII & XXXIV

George[1] Morton, b. 1585 at Yorkshire, Eng.; d. 1624; m. Julianna Carpenter July 23-2, 1612 (Bans. Publ. 6-10 July 1612), in Leyden, Holland. She was a dau. of Alexander Carpenter and was b. abt. 1584; d. Feb. 18, 1665 in 81st yr. at Plymouth, Mass. Julianna m. (2) Menasseh Kempton, Esq., a member of the first, and other assemblies of the Colony, one of the "Old Comers".

George Morton came over in the Ann in 1623, accompanied by his wife and five children - the last, the infant Ephriam, born on shipboard. He acted as financial agent in London for the Plymouth Colony; was one of the original Scrooby congregation; organized "Anne" and "Little" James Cos. As "G. Mourt" signed Bradford's and Winslow's Relation; died impoverished. He was a merchant and trader.

Children: first 4 b. in Leyden, Holland.

Nathaniel[2], b. 1613; d. June 29, 1685; m. (1) Lydia Cooper in 1635; m. (2) Ann, wid. of Richard Templer of Charlestown, Mass.
Patience, b. 1615; d. 1691; m. 1633 John Faunce; (2) Thomas Whitney.
John, b. 1616-17; d. 1673 at Middleboro, Mass.; m. Lettice or Letys ________. She m. (2) Andrew Ring.
Sarah, b. 1616-17; d. 1694 at Plymouth; m. George Bonham.
Ephriam, b. 1623 aboard the "Ann"; d. 1693; m. (1) 1644 Ann Cooper; (2) Mrs. Mary Harlow, wid. of William, and dau. of Robt. Shelley, in 1692.

References:

"Signers of the Mayflower Compact" by Annie Arnoux Haxtun, p. 22, 21, part III; Pope's Pioneers of Mass., p. 321; Savage's Gen. Dict. Vol. III pp. 242, 243; "Saints and Strangers" by George F. Willison pp. 235, 447.

MOTT

Chart IV

John[1] Mott "Oulde John Mott" resided at Portsmouth, R.I. He m. (1) Elizabeth ________. She was bur. 2. Jan. 1610-11, at Saffrone, Walden in Essex Co. Eng.; (2) Catherine; (3) Mary. Catherine was bur. 4 May 1619.

John[1] Mott was adm. a freeman at Aquidneck in 1638. In 8 mo. 1639 John Mott's land is mentioned. Records of the town of Portsmouth, R.I. show that the Town provided for his care for a number of years. On 23 Jan. 1654-55 the town agreed to pay the passage of "Ould John Mott" to Barbados and back again if he cannot be received there, if he live to it, if the ship owners will carrie him" (ib. p. 66). On July 3, 1656, further provision was made for his keep and "the ould man's son Adam" engaged to give a cow and a supply of corn towards it (ib. p. 72). The ould man was evidently held in high esteem, for the order of 9 June, 1652 provided "that there shall be a stone house built for the more comfortable beinge of ould John Mott in the winter". (ib. p. 58).

Children:

Adam, b. 1596; d. 1661; m. (1) 28 Oct. 1615 to Elizabeth Creel; (2) 11 May 1635 to Sarah Lott at Horseheath Co. Cambridge.
Ann, d. 2 Jan. 1616-17.
Elizabeth, bpt. 29 Sept. 1625.

Reference: "The American Genealogist - p. 466 in Austin's Rhode Island Gen. Dict. (Revised edition).

Adam[2] Mott, son of John[1], was b. 1596 at Cambridge, Co. Cambridge, Eng.; d. 1661 - will proved Aug. 31, 1661 at Portsmouth, R.I.; m. (1) Elizabeth Creel, 28 Oct., 1616 at Saffron Walden, Co. Essex, Eng.; m. (2) Sarah Lott, widow, 11 May 1635 at Horseheath, Co. Cambridge.

Adam[2] Mott came over on the "Defense" July 2, 1635, age on passenger list, 39 yrs., and his wife Sarah 31 yrs. He was a Clerk of the Military Co., 1642.

Children:

A son bur. 18 June, 1617.
John, bpt. 6 Sept. 1618; d. young as another John was 14 in 1635.
John[3], b. abt. 1621; res. Portsmouth, R.I.
Adam[3], b. 1623; d. 1673+; m. Oct. 1647 Mary Lott (prob. dau. of Adam[2]'s - 2nd wife by her 1st husb.)

Mott

Children, con't.

Jonathan^3, b. 1626; res. Portsmouth, R.I.
Elizabeth, b. 1629; d. Sept. 2, 1694; m. 1647 Edward Thurston.
Jacob^3, b. 1633, m. Joanna Slocum; d. Nov. 15, 1711.
Eleazer (son of 2nd wife)

References:

Gen. Dict. of R.I. by Austin (Reprint Ed.) p. 344; The American Genealogist Vol. XXXV pp. 107-108; Founders of N.E. by Drake - p. 36.

NORCUTT

Chart II

William^1 Norcutt d. Sept. 18, 1693 - will proved Oct. 18, 1693 - at Marshfield, Mass.; m. Sarah Chapman, dau. of Ralph and Elizabeth (Wills) Chapman. She was b. May 15, 1645.

Children:

William^2, b. Feb. 2, 1662; m. bef. 1690, Experience ________.
John^2, b. Aug. 11, 1664.
Thomas^2, b. June 1, 1670.
Lydia, b. Dec. 5, 1666; m. 17 May, 1699, Ebenezer Jones at Boston, Mass. (Both from Dorchester)
Ralph^2, b. Oct. 5, 1673; d. Dec. 2, 1715; m. Mar. 17, 1714-15, Mary Ro (Worn) both of Marshfield, Mass.
Isaac^2, b. June 10, 1675.
Anne, b. Sept. 20, 1677.
Sarah, b. Nov. 2, 1680.
Ephriam^2, b. Nov. 4, 1683; m. June 30, 1712-13 Elizabeth Bonney in Marshfield, Mass.
Ebenezer^2, b. Mar. 1, 1690-1;
Patience, b. Feb. 9, 1684;
Experience - birth recorded but no date given.

References:

Mayflower Desc. Vol. II pp. 78, 249, 250; Vol. VII p. 120; Vol. VIII pp. 42, 43, 180; Marshfield, Mass. V.R. pp. 12, 31, 40, 37; Births, Deaths & Mar. Boston, Mass. p. 218; Gen. Adv. Vol. III p. 109 (Wm. Norcutt's Will).

Ephriam^2 Norcutt, b. Nov. 4, 1683 at Marshfield; d. aft. Apr. 26, 1757 prob. Middleboro, Mass.; m. Elizabeth Bonney, Jan. 30, 1712-13, at Marshfield, Mass. She was a dau. of Thomas and Dorcas (Sampson) Bonney.

Norcutt

Children of Ephriam^2 Norcutt:

Ebenezer^3, b. at Marshfield, June 11, 1714; m. int. at Kingston, Mass. Sept. 16, 1738, to Susannah Savery.
Elizabeth, b. at Marshfield, Feb. 19, 1715; m. int. at Kingston, to Micah Bryant of Middleboro; d. Jan. 28, 1776 at Middleboro.
Bonney^3, b. at Marshfield, Oct. 7, 1718.
Patience, b. at Marshfield, Dec. 17, 1722; d. at Middleboro, Jan. 3, 1803, age 79.
Ephriam^3, b. July 24, 1725; d. (est. prob.) Apr. 26, 1757, at Middleboro.
John^3, at Duxbury, Mass., Apr. 6, 1732; d. at Middleboro, Mar. 30, 1802, age 70 yrs. Drowned in Saw Mill Flume.

References:

Mayflower Desc. Vol. VII p. 133, Vol. VIII pp. 40, 43, Vol. XXX pp. 151, 155; Kingston, V.R. pp. 258, 187; Marshfield, V.R. pp. 37, 39, 40, 84, 87; Middleboro Deaths pp. 122, 27.

OAKMAN

Chart VII

Samuel^1 Oakman, b. abt. 1630; d. bef. June 30, 1677 when his wid. Mary adm. estate; m. Mary Boaden, dau. of Ambrose & Marie (Lethebridge) Boaden. She was b. Oct. 27, 1634 at Holberton, Co. Devon, Eng. Mary m. (2) Walter Adams bef. March 2, 1689.

Samuel^1 Oakman was a Fisherman; was located on the Spurwink River in Scarboro, Maine, as early as 1657; owned real estate there incl. Oakman's Island at the mouth of said river; owned a large fishing boat. Samuel was selectman of the town 1671, 73, 74, 76; on gr. jury 1673, 74; juryman 1664, 66, 72, 73; took oath of allegiance to Mass. Gov't. July 13, 1658.

Children:

Samuel
Josiah
Susannah, b. abt. 1660; m. (1) Edward Bennett; (2) Peter King.
Tobias, b. abt. 1665 at Spurwink, Maine; d. June 16, 1750 in 86th yr. at Marshfield, Mass.; m. Elizabeth Doty. She was b. Dec. 22, 1673; d. Dec. 17, 1745 - in 72nd yr. at Marshfield.
Marie, (?) bapt. in Quebec, 20 May 1709, then wid. of Thomas Whore (or Hoar); a wid. by 1713.

References:

Oakman Family by Wm. H. Smith, Maine Hist. & Gen. Recorder 1886, pp. 151-158 Vol. III and pp. 229-237; Gen. Dict. of Maine & N.H. by Noyes & Davis, Part IV p. 517; Popes Pioneers of Mass., p.

Oakman

Tobias[2] Oakman, b. 1654 at Spurwink, Maine; d. June 16, 1750 in 86th yr. at Marshfield, Mass., bur. Marshfield Hills Cemetery; m. Elizabeth Doty, dau. of Edward Doty of the Mayflower and his second wife Faith (Clark) Doty.

Tobias Oakman established the boundary line between Falmouth and North Yarmouth. The white rock on the shore of Casco Bay was the point where the line commences between Falmouth and Cumberland. Tobias Oakman made many depositions and many called him the "Swearer". He was a captive among the Indians in 1690; worked for Walter Glendall at the time he was slain by the Indians.

Children:

Faith, b. May 15, 1697; m. Benjamin[3] White, son of Benjamin[2] White of Marshfield, Dec. 2, 1714.
Samuel[2], b. Mar. 15, 1698-99; d. Nov. 21, 1739; m. Elizabeth.
Elizabeth, b. May 10, 1701; d. Nov. 5, 1768; m. Jan. 11, 1719-20, Elisha Ford at Marshfield, Mass.
Sarah, b. 1703; m. May 17, 1722, Benjamin Randall, of Scituate, Mass.
Susanna, b. Jan. 1705-06; m. May 4, 1732, Anthony Collamore, son of Peter.
Mary, b. May 3, 17__; m. Jedidiah Ames May 23, 1724; (2) Joshua Sampson; (3) ________ Sherman.
Mercy, m. (1) March 13, 1740-1 Matthew Simpson; (2) Feb. 5, 1744 John Hamilton.
Edward[3], b. abt. 1716; d. 28 May 1791, age 75, at Marshfield, Mass.; m. bef. 1737, Sarah Daggett.

References:

Maine Hist. & Gen. Reg. 1886 - Vols. 2 & 3; Oakmann Fam. by Wm. H. Smith; Maine Hist. & Gen. Recorder, 1886 - Vol. III pp. 151-158, 229-237; Gen. Dict. Maine & N. H. by Noyes & Davis, Part IV, p. 517; Marshfield, Mass. V. R. pp. 144, 380, 379.

OLDHAM

Chart VIII

John[1] Oldham, b. abt. 1589 in Eng. (40 yrs. of age 1629); killed by Indians, July 20, 1636 at Block Island; name of wife or wives not known.

Mr. John Oldham came to Plymouth on the Anne in 1623; was associated with Lyford in schemes to overthrow the government and substitute Episcopal rule; wrote letters to persons in Eng., who were hostile to the Colony; was detected and banished. He went to Eng., and came again in 1630; settled at Watertown; Freeman May 18, 1631; Deputy 1634-5; was on important committees.

Oldham

While on a trading voyage with Indians at Block Island, was attacked in his vessel by Pequots and murdered (July 20, 1636). Two boys who had accompanied Oldham were rescued uninjured (p. 443 Vol. II Middlesex Co. Hist. by Drake).

The murder of John[1] Oldham, a highly respected citizen of Watertown, its deputy to the first general Court and a member of its church, was the start of the Pequot War. The War ended in the extinction of the warlike Pequot tribe in 1637.

The two boys with John[1] Oldham, may have been his sons though this has not been proved. They were probably:

John, b. abt. 1623 (12 in 1635) res. Duxbury abt. 1643, but no further info.
Thomas, b. abt. 1625; m. Nov. 20, 1656 Mary Witherell.

References:

Hist. of Weymouth, Mass. Vol. I p.104; Chap. XXI pp. 100-106; The English Ancestry and Homes of the Pilgrim Fathers by Banks, pp. 154, 155; Popes Pioneers of Mass. p. 334; Hist. of Middlesex Co. by Drake, Vol. 2 (Watertown) pp. 430, 460; Saints & Strangers by Geo. F. Willison pp. 449, 450.

Thomas[2] Oldham b. abt. 1625; d. March 7, 1711-12 at Scituate, Mass., m. Nov. 20, 1656, Mary Witherell, dau. of Rev. William & Mary (Fisher) Witherell (or Weatherwell). She d. Dec. 12, 1710 at Scituate, Mass.

Thomas Oldham came over on the Elizabeth & Ann in 1635, age 10. His bro. (?) John aged 12 came on the same ship. Thomas was a member of the Duxbury Co., Aug. 1643, Miles Standish Capt. He was a Constable 1691 at Duxbury.

Children:

Mary, b. Aug. 20, 1658.
Thomas[3], b. Oct. 30, 1660; m. June 27, 1683, Mercy dau. of Robert Sprout.
Sarah, b. Mar. 13, 1670-1; m. Jan. 11, 1714-15, Lenix Beverly, of Rehoboth.
Hannah, b. Mar. 7, 1664-5; m. Nov. 6, 1688, Joseph Stetson.
Grace, b. Feb. 13, 1666-7;
Isaac[3], b. Apr. 9, 1669; m. Nov. 21, 1695, Hannah Keen of Duxbury, Mass.
Ruth, b. Dec. 5, 1674; m. Jan. 30, 1711-12 Elias McGoone of Duxbury.
Elizabeth, b. May 5, 1677; m. Mar. 7, 1704-5, Samuel Hatch, Jr.
Lydia, b. Aug. 11, 1679; m. (?) July 2, 1707, Samuel Gardner.

References:

Peirce's Colonial Lists, pp. 43, 75; Scituate V.R. Vol. I p. 276, Vol. II p. 221, 222.

Oldham

Isaac[3] Oldham b. Apr. 9, 1669; m. Nov. 21, 1695 Hannah Keene at Duxbury, Mass. She was a dau. of Josiah and Hannah (Dingley) Keene.

Children:

Hannah, b. June 23, 1700; d. aft. Jan. 17, 1783; m. Sept. 23, 1718, Henry Josselyn.
Alice, b. June 22, 1703; m. Feb. 13, 1723-4, (?) Henry Rickard of Plympton.
Isaac[4], b. Sept. 22; m. Nov. 11, 1731, Mary Stetson.

References:

Duxbury V.R. p. 281; Pembroke V.R. pp. 156, 323.

PACKARD

Charts I & XVI

Samuel[1] Packard, with wife and child and servants, came in Diligent of Ipswich, landing Aug. 10, 1638; went first to Hingham, Mass. Samuel[1] Packard came from Windham, near Hingham, Co. Norfolk, Eng. He was proprietor at Hingham, 1638; Surveyor of Highways at Bridgewater 1672; licensed to keep an Inn, Mar. 8, 1671.

Elizabeth Packard, widow of Samuel[1] m. (2) John[2] Washburn, of Bridgewater.

Children of Samuel & Elizabeth Packard:

Samuel, prob. b. in Eng., bpt. 19 July 1646; m. Elizabeth Lothrop.
Zaecheus, bpt. Apr. 20, 1651; m. Sarah Howard; d. Aug. 3, 1723.
John, b. July 20, 1665.
Nathaniel, m. Margaret, dau. John Smith; d. (will) 1720.
Mary, m. Richard Phillips of Weymouth.
Hannah; bpt. 19 July 1646; m. Thomas Randall; d. Apr. 20, 1727.
Deborah, m. Samuel Washburn, son of John[2].
Deliverence, bpt. July 11, 1652; m. Thomas Washburn, son of John[2].
Jael (or Jane), bpt. Apr. 20, 1651; m. John Smith.
Abigail, bpt. Apr. 20, 1651.
Elizabeth, bpt. July 19, 1646; m. Nov. 14, 1665, Thomas Anger of Taunton.
Israel, bpt. July 19, 1646.
(last 4 not mentioned in father's will. He mentions his gr. ch. Israel & Deliverance Anger.)

References:

Pope's Pioneers of Mass., p. 338; Hist. of Bridgewater, by Mitchell p. 264; Pierce's Colonial Lists, pp. 40, 53; Bridgewater V.R. Vol. II, p. 534; E. Bridgewater V.R. p. 269.

Packard

Ensign Samuel^2 Packard; estate settled 1898 at Bridgewater, Mass.; m. Elizabeth Lothrop, dau. of Mark and Hannah Lothrop. She d. June 19, 1716. Samuel^2 Packard was probably born in Eng. He was an Ensign commissioned Oct. 2, 1689; was in King Phillips War.

Children:

Samuel^3, m. 1705 Elizabeth dau. Samuel Edson; d. Dec. 22, 1749.
Daniel^3, m. 1713, Mary dau. Isaac Harris.
Joseph^3, b. abt. 1697; m. Mary, dau. John Willis; d. Oct. 19, 1760.
Elizabeth
Mary, m. May 2, 1700, Amos Snell of South Bridgewater.
Susanna, m. 1715, John Snell.

References:

Hist. of Bridgewater by Mitchell, p. 264; The Packard and Lothrop Families by C. F. Whitman (article written for the Lewiston, Me. Journal; Bridgewater V.R. Vol. II, pp. 533, 534; Pierce's Colonial Lists p. 71.

Joseph^3 Packard, b. abt. 1697; d. Oct. 19, 1760 in 63rd yr. at Bridgewater, Mass.; m. Mary Willis, Nov. 28, 1723, at W. Bridgewater, Mass. She was a dau. of John and Mary (Brett) Willis; b. Nov. 27, 1699 at Bridgewater, Mass.; d. Dec. 19, 1774 at Bridgewater, Mass. Mary (Willis) Packard m. (2) (?) _________ Hartwell.

Children:

Joseph^4, bpt. May 30, 1725 at W. Bridgewater; m. 1748 Sarah Johnson at East Bridgewater; d. "Quite Aged" at Easton, Mass.
Mary, bpt. Apr. 13, 1729 at W. Bridgewater;
John^4, is a son of Joseph^3.
Susannah, bpt. Oct. 5, 1735; m. Aug. 28, 1760, Joseph Knapp of Norton.

References:

The Packard and Lothrop Families & Connections, by C. F. Whitman - written for the Lewiston, Me. Journal; Hist. of Bridgewater by Mitchell, p. 265; W. Bridgewater V.R.; pp. 84, 85, 165; E. Bridgewater V.R. pp. 267, 269; Bridgewater V.R. Vol. II pp. 533, 534.

Joseph^4 Packard, bpt. May 30, 1725 at W. Bridgewater, Mass.; d. "Quite Aged" at Easton, Mass.; m. Dec. 27, 1748, Sarah Johnson, dau. Capt. David & Rebecca (Washburn) Johnson. She was b. July 19, 1732 at Bridgewater, Mass.; d. (?) Jan. 28, 1775 at Bridgewater, Mass.

Packard

Joseph[4] Packard was a soldier in the French & Indian Wars, serving under Gen. Winslow. He also saw service in Nova Scotia in 1755 (Hist. of Easton, Mass. p. 160).

Children:

Daniel[5], bpt. Oct. 8,1749; m. Aug. 12, 1773, Elizabeth Connolly, an Irish Girl, res. Buckfield, Me.
Anna, b. Oct. 6, 1751; m. Jan. 1, 1778, Benjamin Samson.
Rev. Elijah[5] bpt. Dec. 9, 1754; m. Oct. 21, 1783, Keziah Ames.
Abigail, b. May 20, 1756; m. Apr. 13, 1777, Jacob[4] Whitman of Easton.
Bethiah, bpt. Sept. 24, 1758; m. Simon Record; res. Buckfield, Me.
Martha, bpt. Aug. 24, 1760; m. Joseph Lothrop; res. Buckfield, Me.
Job[5], bpt. Sept. 19, 1762; m. Eunice Bray; res. Buckfield, Me. (Brett Gen. pp. 111 & 125 states that Job m. widow Hannah (Allen) Edson, May 27, 1790).

References:

"The Packard & Lothrop Families and Connections" by C. F. Whitman - Lewiston, Me. Journal; Hist. of Bridgewater, p. 265; Bridgewater, V.R. pp. 274, 275; W. Bridgewater, V.R. pp. 82, 83, 84.

PADDOCK

Charts I & III

Robert[1] Paddock was b. abt. 1605; d. July 25, 1660, at Plymouth; m. (1) bef. 1634 (name of wife not known); m. (2) Mary ________. He was of Duxbury 1638, and Plymouth by 1643; was a Smith; Constable at Plymouth, 1646; sat on grand jury Nov. 1, 1648; was on list of Plymouth Co., Aug. 1643.

Banks Topographical Index gives Robert Paddock as from Hampton High, Co. Devon, Eng.

Children prob. by 1st wife:

Robert, b. 1634.
Zachariah, b. Mar. 20, 1636; d. May 1, 1727 at Yarmouth; m. 1659 Deborah Sears.
Mary, b. Mar. 10, 1638; m. Mar. 24, 1657, Thomas Roberts.
Alice, b. Mar. 7, 1640; d. Sept. 24, 1692; m. May 7, 1663, Zachariah[3] Eddy (Samuel, William).
John[2] Paddock, b. Apr. 1, 1643; d. 1718; m. Dec. 21, 1673, Anna Jones.

Paddock

Children, prob. by 2nd wife:

Susanna, b. 1649; d. Mar. 14, 1670; m. Nov. 12, 1665, John Eddy of Taunton.
George, b. 1650; m. Sarah Ricard.

References:

Mayflower Desc. Vol. 17, p. 185, Vol. 8, p. 254, Vol. 12; N.E.H.G. Reg. Vol. 8, p. 316; Eddy Genealogy, pp. 34, 879.

Zachariah[2] Paddock, b. March 20, 1636 in Plymouth Colony; d. May 1, 1727 at Yarmouth, Mass.; abt. 1659 at Yarmouth, Deborah Sears. She was a daughter of Richard and Dorothy (Thacher) Sears; b. Sept. 1639; d. Aug. 17, 1732 at Yarmouth.

Children:

Ichabod[3], b. Feb. 2, 1661.
Zachariah[3], b. Apr. 14, 1664; d. Apr. 8, 1717-18; m. 1686, Bethiah Hall, dau. of John[2] Hall.
Elizabeth, b. Aug. 1, 1666; d. Apr. 30, 1736; m. Nov. 28, 1688, John Howes.
John[3], b. May 5, 1669; d. Feb. 18, 1717-18; m. 1694 to Priscilla Hall.
Robert[3], b. Jan. 17, 1670-1; m. Mar. 6, 1701-2, Martha Hall.
Joseph[3], b. Sept. 12, 1674; d. Oct. 19, 1732; m. Mar. 5, 1696, Sarah Gardner.
Nathaniel[3], b. Sept. 22, 1677; d. Aug. 1756; m. Dec. 15, 1706, Ann Bunker.
Judah[3], b. Sept. 15, 1681; d. Mar. 31, 1770; m. Dec. 5, 1706, Alethea (Or Alice) Alden.

References:

Sears Gen.; Mayflower Desc. Vol. 3, p. 247; Hist. of Yarmouth by Swift, p. 139; Bearce Gen. (unpublished) in N.E.H.G. Library, Boston.

Note: The Hall girls were sisters.

Capt. John[3] Paddock, b. May 5, 1669 at Yarmouth, Mass.; d. Feb. 18, 1717-18, Barnstable Co. Mass.; m. 1694 Priscilla Hall, dau. of John[2] & Priscilla (Bearce) Hall. She was b. Feb. 1691 at Yarmouth; d. Jan. 2, 1724-5.

Capt. John[3] Paddock took oath of Fidelity at Yarmouth, May 26, 1690; was Constable and Town Treasurer 1696; Representative 1714.

Paddock

Children of John^{3} Paddock:

John^{4}, b. June 24, 1695; d. Sept. 30, 1672; m. (1) Oct. 17, 1617, Rebecca Thacher; (2) Hannah ________.
A son b. Feb. 1, 1696-7; d. Feb. 3, 1696-7.
Elizabeth, b. Apr. 14, 1698; d. June 1772; m. Apr. 17, 1718, Joseph Sears.
Joseph^{4}, b. Mar. 8, 1700; m. Apr. 10, 1768; m. (3) Elizabeth Mayo Nov. 29, 1739; m. (1) Reliance Stone (2) Margaret Crosby.
Priscilla, b. Jan. 30, 1701-2; m. Feb. 22, 1721-2, Thomas Clark, Jr.
(Dea) Ebenezer, b. Mar. 18, 1704; d. Oct. 18, 1767; m. Oct. 21, 1725, Mary Sears.
Child, b. Feb. 25, 1705-6; d. Mar. 6, 1705-6.
Thankful, b. June 26, 1710; d. Nov. 26, 1730.
Josiah, b. Apr. 9, 1712; d. Feb. 1, 1756; m. Feb. 17, 1736-7, Mercy Sears.

References: Sears Genealogy; Mayflower Desc. Vol. 5, pp. 160-1; Barnstable Mass., Families by Swift, Vol. I p. 52 (Bearce-Hall); Bearce Gen. (unpublished) in N.E.H.G. Library, Boston.

Joseph^{4} Paddock, b. March 8, 1700 at Yarmouth, Mass.; d. April 10, 1768 at Lakeville, Plymouth Co., Mass.; m. (1) Mar. 17, 1725-6, Reliance Stone; (2) Nov. 1735, Margaret Crosby; (3) Nov. 29, 1739, Elizabeth Mayo at Eastham, Mass. She was probably a dau. of Thomas^{4} and Elizabeth (Higgens) Mayo, b. May 1, 1702 at Eastham, Mass.; d. Dec. 10, 1761, at Lakeville, Mass.

Joseph^{4} Paddock resided at Yarmouth, Middleboro, and Lakeville, Mass.

Children by Reliance Stone:

Hannah, b. Apr. 20, 1727; m. Mar. 5, 1746-7, John^{5} Richmond (John^{4}, Joseph^{3}, John^{2,1})
Keziah, b. Mar. 9, 1728-9; m. Mar. 13, 1749-50 Joshua Dean.
Reliance, b. Apr. 14, 1731; d. Apr. 29, 1731.
Thomas, b. Sept. 19, 1732; d. Aug. 14, 1820; m. June 9, 1755, ________ Richmond.
Reliance (again), b. June 1, 1735; d. Aug. 14, 1820; m. June 9, 1755 Edward^{5} Richmond (Edward^{4,3}, John^{2,1})

Child by Margaret Crosby:

A daughter b. & d. Nov. 24, 1738.

Paddock

Children by Elizabeth Mayo, b. at Yarmouth:

Elizabeth, b. Sept. 19, 1740; d. 1812; m. May 24, 1764 at Taunton, Mass., Ephriam Hackett.
Margaret, b. Dec. 19, 1741; d. Dec. 15, 1814; m. Nov. 22, 1770 at Taunton, Micah Bryant.
Bathsheba, b. Jan. 28, 1743-4; m. Dec. 9, 1763, Enoch Crowell.

References:

Mayflower Desc., Vol. 19, p. 103; Rec. Yarmouth Town Clerk; Family Rec. Bk. p. 120; Taunton, Mass. V.R. Vol. II p. 350; Mayf. Desc. Vol. 8, p. 218; N.E.H.G. Reg. Vol. 53, p. 249; The Richmond Family by Joshua Bailey Richmond, pp. 43, 47; Middleboro Town Clerk.

PARKHURST

Chart VI

George[1] Parkhurst, b. in Eng.; resided Watertown 1639; and Boston, Mass., 1645; m. (1) Phoebe, a sister of Ruth, wife of Rev. Timothy Dalton (Reg. 68, pp. 370-75); m. (2) Susannah, abt. 1644, widow of John Simpson who d. June 10, 1643.

George Parkhurst from Ipswich, Co. Suffolk, Eng.; was freeman at Watertown, Mass. May 10, 1643; Yeoman, and Proprietor. The earliest seat of any Parkhurst family, so far as is known, was in Guildford, Co. Surrey, where Parish Registers show many of the names from 1541 onward. A George Parkhurst was Mayor of Guildford in 1522, 1529, and 1536.

In the Parish Registers at Ipswich, Co. Suffolk, Eng. the following baptisms of the nine children of George Parkhurst have been found. The 1st in the Parish of St. Stephen; the 2nd in St. Mary at Quay; the 3rd to the 7th incl. & the 9th in that of St. Margaret & the 8th in that of St. Mary le-Tower.

Children:

Phebey, bpt. Nov. 29, 1612; m. Thomas Arnold.
Mary, bpt. Aug. 28, 1614; d. 1687; m. Rev. Thomas Carter.
Sammewell[2], bpt. Feb. 2, 1616-17.
Deborah, bpt. Aug. 1, 1619.
George[2], bpt. June 5, 1621; m. (1) Sarah, dau. John Brown on Dec. 16, 1643; m. (2) Sept. 24, 1650, Mary, perhaps dau. of Wm. Phese or Veazie.
John[2], bpt. Oct. 19, 1623;
Abigail, bpt. Jan. 1, 1625-6.
Elizabeth, born May 18, 1628.
Joseph[2], bpt. Dec. 21, 1629; m. (prop) June 26, 1656 to Rebecca Read at Concord; d. (?) Nov. 30, 1709.

Parkhurst

References:

Savage's Gen. Dict. Vol. III p. 358; Bank's Topographical Index, p. 156; Pope's Pioneers of Mass., p. 345; Gen. Reg. Vol. 68, pp. 370-375; Chelmsford, Mass. V.R. p. 289; Col. Family of U.S.A. by McKenzie, Vol. V, p. 114; Vol. VI, p. 313;

PIERCE

Chart VIII

John[1] Pierce, will probated Oct. 11, 1661; resided Dorchester & Boston, Mass. (1641); m. (1) Parnell _______ who d. 8 (1639); m. (2) Mary ________; m. (3) Rebecca Wheeler, wid. of Boston; m. (4) Rebecca ________.

John[1] Pierce, Cooper, came with the Winthrop Fleet in 1630 with wife Parnell and children Experience, Mercy, and Samuel; freeman May 18, 1631.

Children:

Samuel[2], b. in Eng.
Experience, b. in Eng.
Mercy, b. in Eng.
Exercise,
Joseph, b. 30 (8) 1631;
Abigail, b. 17 (5) 1633; may have m. Charles[2] Stockbridge, bef. 1659.
John, b. 3 (1) 1634-5;
Nehemiah, b. 1637; d. 1639.
Mary, b. 6 (1) 1640
Nehemiah (again) b. 17 (11) 1641.

References:

Planters of the Commonwealth by Banks, p. 79; Popes Pioneers of Mass. p. ; Winthrop Fleet by Banks, p. 87.

PRIEST

Chart II & XXXIII

Degory[1] Priest, Mayflower Passenger; b. abt. 1579 at Londaon; d. 1 Jan. 1620-1 at Plymouth, Mass.; resided Leyden Holland & Plymouth, Mass.; He had been admitted a citizen 16 Nov. 1615 "Hatter from London in the Leyden records; Twenty-ninth Signer of the Mayflower Compact.

Priest

Degory[1] Priest m. Sarah (Allerton) Vincent, widow of John Vincent of London, 4 Nov. 1611 at Leyden, Holland. She m. (3) Godbert Godbertson (frequently written Cuthbert Cuthbertson), 13 May 1621 and came to America with her 3rd husband and children Mary & Sarah, in the Ann. Sarah d. bef. 23 Oct. 1633 at Plymouth, Mass., date of inventory of her estate.

Children:

Mary Priest m. bef. Oct. 1633, Phineas Pratt, d. at Charlestown aft. 4 Mar. 1686-7 & bef. 24 July 1689.
Sarah Priest m. 1630, John Coombs, Gent.

References:

Families of the Pilgrims by Shaw p. 123; Bank's The English Ancestry and Homes of the Pilgrim Fathers (Reprint) p. 75; Signers of the Mayflower Compact by Anne Arnoux Haxtun, Part 2, p. 2.

PRENCE

Chart III

Thomas[1] Prence was b. abt. 1600; d. Mar. 29, 1673 at Plymouth; m. (1) Aug. 5, 1624 Patience Brewster, dau. of Elder William and Mary (Wentworth) Brewster. She d. at Plymouth not long before Dec. 12, 1634. Thomas Prence m. (2) Mary Collier, dau. of Wm. Collier of Duxbury; m. (3) in 1662, Mary, wid. of Samuel Freeman, Jr.; m. (4) Mary, wid. of Thomas Howes of Yarmouth.

Thomas[1] Prence came on the Fortune in 1621, to Plymouth. He was the son of Thomas Prence of all Hallows, Barking, London, Carriage maker and had just reached his majority when he emigrated. His father had lived at Lechlade, Gloucestershire before coming to London.

He was chosen Governor's Asst. 1632, 1635-1637, 1639-1656; Governor June 3, 1657 to Apr. 8, 1673; was a worthy Gentleman, very pious; and very able for his office and faithful in the discharge thereof, studious of peace, a welwiller to all that feared God and a terror to the wicked. His death was much lamented.

Children by Patience Brewster:

Thomas[2], b. bef. May 22, 1627; d. in Eng. bef. Mar. 13, 1672, left a widow and dau. Susanna.
Rebecca, b. bef. May 22, 1627; d. bef. July 1651 at Plymouth; m. Apr. 22, 1646, Edmund Freeman, Jr. He m. (2) at Sandwich, July 18, 1651 Margaret Perry.
Mercy, b. at Plymouth abt. 1631; d. at Eastham, Sept. 28, 1711; m. Feb. 13 or 14, 1649 at Eastham, John Freeman.

Prence

Children by Patience Brewster, con't.

Hannah, b. bef. 1635; d. bef. Nov. 23, 1698; m. (1) at Eastham, Nathaniel[2] Mayo (John[1]); m. (2) betw. June 5, 1667 & Sept. 11, 1671, Jonathan Sparrow.
Sarah, m. Jeremiah Howes of Yarmouth in 1650.

Children probably by Mary Collier:

Jane, b. at Eastham, Nov. 1, 1637; m. Jan. 6, 1660, Mark Snow.
Elizabeth, m. Arthur Howland, Jr. Dec. 9, 1667.
Mary, m. John Tracy of Duxbury.
Judith, m. Isaac Barker of Duxbury, Dec. 28, 1685.

References:

Families of the Pilgrims by Shaw, pp. 51, 53, 54; Popes Pioneers of Mass. p. 372; Savage's N.E. Dict. Vols. 3, p. 432; Mayflower Desc. Vol. VI, p. 127, 157; Vol. 7, p. 14; Mar. Rec. bef. 1699 by Clemens, p. 176; Hist. of Duxbury by Winsor, p. 293; The English Ancestry and Homes of The Pilgrim Fathers by Banks, p. 125; Pierces Colonial Lists pp. 3, 4, 6.

RECORD

Charts I & XV

John Record[1] was of Weymouth, Mass., by 1676 as he was a Soldier on Conn. River in Phillips War 1676; d. Jan. 23, 1713 at Pembroke, Mass.; m. (1) Hannah (Burr) Hobart, widow at Hingham, Mass. July 1677; m. (2) Grace _______. She m. (2) Thomas Parris Jan. 31, 1714-15 at Pembroke. We do not know the maiden name of Grace.

Children by Hannah (Burr) Hobart b. at Hingham:

John[2] b. Apr. 30, 1678.
Simon[2] b. Apr. 2 or 9, 1680.
Jonathan[2] b. Feb. 3, 1681-2; d. June 1, 1742 at Little Compton, R.I.; m. Feb. 28, 1705 at Little Compton, R.I. Mary Wilbore.

Children by Grace, b. at Pembroke, Mass.

Thomas[2], b. June 16, 1692; d. 1770; m. Oct. 5, 1715, Mary Dawes (Douce).
Isaac[2], b. Jan. 25, 1693.
Joseph[2], b. abt. 1700; m. (1) Mercy ______ res. Abington; m. (2) Lydia Hall.
Elisha, d. abt. 1636.
Daughter m. Theophilus Witherell (mentioned in her bro. Elisha's will)
Ruth, b. May 31, 1702; m. Apr. 8, 1724 Elisha Boney.
Daughter m. William Gould (mentioned in her bro. Elisha's will)

Record

Children by Grace, b. at Pembroke, Mass. (con't)

Hannah, m. John Franklin of Rehoboth (mentioned in her bro. Elisha's will)
Ebenezer, b. Oct. 7, 1712; d. bef. 1797; m. Mar. 7, 1744, Johanna Bowles.

References:

N.E.H.G. Reg. Jan. 1968, pp. 20-27; Hist. of Buckfield, Me. by Cole, 1915, pp. 659-663; Pembroke, Mass. V.R. pp. 175, 336, 440; Hist. of Hingham, Mass. 1893; Hist. of Weymouth Chapt. XXII.

Ebenezer[2], b. Oct. 7, 1712; d. before 1797; m. Mar. 4, 1744 at Pembroke, Joanna Bowles, dau. of Samuel[3] and Lydia (Balch) Bowles. She was b. June 12, 1727 at Rochester, Mass.; d. aft. Feb. 15, 1797, prob. at Buckfield, Maine.

Children:

Dominicus, b. 1745; d. Feb. 4, 1810 at Buckfield, Maine; m. (1) Aug. 19, 1768, Martha Dailey, (2) Sept. 10, 1770, Jane Warren at Turner, Me.
Jonathan, b. 1749; d. Jan. 17, 1855; m. Feb. 8, 1781, Remember Briggs of Halifax, Mass.; (2) Abigail Cobb.
David, b. 1749; d. Mar. 20, 1832; m. Sept. 9, 1781, Abigail Damon of Pembroke.
Simon, b. 1756; d. Oct. 5, 1843; m. bef. 1779, Bethiah Packard, res. Buckfield, Maine.
Olive, m. Nov. 8, 1768, Daniel Merrill, res. Buckfield.
Deborah, m. John Walker, res. Pembroke, Mass.

References:

Hist. of Buckfield, Maine, by Cole & Whitman, pp. 659-663; Bridgewater, Mass. V.R. p. 316, V. 2; Hist. of Turner, Me. by French, p. 159; Halifax, Mass. V.R. pp. 10 & 28;

Simon[3] Record, son of Ebenezer & Joanna (Bowles) Record, b. 1756; d. Oct. 5, 1843 aged 87, at Buckfield, Maine; m. 1777 at Bucktown, Maine, Bethiah Packard. She was a dau. of Joseph & Sarah (Johnson) Packard; b. 1758 at Bridgewater, Mass.; d. June 8, 1829.

Simon Record of Pembroke and Easton, Mass. Pvt. Capt. Ichabod Leonard's Co., Vol. Thomas Carpenter's Regt.; Service 1 mo., 13 days. Co. marched from Bristol Co. R.I. in July of 1778 to serve for 6 weeks.

Children:

Cynthia, b. 8/20/1778; d. Sept. 20, 1819; m. Jan. 28, 1798, Thomas[4] Bray.
Simeon[4], b. May 15, 1781; m. Eliza Stroud.
Bathiah, b. July 20, 1783; m. Stephen Spaulding.

Children of Simon[3] Record; con't.

Joanna, b. Apr. 3, 1786; m. Eliphalet Noyes.
Ebenezer[4], b. May 18, 1788; m. Nancy Manley.
Charles[4], b. May 18, 1788; m. Sally Noyce.
Cyrus[4], b. Sept. 19, 1790; d. Dec. 12, 1876; m. Arvella Spaulding.
Simon[4], b. Dec. 19, 1792; m. Catherine Fernold.

References:

Soldiers & Sailors of Mass. Vol. 13, p.. 39; Hist. of Buckfield, Me. p. 663; Seven Generations of Brays by Wm. M. Bray, pp. 7, 8.

RICHMOND

Chart IV

John[1] Richmond b. 1594; d. March 20, 1664, age 70, at Taunton, Mass. Will dated 14 Dec. 1663. Name of wife unknown. He resided at Wiltshire, Eng. (prob. town of Amesbury); Duxbury, Mass. and Taunton, Mass.

John[1] Richmond was a large landowner and quite wealthy for that time; was one of the purchasers of Taunton, Mass. in 1657.

Children:

John[2], b. abt. 1627; m. Abigail Rogers, dau. of John[2] Rogers of Duxbury & gr. dau. of Thomas Rogers of the Mayflower.
Capt. Edward[2], b. abt. 1632; d. Nov. 1696; m. (1) Abigail, dau. of James Davis; (2) Amy, dau. of Gov. Henry and Elizabeth Bull.
Sarah, b. 1638; d. 1691; m. (1) Edward Rue; (2) Nov. 4, 1678, James Walker, the immigrant; (3) Nicholas Stoughton.
Mary, b. 1639; d. Oct. 13, 1715; m. William Paul, of Berkley, Mass.

References:

Richmond Family by J.B. Richmond; pp. 3, 5, 6, 7. N.E.H.G. Reg. VII p. 180; Mayflower Index Vol. 1 & 2, pp. ; Families of the Pilgrims (Rogers) by the Mass. Mayflower Soc.

John[2] Richmond; b. abt. 1627; d. Oct. 7, 1715 age 88, at Taunton, Mass.; m. Abigail Rogers abt. 1663. She was a dau. of John[2] and Ann (Churchman) Rogers, and a gr. dau. of Thomas Rogers of the Mayflower. She was b. 1641; d. Aug. 1, 1727 at Taunton, Mass.

Richmond

John[2] Richmond was on Town Council Feb. 29, 1675-6 also 1690; was Constable, Commissioner & Surveyor. He was a member of every important committee in Taunton; for the purchase, division and settlement of the land and other matters of public interest.

John[2] Richmond probably had a previous wife who d. in 1662.

Children of 1st mar.

Mary, b. June 2, 1654 at Bridgewater; d. Mar. 5, 1732; m. Jan. 1, 1679-80, Richard Godfrey.
John[3], b. June 6, 1656 at Bridgewater; d. Sept. 20, 1672.
Thomas[3], b. Feb. 2, 1659 at Newport, R.I.; d. Dec. 14, 1705 at Middleboro, Mass.; unmarried.
Susanna, b. Nov. 4, 1661 at Bridgewater; d. Aug. 18, 1725; m. Apr. 18, 1683 James Reed, son of Wm. Reade the immigrant.

Children by Abigail Rogers:

Joseph[3], b. Dec. 8, 1663 at Taunton; m. June 26, 1685 Mary Andrews, dau. Henry & Mary Andrews of Taunton.
Edward[3], b. Feb. 8, 1665; d. 1741; m. (1) Mercy ________; (2) Rebecca Thurston; (3) Mary ________.
Samuel[3], b. Sept. 23, 1668; d. 1736; m. (1) Mehitable Andrews, dau. Henry & Mary Andrews; (2) Elizabeth (King) Hall, wid. John Hall, dau. Phillip & Judith (Whitman) King.
Sarah, b. Feb. 26, 1671; d. Sept. 12, 1749; m. Oct. 6, 1699, James Walker, son James & Bathsheba (Brooks) Walker.
John[3], b. Dec. 5, 1673; m. Nov. 28, 1709, Hannah Otis, dau. Stephen & Hannah (Ensign) Otis.
Ebenezer[3], b. May 12, 1676 at Newport, R.I. d. 1729; m. bef. 1701, Anna Sproat, dau. Robert & Elizabeth (Sampson) Sproat.
Abigail, b. Feb. 26, 1679; m. July 29, 1708, Nathan Walker, son James & Bathsheba (Brooks) Walker.

Note: The first five children of John[2] & Abigail (Rogers) Richmond, were born at Taunton, Mass., the last two at Newport, R.I.

References:

The Richmond Family by J.B. Richmond, pp. 3,4,5,9,10,11,12,13; Families of the Pilgrims, Mass. Mayflower Soc.; Mayflower Index pp. 619 (28834), 603, 604, 605, 608; Pierce's Colonial Lists pp. 32, 36, 98.

Edward[3] Richmond, b. Feb. 8, 1665 at Taunton, Mass.; d. 1741; will dated June 3, 1738, Prob. Dec. 9, 1741; m. (1) Mercy ________; (2) Rebecca Thurston, dau. Jonathan & Sarah (   ) Thurston. She was b. Nov. 28, 1689. Edward[3] Richmond m. (3) Mary ________.

Edward[3] Richmond & his bro. Joseph bought 150 acres of land in Middleboro, of John Rogers of Duxbury in 1687.

Richmond

Children of Edward[3] & Mercy, 1st wife:

Mercy, b. 1693; d. June 27, 1760; m. Edward Walker, son Peter & Hannah Walker.
Edward, b. 1695; d. Feb. 16, 1771; m. (1) Elizabeth Deane, dau. Benj. & Sarah (Williams) Deane; m. (2) Nov. 6, 1750, Mrs. Elizabeth (Shaw) Sampson, wid. Isaac Sampson of Plympton.
Richard
Josiah, b. 1697; d. 1763; m. (1) Mehitable Deane, dau. Benj. & Sarah (Williams) Deane; (2) Mrs. Lydia Crocker.
Nathaniel, b. 1700; d. 1763; m. Alice Hackett, dau. John & Elizabeth (Elliott) Hackett.
Seth, m. Lydia Haskins, dau. Wm. Haskins.
Elizabeth, m. __________ Hathaway.
Phebe, b. 1706; d. Mar. 9, 1741-2; m. Noah Elliott, son Thomas & Mercy (Walker) Elliott.

Children by Rebecca, 2nd wife, b. at Little Compton, R.I.

Sarah, b. Dec. 20, 1711; m. (1) Josiah Washburn, son John & Rebecca (Lapham) Washburn; (2) 1738, Samuel Crane.
Mary, b. 1714, m. Edmund Burt.
Priscilla, b. Feb. 27, 1718; m. 1739 John Hackett as his 3rd wife.
Eunice, b. Sept. 23, 1722; d. young; not mentioned in father's will.

References:

The Richmond Family by J.B. Richmond, pp. 10, 11, 27, 28, 25, 26; Mayflower Index Vols. 1 & 2, pp. 604, 607, 608.

RIGGS

Chart XIV

Thomas[1] Riggs d. Feb. 26, 1722 age 90, at Gloucester, Mass. age 90; m. (1) Mary Millett, dau. Mr. Thomas and Mary (   ) Millett, June 7, 1658. She was b. 1639; d. Jan. 23, 1694-95 at Gloucester, Mass.; Thomas[1] Riggs m. (2) Eliz. Frese, Oct. 30, 1695.

Thomas[1] Riggs was educated in Eng. for the profession of a scrivener. He was town clerk 51 yrs.; selectman 20 yrs. sometimes schoolmaster; representative 1700; often served on various committees.

Children:

Mary, b. Mar. 6, 1659; m. Nov. 1677, Benjamin Haskell.
Thomas[2], b. Jan. 23, 1660; d. Feb. 1, 1660.
Sarah, b. Feb. 16, 1661; m. May 9, 1661, John Tucker.
Anna, b. Apr. 27, 1664; d. Dec. 7, 1701; m. Jan. 30, 1683, Nathaniel[2] Wharff at Gloucester.

Riggs

Children of Thomas[1] Riggs: (con't)

Thomas[2], b. Dec. 7, 1666; d. Aug. 1756; m. (1) Nov. 22, 1687, Ann Wheeler of Salisbury; m. (2) Mar. 5, 1723, Elizabeth Wood.
John[2], b. Feb. 25, 1670; d. Jan. 12, 1748; m. Jan. 1, 1689-90, Ruth Wheeler.
Eliz. b. Apr. 22, 1672; d. Apr. 28, 1728; m. Apr. 28, 1692, Ezekiel Collins.
Abigail, b. Dec. 29, 1678.
Andrew, b. Jan. 8, 1682; living in 1771; m. Jan. 24, 1703-4, Mary Richardson of Newbury at Newburyport.

References:

Hist. of Gloucester by Babson, p. 131; Gloucester V.R. Vol. I, pp. 578, 579, 581, 582, 583, 584; Vol. II pp. 452-456; Vol. III p. 256-258; Savage's N.E. Dict. p. ; Pope's Pioneers of Mass. p.

ROBBINS

Chart XVI

Nicholas Robbins of Duxbury, Mass. 1638; Shoe Maker; made his will Feb. 9, 1651; m. Ann _______; an original Proprietor of Bridgewater but never resided there.

Children:

John, m. Dec. 14, 1665, Jehosabeth Jourdaine (res. at Duxbury & Bridgewater.
Katherine
Mary, m. George Turner.
Hannah

References:

N.E.H.G. Reg. IV p. 319; Popes Pioneers of Mass.; p. 386; Winsor's Hist. of Duxbury, p. 297.

ROGERS

Chart III & IV

Thomas Rogers, Mayflower Passenger, b. ; d. 1620 at Plymouth, in "first sickness".

Thomas Rogers & his son Joseph came over on the Mayflower. Thomas[1] was the Eighteenth Signer of the Compact.

Rogers

Children:

John, d. bef. Sept. 20, 1692; m. at Plymouth, Ann Churchman, Apr. 16, 1639.
Joseph, d. at Eastham betw. 2 & 15 Jan. 1677/8; m. Hannah ____.

Reference: Families of the Pilgrims by Shaw, pp. 126, 127.

John[2] Rogers d. bef. Sept. 20, 1692 (Prob.); m. Ann Churchman, Apr. 16, 1639, dau. of Hugh Churchman.

Children:

John[3], b. abt. 1640; d. 28 June, 1732; m. (1) Nov. 1666 at Duxbury, Elizabeth Pabodie; (2) Oct. 21, 1679 Hannah (Hobart) Brown.
Anna, b. aft. 1640, bef. 1650; d. aft. July 24, 1710; m. (1) 23 Nov. 1664 at Taunton, John Tisdale; (2) Thomas Terry, (3) Samuel Williams.
Abigail, b. abt. 1641; d. Aug. 1727; m. abt. 1663 John Richmond.
Elizabeth, b. 1653; d. aft. July 25, 1698; m. Nov. 17, 1668, at Taunton, Nathaniel Williams.

Reference: Families of the Pilgrims by Shaw, pp. 127, 128.

Joseph[2] Rogers d. in 1678 (will dated Jan. 2, 1666/7, proved Mar. 5, 1677/8); Resided Duxbury & Eastham, Mass.

Lieut. Joseph Rogers came over on the Mayflower with his father abt. 1655; he moved to Eastham where he died. His wife was Hannah __________.

Children:

Sarah, b. Aug. 6, 1633 at Duxbury; d. Aug. 15, 1633.
Joseph, b. July 19, 1635 at Duxbury; d. at Eastham Dec. 27, 1660; m. Apr. 4, 1660, Susanna Deane at Eastham.
Thomas, b. Mar. 29, 1638; d. betw. Mar. 5, 1677/78 and (bef) Oct. 30, 1678; m. Dec. 13, 1665 at Eastham, Elizabeth Snow.
Elizabeth, b. Sept. 29, 1639; d. aft. Jan. 2, 1667/68, & bef. July 4, 1674; m. Jan. 9, 1660, at Eastham, Jonathan Higgins. He m. (2) her sister Hannah Rogers.
John, b. Apr. 3, 1642 at Duxbury; d. at Eastham bef. Aug. 10, 1714; m. Aug. 19, 1669, Elizabeth Twining.
Mary, b. Sept. 22, 1644 at Sandwich; d. at Barnstable, Mass., John Phinney Aug. 10, 1664.
James, b. Oct. 18, 1648; d. Apr. 13, 1678; m. Jan. 11, 1670, at Eastham, Mary Paine.
Hannah, b. at Sandwich; d. aft. Oct. 17, 1680, Jonathan Higgins (he m. (1) her sister Elizabeth Rogers.)

Reference: Families of the Pilgrims by Shaw, pp. 126-219.

ROWLANDSON

Chart V

Thomas[1] Rowlandson (Rolenson or Rowlinson) d. Nov. 17, 1657 at Lancaster, Mass. He resided at Ipswich, Mass., 1637; removed to Lancaster in 1655; was proprietor 1637; Freeman May 2, 1638; Constable 1645.

He m. Bridget, wid. of Robert Mussey, between 1644 & 1648. She m. (3) May 31, 1659, William Kerley, Sr. at Lancaster; d. June 14, 1662 at Lancaster, Mass.

Children:

Thomas[2], m. Dorothy Portland, May 17, 1653; d. July 7, 1682.
Elizabeth, m. (1) Dea. Richard Wells of Salisbury; (2) Oct. 24 or 27, John Harris of Rowley, Mass.
Martha, m. John[2] Eaton (John[1])
Joseph[2], b. abt. 1631 in Eng.; d. Nov. 23 or 24, 1678 at Wethersfield; m. 1656, Mary, dau. of John White. Joseph[2] grad. Harvard 1652; was minister; resided at Lancaster, Boston and later Wethersfield.

References:

Old Families of Salisbury & Amesbury by Hoyt, Vol. I, pp. 306, 307; Lancaster, Mass., Births, Mar. & Deaths, pp. 11, 12; Popes Pioneers of Mass. p. 393.

ROYAL

Chart II

William[1] Royal, d. June 15, 1676 (est. settled 1722-3); resided North Yarmouth, Me., Salem, Mass., Wescustogo 1636, Dorchester. He was a Cooper; engaged by Mass. Bay Co. March 23, 1628 to go to N.E.; arrived at Salem 1629, where he gave his name to "Royal's Side". Thomas Gorgas granted him 250 acres bordering on Royal River in 1643. He was Clerk of the Writs in No. Yarmouth 1667; was a leading citizen of No. Yarmouth; left there for Dorchester at beginning of Phillips War. His neighbors deposed that he was about 80 years of age when he arrived there.

William[1] Royal m. Phebe Greene. She d. July 16, 1678.

Children:

William[2], b. abt. 1640; d. Nov. 7, 1724 aged 85th yr.; m. Mary ________.
John[2], d. bef. May 9, 1699; m. Elizabeth Dodd. (She m. (2) May 9, 1699, Thomas Southerin)
Samuel[2], of Boston, Cooper, was wounded at Black Pt. Garrison 1675; m. Sarah ________.
Isaac of Dorchester, Carpenter; m. (1) Ruth Tolman, m. (2) Waitstill Spurr.

Royal

Children of William[1] Royal: (con't)

Joseph of Boston, Sailmaker, b. abt. 1645; d. Jan. 14, 1728 age 83; m. Mary ________.
Elizabeth (probably) m. (1) Thomas Barlow, (2) John Coombs, (3) John Warren. Her children by 2nd & 3rd husbands, called Joseph Royal "Uncle".
Margaret, m. (1) Thomas Watkins (?), (2) Thomas Stevens.
Mary)
Mehitable) these named in "Pioneers on Maine Rivers".

References:

Gen. Dict. of N.H. Vol. IV pp. 599, 600; Pioneers on Maine Rivers, pp. 213, 228, 234-8, 250, 252; Maine Hist. & Gen. Reg. Vol. I, p. 150; Vol. II, p. 265; Hist. of Salem by Perley, pp. 119, 120, 128.

SAMPSON

Chart II

Henry[1] Sampson, Mayflower Passenger; came with Edward Tilley and his wife. He was too young to sign the compact, but was included in the assignments of lands 1623 and in the division of cattle in 1627. He removed to Duxbury early and was one of the original grantees of Bridgewater 1645, although he never moved there.

Henry[1] Sampson d. Dec. 24, 1684 at Duxbury (will and inv. in May. Desc. Vol. 2, p. 142); m. Anne Plummer on Feb. 6, 1635 at Plymouth. She was b. bef. 1620 & d. bef. 1684.

He was Constable at Duxbury in 1661; Gr. juryman 1649 & 1663; Collector of The Excise at Dusbury June 5, 1667; Member of the Duxbury Co. Aug. 1643; Vol. for Piquot War June 7, 1637.

Children:

Stephen, d. bef. Jan. 3, 1714; m. bef. 1686, Elizabeth ______.
John, d. aft. May 27, 1702, unmarried.
James, d. bef. July 7, 1718; m. bef. Oct. 12, 1694, Hannah ( ) Wait.
Caleb, b. bef. 1670; d. aft. July 9, 1744; m. (1) bef. 1685 Mercy Standish; m. (2) Jan. 30, 1728/9 at Duxbury, Rebecca Stanford.
Elizabeth, b. bef. 1647; d. bef. Oct. 17, 1750 & aft. Nov. 23, 1711; m. Robert Sprout.
Hannah, b. bef. 1650; m. Mar. 20, 1665 at Duxbury, Josiah Holmes.
__________ dau. m. John Hammer.
Mary, m. John Summers.
Dorcas, b. bef. 1669; d. aft. Dec. 24, 1684; m. bef. 1684, Thomas Bonney. He m. (2) July 18, 1695 Sarah Studley.

Sampson

References:

Families of the Pilgrims pp. 131, 132; Pierces Colonial Lists, pp. 42, 53, 60, 75, 84; May. Desc., Vol. 2, p. 142.

SEARS
Chart III

Richard[1] Sears (Sares, Sayre) b. abt. 1590, son of John Bouchier and Marie (Lemoral) Sayer; d. 1676 age 86, at East Dennis, Mass.; will dated 10 (3) 1667, wills to Bro. Thasher, Codicil Feb. 3, 1675; m. Dorothy Thacher, sister of Anthony Thacher, in Plymouth, Mass., 1632.

Richard[1] Sayre joined the Scrooby Co., at Leyden, Holland, & upon the death of his father in 1629 came into possession of a large property & subsequently accompanied the remnant of the congregation to Plymouth.

He resided at Plymouth, Mass. 1630 (taxed there in 1632); Salem, Mass., 1638 (recd. a land grant there); East Dennis 1643; one of the founders of Yarmouth, Mass., 1639. He was Constable of Sesuit (now E. Dennis) in 1660; Deputy of the Court 1662; Representative at Yarmouth, 1661; Gr. Juryman at Yarmouth, 1652; Freeman June 7, 1653; member of the Yarmouth Co., Lieut. Wm. Palmer; was a trader.

Children:

Knyvet[2] b. 1635; d. in Eng. 1686; m. Eliz. Dimmock.
Paul[2] b. 1637; m. Deborah Willard.
Silas[2] b. 1639;
Deborah, b. abt. 1640; m. 1659 Zachariah Paddock (Richard Sears willed to son-in-law Zachariah Paddock & his wife Deborah).

References:

Gen. Dict. of N.E. by Savage, Vol. p. ; Hist. of Yarmouth, Mass., by Swift, 1884, p. 59; Hist. of Salem, Mass., Vol. II p. 247; Pope's Pioneers of Mass. p. 406; Soc. Col. Wars, Index to Ancestors Publ. 1922, p. 421; Pierce's Col. Lists pp. 15, 20, 74; Mar. Rec. by Clemens, p. 193.

SHAW
Chart XXII

Abraham[1] Shaw, clothier, came from the Village of Northowran in the parish of Halifax, Eng., to Watertown, Mass.; was a proprietor 1636; His house burned in Oct. 1636 and he removed to Dedham; was made freeman Mar. 9, 1636-7; was Constable 6 (7) 1638; had liberty to erect a corn mill Feb. 12, 1636-7; had grant of coal or iron stone which may be found in any common ground at this country's disposing Nov. 2, 1637.

Shaw

Abraham[1] Shaw made his will abt. Nov. 1638; m. Bridget Best on June 24, 1616, at Northowram, Parish of Halifax, Eng. She was bpt. Apr. 9, 1592 at Ovenden, a dau. of Henry Best.

Children, Records of baptisms Northowram, Parish of Halifax, Yorkshire.

Joseph, bpt. Mar. 14, 1618; d. at Weymouth, Mass., Sept. 16, 1704.
Susannah, m. bef. Oct. 1638, Nicholas Byram of Weymouth, d. 1699 - will proved Dec. 18, 1699.
Grace, bpt. Aug. 15, 1621; m. William Richards of Weymouth.
Martha, bpt. Dec. 1, 1623; d. Mar. 31, 1625.
John, bpt. Nov. 16, 1628; d. Apr. 12, 1629.
Marie, bpt. June 18, 1626; m. John Bicknell of Weymouth. She was adm. Church of Charlestown July 1, 1645.
John, bpt. May 13, 1630; d. Sept. 16, 1704; m. June 7, 1658, Sarah Waters (?) at Weymouth, Mass.
Martha, bpt. Jan. 6, 1632; m. Thomas Vinson of Weymouth.

References:

N.E.H.G. Reg. Vol. 48, p. 346; Reg. Vol. 2, p. 180 (Will)
Reg. Vol. 49, p. 64; Hist. of Weymouth, Mass. Vol. 4, p. 611.

SHAW

Chart II & XIX

John[1] Shaw, planter, Plymouth, one of the "purchasers or old comers" had share in division of cattle 1627; freeman of Plymouth 1636; juryman 1648. He was one of those who undertook to cut a passage from Green's Harbor to the Bay, bef. July 1, 1633. In 1645 he was one of eight men who went out against the Narragansetts.

John Shaw, the Elder, as his name appears in Plymouth Colony Records, bought land in the Twenty-six Men's Purchase prior to the breaking out of the War and was one of the inhabitants of Middleboro in the Fort at that time. He was one of the Purchasers of Dartmouth in 1652 and one of the original owners of Bridgewater and of the Purcade Purchase.

John[1] Shaw d. Oct. 24, 1694. His wife Alice d. March 6, 1655 at Plymouth.

Children:

John[2] went to Eng. unmarried.
James[2] m. Dec. 24, 1652, Mary, dau. Experience Mitchell
Jonathan[2], m. Jan. 22, 1657, Phebe, dau. George Watson; (2) Persis, wid. Benjamin Pratt & dau. John Dunham.
Abigail, b. bef. 1632; d. Oct. 24, 1694 (?); m. Stephen Bryant.

Shaw

References:

Hist. of Middleboro, Mass. by Thomas Weston, p. 53; Savage's Gen. Dict., Vol. 4, pp. 5, 6; Pope's Pioneers of Mass., p. 410; Pierce's Col. Lists pp. 76, 88; Mayflower Desc. Vol. 10, p. 33.

SIMONDS

Chart X

William[1] Simonds was in Concord, Mass. 1639, removed to Woburn 1644. His first wife Sarah was buried at Concord 3 (2) 1641. He was taxed at Woburn 1645; Deposed in 1658, age abt. 47 yrs.

William[1] Simonds was b. abt. 1611; d. June 7, 1672 at Woburn; m. (2) at Woburn, Mass., Judith (Phippen) Hayward, wid. of James Hayward, Jan. 18, 1644 (or March 18, 1643 - County Rec.). Judith Phippen, age 16, came in the Planter, March 22, 1634, cert. from the Parish of Stepruy. She was b. ab.t 1618; d. Jan. 3, 1689-90, at Woburn, Mass.

Children, all born at Woburn, Mass.

Sarah, b. July 28, 1644; m. Nov. 30, 1665 at Concord, John Heywood.
Judith, b. Mar. 3, 1646; m. Dec. 9, 1668 at Concord, John Barker.
Mary, b. Dec. 9, 1647; d. Aug. 29, 1728; m. Apr. 25, 1671, Roger Chandler of Concord.
Caleb[2], b. Aug. 16, 1649; d. Nov. 4, 1712; m. Sept. 25, 1677, Sarah Bacon.
William[2], b. Apr. 15, 1651.
Joseph[2], b. Oct. 18, 1652; was a carpenter, settled at Cambridge Farms or Lexington.
Benjamin[2], b. Mar. 18, 1654; m. Rebecca. She d. Apr. 1713.
Tabitha, b. July 20, 1655; d. Aug. 20, 1655.
Joshua[2], d. July 16, 1657.
James[2], b. Nov. 1, 1658; d. Sept. 15, 1717; m. Dec. 29, 1685 to Susanna Blogget, dau. Samuel & Ruth Blogget.
Bethiah, b. May 9, 1659; m. Aug. 13, 1696, John Walker, Sr.
Huldah, b. Nov. 20, 1660; m. Apr. 30, 1683, Samuel Blogget, Jr.

References:

Hist. of Woburn, Mass. by Sewell, pp. 637, 638; Concord, Mass. V.R. pp. 3, 12, 13, 15; Pope's Pioneers of Mass.; p. 445.

SOMES

Chart XIV

Morris[1] Somes, b. abt. 1600 (Deposed in 1658, age abt. 58); d. Jan. 16, 1689 at Gloucester, Mass.; Adm. granted Dec. 28, 1692; m. (2) Elizabeth Kendall, dau. of John & Elizabeth (   ) (Holley) Kendall of Cambridge. She d. Jan. 4, 1696-7 at Gloucester, Mass.; m. (1) Marjorie ________ who d. Jan. 22, 1646 at Gloucester, Mass.

Children by 1st wife:

Marie, b. Mar. 1, 1641-2; m. Oct. 17, 1660 John Heman (or Hammond).
Sarah, b. June 15, 1643; m. June 15, 1665 Henry Witham.
Timothy[2], m. (1) Apr. 2, 1673, Jane Stanwood (she d. Oct. 30, 1696); m. (2) Hannah Despar, Mar. 11, 1697.

Children by 2nd wife:

John[2], b. Apr. 22, 1648; m. Hannah Shattuck, dau. of Samuel Shattuck of Salem. He resided Boston.
Lydia, b. Oct. 3, 1649.
Nathaniel[2], b. July 27, 1651; d. (?) July 12, 1690.
Patience, b. Mar. 10, 1652.
Abigail, b. May 6, 1655; may be the one who m. Anthony[1] Bennett bef. 1679. She d. Oct. 26, 1733 betw. 70 & 80 yrs. of age. Abigail Somes would have been 78 yrs. of age in 1733. Her brother Timothy[2] Somes signed as security & the inventory, to est. of Anthony[1] Bennett 1690.
Hannah, b. Sept. 3, 1658.
Joseph, b. Dec. 3, 1654.

References:

Gloucester, Mass. V.R. Vol. I pp. 665-669; Vol. II, pp. 508, 510; Vol. III pp. 290, 291; Hist. of Gloucester by Babson, p.166; Clemen's M. Rec. bef. 1699 (Revised) p. 200; Savage's N.E. Dict. Vol. IV p. 140; Pope's Pioneers of Mass., p. 425.

SPAULDING

Chart I & IX

Edward[1] Spalding, tailor, came over from England in 1619 with Sir George Yeardley. He was in James City, Va. Feb. 16, 1623, with a son and a daughter. About 1634 Edward and Margaret Spalding, from Jamestown, Va.; were in St. Mary's Co. Maryland; proprietor of Braintree, Mass., 1640; Freeman May 13, 1640; an original incorporator of Chelmsford, Mass. 1653. He was in Wenham, Mass. 1645. He was selectman of Chelmsford 1654, 1656, 1660 & 1661; Surveyor of Highways 1663; juryman 1648.

Spaulding

Edward[1] Spalding's 1st wife was Margaret. She d. in Braintree, Mass., Aug. 1640. He m. (2) Rachel. He d. Feb. 26, 1669 or 1670, age about 72 yrs. (Court rec. gives the latter date) Will dated Feb. 13, 1667; was probated Apr. 6, 1670. His widow died shortly after.

Children: by 1st wife

John[2], b. 1631; d. 1721; m. May 18, 1658, Hannah Hale.
Edward[2], b. 1635; d. Jan. 1708; m. (1) July 6, 1663, Priscilla Underwood at Chelmsford; (2) Margaret Barrett, Nov. 22, 1681.
Grace, d. at Braintree, Mass., May 1641.

Children: by 2nd wife

Benjamin[2], b. at Braintree, Mass., Apr. 7, 1643; m. Oct. 30, 1668, Olive Farwell, dau. Henry & Olive Farwell. They resided at Canterbury, Windham Co. Coun.
Joseph[2], b. Oct. 25, 1646; d. Apr. 3, 1740 in Plainfield, Mass.; m. Mercy Jewell, dau. Thomas and Grizell Jewell.
Dinah, b. Mar. 14, 1648; m. Feb. 9, 1674, Eliazer Brown.
Andrew, b. Nov. 19, 1652; d. May 5, 1713; m. Apr. 30, 1674; Hannah Jefes, dau. Henry Jefes of Billerica.

References:

The Spaulding Memorial by Charles Warren Spalding; Chelmsford V.R. pp. 141, 142, 319, 320, 323; Hotten's Lists of Emigrants to America 1600-1700, p. 176; McKenzies Am. Ancestry, Vol. IV p. 259; Bulkeley Gen. by Jacobus, p. 23.

Andrew[2] Spaulding was the youngest child of Edward and Rachel Spaulding, and by the will of his father, heir to the paternal estate. He was b. Nov. 19, 1652; d. May 5, 1713 at Chelmsford, Mass.; m. Hannah Jefes, dau. Henry and Hannah (Births) Jefes. She was b. Feb. 4 (or 14) 1654-5 at Billerica, Mass.; d. Jan. 21, 1730; bur. in Forefathers Cemetery, Chelmsford, Mass. Andrew[2] Spaulding was deacon of the church until the time of his death.

Children:

Hannah, d. Mar. 10, 1677.
Andrew[3], b. Mar. 25, 1678; d. Nov. 7, 1753; m. Feb. 5, 1701, Abigail Warren.
Henry[3], b. Nov. 2, 1680; d. Apr. 5, 1718; m. 1701 or 2 at Dunstable, Mass. M. Elizabeth Lund.
John[3], b. Aug. 20, 1682; d. Mar. 7, 1760; m. Feb. 6, 1705, Mary Barrett.
Rachel, b. Sept. 26, 1685; m. Dec. 7, 1703, Samuel Butterfield.
William[3], b. Aug. 3, 1688.
Joanna, b. Oct. 8, 1689-90; m. Joseph Fletcher.
Benoni[3], b. Feb. 6, 1691; d. Dec. 17, 1752 at Chelmsford; m. (1) Rebecca; (2) Esther Chamberlain, Dec. 21, 1743; Resided Billerica, Mass.
Mary, b. Dec. 5, 1695; d. July 18, 1698.

Spaulding

References:

The Spaulding Memorial by Charles Warren Spaulding; Chelmsford V.R. pp. 141, 144, 142, 146-148; 320, 322, 323; Dunstable Families.

Henry[3] Spaulding, b. Nov. 2, 1680; d. Apr. 5, 1718, age 38 yrs. 5 mos. 3 days, bur. in Forefathers Cemetery in Chelmsford, Mass.; m. Elizabeth Lund abt. 1701-3, dau. of Thomas and Eleanor Lund of Dunstable. She was b. Sept. 29, 1684; d. April 17, 1781. She m. (2) Samuel[2] Scripture of Groton, Mass., Int. Feb. 6, 1723-4. Elizabeth had a son of this marriage, Samuel[3] Scripture b. Apr. 27, 1727. He m. Mary Green Oct. 9, 1746 at Groton, Mass.

Elizabeth Scripture, wid. was bur. Apr. 17, 1781, age 98 yrs. 4 mos. at the Forefathers Cemetery, Chelmsford, to the side and back of her 1st husband Henry Spaulding. Henry Spaulding served in the Colonial Wars.

Spaulding Children - b. at Chelmsford:

Henry[4], b. Nov. 22, 1704; d. Apr. 29, 1792; m. (1) May 19, 1725 Lucy Proctor; m. (2) Apr. 27, 1743, Mariah Adams.
Thomas[4], b. July 30, 1707; d. Aug. 13, 1795; m. int. March 13, 1730-31, Mary Adams; res. Carlisle, Mass.
William[4], b. Mar. 17, 1711; d. June 21, 1790; m. Jan. 6, 1731 Hepzibah Blood, dau. Joseph Blood of Groton, Mass.
Leonard[4], b. Dec. 1, 1713; d. Feb. 1758; m. (int.) Dec. 18, 1737, Elizabeth Durant. She m. (2) Dr. Ezekiel Chase & d. in Buckfield, Me. age 80 yrs.
Eleazer, b. May 27, 1717; m. Oct. 30, 1753, Elizabeth Proctor.

References:

The Spaulding Memorial by Chas. Warren Spaulding; Chelmsford, Mass., V.R. pp. 145, 147, 151, 323, 324, 327; Hist. of Groton, Mass., by C. Butter, 1848, p. 434; Groton, Mass. V.R. p.

Leonard[4] Spaulding, b. Dec. 1, 1713 at Chelmsford, Mass., d. Feb. 1758 at Concord, Mass.; m. Elizabeth Durant (int.) Dec. 18, 1737 at Chelmsford. She was b. abt. 1719, dau. of Thomas[2] and Sarah (Jaquith) Durant of Billerica, Mass. She m. (2) Dr. Ezekiel Chase, July 20, 1768; d. 1799 ae. 80 at Buckfield, Maine.

Children:

Benjamin[5], b. Feb. 5, 1739 at Chelmsford, Mass.; d. Oct. 14, 1811 at Buckfield, Maine; m. Nov. 24, 1764, Chelmsford, Mass., Patty Barrett.
Elizabeth, b. Dec. 29, 1740; m. Jan. 24, 1760, John Green.
Rachel, bpt. Chelmsford, Nov. 14, 1742; m. Sept. 21, 1761, James Pemberton.
Thankful, bpt. Chelmsford, Oct. 21, 1744; m. John Walker.
Sarah, b. Concord, Mass., Oct. 29, 1745; m. Oct. 30, 1766, James Nicholas of Billerica.

Spaulding

Children of Leonard[4] Spaulding: (con't)

Abel, b. Dec. 29, 1752, Concord, Mass.; m. Mary Warren at Chelmsford.
Esther, b. Jan. 21, 1755.
Lucy, b. Jan. 21, 1757; m. Apr. 6, 1779 at Concord, William Spaulding; d. Apr. 15, 1821 at Carlisle, Mass.

References:

Chelmsford, Mass., V.R. pp. 144-149, 322, 324; Concord, Mass. V.R. pp. 200, 204, 221; Early Church Recs. of Hudson, N.H. in N.E.H.G. Reg. 1937;

Benjamin[5] Spaulding, b. Feb. 5, 1738-9 at Chelmsford, Mass.; d. Oct. 14, 1811 at Buckfield, Maine; m. Nov. 29, 1764 at Townsend, Mass., to Patty Barrett. She was b. Jan. 20, 1740-1 at Chelmsford, Mass., dau. of John[4] & Martha (Heald) Barrett; d. Oct. 4, 1819 at Buckfield, Maine.

Benjamin[5] Spaulding resided Chelmsford, Ashby and Townsend, Mass., and Buckfield, Maine. He served in Capt. Oliver Barrow's Co. in the French and Indian War. It is believed that this Benjamin Spaulding was one of the many of his surname who marched to Cambridge on the occasion of the Lexington Alarm in April 1775. There were five Spaulding's all of Chelmsford, Mass., in Capt. Oliver Baron's Co., and one of them was Benjamin. He was one of the famous minute men of Boston.

The first improvements made in the town of Buckfield, Maine, were made by Benjamin Spaulding in 1776. He at one time owned 800 acres of land and was very prominent in town affairs. Hist. of Buckfield says "The descendents of this worthy couple (Benjamin and Patty Spaulding) of every generation, have always been considered as of the very best people of the town and have ever been honored with offices and positions of trust within their gift." Mr. Spaulding became one of the three leading spirits in the Management of the town and the most prosperous and wealthy of them all.

The poor and the needy came to Benjamin and Patty Spaulding's home and it was not unusual for them to go home with a hundred weight of corn and half a cheese.

Children:

Patty, b. Sept. 14, 1765; m. Joseph Robinson.
Rebecca, b. Nov. 10, 1766; d. June 10, 1858; m. 1785 Benjamin[6] Heald, son of Israel[5] (John[4,3,2,1])
Benjamin Jr., b. Aug. 15, 1768; d. Feb. 18, 1858, ae. 89; m. (1) Oct. 15, 1790, Myrtle Robinson of Sumner, Maine, dau. Increase & Rebecca Robinson; m. (2) Mrs. Mary Sturtevant/Bampas of Hebron, Maine.

Spaulding

Children of Benjamin[5] Spaulding (con't):

Leonard[6], b. Feb. 13, 1770; d. Aug. , 1854 ae. 84; m. Margaretta Warren.
Elizabeth, b. Jan. 18, 1772; m. John Fletcher.
Abel, b. Oct. 15, 1777; d. Sept. 1, 1809; m. 1799, Phebe Proctor.
Esther, b. Oct. 28, 1779; m. Alexander Thayer.
Stephen[6], b. Oct. 13, 1782; d. Apr. 28, 1865 ae. 85 yrs., m. (1) Feb. 5, 1804, Bethiah Record; m. (2) Sophia Morrill.
Thankful, b. Aug. 16, 1787; m. Caleb Cushman.

References:

Hist. of Buckfield, Maine by Alfred Cole & Charles F. Whitman; The Spaulding Memorial by Charles Warren Spaulding; Hist. of Townsend, Mass. by Sawtelle, p. 424; Mothers of Maine by Helen Coffin Beedy, 1895, p. 269; Cutter, Vol. II, p. 269; Chelmsford, Mass. V.R. pp. 144, 145, 147, 149;

Capt. Leonard[6] Spaulding, b. Feb. 13, 1770 at Chelmsford, Mass.; d. Aug. 27, 1854 at Buckfield, Maine; m. Margaretta Warren, dau. of Capt. John & Jane (Johnson) Warren. She was b. Jan. 11, 1774; d. July 13, 1856 at Buckfield, Maine.

Capt. Spaulding was a prosperous farmer and good Citizen. In planting time, when seed was scarce, it is said of him that he would sell to those who had no money and take his pay in work; but would tell those that had money that they must buy elsewhere. His granddaughter, Emma Frances Spaulding Bryant, said he served in the old French War.

Children:

Sally, b. Nov. 22, 1794; d. Dec. 11, 1836; m. June 5, 1814, Increase Spaulding.
William[7], b. Apr. 2, 1796; d. Sept. 17, 1848 at Swanton, Ohio; m. Jan. 17, 1820 to Rebecca Swallow, dau. Leonard and Olive F. Swallow of Buckfield, Maine.
Zilpha, b. July 25, 1799; d. Jan. 30, 1844; m. May 21, 1821, Hon. Job Prince.
James[7], b. June 10, 1802; d. Oct. 31, 1886; m. June 5, 1825 to Cynthia Bray at Turner, Maine.
Africa[7], b. May 10, 1804; d. Jan. 5, 1886; M. Oct. 12, 1834 to Harriet Swett.
Almeda, b. Aug. 28, 1807; d. Feb. 11, 1843; m. Sept. 1825 to Winchester Spaulding.
Abel[7], b. July 29, 1809; m. July 1, 1868 to Marcia Geer, res. Swan Creek, Fulton Co. Ohio.
Jane, b. Sept. 20, 1811; m. Mar. 3, 1844, Winchester Spaulding.

Spaulding

Children of Capt. Leonard[6] Spaulding, (con't):

Benjamin Franklin, b. Dec. 1, 1814; m. Nov. 29, 1840, Lydia Stetson Fletcher, dau. Daniel & Mary Fletcher; res. Forest City, Meeker Co., Minn.
Diantha, b. Aug. 20, 1817; m. Oct. 5, 1834 to Arretus Farrar.

References:

Hist. of Buckfield, Maine by Alfred Cole & Charles F. Whitman; The Spaulding Memorial by Charles Warren Spaulding.

Capt. James[7] Spaulding, b. June 10, 1802 at Buckfield, Maine; d. Oct. 31, 1886 at Earville, Ill.; m. June 5, 1825 to Cynthia Bray at Turner, Maine. She was a dau. of Thomas and Cynthia (Record) Bray; b. March 25, 1802 at Turner, Maine; d. Dec. 11, 1864, Buckfield, Maine.

Capt. James[7] Spaulding was greatly respected by all who knew him. It was said of him that "his was as good as his note". His wife d. in 1864 and he went to live with his son-in-law Jacob W. Browne, where he lived until his death, engaging actively in farming as long as he lived. His dau. Zelpha was very beautiful and his son Greenleaf was a very fine mathematician, being United States Coast and Geodetic Surveyor for many years at North Haven Island, Maine; Sandy Hook, New Jersey; and Fort Hamilton, N.Y.

Children:

Margaretta Jane, b. Sept. 8, 1826; d. Oct. 4, 1894; m. (1) Ezra Bisbee; m. (2) Jacob W. Browne.
Zilpha Prince, b. Apr. 10, 1832; d. Jan. 14, 1862 to Christopher C. Packard.
James Greenleaf, b. July 4, 1834; d. Apr. 8, 1910; m. (1) Jan. 9, 1865 to Nancy Woodsum Hines; (2) Feb. 8, 1893, Cora Ada Smith.
Emma Frances, b. Feb. 16, 1844; d. May 2, 1901; m. June 26, 1864, Col. John Emory Bryant.

References:

History of Buckfield, Maine, by Cole & Whitman; The Spaulding Memorial by Charles Warren Spaulding; Spaulding Bible Record.

STOCKBRIDGE

Chart VIII

John[1] Stockbridge b. abt. 1608 in Eng.; d. 13 (8) 1657, will dated 4 (7) 1657, prob. Apr. 8, 1658; m. (1) bef. 1634 Ann; m. (2) at Scituate, Elizabeth Sone, Oct. 9, 1643; m. (3) Mary ________ who survived him. She m. (2) Daniel Henricke, April 8, 1660.

John[1] Stockbridge was a wheelwright; at age 27, he, his wife Ann, age 21 and Charles age 1, came in the Blessing in July 1635. He owned and operated a water mill at Scituate, Mass.; took oath of allegiance Feb. 1, 1638; Constable 1643; Grand Juryman, 1648; member of Scituate Co. 1643;

Children: by 1st wife Anne

Charles, b. in Eng. abt. 1634; m. 1669 or before Abigail Pierce.
Hannah, bpt. Oct. 8, 1637; d. July 5, 1665; m. 29 (8) 1656 William Ticknor.
Elizabeth, b. abt. 1639; m. Jan. 1, 1661, Thomas Hyland.

Children: by 2nd wife Elizabeth

Sarah, bpt. Mar. 15, 1645-6; m. Jan. 6, 1669 Joseph Woodworth at Scituate.
Hester, bpt. July 11, 1647;

Children: by 3rd wife Mary

John, b. July 19, 1657;
Mary, b. Apr. 29, 1655;

References:

Pope's Pioneers of Mass. p. 435; N.E.H.G. Reg. VII, p. 352; Bank's Planters of the Commonwealth, p. 177; Pierce's Colonial Lists pp. 51, 58, 74; Boston Births, Mar. & Deaths 1630-1699, pp. 14, 57, 61, 62, 76; Scituate V.R. Vol. II pp. 274, 445, 451; Vol. II pp. 337, 338;

Charles[2] Stockbridge, b. abt. 1634 in Eng.; d. Dec. 28, 1683 at Scituate, Mass.; res. Charlestown, Boston, Scituate; m. by 1659, Abigail Pierce, sister of Michael Pearse (in his will dated Jan. 15, 1675 Michael Pierce calls Charles Stockbridge "brother").

Charles[2] Stockbridge, wheelwright, inherited the water mill from his father; was constable at Scituate 1669; soldier at Scituate & received land for his services.

Stockbridge

Children of Charles[2] Stockbridge:

John[3], b. at Boston, Dec. 2, 1659; d. Feb. 1, 1659-60.
Abigail, b. at Charlestown, Mass.; d. July 15, 1743; m. Nov. 4, 1676, Henry Josselyn.
John[3] (again), b. at Boston, Sept. 29, 1662.
Charles[3], b. Feb. 4, 1663; d. Apr. 7, 1731; d. bef. 1699.
Sarah, b. May 30, 1665; m. Israel Turner.
Thomas[3], b. Apr. 6, 1667; m. July 28, 1697 Sarah Poole, dau. of Thomas of Weymouth.
Elizabeth, b. Apr. 13, 1670; m. David Turner.
Joseph[3], b. June 28, 1672; d. Mar. 11, 1773 at over 100 yrs. age age; m. Margaret Turner, dau. of Joseph Turner; resided Scituate.
Benjamin[3], b. Oct. 9, 1677; m. July 23, 1701; m. Marcy Tilden.
Samuel[3], b. July 9, 1679; m. Aug. 5, 1703, Liddia Barrell, dau. of William.

References:

Pope's Pioneers of Mass., p. 435; Scituate V.R. Vol. I pp. 336, 337, 339; Vol. II pp. 272, 273, 274, 445; Hist. of Duxbury by Winsor, p. 323; Pierce's Colonial Lists pp. 52, 101, 102; Boston Births, Mar. Deaths 1630-1699, pp. 69, 71; Savage's N.E. Dict. Vol. IV pp. 197, 198.

THURSTON

Chart IV

Edward[1] Thurston, b. abt. 1617 in Eng.; d. Mar. 1, 1707 at Newport, R.I., (will made Jan. 11, 1704; proved Mar. 12, 1707); m. Elizabeth Mott, dau. of Edward and Elizabeth (Creel) Mott, on June 1647 at Portsmouth, R.I. (their m. 3rd on rec. of Soc. of Friends at Newport, R.I.). Elizabeth was b. in 1629 and d. Sept. 2, 1694 at Newport, R.I. She was bur. at Coddington Burial Ground.

Edward[1] Thurston was a Quaker; freeman 1655; Commissioner 1663; Deputy 1667-71, 71-74 incl., 80-85 incl.; Assistant 1675, 86, 90, 91; Aug. 26, 1686 signed an address, with other Quakers, to the King, asking to be excused from bearing Arms; Jan. 30, 1690, he, with 5 other assistants & Deputy Gov. Gen. Greene, wrote a letter to William & Mary, congratulating them on their accession to the Crown - mentioned the seizure of Andros in R.I. and his return to Mass.

Children:

Sarah, b. Mar. 10, 1648.
Elizabeth, b. Feb. 1650.
Edward[2], b. Apr. 1, 1652; m. Susanna Jeffrey, dau. Wm. & Mary (Gould) Jeffrey. Res. Newport.
Eleanor, b. Mar. 1655; d. 1724; m. (1) 1674 _______ Jeffrey; m. (2)

Thurston

Children of Edward[1] Thurston, (con't):

Mary, b. Feb. 1657; d. Nov. 16, 1732; m. Rev. Ebenezer Slocum, son of Giles & Joan Slocum.
Jonathan[2], b. Jan. 4, 1659; d. 1740; m. Sarah abt. 1678.
Daniel[2], b. Apr. 1661; d. 1712; m. Mary Easton, dau. John & Mehitable (Gaunt) Easton, res. Newport.
Rebecca, b. Apr. 1662; d. Sept. 15, 1737; m. (1) Peter Easton, son of Peter & Ann (Cogswelle) Easton; m. (2) Nov. 21, 1691 Weston Clarke, son of Jeremiah & Frances (Latham) Clarke.
John, b. Dec. 1664; d. Oct. 22, 1690; m. Elizabeth ________; res. Newport, both bur. Clifton burial grounds.
Content, b. June 1667.
Samuel[2], b. Aug. 24, 1669; d. Oct. 27, 1747; m. Abigail Clarke, dau. Latham & Hannah (Wilbur) Clarke; res. Newport.
Thomas[2], b. Oct. 8, 1671; d. Mar. 22, 1730; m. Mehitable Tripp, dau. Peleg & Ann (Sisson) Tripp.

References:

Austins Gen. Dict. of R.I. p. 201; Am. Gen. Vol. 17, p. 194, Vol. 20, p. 118; Arnolds V.R. of R.I. Vol. 4, pp. 64, 66; Little Compton R.I. Families by L. C. Hist. Soc. p. 673; Thurston Gen. by Brown Thurston pp. 673-676.

Jonathan[2] Thurston, b. Jan. 4, 1659; d. (will prov.) Apr. 15, 1740 (written Aug. 22, 1735) at Dartmouth, Mass.; m. (1) Sarah __________, 1679 or before. She d. before Jonathan made his will as she is not mentioned. Jonathan[2] Thurston resided at Newport & Little Compton, R.I., and Dartmouth, Mass. He was a Grand Juryman at Little Compton, June 3, 1684.

Children:

Edward[3], b. Oct. 18, 1679; m. (1) Dec. 19, 1706; Susanna Pearce, dau. George & Alice (Hart) Pearce; m. (2) Oct. 11, 1712, Sarah Carr, dau. Ezek & Susanna Carr.
Elizabeth, b. Nov. 29, 1682; m. Jan. 6, 1703 in Little Compton, Jonathan Wood, son of Col. Thomas & Rebecca Wood.
Mary, b. Mar. 20, 1685; m. July 6, 1706 Lt. George Brownell, son of Thomas & Mary (Pearce) Brownell of Little Compton.
Jonathan, b. July 5, 1687; m. Hannah.
Rebecca, b. Nov. 28, 1689; m. May 6, 1711 Capt. Edward Richmond, son of John[2] & Abigail (Rogers) Richmond.
Content, b. Aug. 18, 1691; m. Sept. 14, 1715 Henry Wood.
Sarah, b. Nov. 9, 1693; m. June 26, 1712 ________Farraday.
John[3], b. July 12, 1695; d. bef. 1735.
Eleanor, b. Nov. 26, 1696; m. ___________ Peters.
Abigail, b. May 7, 1700; m. Oct. 2, 1729, William White of Dartmouth.
Hope, b. Nov. 26, 1698; d. Feb. 1716.

Thurston

Children of Jonathan[2] Thurston: (con't)

Patience, b. Feb. 16, 1702; m. Feb. 21, 1723, Thomas Southworth.
Amey, b. Jan. 29, 1705; d. bef. 1735.
Peleg[3], b. July 8, 1706; d. bef. 1735.
Jeremiah[3], b. May 8, 1710; d. bef. 1735.
Susanna, b. Aug. 20, 1712; m. ___________ Carr.
Joseph[3], b. Apr. 25, 1714; m. June 1, 1738, Mary Burgess, dau. of Thomas & Patience Burgess.
Job, b. July 1, 1717.

References:

Little Compton Families, pp. 673-675; Thurston Gen. by Brown Thurston pp. 673-676; Austins Gen. Dict. of R. I, p. 201.

TILDEN

Chart VI & XXIII

Nathaniel[1] Tilden bapt. July 28, 1583 at Tenterden, Eng.; made his will May 25, 1641 (will prob. July 31, 1641); m. Lydia Huckstep, dau. Stephen & Winifred (Hatch) Huckstep, abt. 1606-7; She was b. Feb. 11, 1587-8; d. after July 31, 1641.

Nathaniel[1] Tilden came in the Hercales of Sandwich in March 1634, bringing wife Lydia, 7 children & 7 servants; settled in Scituate; was Town Officer & Ruling Elder; resided, Stepney or Tenterden, near Cranbrook, Co. Kent Eng., & Scituate, Mass. He was called "Mr." and "Gentleman" in both old and new England Records; was Mayor in 1622 & jurat 1624, 25, 27 & 29.

Children: Bapt. at Tenterden, Eng.

Thomas, bpt. Oct. 23, 1608; bur. Jan. 19, 1618-19 at Tenterden.
Mary, bpt. May 20, 1610; m. (1) Mar. 13, 1636-7, Thomas Lapham; (2) William Bassett.
Joseph, bpt. Jan. 12, 1611-12; bur. Mar. 15, 1611-12 at Tenterden.
Sarah, bapt. June 13, 1613; m. Mar. 13, 1636-7 Geo. Sutton.
Joseph[2], bpt. Apr. 29, 1615; m. Nov. 20, 1649, Alice, dau. John Twisden of Marshfield, Mass.
Stephen, bpt. Mar. 31, 1617; bur. Oct. 21, 1619 at Tenterden.
Thomas[2], bapt. Jan. 19, 1618; m. Elizabeth (Bourne) Waterman, dau. Thomas Bourne of Marshfield.
Judith, bapt. Oct. 22, 1620; d. abt. Mar. 30, 1663; m. Jan. 3, 1641, Abraham Preble; res. York, Me.
Winifred, bpt. Oct. 20, 1622; bur. Sept. 14, 1627 at Tenterden.
Lydia, bpt. May 30, 1624; bur. Sept. 15, 1624 at Tenterden.
Lydia, bpt. Sept. 28, 1625; m. Richard Garrett.
Stephen[2], bpt. Oct. 11, 1629; m. Jan. 25, 1661-2, Hannah Little, dau. Thomas Little.

Tilden

References:

N.E.H.G. Reg. Vol. 65, pp. 322-333, Vol. 67, pp. 44-48; Vol. IV p. 173; XXXVIII p. 322; Hist. of York, Me., by Banks, Vol. I p. 149; Dean's Hist. of Scituate; Water's Gen. Gleanings in Eng., Vol. I, pp. 71, 72, 500; Pope's Pioneers of Mass., p. 454; Plym. Col. Rec. XII;

TURNER

Chart XVI

George Turner d. Dec. 7, 1695 at Bridgewater, Mass.; m. Mary Robbins, dau. Nicholas and Ann (   ) Robbins of Duxbury; settled early in W. Bridgewater, Mass.

Children:

John, m. Hannah
Ann, m. bef. 1679, Elihu Brett.

References:

Hist. of Bridgewater by Mitchell, p. 333; The Brett Gen. by L. B. Goodenow, p. 48.

TYBBOT

Chart XIII

Walter[1] Tybbot, b. 1584; d. at Gloucester, Mass. 14:6m;1652 ae. 67. The name of his wife is not known. She m. (2) John Harding (or Hardin), April 22, 1652.

Walter[1] Tybott came to Gloucester with Rev. Richard Blynman, Minister from Wales; came to Greens Harbor; in Marshfield, Mass. 1640; Removed to Gloucester, of which he was one of the Founders; admitted Freeman May 19, 1642; Selectman 1642 and in several subsequent years; May 26, 1647 he was licensed to sell wine and exempted from common training. Walter Tybbott was one of the largest proprietors of land which he cultivated well. He was Constable in 1643.

In his will dated 5 (4 mo.) 1651, he mentions his "son-in-law Edward Clarke"; and Elizabeth Dick; Elenor Bapsene (Babson) wife of James Bapsene; Sebelone Hill and John Hill - with the exception of Edward Clark, the relationship is not given. The only child mentioned was Mary Haskell, the wife of William Haskell.

Tybbot

Child (only one proved):

Mary, m. Nov. 6, 1643, William Haskell.

Agnes, wife of Edmond Clark, may have been a dau. as her husb. is called "son-in-law" of Tybbot. She had a previous husb. Dike, by whom she had a dau. Elizabeth.

References:

Hist. of Gloucester, Mass. p. 173; Notes and Additions No. 1, by Babson; Gloucester, Mass. V. R. Vol. 2 p. 556, Vol. 3 p. 309; Essex Co. Mass., Probate Rec., Vol. 1, p. 132.

WARREN

Charts I & XI

James[1] Warren, b. abt. 1620 (deposed upward of 80 in 1702); will proved Dec. 24, 1702; m. Margaret. Her will was proved Oct. 15, 1713.

James[1] Warren is said to have come from Birwick, Scotland to Kittery, Me. from York, Me. He settled in the Parish of Unity, Kittery, Me., July 15, 1656 there was land laid out to him. He was probably a Scotch Prisoner, taken by Cromwell in the battle of Dunbar in 1651 & sent to Boston. His wife was from Ireland. He held various town offices being selectman for several years.

Children:

Gilbert, b. 1654; m. Sarah Thompson, widow.
Margaret, m. James Stackpole.
Grizel, b. Feb. 24, 1661; d. Oct. 27, 1750; m. (1) Richard Otis of Dover, N. H.; m. (2) Oct. 15, 1693, Philip Robitaile in Canada. She was captured by Indians in 1688.
Jane, m. Aug. 4, 1690, William Grant.
James, b. 1658; d. June or July 1725; m. 1691, Mary Fost (Foss or Frost).

References:

Old Kittery Maine & Her Families by Everett S. Stackpole, pp. 785-787; Gen. Dict. of Maine & N. H. Vol. 5, pp. 720-721.

James[2] Warren, b. 1658; est. Adm. July 6, 1725; m. Mary Foss (or Frost) abt. 1691. She was a dau. of John & Mary (Chadbourne) Foss (or Frost); b. Oct. 1665 at Boston, Mass.; d. aft. June 1750.

Warren

James^2 Warren was often one of the Selectmen and prominent in Town Affairs; Surveyor of highways & fences 1692-3, 1698-9; Constable 1693-4; Gr. jury 1695; foreman Gr. jury 1702; Auditing Committee 1696-1699; On committee to divide Kittery from Berwick lands, Feb. 1713-14; Resided Kittery, Maine.

Children:

Mary, b. Feb. 23, 1692; m. John Field.
Margaret, b. Nov. 5, 1694; m. Dec. 18, 1718, Nathaniel Heard.
James^3, b. June 8, 1698; m. Mary Goodwin.
Rachel, b. Aug. 29, 1700; d. Sept. 3, 1703.
Gilbert, b. Apr. 30, 1703; d. (will) 1755. He was a Quaker; m. Abigail ________.
John^3, b. Dec. 16, 1705; d. 1769; m. Mary Heard.

References:

Old Kittery and Her Families by Everett S. Stackpole, pp. 785-787.

John^3 Warren, b. Dec. 16, 1705; will proved Feb. 24, 1764; m. abt. 1728, Mary Heard. She was a dau. of Tristram and Abigail (Waldron?) Heard of Dover, N. H.; b. June 10, 1709.

John^3 Warren was on the Grand Jury & also at the inferior Court at York, Me., 1630-37; Held various offices in Berwick, Me., up to 1762; owned considerable real estate; his house was standing in 1898.

References:

Old Kittery Maine & Her Families by Stackpole, pp. 785-787; Landmarks of Ancient Dover, N. H. p. 56; Hist. of Durham, Me., p. 279.

Capt. John^4 Warren, b. Mar. 5, 1731 at Berwick, Me.; d. Jan. 30, 1807 at Stroudwater, Me.; resided Westbrook, Me.; m. Dec. 25, 1755 Jane Johnson. She was a dau. of John & Jane (Maxwell) Johnson, b. June 15, 1740 at Westbrook, Me.; d. Nov. 3, 1809.

John^4 Warren was a farmer and blacksmith; was a Priv. in Capt. John Brackett's Co., Col. Edmond Phinney's (31st) regt. Co. return dated Sept. 29, 1775; enlisted May 10, 1775; also Capt. James Johnson's Co., Col. Phinney's regt., order for bounty coat dated Cambridge, Fort No. 2; Oct. 24, 1775.

Warren

Children of John[4] Warren:

John[5], b. Nov. 9, 1756; d. May 23, 1776.
Polly, b. Mar. 7, 1758.
David[5], b. Nov. 17, 1760.
Elizabeth, b. June 28, 1753; d. June 23, 1846; m. Mar. 27, 1788 John Sweet, gr. father of Lincoln's law partner, Leonard Sweet.
Sally, b. June 9, 1766; m. June 27, 1791, Moses Fickett.
James[5], b. Jan. 25, 1770.
Margaretta, b. Jan. 11, 1774; m. Leonard Spaulding; d. July 13, 1856 at Buckfield, Me.
John[5], b. May 23, 1776; m. Eleanor Lamb; d. Sept. 10, 1845.
Robert[5], b. June 10, 1778; d. Apr. 19, 1845; m. Apr. 1845.
Nathaniel[5], b. Feb. 28, 1781.
Nancy, b. Oct. 24, 1782.

References:

Old Kittery Maine & Her Families by Everette S. Stackpole, pp. 785-787; Gen. of Warren Family by Orin Warren, Chase Press, Haverhill, Mass. 1902; Stackpole's Hist. of Durham, Me.; Mass. Soldiers & Sailors, Vol. 16, p. 620.

WASHBURN

Charts XVI & XXVI

John[1] Washburn, son of John & Martha (Timbrell) (Stevens) Washburn, bpt. July 2, 1597 at Evensham, Worstershire, Eng.; d. before 1670 at Bridgewater, Mass.; m. Nov. 23, 1618 at Bengeworth, Co. Worcester, Eng., Marjorie Moore. She was a dau. of Robert & Ellen (Taylor) Moore; b. abt. 1586 (49 in 1635).

John[1] Washburn came to Plymouth Col. between 1625 & 1631 as he was Churchwarden of Bengeworth Parish, Worcester, Eng., and at Duxbury, Mass. 1631. His wife came on the Elizabeth & Ann in 1635, with sons John age 14 & Philip age 11.

John[1] Washburn was 12th generation from Sir Roger de Washburn of Little Washbourne, Worcestershire, resident of Eng. in later half of thirteenth century. He was Freeman June 2, 1646; Member of Gr. Enquest at Plym. June 4, 1645; Took Oath of Loyalty at Duxbury, 1657; Surveyor of Highways 1649; Constable at Duxbury 1659; An original proprietor of Bridgewater 1645. He was a tailor and was taxed at Duxbury in 1632.

Children:

Mary, bpt. 1619; d. at Bengeworth.
John, bpt. Nov. 26, 1620; b. abt. 1621; m. 1645 Elizabeth Mitchell, dau. Experience & Jane (Cooke) Mitchell.
Phillip, bpt. 1622; d. at Bengeworth.
Phillip (again), b. abt. 1624;

Washburn

References:

Packard & Lothrop Fam. p. 4; Pope's Pioneers of Mass., p. 480; Founders of N. E. by Drake, p. 22; Bank's Topographical Index, p. 184; Crozier's Gen. Armory, p. 133; Pierce's Col. Lists, pp. 42, 53; Washburn Fam. by Mabel Thacher Washburn 1953, pp. 56-60; Ancestral Heads of N. E. Fam. by Holmes.

John[2] Washburn, bpt. Nov. 26, 1620 at Bengeworth, Worcestershire, Eng.; d. Nov. 12, 1686 (will dated Oct. 30, 1686) at Bridgeworth, Mass.; m. (1) Dec. 6, 1645, Elizabeth Mitchell, at Plymouth, Mass. She was a dau. of Experience & Jane (Cooke) Mitchell, b. at Plymouth, Mass. 1628; d. bef. Oct. 1686; m. (2) betw. 1684 & 1686, Mrs. Elizabeth Packard, widow of Samuel Packard of Bridgewater.

John[2] Washburn was a Soldier in Narragansett War; Gr. Juryman 1684; Memb. Duxbury Co. Aug. 1643; Memb. Gr. Inquest June 7, 1665; an original Proprietor of Bridgewater 1645.

Children:

John[3], m. 1679, Rebecca Lapham, dau. Thomas Lapham; d. Oct. 1719.
Thomas[3], m. (1) Deliverance, dau. Samuel Packard; (2) Abigail, dau. Jacob Leonard.
Joseph[3], m. Hannah, dau. Robert Latham.
Samuel[3], b. 1651; m. Deborah, dau. Samuel Packard.
Jonathan[3], m. 1683 Mary, dau. George Vaughan of Scituate.
Benjamin[3], lost his life in exped. of Sir Wm. Phips against Quebec, Aug. 1690.
Mary, b. 1661; m. Samuel Kensley.
Elizabeth, m. (1) James Howard; (2) Edward Sealey.
Jane, m. William Orcutt, Jr.
James[3], b. 1672; m. Dec. 20, 1693, Mary Bowden of Bridgewater, Mass.
Sarah, m. Jan. 12 1697, John Ames.

References:

Pope's Pioneers of Mass.; Packard & Lothrop Fam. by Whitman, p. 4; Clemen's Mar. Rec. bef. 1699 (reprint) p. 226; Gen. Adv. Vol. 2, pp. 25, 26; Scituate, V. R. Vol. I, p. 216; Pierce's Col. Lists, pp. 75, 88; Washburn Fam. 1953, pp. 56-60.

John[3] Washburn, b. 1646; d. Oct. 1719, age 73, at Bridgewater, Mass.; m. Apr. 16, 1679 at Bridgewater, Mass., Rebecca Lapham, dau. Thomas[1] and Mary (Tilden) Lapham, bpt. Mar. 15, 1645 at Scituate, Mass.; d. 1719 ae 73. John & Rebecca were bur. Ames Fam. Bur. Gr.; W. Bridgewater, Mass.

Washburn

Children of John[3] Washburn:

Josiah[4], b. 1680; m.
John[4], b. 1682; m. Feb. 16, 1709-10, Margaret, Dau. of Nathaniel[2] Packard.
Joseph[4], b. 1683;
William[4], b. 1686;
Abigail, b. 1688;
Rebecca, b. abt. 1690; m. Jan. 7, 1719, Capt. David Johnson of Bridgewater.

References:

Packard & Lothrop Families, p. 4; Bridgewater V. R. Vol. I p. 330, Vol. II p. 571.

WHARFE

Chart XIV

Nathaniel[1] Wharfe, d. bef. June 23, 1673; resided Casco Bay and Falmouth; m. bef. 1661, Rebecca Macworth, dau. Arthur and Jane (   ) (Andrews) Macworth. Rebecca (Macworth) Wharfe, m. (2) William Rogers, as shown by mother's will dated May 20, 1676 at Boston, Mass.

Nathaniel[1] Wharfe signed a Falmouth petition 1663. Was fined 1665 for absence from court; with wife quit claimed interest in cert. Marsh to Francis Neal 1666 and appraisers est. of Richard Martin Feb. 21, 1672-3. His own est. was appraised by Robert Corbin & Jenkin William June 23, 1673; Administration to wid. Rebecca.

Children:

Nathaniel[2], b. 1661; m. Jan. 30, 1683, Anna Riggs.
Rebecca, m. Feb. 15, 1693, Francis Holmes at Boston.
Arthur[2], b. abt. 1664.
Isaac
John

References: Gen. Dict. Maine & N. H. Part V p. 742.

Nathaniel[2] Wharfe, b. 1661; living Apr. 12, 1736 upward of 75. Resided Gloucester and Falmouth; m. Jan. 30, 1683, Anna Riggs, dau. Thomas and Mary (Millett) Riggs. She was b. Apr. 27, 1664 at Gloucester, Mass.; d. Dec. 17, 1701 at Gloucester.

In 1735 Nathaniel deeded all interest in Falmouth to Nathl. Noyes; he was near 70 in Oct. 1730, 71 in Apr. 1732, + 72 in July 1733; deposed that he lived at Falmouth from earliest recollection until the first Ind. War, and for 7 years between the Wars & built a home on his father's farm, Wharfe's Point up Presumpscot River next above Macworth's.

Wharfe

Children of Nathaniel[2] Wharfe:

Nathaniel[3], b. Mar. 8, 1684-5; m. Feb. 7, 1714, Hannah Stevens.
Rebecca, b. Apr. 21, 1686; m. (1) probably July 13, 1704, Anthony Bennett; m. (2) probably Ezekiel Woodward Nov. 24, 1740.
Mary, b. Apr. 7, 1687; m. Dec. 25, 1705, Ebenezer Davis.
Charrity, b. Feb. 22, 1687-8; d. Feb. 24, 1687-8.
Thomas[3], b. Jan. 30, 1688; lost at sea 1753; m. Nov. 16, 1738, Dorcas Lane.
Experience, b. June 15, 169_; d. June 15, 169_.
Mercy, b. June 15, 169_; d. June 15, 169_.
Hannah, b. July 29, 1691; m. May 30, 1711, Joseph Witson.
Arthur[3], b. Mar. 5, 1693-4; m. Mar. 24, 1636-37, Martha Lee.
John[3], b. Jan. 15, 1695-6; m. (int) Mar. 5, 1718-19, Hannah Cleigh.
Patience, b. Oct. 17, 1697; d. Dec. 9, 1697.
Abraham, b. Oct. 11, 1699; d. Mar. 19, 1706-7.
Lydia, b. Mar. 25, 1701; d. Jan. 20, 1701-2.

References:

Hist. of Gloucester, Mass. by John J. Babson, 1860, p. 178; Additions to Hist. of Gloucester, p. 86; Gen. Dict. of Maine and N. H., Part V, p. 742; Gloucester V. R. Vol. I pp. 752, 754, 755; Vol. II pp. 82, 84, 568, 569, Vol. III pp. 319, 320, 321.

WILLIS

Charts XVI & XXI

Deacon John[1] Willis d. at Bridgewater, Mass.; will dated June 4, 1692, proved Sept. 29, 1693; m. Elizabeth (Hodgkins) Palmer, wid. of Wm. Palmer, Jr. She d. 1681.

Deacon John[1] Willis was a Puritan of great respectability and considerable distinction; came over prior to 1637 and settled in Duxbury, Mass., then was an organizer and proprietor of Bridgewater; holding various town offices; appointed to solemnize marriages and administered oaths; served as representative to the old Colony Court for a period of 25 years.

Deacon John[1] Willis had four brothers, Nathaniel, Lawrence, Jonathan and Francis. Nathaniel's estate was settled in 1686; Lawrence's estate settled at Boston, 1703; Francis' estate also settled at Boston abt. 1704. Jonathan was at Duxbury "for cure" and then was sent to Sandwich, whence he came. John & Nathaniel appear to be the only two of the five brothers who left descendents.

Willis

Children of John[1] Willis:

John[2], d. 1712; m. Experience Byram.
Nathaniel[2], d. 1716; m. Lydia ________.
Jonathan[2]
Comfort[2], served in Calvary in part of Phillip's War.
Benjamin[2], will dated 1696; m. Susanna, dau. of Thomas Whitman of Bridgewater.
Hannah, m. Nathaniel Hayward.
Elizabeth, m. ________ Harvey.
Sarah, m. John Ames.

References:

Will of John[1] Willis in Gen. Adv. Vol. 3, p. 93; Savage's Gen. Dict. of N. E. Vol. IV p. 575; Pope's Pioneers of Mass., p. 502; Hist. of Bridgewater by Mitchell, pp. 363, 364.

John[2] Willis, d. 1712; m. bef. 1671-2, Experience Byram. She was a dau. of Dr. Nicholas and Susanna (Shaw) Byram.

Children:

John[3], b. 1671-2; d. Nov. 1, 1632; m. 1698, Mary Brett.
Samuel[3], b. 1688; d. June 19, 1797; m. Mar. 18, 1705-6, Margaret Brett at Bridgewater.
Experience
Mary, m. Jan. 25, 1701 Israel Randall.
Nathaniel

Reference: Hist. of Bridgewater, Mass., by Mitchell, pp. 364, 365.

John[3] Willis, b. 1671-2; d. Nov. 1, 1732 in 61st yr. at Bridgewater, Mass., m. 1698 Mary Brett at Bridgewater. She was a dau. of Judge Elihu and Ann (Turner) Brett, b. 1678-9; d. Jan. 14, 1756, in 78th yr., at Bridgewater. She and her husband were buried in the Old Graveyard, South St., Bridgewater, Mass.

Children: 1st 3 born in Bridgewater, Mass.

Mary, b. Nov. 27, 1699; d. Dec. 19, 1774; m. Nov. 28, 1723, Joseph Packard.
John, b. Dec. 24, 1701; d. July 17, 1776; m. Dec. 9, 1724, Patience Hayward.
Margaret, b. Sept. 15, 1704; d. Apr. 12, 1771, ae. 76; m. July 4, 1733 Nathaniel Harvey.
Experience, b. 1706; m. May 4, 1732, John Randall of Easton.
Martha, b. 1708; m. Nov. 22, 1733, James Pratt of Easton.
Mehitable, b. 1715; m. Apr. 21, 1743, James Stacey of Easton.

Willis

References: Brett Gen. by L. B. Goodenow, 1915, pp. ; Bridgewater V. R. Vol. I pp. 352, 353; Vol. II pp. 410; Hist. of Bridgewater by Mitchell, p. 365.

WILSON

Chart X

Roger Wilson, b. abt. 1588 at Scrooby, Nottinghamshire, Eng.; m. Mary Fuller, prob. dau. of Nicholas Fuller of Stepney, Eng., a barrister and memb. of Parliament for St. Maines in 1601. Mary was a sister of Dr. Samuel Fuller of the Mayflower.

Roger Wilson had much to do with the establishment of the band of Pilgrims. He was the chief instigator and supporter of the movement that led to the undertaking and stood as bondsman for William Bradford, Isaac Allerton, and Degory Priest. He was a member of John Robinson's Church - one of the three Friends who provided a house for the comfort and convenience of the growing Separatist Congregation and cooperated with Cushman, Bradford, Brewster, and others in the removal of the able-bodied members of the congregation to America in 1620. Was one of the wealthier of the congregation. He helped to fit out the Mayflower for its voyage.

Roger Wilson remained in Leyden with Rev. John Robinson. After the death of the Pastor, the remainder of the congregation returned to Eng., as persecution of the Separatists had subsided.

Roger Wilson did not come to America, however John, his youngest son b. in Leyden, Holland or in Scrooby, Nottinghamshire, Eng. (if his father returned to Eng.) in 1631 came to N. E.

Reference: Maine Genealogies by Little, Vol. III pp. 1565.

John[1] Wilson, youngest son of Roger and Mary (Fuller) Wilson, b. abt. 1631 in Leyden, Holland, or Scrooby, Nottinghamshire, Eng.; d. in Woburn, Mass., July 2, 1687; m. (2) Hannah (James) Palmer, bef. 1666. She may have been a dau. of Walter and Rebecca ( ) Palmer, bapt. 15 (4) 1634 prob. in Eng. She m. (3) Thomas Fuller of Woburn, Mass.

John[1] Wilson came in the Sarah and John from London, 1651; first appears on the tax list of Woburn, Mass., Aug. 26, 1666. He was a valient and sturdy Pioneer and a soldier of the early Wars; Lieutenant in the Indian Wars; a soldier in King Philips War.

Children prob. of 1st wife:

John[2], b. Jan. 3, 1653; d. aft. 1725; m. bef. 1672, Mary Lyon.
Dorcas, b. 1655; d. Nov. 29, 1714; m. Sept. 26, 1675, Aaron Cleveland in Woburn (ancester of Grover Cleveland).

Wilson

Children prob. of 1st wife: (con't)

Samuel, b. Dec. 29, 1658; d. Nov. 21, 1729; m. Feb. 24, 1681-2, Elizabeth, dau. Robert Pierce.

Children by Hannah:

Abigail, b. Aug. 8, 1666; m. (1) Joseph Hildreth Dec. 12, 1683; m. (2) abt. 1708, Jonathan Barrett of Chelmsford, Mass. She was bur. at Chelmsford Nov. 27, 1747.
Elizabeth, b. Aug. 6, 1668; m. Nov. 12, 1685, Isaac Hildreath at Chelmsford.
Benjamin[2], b. Oct. 15, 1670; m. Elizabeth ______ in 1691.
Hannah, b. May 31, 1672; m. Jonathan Pierce, Nov. 19, 1689.
Francis[2], d. Aug. 1724; m. Ruth Duntlen, Mar. 6, 1683.
James, b. abt. 1658 (prob. son of 1st wife); d. bef. 1749; m. (1) Jan. 19, 1687-8, Deborah Pierce; m. (2) Apr. 17, 1704, Margaret (Russ) Peters.

References:

Gen. & Fam. Hist. of Maine, by Little; Hist. of Woburn, Mass. by Sewell, p. 648; Cleveland Gen. Vol. I, pp. 38, 39; Fuller Gen. p. 13 (publ. 1909); Woburn, Mass. V. R. Part 3, pp. 303, 304; Cincinnati Enquirer, Aug. 1, 1915; Boston Evening Transcript, Apr. 7, 1932 (#3134);

WITHERELL

Chart VIII

Rev. William[1] Witherell (Weatherwell) M. A. was b. abt. 1602; will dated June 4, 1684 at Scituate, Mass.; m. March 26, 1627 at St. Mildred's Church, Canterbury, Co. Kent, Mary Fisher of Boughton, Monchelsea, Co. Kent. She was b. abt. 1605, a dau. of ________ Fisher & Joan (later wife of John Martin).

Rev. William[1] Witherell received B. A. & M. A. degrees at Corpus Christi College, Cambridge, Eng., where he was admitted in 1619. He was schoolmaster at Maidstone, Co. Kent, Eng.; came on the "Herculese" of Sandwich, with wife Mary and 3 children and 1 servant; was schoolmaster at Charlestown, Mass., 1635; at Cambridge, Mass., 1636, 1637; Proprietor at Duxbury, Mass., Aug. 31, 1640; called to be pastor of the 2nd Church of Scituate, Mass.; was ordained Sept. 2, 1645. He was minister at Scituate until April 9, 1684.

Rev. Witherell is thought to be a grandson of John Rogers, the Smithfield Martyr. If one wishes to know more about the Rev. John Rogers, see pp. 420-423 of "Foxe's Christian Martyrs of the World. Chicago: Moody Press.

Witherell

Children of William[1] Witherell:

Samuel[2] bpt. Dec. 5, 1628, All Saints, Maidstone, Co. Kent, Eng.; d. bef. Mar. 4, 1683 (date of inv. of his estate); m. Isabel ______; she m. (2) Josiah Torrey, Oct. 6, 1684.
Daniel[2] bpt. Dec. 3, 1630 at All Saints, Maidstone; d. Apr. 14, 1719, age 88 at New London, Conn.; m. Aug. 4, 1659, Grace dau. of Jonathan & Lucretia (Oldham) Brewster.
Thomas[2], bpt. Apr. 28, 1633 at All Saints, Maidstone;
John[2], d. (will dated) July 13, 1690; inv. dated Feb. 6, 1690/1; m. Hannah (Pincin) Young, wid. George Young & dau. of Thomas & Jane (Standlake) Pincin. She m. (3) ______ Morey.
Mary, m. Thomas Oldham of Scituate, Nov. 20, 1656; d. Dec. 12, 1710 at Scituate.
Elizabeth, m. Dec. 22, 1657, John Bryant as his 2nd wife.
Theophilus[2], m. Nov. 9, 1675, Mary, dau. of William & Mary (Rowlins) Parker; m. (2) Lydia, dau. of William & Mary (Turner) Parker. Mary & Lyida were half sisters.
Sarah, b. Feb. 10, 1644 at Scituate; m. Dec. 21, 1669, Israel Hobart, son of Rev. Peter Hobart of Hingham, Mass.
Hannah, b. Feb. 20, 1646 at Scituate; probably d. young.

References:

Gen. Adv. Vol. II pp. 61, 62; Canterbury Mar. Lic. 2nd Series, p. 1087; Drake's Founders of N. E., p. 82; Planters of the Commonwealth by Banks, p. 115; Gen. Adv. Vol. I, p. 21; Hist. New London, Conn. p. 363; Hist. of Cambridge, Mass., by Paige p. 701; Winsor's Hist. of Duxbury, p. 346; Dean's Hist. of Scituate, p. ; Pierce's Col. Lists, p. 112; Savage's Gen. Dict. of N. E. Vol. IV pp. 491, 492; Scituate V. R. Vol. I pp. 414, 415, Vol. II pp. 322, 332, 333, 467, 427.

The following elegy which was written in December 1680 is one of the few remaining examples of Rev. William Witherell's poetry. This was written when the author was 80 years of age and affords good evidence of his good scholarship, it being good, not only for his time, but for today. Cotton Mather commended upon his writings and rated his verse superior to Dunster.

Upon the much to be lamented Death of the thrice three times Honoured Josiah Winslow, Esq. late Governor, of New Plymouth and Chrlo Charus, beloved of his Prince.

Within this Sacred Urn doth lie,
The Quintesence of the Colonie
New England's Phoenix, Plymouth's glory,
Meet subject for a compleat story
To whom at helm, we yield the praise
Of blissful times of peaceful dayes;
The Halcyon which contrould our seas
Of civil storms and broiles appease.

Would you have me, him to discrie,
Angels must limn him out, not I;
A Sophoclean quill comes short,
His worth and merits to report:
Where Wisdom, Valor, Eloquence,
Were center'd in great Eminence
Faith, Justice, Patience, every grace
In this frayl clay tent had their place.
On these two pillars founded are,
The firmest States for Peace or War:
Christ was his all, him might he gain,
Far wealthier he than either Spain.
But why do I burn Tapers in the Sun:
Or midst great Cannons, let fly my pop-gun;
His worth transcends the weakness of my quill,
As lofty mounts o'ertops the pismire hill.

The goodliest Cedar which this land e'er bore
Is hewn flat down and level'd with the shore:
Under whose shade and boughs we shelter'd were,
'Gainst storms of outrage, wrongs oppression, feare.
Blessed with good Government, thrice happy we
Had we had eyes our happiness to see.
The sweetest Rose that e'er in Plymouth grew
Frost nips - dried up - like morning dew
Yet leaving a sweet scent, mongst great and small,
Perfum'd his name from Carswell* to White-Hall;
Whereby great Charles enamored of his worth,
Lets the warm glances of his love shine forth
Upon New Plymouth: grac'd with Royal favour,
Let us be Loyal bound t'our good behavior.
Strong were my feares, lest this strange blazing stream;+
Would be prognostick of some tragick theme;
Yet what it doth portend I cannot tell,
But here I come to ring the funeral Knell
Of a choice Worthy, and the people call
To come and solemnize the Funeral,
Of him who late was foremost for his worth
Close lock't in Prison, cannot now step forth.

* Carswell or Carsrull was the name of Gov. Winslow's seat in Marshfield, so called from a castle of his ancestors in England.

\+ The great Comet in 1680 which our venerable Author seems half inclined to believe, was sent to foretell Gov. Winslow's death.

How many dangers hath this gentleman,
In's life escaped, both by Sea and Land;
Fort-fights*, Sholes, Quicksands, Quag-mires, Boggs
  and Sloughs,
Enought to plunge an hundred strong team'd Ploughs:
Yet in brake through: but now we see him have
Mir'd and stuck fast in a dry upland grave.
The Pitcher that went oft whole to the well,
Comes home at last, crack'd like a broken shell.

Our Court of Justices sits in Widowhood:
The Judge arrested - Baile will do no good
Judges are stayes of States; when such stayes fall
It bodes the weak'ning of the Judgment Hall. (Isaiah 111-2)

Somewhat above thrice compleat seven years since,
Plymouth hath lost blest Bradford, Winslow, Prince.
Three skilled Pilots, through this Wilderness,
To conduct Pilgrims, all three call'd t'undress
Upon the top of Pisgah; while we here (Dur. XXXIV 4,5,6)
Left Pilot-less, do without Compass steer.

* The "Naraganset Fort fight" is meant.

Thrice honored Rulers, Elders, People all,
Come and laments this stately Cedar's fall,
Cut down at's height, full noontide, blest with shine
Of Royal favour, and (no doubt) Divine;
Freighted with tunns of honor. Every man,
At's best estate is altogeather vain, (Psalm XXXIX 5)
Ye birds of Musick, Lark, Thrush, Turtle, Quaile,
Ye pretty humming birds, and Nightingale,
Your doleful notes sigh over this sad hearse,
Sighs more suit Fun'ralls than a golden verse.

You that have skill in Verse, let every line
You here present, first pickled be in brine,
Had but the Muses heard thou hence wurt gone,
T'attend thy hearse, they had left Helicon;
Thrice Royal Charles, were he person here,
Into this Urn, would drop a sacred tear.
Had I a hundred eyes like Argus, I
Would weep them all purblind, pump them dry,
I'd rather drink the tears of my old, eyes
For sweet Josiah, than quaff muskadine.
Old eyes can shed few tears; but my old heart
More ready is to break, than eyes to smart.
Slight grief have tears, in troops that ready stand
To sally forth and but expect command:
But deep ingulphing sorrow strikes men dumb,
As frosty Winters do their joints benumb.

Methinks I see Cape Cod, Manamoit high land,
Our Scituate Cliffs, and the Gutnet weeping stand,
All clad in mourning sable; brinish streames
Venting, to float a gallant Ship to 'th Thames.
All creatures crowd to fetch so deep a groan,
Able to break an heart of hardest stone,
And all because their dear Josiah's gone.

Postscript
I wish that, He, who thee succeedeth next
May, like to thee, keep close unto the Text,
Sacred and Civil; He shall have my vote
While I am worth a Tester or Gray Groat.

Moestus posiut
William Witherell
Octogenarius

WOODMAN

Charts VI & XXXI

Mr. Edward[1] Woodman, bpt. Dec. 27, 1606 at Corsum, Co. Wilts, Eng.; d. 1694; m. bef. 1628 Joanna Bartlett. She was b. abt. 1614 (was 74 in 1688).

Mr. Edward[1] Woodman, his wife and two sons, Edward and John, came in the "James" of London in 1635. He was one of the 91 grantees who settled Newbury, Mass., and one of the 15 of that number entitled to be called "Mr." Edward[1] Woodman, Husbandman, was a man of influence, decision and energy; was Freeman May 25, 1636; Deputy to Gen. Court 1636-1639, 1643, 59, 60, 64; appointed one of three Commissioners in Newbury to end small causes, by Gen. Court, May 6, 1646; Granted 300 acres of land by Gen. Court 1660.

Children:

Edward[2], b. 1628; d. (will) Dec. 16, 1693 at Newbury; m. Dec. 20, 1653 at Newbury, Mary Goodridge.
John[2], b. 1630 or bef. in Eng.; d. Sept. 17, 1706, at Dover, N. H.; m. (1) Mary Field at Oyster River, N. H. July 15, 1656; m. (2) Oct. 17, 1700, Sarah Huckins.
Joshua[2], b. Jan. 12, 1636 (1st Eng. male child b. at Newbury); d. May 30, 1703, Newbury, Mass.; m. Elizabeth Stevens at Andover, Mass., Jan. 22, 1665-66.
Sarah, b. Jan. 12, 1641 at Newbury; m. John Kent, Jr. Mar. 13, 1665.
Jonathan[2], b. Nov. 5, 1643; d. Nov. 21, 1706 (will Nov. 15, 1706); m. July 2, 1668 at Newbury, Hannah Hilton. He was a Shipbuilder and resided at Newbury.
Ruth, b. Mar. 28, 1646; m. Oct. 17, 1666, Benjamin Lowle at Newbury.
Mary, m. Feb. 20, 1660, John Brown at Newbury.

References:

N. E. H. G. Reg. Vol. LXXXVI p. 345; Old Fam. Salisbury & Amesbury, Vol. I p. 365, 366, 234; Newbury V. R. Vol. I p. 556, Vol. II p. 522; Little's Gen. of Maine, Vol. I, p. 109; Clemen's M. Rec. bef. 1699, (revised ed. 1967), p. 237; Gen. Dict. Maine & N. H. Part V p. 770.

WRIGHT

Charts X & XL

Edward[1] Wright, son of Francis and Mary (Wiggins) Wright, of Castle Bromwich, Co. Warwick, Eng., b. abt. 1626; d. Aug. 28, 1691 at Concord, Mass., m. abt. 1653, Elizabeth (Mellows) Barrett, wid. of Thomas[2] Barrett of Concord, Mass. She was a dau. of Oliver and Mary (James) Mellowes, bpt. Dec. 10, 1625 at Sutterton, Co. Lincoln, Eng.; d. Feb. 15, 1690/1 at Concord, Mass.

Wright

Edward[1] Wright of Concord, Mass. sold to John Hoare, Mar. 4, 1671-2, all his right & title to an estate in Castle Bromwich, Co. Warwick, Eng., which fell to him as only son & heir of Francis Wright. The estate was given to Francis June 27, James (1613) (James, King of Eng. 1603-25) on his marriage to Mary, dau. of John Wiggins of Aldridge, Co. Stafford, by his father Edward Wright of Castle Bromwich, whose heir apparent he was. He refers to having been in Eng. a year before the date of the sale. He rec'd in part payment a house in Concord, Mass., of which John and Alice Hoare made full deed Aug. 1, 1682. He deeded lands Jan. 26, 1683, his wife Elizabeth, joining, to sons Samuel and Edward they to pay certain sums to their three sisters. Conditions incl. life income for himself and wife. He also gave land Dec. 31 to his son Peter on the occasion of his m. to Elizabeth, dau. wid. Elizabeth Lambson, an agreement was signed by all heirs at a later day, Robert Blood joining in. Peter agreed to pay a certain sum to his sister Sarah.

Children:

Elizabeth, b. abt. 1655; d. Dec. 16, 1704 at Concord; m. Oct. 23, 1682, John Hartwell as his 2nd wife.
Edward[2], b. Jan. 22, 1657-8; d. Jan. 22, 1725; m. Lydia Danforth.
Martha, b. June 18, 1659; d. June 14, 1746 at Stow, Mass.; m. Israel Heald.
Samuel[2], b. Apr. 12, 1661; d. Oct. 1, 1741; m. (1) Mary Hosmer; m. (2) Sarah _______.
Peter[2], b. abt. 1665; d. Jan. 15, 1717/18; m. May 5, 1684, Mary Lamson.
Sarah, b. abt. 1670; d. May 3, 1726 at Boston; m. Timothy Wales.

Children of Elizabeth (Mellows) & Thomas Barrett (son Humphrey Barrett)

Oliver Barrett, d. Sept. 1671 at Concord.
Mary, b. abt. 1651; d. July 18, 1717; m. Dec. 4, 1671 at Concord, James Smedley.

References:

Pope's Pioneers of Mass., p. 516; Savage's N. E. Dictionary, Vol. IV p. 655; Births, Mar., Deaths, Concord, Mass., pp. 9, 10, 25, 29, 55, 93, 144; Stow, Mass. V. R. p. 249; Deeds, Mdx. Co. Mass. Bk. 4, pp. 409-413; Family of Rev. Peter Bulkley by Donald L. Jacobus pp. 24-28 incl.

ZELLER

Chart No. I

Anthony Zeller, son of Mathiew, was b. 1805 at Pfaffenhoffen, Germany; d. 1873 Pfaffenhoffen, Bavaria (now known as Boblingen - is located south of Stuttgart (capitol of Wurttemberg in southern Germany. He m. Josepha Zeller, dau. of Johan Martin and Theresa (Probstlin) Zeller.

Anthony Zeller was Burgo-Master for many years and second largest land owner in village of Volshafen.

Johan Martin Zeller and Theresa Probstlin, m. June 30, 1807 at Beblinger, Bavaria, the same town in which she was born 1/1/1772. She d. there 1/6/1812.

Children: only two known but probably others

John George, b. Dec. 10, 1828 in Bavaria; d. June 17, 1893 at Spring Bay, Ill.; m. (1) Frederica Caroline Nicolas, March 8, 1855; m. (2) Caroline Winkler, Sept. 20, 1865.
Mathew,

Reference: Family Records.

Dr. John George[1] Zeller, was b. Dec. 10, 1828 near the city of Ulm on the Swiss border in Southern Bavaria, Germany; d. June 17, 1893 at Spring Bay, Ill.; m. (1) Frederica Caroline Nicholas on March 8, 1855. She d. May 15, 1865 and he m. (2) Caroline Winkler, Sept. 20, 1865. She was b. July 10, 1846 at Worth Twp., Woodford Co. Ill.; d. Jan. 20, 1923 ae 76 yrs. 6 mo. 10 days at Spring Bay, Ill.; dau. of Christian and Elizabeth (Snyder) Winkler.

Dr. John George Zeller, was Physician, Surgeon, Naturalist & Horticulturist. He came to America in 1847. After two years of travel and study he returned to Bavaria where he spent four years. He returned to America and in 1855 he graduated from St. Louis Medical College, in St. Louis, Mo. The same year he settled in Spring Bay, Ill.

As a medical man he took front-rank and was well informed of the latest advances in the field of medicine. He was a man of extraordinary business ability. He was a well loved physician whose many years of faithful toil in his profession made his name a household word in the community.

Children by 1st wife:

Charles Alexander[2], b. July 6, 1857; d. abt. 1908; m. Kate ____.
George Anthony[2], b. Nov. 7, 1858; d. June 1938; m. Sophie Kline. He was an outstanding Psychiatrist.
Josephine Matilda, b. Jan. 8, 1861; d. 1954; graduated in law at U. of Ill.; never practiced law; never married.
Frederica Caroline, b. Oct. 17, 1864; d. 1944, unmarried. She graduated in medicine at Woman's Medical College in Chicago.

Zeller

Children of Dr. John George[1] Zeller & his 2nd wife:

Catherine, b. Aug. 2, 1867; d. in infancy.
John Henry, b. June 15, 1869; d. Jan. 23, 1872.
Julius Christian, b. Dec. 15, 1871; d. March 10, 1938; m. Emma Alice Bryant, Jan. 1, 1871.
Christine, b. Feb. 6, 1878; d. Nov. 22, 1954; m. 1900, Everett W. Oglevee.
William L.[2], b. June 2, 1882; d. Sept. 10, 1957; m. abt. 1913, Minnie Koopman. He was a well known ornothologist and lecturer.

The Coat of Arms is the Zeller armorial of original grant, dating from the first Crusade A. D. 1096, in which it was first borne by a Sir Knight Crusader Ivhan Von Zeller.

References:

Obituary Notices; Hist. of Woodford Co. Ill.; Biographical Record of Livingston & Woodford Cos. Ill., p. 607.

Julius Christian[2] Zeller, b. Dec. 15, 1871 at Spring Bay, Ill.; d. March 10, 1938 at Kansas City, Mo.; m. Jan. 1, 1895 at Mt. Vernon, N. Y. to Emma Alice Bryant, dau. John Emory and Emma Frances (Spaulding) Bryant. She was b. in Atlanta, Georgia, Nov. 16, 1871; d. at East Orange, N. J. April 26, 1946. Both Julius Christian and Emma Alice Zeller, are buried at Spring Bay, Ill. (Peoria, R. #6), the same cemetery where his parents and many other relatives are buried.

He was a minister, Educator, Planter and Politician. During World War I, he was a Four Minute Man, an enrolling officer and a frequent speaker in connection with the Liberty Loan drives.

Dr. Zeller had numerous degrees: B. A. University of Chicago 1903; B. D. University of Chicago 1904; M. A. University of Chatanooga 1905; D. D. University of Chatanooga 1909; D. C. L. Illinois Weslyan University 1910; completed scholastic for Ph. D. at University of Chicago. He entered the ministry of the Methodist Episcopal Church in 1893, after receiving B. A. & B. O. degrees from the U. S. Grant University at Athens, Tenn. that same year. He served charges at Magnolia, Chebanse and Manteno, Ill. In 1904 he accepted the chair of Philosophy & Education in Ill. Weslyan University. In the fall of 1909 he became President of the University of Puget Sound, Tacoma, Wash. He resigned in 1914 and spent some time at the Graduate School of the University of Chicago, where he completed the scholastic work for his Ph. D. but did not complete his thesis because he became too much occupied with rural life problems in Mississippi where he had large plantations.

Zeller

Dr. Zeller was a member of the Miss. Senate for twelve or more years from 1916 to about 1930. From 1930 to 1932 he was Vice Chancellor, Dean of Men, and head of the Dept. of Philosophy and Ethics of the Univ. of Miss.

Children of Julius Christian & Emma Alice (Bryant) Zeller:

Miriam Irene, b. Oct. 28, 1895; m. (1) 1918, Frank Ogden; who d. 1918; (2) 1927 Russell Charles Gross.
Dorothy Spaulding, b. June 2, 1898; m. Aug. 1, 1926, Harry Francis Smith at New Vineyard, Maine.
Raymond Bryant, b. June 27, 1900; m. June 26, 1930, Elenor Gehrels; d. June 4, 1959.
Julius Cornelius, b. June 27, 1900; d. at birth.
Margaret Louise, b. Nov. 26, 1902; m. June 3, 1950, Clarence Jasper Garrett.
Ethel Frances, b. Nov. 26, 1902; d. age 2 yrs.
Rachel Elizabeth, b. July 4, 1906; m. Sept. 14, 1935, Ralph Blanchard Nelson.
James Greenleaf, b. abt. 1908; d. at birth.
Alice Caroline, b. Aug. 3, 1910; m. abt. 1933, William Lacey.
Letitia Josephine, b. June 1, 1912; m. (1) Edward R. Schauffler; m. (2) Clarence I. Brant; d. June 7, 1953, just one month before her dau. Marnee was three years old.

References:

Miss. Register 1920-24, p. 141; 1924-28 p. 150; Ntl. Encyclopedia of American Biography, Vol. 47, p. 559; Who's Who in America 1938 and before; Who Was Who in America 1938-42.

LINEAL ORGANIZATIONS

To which one or more of my sisters and I belong

(Margaret Zeller Garrett)

Order of Three Crusades, 1096-1192
National Society Magna Charta Dames
National Society Daughters of the Barons of Runnymede
Order of the Crown of Charlemagne in The U. S. A.
Society of Descendents of King William I The Conquerer
The National Huguenot Society
National Society of Mayflower Descendents
Daughters Founders and Patriots of America
National Society Women Descendents of the Ancient and Honorable Artillery Co.
Society of the Descendents of Colonial Clergy
Hereditary Order of the Descendents of Colonial Governors prior to 4 July 1776
Daughters of Colonial Wars Inc.
The National Society Colonial Dames XVII Century
Daughters of the American Colonists
National Society of New England Women
Order of Americans of Armorial Ancestry
Daughters of American Revolution
National Society U. S. Daughters of 1812
Dames of Court of Honor

The Order of The Three Crusades, 1096-1192

The American Ancestor, Joseph Bowles (Bolles) of Wells, Maine

The Crusader Ancestor, Simon St. Lis, Earl of Huntingdon. He lived in Huntingdon, Northemberland, England. He died abt. 1111.

Joseph Bowles (Bolles) was a son of Thomas Bolles of Osberton Manor in 1614 m. Elizabeth Perkins of Fishlake, Yorkshire - Proof: Libby's Gen. Dict. of Maine and N. H. p. 352; Adams & Weis, Magna Charta Securities Line 82, p. 68.

Benjamin Bolles of Osberton, Co. Notts, m. Ann Goodrich. Proof: Adams & Weis, Line 82 p. 68.

Lionell Goodrick of Kirby, Co. Lincs, m. Winifred Sapcott (?) Proof: Ibid.

John Goodrick of Kirby, Notts, m. Ann Dymoke. Proof: Ibid.

Sir. Lionel Dymoke d. 17 Aug. 1519; m. Johane Griffith (?) Proof: Ibid.

Sir Thomas Dymoke of Schrivelsby, Co. Lincs, m. Margaret de Welles. Proof: Ibid.

Sir Lionel de Welles, K. G. d. at Towton on 29 March 1461; m. ca 1426 to Joan de Waterton b. at Co. York. Proof: Ibid.

Eudo de Welles m. Maud de Greystock. Proof: Ibid & M. C. S. Line 63; Cockayne's Complete Peerage, Vol. XII, pt. 11, p. 443.

John de Welles b. at Conisholme, Lincs. on 20 April 1352; m. to Eleanor de Mawbray. Proof: Ibid - C. P. Ibid. p. 443 - footnote (J) and IX; p. 780; Weis 8 Ancestral Roots Supplement 1952, line 202.

John de Mawbray, b. at Epworth on 25 June 1340; d. at Thrace as a Crusader on 1368; m. ca 1349 to Elizabeth de Seagrave who d. 24 March 1398/99; Proof: Ibid. Line 63 and C. P. IX; pp. 383/4 & 720.

John de Mawbray, b. at Hovingham, Yorks., on 29 Nov. 1310; d. at York on 4 Oct. 1361; m. ca 29 Nov. 1326/7 to Joan Plantagenet. She d. ca 1349. Proof: Ibid. C. P. IX; pp. 380/83 & Von Riddlech's Charlemagne's Desc. pp. 160 & 174.

John de Mawbray, b. 4 Sept. 1286; d. at York, 23 March 1321/22; m. 1298 to Aline/Eleanor de Braoise, b. at Wales; d. ante 20 July 1331; m. at Swansea; Proof: Ibid. & M. C. Sureties & C. P. IX; pp. 377/8.

Roger de Mowbray b. at Thirsk / Hovingham; d. at Glient, ante 21 Nov. 1297; m. to Roese de Clare, livg. 1316. Proof: Ibid.

Sir Richard de Clare b. 4 Aug. 1222; d. 16 July 1262; m. (2) 25 July 1237/8 to Maud de Lacy; She was b. at Co. Lincoln Proof: M. C. S. Lines 28-63 & 107.

John de Lacy, Earl of Lincoln, Surety for Magna Charta, d. 22 July 1240; m. ante 21 June 1221 to Margaret de Quincy. She d. ante 30 March 1288/9. Proof: M. C. S. Lines 54 & 107.

Robert de Quincy, brother and not son of Saire de Quincey, Surety for M. C., both Crusaders; d. ante 1222; m. to Haivise of Chester, Countess of, b. at Lincoln 1180; Proof: M. C. S. Line 107 & C. P. Vol. XII, pt. 11, pp. 748/9 - footnote (g).

Robert de Quincy I d. ante 1127; m. Orabel Louchars. Proof: Cockayne, C. P. Ibid.

Saire de Quincey d. lvg. Jany. 1145/6, dcd. abt. 1156/8; m. Maud de St. Lis; lvg. 1156 - dead 1163; Proof: Ibid; pp. 745/6.

Simon de St. Lis d. ca. 1111; m. ca. 1090 to Maud of Huntingdon b. ca 1073; Proof: Cockayne C. P. XII; pt. ii, p. 745 & Ancestral Roots, Weis, Line 148 - The said Crusader Ancestor.

The Order of the Crown of Charlemagne in the U.S.A.

Joseph Bowles (Bolles) of Wells, Maine, American Ancestor. Line of descent same as "The Order of The Three Crusades" through:

Simon de St. Lis, Earl of Huntington - Crusader; d. 1111; m. ca 1090 to Maud of Huntington who was a dau. of:

Waltheof, Earl of Huntington; d. at Winchester 31 May 1076; m. Judith of Leus. Proof: Ancestral Roots - Weis - Line 148.

Lambert of Boulogne, Count of Leus; d. at Battle of Lille, 1054; m. Adelaide of Normandy, sister of the Conqueror on 1030. Proof: Ancestral Roots, Weis - Line 148 & Cokayne C. P. Vol. #1; pp. 350 & 353.

Eustice II, Count of Boulogne; m. Maud of Louvain. Proof: Ibid.

Lambert I, County of Louvain; d. subs. 1017; m. ca 990 Gerberga of Lorraine b. c 975; d. subs. 1017. Proof Ancestral Roots - Weis, Line 148 & Turton's Plantagogenet Ancestry, p. 171.

Charles, Duke of Lower, b. 953; d. 994; m. Bonne d' Ardennes & Verdun. Proof: Ancestral Roots, Line 148.

Louis IV (d' Autre Mer), King of France, b. 919; d. 10 Sept. 954; m. 939 to Gerberga of Saxony. She d. 25 May, 984. Proof: Ancestral Roots - Weis, Lines 142 & 148.

Charles III (The Simple) King of France, b. 17 Sept. 879; d. at Peronne on 7 Oct. 929; m. (3) Eadgifn or Edgwa, granddaughter of Alfred the Great of Eng. Proof: Ancestral Roots - Weis, Line 148.

Louis II (The Stammerer) King of France, b. 844; d. at Compiegna on 10 April 879; m. (2) ca. 868, to Adelaide (not named). She d. Subs. 901. Proof: Ibid.

Charles II, King of France, b. 13 June 828; d. near Mount Cenis in the Alp. on 8 Oct. 877; m. (1) Dec. 842 to Ermentrude of Orleans. She d. 6 Oct. 869. Proof: Ibid.

Louis I, King of France, b. 778; d. 20 June 840; m. Judith of Bavaria. Proof: Ibid.

Charles the Great (Charlemagne), King of France, Holy Roman Emperor; d. at Aix le Chapelle, on 28 June 813/14; m. to Hildegarde of Swabia. She was b. 758; d. 30 April 783. Proof: Ancestral Roots, Lines 50, 148 & 182, von Redlich's Charlemagne's Descendents, pp. 132 & 164.

Martha Bulkeley (wife of Abraham Mellowes) our American Ancestor. The Bulkeley Genealogy by Jacobus, p. 24; Charleston Estates, p. 665.

Rev. Edward Bulkeley of Odell, England, m. Olive Irby. Proof: The Bulkeley Genealogy by Jacobus, p. 13; Marcellus Donald R. Von Redlich "Pedigrees of Some of Emperor Charlemagne's Descendents", Vol. I, 1972, p. 134 reprint; The American Genealogist, V. 35 (1959), pp. 32, 106.

Elizabeth Grosvenor m. Thomas Bulkeley of Woore, Salop. Proof: "Pedigrees of Some of the Emperor Charlemagne's Descendents:, supra p. 134; TAG. op. cit. V. 31, 106. Jacobus, op cit., pp. 5, 9.

Randall Grosvenor m. Anne Charlton. Proof: Von Redlich; Ibid.; Jacobus, op. cit. pp. 5, 9, 11.

Richard Charlton m. Anne Mainwaring. Proof: Von Redlich, Ibid.; TAG, op. cit., V. 35, pp. 31, 106; Jacobus, op. cit.

Robert Charlton m. Mary Corbet. Proof: Von Redlich, Ibid.; TAG, op. cit., V. 35, pp. 29, 31, 104; Jacobus, Ibid.

Thomas (De Knightley) Charlton m. Elizabeth Francis. Proof: Von Redlich, Ibid.; Jacobus, Ibid.

Anne De Charlton m. William De Knightley. Proof: Von Redlich, Ibid; Jacobus, Ibid.

Thomas De Charlton. Proof: Von Redlich, Ibid.; Jacobus, op. cit. p. 12.

Alan De Charlton m. Margery Fitzaer. Proof: Von Redlich, Ibid. Jacobus, Ibid.

Elena La Zouche m. Sir Alan De Charlton. Proof: Von Redlich, Ibid; Cokayne, G. E. "The Complete Peerage", V. 12, Pt. 2 (1959) pp. 936, 937.

Alan La Zouche, Baron Zouche of Ashby, Leicester, m. Eleanor Seagrave. Proof: Von Redlich, op. cit. pp. 133, 134; Jacobus, Ibid.; Cokayne, op. cit. V. 12, Pt. 2, pp. 935-936.

Sir Roger La Zouche, Baron Zouche, m. Ela Longspee. Proof: Von Redlich op. cit. p. 133; Jacobus, Ibid.; Cokayne, op. cit. Vol. 12, Pt. 2, pp. 934-935.

Elena (Helen) De Quincy m. Alan La Zouche. Proof: Von Redlich, Ibid.; Jacobus, Ibid.; Cockayne, op. cit., V. 12, Pt. 2, pp. 753, 932, 934.

Roger De Quincy, Earl of Winchester, m. Helen of Galloway. Proof: Jacobus, Ibid; Cokayne, op. cit. V. 12, Pt. 2, pp. 751, 754.

Margaret (Fitzpernel) De Beaumont, m. Saier De Quincy, Earl of Winchester. Proof: Jacobus, Ibid; Cokayne, op. cit. V. 12, Pt. 2, pp. 748, 750.

Robert De Beaumont III, Earl of Leicester, m. Pernel of Grandmesnil. Proof: Cokayne, op. cit. Pt. 2, pp. 749-750; V. (1959) pp. 530-533.

Robert De Beaumont II, m. Amice De Montfort. Proof: Cokayne, op. cit. V. pp. 577, 530.

Isabel (Elizabeth) De Vermandois, m. Robert De Beaumont. Proof: Cokayne, op. cit. V. 7, pp. 523, 526.

Adelaide De Vermandois m. Hugh The Great, Count of Vermandois. Proof: Cokayne, op. cit. V. 7. p. 526.

Herbert IV, Count of Vermandois m. Adele De Valois. Proof: Brandenburg, Erich, "Die Nachkommen des Grossen" (1935), p. 5.

Otho, Count of Vermandois m. Pavie. Proof: Brandenburg, Ibid.

Herbert III, Count of Vermandois, m. Irmegard of Bar. Proof: Brandenburg, op. cit. p. 4.

Albert I, Count of Vermandois, m. Gerberga of Lorraine. Proof: Brandenberg, Ibid.

Herbert II, Count of Vermandois. Proof: Brandenberg, op. cit., pp. 3-4.

Herbert I, Count of Vermandois. Proof: Brandenberg, op. cit. p. 3.

Peppin, Count of Vermandois. Proof: Brandenburg, op. cit. p. 2.

Bernhard, King of Italy m. Cunigunde, Proof: Brandenburg, Ibid.

Pippin. Proof: Brandenburg, Ibid.

Charlemagne, King of the Franks and Emperor of the West, m. Hildegarde, The Swabian Princess. Proof: Brandenburg, Ibid.

<u>The Order of the Crown of Charlemagne in the U. S. A.</u> *

The American Ancestor Thomas Josselyn b. at Boxwell (prob.) Essex, Eng., late in 1591; d. Lancaster, Mass., Jan. 3, 1660/1; m. 1615 Rebecca Marlow. Proof: "Josselyn Family" Wessler, pp. 77-81, # 34, Hist. of Hingham, Mass., p. 264; Annals of Lancaster, Mass.

#31 Ralph Josselyn, prob. b. Boxwell-Chignal, Smealey Church, 1556; bur. Roxwell, Co. Essex, Mar. 19, 1631/2; m. (1) May 21, 1583 to Mary Bright, at Roxwell, Co. Essex. Proof: "Josselyn Family" Wessler, pp. 77, 65, 66, 60, 61, 58; N.E.H.G.R. 71:232, 247, 250.

John Josselyn of Fyfield, Smealy & Roxwell; b. Co. Essex, Eng. ca 1525; bur. Roxwell, Co. Essex, Feb. 18, 1578/9; m. Jan. 15, 1544/5, Alice Nevell, widow, at Fyfield Co. Essex; bur. Roxwell, Co. Essex, prob. Jan. 31, 1600/1. Proof: Wessler, 60, 61, 64, 58.

#26 Ralph Josselyn of Much or Great Canfield, Co. Essex; b. ca 1503; d. at Co. Essex, Eng. ante 1540; m. (name not known) prob. Co. Essex, Eng. Proof: Wessler, pp. 58, 60, 61, 55; N.E.H.G.R. 71;20, 21, 245, 242; will of father names Ralph.

Ralph Josselyn I of Moche or Great Canfield, Co. Essex, b. ca 1475; bur. Church of St. Savior after May 30, 1525; m. Elizabeth Cornish, dau. and heiress of William Cornish. She d. after May 30, 1525. Proof: Wessler, pp. 55, 56, 58, 53, 52. Will. N.E.H.G.R. 71:20, 21, 242, 241.

*Also Soc. of Desc. of King William the Conqueror - see p. 4.

John Josselyn of Sheering, Co. Essex, b. ca 1430; d. bef. Aug. 1524; m. Anne Lavenham, dau. of John Lavenham of Uphall. Proof: "Josselyn Family" Wessler, pp. 52, 53, 54, 55, alt.; N.E.H.G.R. 71:241.

Geoffrey Josselyn b. ca 1400; d. Jan. 2, 1470/1, bur. in the church yard at Saxbridgeworth, Herts; m. Katherine (maybe le Braye); bur. at church at Saxbridgeworth. Proof: "Josselyn Family" Wessler, pp. 52, 50, 51, att. N.E.H.G.R. 71:240-239.

Geoffrey Josselyn, Esq. of Hide Hall in Saxbridgeworth; b. at Co. Herts ca 1375; d. on W.D. 1424, 1425, bur. at Saxbridgeworth, Co. Herts; m. prob. Katherine, maybe dau. of Thomas, Lord Bray. Proof: Wessler, p. 50; N.E.H.G.R. 71:239; Calendar of Patent Rolls, 1391-1396, p. 494; Harl. Ms. 4944 in British Museum.

<u>The Order of the Crown of Charlemagne in the U. S. A.</u>, (con't)

Ralph Jocelyn b. ca 1340 at Co. Herts; d. 1383, prob. at Hide Hall; m. Margaret de Patmore, dau. of Sir John Patmore, son of John & Sarah de Patmore & grandson of Philip of Patmore Hall. Proof: N.E.H.G.R. 71: 238; Patmer Gen. in Harl. Soc. C 13, p. 227, 235. Wessler, op. cit. p. 50.

Geoffrey Jocelyn b. at Schellow-Jocelyn, Co. Essex, ca 1310; d. betw. 1360-1373, prob. at Cockenhatch; m. to Margaret Rokell, dau. of Sir Robert Rokell. Proof: Wessler - p. 49, 50. N.E.H.G.R. 71:238.

Ralph Jocelyn b. at Shallow-Bowels, Co. Essex, on Dec. 13, 1275; d. betw. 1312/3-1323; m. (2) Maud de Sutton. Proof: Wessler p. 49; Herald & Genealogist U. 5. p. 111; Calendar of fine rolls U. I. - p. 392. Calendar of Inquisitions Post Mortems, Edward I p. 323; N.E.H.G.R. 71:238.

Thomas Jocelyn b. at Sawbridge, Hide Hall, Co. Herts., ca 1249; d. ca 1284; m. ca 1270 to Alice Liston, dau. of William Liston. Proof: Wessler p. 49; Ancient Deeds, V. 3 #A5130 Pub. by British Government; N.E.H.G.R. 71:237.

Thomas Jocelyn d. after 1277; m. ca 1248, Maud Hide (Hyde) dau. & Co-Heiress of Sir John Hide of Hide, Knt. She was b. ca 1240 at Sawbridgeworth, Co. Herts; d. after 1277. Proof: Wessler, p. 48; Harl. Soc. V. 13 - p. 235; N.E.H.G.R. 71:237.

Sir John Hide (Hyde) Knt. of Sawbridgeworth, Herts. Hide Hall; m. Elizabeth Sudley, dau. of John Lord Sudley. Proof: N.E.H.G.R. 71:237; Wessler, op. cit. 48. Harl. Soc., op. cit. p. 235.

John, Lord Sudley of Sudley & Toddington, Co. Gloucester, 1140; b. at Gloucester; d. after 1140; m. by 1130 to Grace de Tracy, dau. of William de Tracy. Proof: Wessler, p. 48; Harl. Soc. 13:235; A.R. 1964 (222-27); VCH Warwick, V. 70. AR 1969 (25-26) (222-27) (235-23); CP V1 446-7, XI app D. 109-110 Note (1) p. 109. Brandenburg.

William de Tracy of Barnstable, son of Henry I King of Eng., d. ca 1135; name of wife not known. Proof: Ar 1964 (222-26); CPXI ap. D., 1909-10 Brandenburg; AR 1969 (222-26).

Henry I, King of England, b. 1070; d. Dec. 1, 1135 (King 1100-1135); m. Nov. 11, 1100 to Matilda of Scotland. She was b. 1079; d. May 1, 1118. Proof: Ar 1964 (222-25); CPXI Ap. d. 109-110 note; Brandenburg. AR (121-25) 1964.

William I the Conqueror, Duke of France, b. at Falaise, France, 1027; d. at Rouen, France, Sept. 9, 1089. He was King of England 1066-1087; m. 1053 (Maud) Matilda of Flanders, dau. Count of Flanders. She was b. 1032; d. Dec. 1, 1135. Proof: AR 1961 (121-25) (222-25); CCN 494 (162-23); "Falaise Roll" Crispin 1938 p. 186-187.

<u>The Order of the Crown of Charlemagne in the U. S. A.</u>, (con't)

Baldwin V. de Lille, Count of Flanders b. 1012; d. at Lillie Sept. 1, 1067; m. 1028 to Adele de France. She d. Jan. 8, 1079. Proof: AR 1969 (162-22) (128-22); CCN 112; Crispin "Falaise Roll" London, 1938, p. 186-7.

Baldwin IV, the Bearded, Count of Flanders, Count of Valenciennes 1007; b. 980; d. May 30, 1036; m. (1) 1012 to Ogive of Luxembourg, dau. of Frederick I, Count of Luxembourg. She d. Feb. 21, 1030. Proof: AR 1969 (162-21).

Arnold II the Young, Count of Flanders, d. Mar. 30, 987; m. 968 to Rosele (or Susanna). She d. Jan. 26, 1003. Proof: AR 1969 (162-20) (146-19); Falaise Roll, p. 186-187.

Baldwin III Count of Flanders d. Jan. 1, 961/2; m. to Matilda Billing, dau. of Hermann Billing, Duke of Saxony and Hildegarde. She d. at Westerbourg on May 25, 1008. Proof: AR 1969 (162-19)

Arnold I, the old Count of Flanders and Artois, b. ca 890; d. Mar. 27, 965/6; m. 934 to Alix de Vermandois. She d. at Bruges on 960. Proof: AR 1969 (162-18).

Baldwin II, the Bald, Count of Flanders & Artois, b. ca 865; d. on Jan. 12, 918; m. 884 to Alfthryth, dau. of Alfred the Great of England. She d. June 7, 929; Proof: AR 1969 (162-17) (44-16) CCN 112 (1-15).

Baldwin I "Bras de Fer", Count of Flanders, d. 879; m. 862 to Judith, dau. Charles II King of France, b. ca 846. Proof: AR 1969 (162-16); CCN 112.

Charles II, the Bald, King of France 840-887; b. at Frankfort on the Main on June 13, 828; d. near Mt. Cenis in the Alps, on Oct. 6, 877; m. (1) Dec. 842 to Ermentrude, dau. of Odo, Count of Orleans, and Engeltrude. She d. Oct. 6, 869. Proof: AR 1969 (162-15) (148-15); CCN 236, 642.

Louis, The Fair, Emperor 814-840, b. Aug. 778; d. near Mainz on June 20, 840; m. (2) Feb. 819 to Judith of Bavaria, dau. of Walf I, Duke of Bavaria. She d. Apr. 19, 843. Proof: AR 1969 (162-14) (140-14); CCN 623.

Charlemagne b. at Ingelheim, Apr. 2, 742/7; d. at Aix la Chapelle on Jan. 28, 813/4; m. ca 771, Hildegarde, dau. of Count Geroud of Swabia. She d. Apr. 30, 783. Proof: AR 1964 (50-13).

National Society Daughters of the Barons of Runnemede

and

National Society Magna Charta Dames

American Ancestor Joseph Bolles (Bowles) of Winter Haven Maine in 1640 - later of Wells, Maine.
Magna Charta Ancestor Richard de Clare, Earl of Clare & Hertford.

Richard De Clare, Sixth Earl of Clare and Third Earl of Hertford, a Surety for Magna Charta, b. ca 1150; d. betw. 30 Oct. and 28 Nov. 1217; ca 1173 he m. Amice (Amitia) dau. William Fitz Robert, Second Earl of Gloucester, and a grandson of King Henry I of England. She d. 1 Jan. 1224/5. Proof: The Complete Peerage, Vol. VI, p. 501-503 & Vol. V, p. 687-689.

Gilbert De Clare, Seventh Earl of Clare, Fourth Earl of Hertford and Fourth Earl of Gloucester, also a Surety for Magna Charta; b. ca. 1180; d. at Penros, Brittany on 25 Oct. 1230; m. 9 Oct. 1217 to Isabel Marshall, dau. of William Marshall, Earl of Pembroke and Striguil and Regent of England 1216-1219. She d. at Berkhamstead on 17 Jan. 1239/40. Proof: The Complete Peerage, Vol. V, p. 694-696.

Richard De Clare, Eighth Earl of Clare, Fifth Earl of Hertford and Fifth Earl of Gloucester; b. 4 Aug. 1222; d. at Ashenfield on 15 July 1262; m. (2) on or bef. 25 Jan. 1237/8 to Maud de Lacy, dau. John de Lacy, Earl of Lincoln and Constable of Chester, also a Surety for Magna Charta and a Crusader of 1218-1220 (Fifth Crusade). She d. bef. 10 Mar. 1288/9. Proof: The Complete Peerage, Vol. V, p. 696-702 & Vol. VII, p. 676-679.

Roese De Clare, dau. of Richard De Clare, b. 17 Oct. 1252; d. aft. 1316; m. in 1270 to Roger de Mowbray, First Lord Mowbray, grandson of William de Mowbray, Lord of Axholme, a Surety for Magna Charta. Roger was b. ca. 1257; d. bef. 21 Nov. 1297. Proof: The Complete Peerage, Vol. V, p. 700 and note (h) on p. 701; & Vol. IX p. 376-377.

John De Mowbray, Second Lord Mowbray; b. 4 Sept. 1286; hanged at York on 23 March 1321/2; m. at Swansea in 1298, to Aline de Braose (Brewes), dau. of William de Braose (Brewes), Lord Braose (Brewes), and Lord of Gower and Bramber. She d. by 20 July 1331.

John De Mowbray, Third Lord Mowbray, b. at Hovingham in Yorkshire on 29 Nov. 1310; d. 4 Oct. 1361; m. (1) Princess Joan Plantagenet, dau. of Prince Henry Plantagenet, Earl of Lancaster, grandson of King Henry III of England. She d. on 7 July ca. 1349. Proof: The Complete Peerage, Vol. IX, p. 380-383.

<u>Barons of Runnemede & Magna Charta Barons</u> (con't)

John De Mowbray, Fourth Lord Mowbray, b. at Epworth, 25 June, 1340. Slain by Saracens in Sept. or Oct. 1368, while on an expedition to the Near East; m. ca 1349 to Elizabeth de Segrave, dau. of John de Segrave, Lord Segrave and his wife Princess Margaret Plantagenet of Brotherton, Earl of Norfolk and Marshall of England, oldest son of King Edward I of England by his 2nd wife and Queen, Princess Marguerite of France, elder dau. of King Phillip III, the son of Saint Louis (King Louis IX), and Crusader of 1270 (Eighth Crusade). Through her mother Marie of Brabant the second wife and Queen of King Phillip III, Princess Marguerite, and her great granddaughter Elizabeth de Segrave were descended from the Holy Roman Emperor Frederick I Barbarossa, leader of the Third Crusade until his death in 1190, and from the Byzantine Emperor Alexius I Comnenos (1081-1118), who was largely responsible for the First Crusade (1096-1099). Elizabeth de Segrave was b. 25 Oct. 1338 at Croxton Abbey; d. before her husband, betw. 1364 & 1368, prob. ca 1367. Proof: The Complete Peerage, Vol. IX, p. 383-384.

Alienore (Eleanor) De Mowbray, b. shortly bef. 25 March 1364; Prob. living in 1399 but d. some years bef. 1417; m. bef. May 1386 as his first wife, John de Welles (Welle), Fifth Lord of Welles b. at Conesholme, Lincolnshire, 20 April 1352; d. 26 Aug. 1421. Proof: The Complete Peerage, Vol. IX, p. 384, Note (g); and Vol. XII part II, p. 441-443.

Ivis (Eude or Ean) De Welles, d. bef. 1421; m. Maud de Greystoke, dau. of Ralph de Greystoke, Third Lord Greystoke, and his wife Katherine de Clifford, dau. of Roger de Clifford, Fifth Lord Clifford, descended from the Magna Charta Sureties Saher IV de Quincy, Roger II Bigod, Hugh II Bigod, Richard de Clare Gilbert de Clare and John de Lacy. Proof: The Complete Peerage, Vol. XII, part II, p. 443; Vol. VI, p. 195-196; & Vol. III, p. 290-292.

Lionel De Welles, Sixth Lord Welles, b. in 1406; killed at the Battle of Towton, while commanding troops for King Henry VI of the House of Lancaster, on March 29, 1461, during the Wars of the Roses. Installed as a <u>Knight</u> of <u>The Garter</u> on 14 May 1457, being number 176; m. 1st on 15 Aug. 1417, at Saint Oswald's Methley, Yorkshire, to Joan (or Cecily) Waterton, dau. and heiress of Robert Waterton of Methley. She was living in 1434, but d. bef. 1447. Proof: The Complete Peerage, Vol. XII, part II, p. 443-444.

Margaret De Welles, d. 3 July 1480; m. as her 1st husband Sir Thomas Dymoke of Schrivelsby, Lincolnshire. He was b. ca. 1428 and beheaded 12 March 1470 by the Yorkists during the Wars of the Roses. Proof: The Complete Peerage, Vol. XII, part II, p. 449-450, Note (j); Ancestral Roots of Sixty N. E. Colonists by Dr. F. L. Weis; 4th Edition, 1969, revised and edited by W. L. Sheppard, Jr., hereafter called A. R. 1969, Line 202, generation 36.

Barons of Runnemede & Magna Charta Barons (con't)

Sir Lionel Dymoke, d. 17 Aug. 1519; m. twice. One of his wives was Joan Griffith, dau. of Richard Griffith. Proof: A. R. 1969, 202-37.

Anne Dymoke, m. John Goodrick of Kirby, Lincolnshire. Proof: A. R. 1969, 202-38.

Lionel Goodrick, prob. m. Winifred Sapcott, dau. of Henry Sapcott of Lincolnshire. Proof: A. R. 1969, 202-39.

Ann Goodrick, m. Benjamin Bolles of Osberton, Nottingham. Proof: A. R. 1969, 202-40.

Thomas Bolles, living at Osberton in 1614; m. Elizabeth Perkins, dau. of Thomas Perkins of Fishlake, Yorkshire. Proof: A. R. 1969, 202-41; Gen. Dict. of Maine & N. H. by Charles Thornton Libby, Noyes & Davis, p. 101.

Joseph Bolles (Bowles) the American Ancestor.

Magna Charta Barons

Richard de Clare, Gilbert de Clare, John de Lacy, William de Mowbray, Saher IV de Quincy, Roger II Bigod, Hugh II Bigod.

Knights of the Garter

Sir Lionel de Welles, Sixth Lord Welles. Installed 14 May 1457, being no. 176.

The National Huguenot Society

Hester Mahieu m. Francis Cooke of the Mayflower
Jane Cooke m. Experience Mitchell
Elizabeth Mitchell m. John Washburn
John Washburn, Jr. m. Rebecca Lapham
Rebecca Washburn m. Capt. David Johnson
Sarah Johnson m. Joseph Packard
Bethiah Packard m. Simon Record
Cynthia Record m. Thomas Bray
Cynthia Bray m. Capt. James Spaulding
Emma Frances Spaulding m. Col. John Emory Bryant
Emma Alice Bryant m. Julius Christian Zeller

Daughters of Colonial Wars, Inc.

Elder William Brett m. Margaret Ford
Judge Elihu Brett m. Ann Turner
Mary Brett m. John Willis
Mary Willis m. Joseph Packard
Joseph Packard m. Sarah Johnson
Bethiah Packard m. Simon Record
Cynthia Record m. Thomas Bray
Cynthia Bray m. Capt. James Spaulding
Emma Frances Spaulding m. Col. John Emory Bryant
Emma Alice Bryant m. Julius Christian Zeller

Mayflower Lines - 5

Francis Cooke of the Mayflower - dau.
Jane Cooke m. Experience Mitchell - dau.
Elizabeth Mitchell m. John Washburn - son
John Washburn, Jr., m. Rebecca Lapham - dau.
Rebecca Washburn m. Capt. David Johnson - dau.
Sarah Johnson m. Joseph Packard - dau.
Bethiah Packard m. Simon Record - dau.
Cynthia Record m. Dr. Thomas Bray - dau.
Cynthia Bray m. Capt. James Spaulding - dau.
Emma Francis Spaulding m. Col. John Emory Bryant - dau.
Emma Alice Bryant m. Julius Christian Zeller

Edward Doty of the Mayflower - son
Edward Doty m. Sarah Faunce - dau.
Elizabeth Doty m. Tobias Oakman - dau.
Elizabeth Oakman m. Elisha Ford - son
Isaac Ford m. Lucy Josselyn - dau.
Elizabeth Ford m. Joseph French - dau.
Lucy Ford French m. Benjamin Franklin Bryant - son
Col. John Emory Bryant m. Emma Frances Spaulding - dau.
Emma Alice Bryant m. Julius Christian Zeller

Francis Eaton of the Mayflower - son
Benjamin Eaton m. Sarah Hoskins - son
Benjamin Eaton m. Mary Coombs - dau.
Hannah Eaton m. Benjamin Bryant - son
Micah Bryant m. Elizabeth Norcut - son
Micah Bryant m. Margaret Paddock - son
Elias Bryant m. Bethsheba Hackett - son
Benjamin Franklin Bryant m. Lucy Ford French - son
John Emory Bryant m. Emma Frances Spaulding - dau.
Emma Alice Bryant m. Julius Christian Zeller

Mayflower Lines - con't.

Degory Priest of the Mayflower - dau.
Sarah Priest m. John Coombs - son
John Coombs m. Elizabeth (Royal) Barlow. - dau.
Mary Coombs m. Benjamin Eaton - dau.
Hannah Eaton m. Benjamin Bryant - son
Micah Bryant m. Elizabeth Norcut - son
Micah Bryant m. Margaret Paddock - son
Elias Bryant m. Bethsheba Hackett - son
Benjamin Franklin Bryant m. Lucy Ford French - dau.
John Emory Bryant m. Emma Frances Spaulding - dau.
Emma Alice Bryant m. Julius Christian Zeller

Henry Samson of the Mayflower
Dorcas Samson m. Thomas Bonney - dau.
Elizabeth Bonney m. Ephriam Norcut - dau.
Elizabeth Norcut m. Micah Bryant - son
Micah Bryant m. Margaret Paddock - son
Elias Bryant m. Bethsheba Hackett - son
Benjamin Franklin Bryant m. Lucy Ford French - son
John Emory Bryant m. Emma Frances Spaulding - dau.
Emma Alice Bryant m. Julius Christian Zeller

Daughters Founders & Patriots of America

John[1] Bryant m. Mary Lewis
Lieut. John[2] Bryant m. Abigail Bryant
Benjamin[3] Bryant m. Hannah Eaton
Micah[4] Bryant m. Elizabeth Norcut
Micah[5] Bryant m. Margaret Paddock
Rev. Elias[6] Bryant m. Bathsheba Hackett
Benjamin Franklin[7] Bryant, M.D. m. Lucy Ford French
Col. John Emory[8] Bryant m. Emma Frances Spaulding
Emma Alice[9] Bryant m. Julius Christian Zeller

Descendents of Colonial Governors

William[1] Hooke m. Elenor (Knight) Norton
William[2] Hooke m. Elizabeth Dyer
William[3] Hooke m. Mary (Fallonsbee) Pike, wid.
Mary[4] Hooke m. Stephen Bennett
Judith Bennett m. Ebenezer Bray
Dr. Thomas Bray m. Cynthia Record
Cynthia Bray m. Capt. James Spaulding
Emma Frances Spaulding m. Col. John Emory Bryant
Emma Alice Bryant m. Julius Christian Zeller

Women Desc. Ancient & Honorable Artillery

Mr. Edward Woodman m. Joanna Bartlett
Mary Woodman m. John Brown
Judith Brown m. Zachariah Davis
Elizabeth Davis m. Samuel Batchelder
Mary Batchelder m. Nathaniel Dearborn
Mary Dearborn m. Moses French
Joseph French m. Elizabeth Ford
Lucy Ford French m. Benjamin Franklin Bryant, M.D.
John Emory Bryant m. Emma Frances Spaulding
Emma Alice Bryant m. Julius Christian Zeller

John Johnson m. Marjorie Heath
Humphrey Johnson m. Ellen Cheney
Capt. Isaac Johnson m. Abigail (Leavitt) Lazell, wid.
Capt. David Johnson m. Rebecca Washburn
Sarah Johnson m. Joseph Packard
Bethiah Packard m. Simon Record
Cynthia Record m. Dr. Thomas Bray
Cynthia Bray m. Capt. James Spaulding
Emma Frances Spaulding m. Col. John Emory Bryant
Emma Alice Bryant m. Julius Christian Zeller

Rev. Joseph Hull m.
Elizabeth Hull m. John[1] Heard
Tristram[2] Heard m. Abigail
Mary[3] Heard m. John Warren
Capt. John Warren m. Jane Johnson
Margaretta Warren m. Capt. Leonard Spaulding
Capt. James Spaulding m. Cynthia Bray
Emma Frances Spaulding m. Col. John Emory Bryant
Emma Alice Bryant m. Julius Christian Zeller

Colonial Dames XVII Century

John[1] Balch m. Margaret Lovell
Benjamin[2] Balch m. Grace (   ) Mallett, wid.
Lydia[3] Balch m. Samuel[3] Bowles
Joanna Bowles m. Ebenezer Record
Simon Record m. Bethiah Packard
Cynthia Record m. Dr. Thomas Bray
Cynthia Bray m. Capt. James Spaulding
Emma Frances Spaulding m. Col. John Emory Bryant
Emma Alice Bryant m. Julius Christian Zeller

Descendents of Colonial Clergy

Rev. Joseph Hull m. Agnes
Elizabeth Hull m. John Heard
Tristram Heard m. Abigail
Mary Heard m. John Warren
Capt. John Warren m. Jane Johnson
Margaretta Warren m. Capt. Leonard Spaulding
Capt. James Spaulding m. Cynthia Bray
Emma Frances Spaulding m. Col. John Emory Bryant
Emma Alice Bryant m. Julius Christian Zeller

Rev. Stephen Batchelder m. Anne Batte
Nathaniel Batchelder m. Hester Mercer
Nathaniel Batchelder m. Mary (Carter) Wyman, wid.
Samuel Batchelder m. Elizabeth Davis
Mary Batchelder m. Nathaniel Dearborn
Mary Dearborn m. Moses French
Joseph French m. Elizabeth Ford
Lucy Ford French m. Benjamin Franklin Bryant
Col. John Emory Bryant m. Emma Frances Spaulding
Emma Alice Bryant m. Julius Christian Zeller

William Witherell m. Mary Fisher
Mary Witherell m. Thomas Oldham
Isaac Oldham m. Hannah Keen
Hannah Oldham m. Henry Josselyn
Lucy Josselyn m. Isaac Ford
Elizabeth Ford m. Joseph French
Lucy Ford French m. Benjamin Franklin Bryant
Col. John Emory Bryant m. Emma Frances Spaulding
Emma Alice Bryant m. Julius Christian Zeller

Rev. Thomas Carter m. Mary Parkhurst
Mary (Carter) Wyman m. Nathaniel Batchelder
Samuel Batchelder m. Elizabeth Davis
Mary Batchelder m. Nathaniel Dearborn
Mary Dearborn m. Moses French
Joseph French m. Elizabeth Ford
Lucy Ford French m. Benjamin Franklin Bryant, M.D.
Col. John Emory Bryant m. Emma Frances Spaulding
Emma Alice Bryant m. Julius Christian Zeller

Daughters of The American Colonists

Abraham Mellowes m. Martha Bulkley
Oliver Mellowes m. Mary James
Elizabeth (Mellowes) Barrett, wid. m. Edward Wright
Martha Wright m. Israel[2] Heald
Mary Heald m. John[4] Heald
Martha Heald m. John Barrett
Patty Barrett m. Benjamin Spaulding
Capt. Leonard Spaulding m. Margaretta Warren
Capt. James Spaulding m. Cynthia Bray
Emma Frances Spaulding m. Col. John Emory Bryant
Emma Alice Bryant m. Julius Christian Zeller

William Hooke, Gov. m. Elenor (Knight) Norton, wid.
William Hooke, m. Elizabeth Dyer
William Hooke, m. Mary (Fallonsbee) Pike, wid.
Mary Hooke, m. Stephen Bennett
Judith Bennett m. Ebenezer Bray
Dr. Thomas Bray m. Cynthia Record
Cynthia Bray m. Capt. James Spaulding
Emma Frances Spaulding m. Col. John Emory Bryant
Emma Alice Bryant m. Julius Christian Zeller

National Society of New England Women

Mother's Father's Ancestry

John[1] Bryant m. Mary Lewis
Lieut. John[2] Bryant m. Abigail Bryant
Benjamin[3] Bryant m. Hannah Eaton
Micah[4] Bryant m. Elizabeth Norcut
Micah[5] Bryant m. Margaret Paddock
Elias[6] Bryant m. Bathsheba Hackett
Benjamin[7] Bryant m. Lucy Ford French
John Emory[8] Bryant m. Emma Frances Spaulding
Emma Alice Bryant m. Julius Christian Zeller

Mother's Mother's Ancestry

Edward[1] Spaulding m. Rachel
Andrew[2] Spaulding m. Hannah Jeffs
Henry[3] Spaulding m. Elizabeth Lund
Leonard[4] Spaulding m. Elizabeth Durant
Benjamin[5] Spaulding m. Patty Barrett
Capt. Leonard[6] Spaulding m. Margaretta Warren
Capt. James[7] Spaulding m. Cynthia Bray
Emma Frances[8] Spaulding m. Col. John Emory Bryant
Emma Alice Bryant m. Julius Christian Zeller

Order of Americans of Armorial Ancestry

John[1] Washburn m. Marjorie Moore
John[2] Washburn m. Elizabeth Mitchell
John[3] Washburn m. Rebecca Lapham
Rebecca Washburn m. Capt. David Johnson
Sarah Johnson m. Joseph Packard
Bethiah Packard m. Simon Record
Cynthia Record m. Thomas Bray
Cynthia Bray m. Capt. James Spaulding
Emma Frances Spaulding m. Col. John Emory Bryant
Emma Alice Bryant m. Julius Christian Zeller

Daughters of The American Revolution

Simon Record m. Bethiah Packard
Cynthia Record m. Thomas Bray
Cynthia Bray m. Capt. James Spaulding
Emma Frances Spaulding m. Col. John Emory Bryant
Emma Alice Bryant m. Julius Christian Zeller

National Society U. S. Daughters of 1812

Benjamin Spaulding m. Patty Barrett
Capt. Leonard Spaulding m. Margaretta Warren
Capt. James Spaulding m. Cynthia Bray
Emma Frances Spaulding m. Col. John Emory Bryant
Emma Alice Bryant m. Julius Christian Zeller

Dames of The Court of Honor

Col. John Emory Bryant m. Emma Frances Spaulding
Emma Alice Bryant m. Julius Christian Zeller

INDEX

www.ingramcontent.com/pod-product-compliance
Lightning Source LLC
Chambersburg PA
CBHW061758260326
41914CB00006B/1151

* 9 7 8 1 5 9 6 4 1 3 6 7 2 *